Steve Cioccolanti has written a different numbers may represent in tue ᴅɪᴅɪᴇ and in prophecy. He has assembled an impressive range of prophetic theories about the timing of end-time events. His book is highly readable, carefully researched, and provocative. The fact that he is not dogmatic in pushing any one specific prophecy is refreshing. He gives each reader credit for being able to make up their own mind based on the information he has presented.

—R. Edwin Sherman
President of Isaac Newton Bible Code Research Society
President of *Bible Code Digest*
Member of American Academy of Actuaries

Bible numerics is a subject that will never be exhausted. *The Divine Code* by Steve Cioccolanti certainly adds to this amazing and fascinating subject.

—Kevin Conner
Former Senior Pastor of City Life, Melbourne
International Author and Teacher

Over the past several decades many Christian authors have written books on biblical numbers and their meanings, and some have even taught a complicated and controversial system of numerology. Then a few years ago the Bible Code books caused a sensation; and now we have Jesus codes, Buddha codes, Torah codes, etc. However, much of this is simply speculation focusing on conspiracy theories and strange doctrines that do not edify anyone. They only lead people away from the revelation of the Word of God.

The Divine Code: from 1 to 2020 by Steve Cioccolanti is an excellent reference book that is extremely informative, inspirational, and practical in every way. Above all, the teaching in this book is based on solid Biblical exegesis and accepted and proven evangelical doctrines. Steve has an accepted and proven teaching ministry and deals with many more complicated subjects such as Christianity and postmodern philosophy, evolution and creationism, reconciling Biblical history with science and secular accounts, and many other subjects relevant to twenty-first century believers.

This excellent book has reconciled the extremes in doctrines and practices we see all around us, and brings forth the proper balanced Biblical perspective. More than that, the teaching is very practical and is extremely helpful in the daily lives of the reader. I highly recommend this to every follower of Jesus, and Christian teachers and leaders will find this teaching valuable as they build the Church on the foundation of God's Word.

—Pastor Dennis Balcombe
Founder of Revival Chinese Ministries
International Senior Pastor of Revival Christian Church,
Hong Kong
Missionary to Hong Kong since 1969
Pioneer in China since 1978

Steve Cioccolanti's book is both stimulating and thought provoking. It is thoroughly Biblical in its approach and examines issues facing us in our twenty-first-century world. I have always been cautious about end times as so many people and Churches get sidetracked from the real issues. Steve's book cuts to the core by giving us a solid practical platform to approach this subject. When it comes to addressing the subject of end times, this book focuses on what we need to do so that we are not caught up in the grip of a world that is under the control of the "god of this world." I highly recommend it to all who are seeking to understand end times.

—David Boyd
Senior Pastor, Jesus Family Center
Sydney, Australia
Author, *You Don't Have to Cross the Ocean to Reach the World*

The

DIVINE CODE

FROM ONE TO

2020

STEVE CIOCCOLANTI

CREATION
HOUSE

THE DIVINE CODE: FROM 1 TO 2020 by Steve Cioccolanti
Published by Creation House
A Charisma Media Company
600 Rinehart Road
Lake Mary, Florida 32746
www.charismamedia.com

Unless otherwise noted, all Scripture quotations are from the New King James Version of the Bible. Copyright © 1979, 1980, 1982 by Thomas Nelson, Inc., publishers. Used by permission.

Scripture quotations marked AMP are from the Amplified Bible. Old Testament copyright © 1965, 1987 by the Zondervan Corporation. The Amplified New Testament copyright © 1954, 1958, 1987 by the Lockman Foundation. Used by permission.

Scripture quotations marked KJV are from the King James Version of the Bible.

Scripture quotations marked NAS are from the New American Standard Bible—Updated Edition, Copyright © 1960, 1962, 1963, 1968, 1971, 1972, 1973, 1975, 1977, 1995 by The Lockman Foundation. Used by permission. (www.Lockman.org)

Scripture quotations marked NIV are from the Holy Bible, New International Version. Copyright © 1973, 1978, 1984, International Bible Society. Used by permission.

Scripture quotations marked NLT are from the Holy Bible, New Living Translation, copyright © 1996. Used by permission of Tyndale House Publishers, Inc., Wheaton, IL 60189. All rights reserved.

Scripture quotations marked WEY are from the Weymouth Bible, *The New Testament in Modern Speech*, by Richard Francis Weymouth. Copyright © 1939 by James Clarke Co., publishers.

Design Director: Bill Johnson
Cover design by Justin Evans

Visit the author's Web site: www.Discover.org.au

Library of Congress Control Number: 2011921016
International Standard Book Number: 978-1-61638-448-7
First Edition
11 12 13 14 15 — 987654321
Printed in Canada

DEDICATION

Dedicated to the love of our lives,
Alexis Bethany Cioccolanti. You inspired us from the
moment God gave you on 19-1-9.

Your loving parents,
Papa and Mama

CONTENTS

PREFACE

In the beginning was the Word [Logos], and the Word [Logos] was with God, and the Word [Logos] was God.

JOHN 1:1

HOW TO USE THIS BOOK

You can read these chapters in any order, except for some of the last few which build on your knowledge of numbers. It may behoove you to read most of the book first before venturing into end-time chronology.

If you are interested in all the divine codes, then you will enjoy this book from cover to cover. Or you may be interested in certain numbers only; then you can use this book as a handy reference. Many will want to specifically read about 666 or 2020, so I have devoted more attention to them for the readers' sake.

SUMMARY ABOUT THE BOOK

This is a book about numbers—their meanings and patterns in Scripture, nature, history, and prophecy. They are "divine codes" simply because if God did not exist, none of these numbers and patterns would recur in logical fashion at multiple levels of the observable cosmos. God is logical.

Numbers can tell us a lot. While visiting Greece once, a local tour guide informed me that by studying nature, the Greeks believed creation was mathematical. They reasoned that a mind that understands mathematics—a mind similar to ours—created the universe, because we can understand it on mathematical terms. But of course, they said, His mind must be greater than ours. Furthermore, they postulated that He can't be double-minded (or "bi-polar," we might say), so He can't be many. Through sheer mathematics, they arrived at the conclusion that there must be—behind everything—one single great God. This is monotheism by mathematics.

This is *not* a book about mathematics or numerology in the sense that it is not too technical or theoretical. It is a *practical* book about numbers, what they tell us, and how we can apply their meanings to have a richer, deeper, more meaningful life.

THE HEART NOT HEAD OF NUMBERS

The apostle John opens his Gospel with a classic statement: "In the beginning was the Word, and the Word was with God, and the Word was God." Here the Greek word *logos* is translated *word* in English, but *logos* means more than just *word*. The Greeks actually use *lexis to* convey "word." Some Christians say *logos* means the "written word." But the Greeks use *gramma* to convey "written word," "writing," or "letter" (from which we get our English word *grammar*).

What does *logos* really mean? On a cursory look we call tell the Greek *logos* looks very similar to some of our English words: logic, logical, logistics. *Logos* can mean *word*; but it also means logic, thought, reason, intelligence, planning, carrying out activity, and creative power. By extension, one who thinks also utters and speaks. With this understanding, we can read what John was saying, "In the beginning was Logic, and Logic was with God, and the Logic was God." In other words, God is logical.

There is a *reason* behind everything God does, behind everything He creates, behind every word He writes, behind every number He uses. This is what the world has not understood and what the Church has largely forgotten. Our modern services tend to appeal to emotions. Our feel-good sermons skirt the issues and dodge the questions. Christians expect others to accept Bible claims on demand: "Just believe!" Believe in what? And why should one believe?

Paul said "the letter (*gramma*) kills" (2 Cor. 3:6). That means you can read a written word or hear a spoken word, but not understand the thought, intent, and *heart* behind the words. It is possible to hear, know, even obey something that is written or spoken, but not understand the *logic* of what is being said. This is the crux of tradition and legalism. Religion is not mindless, it is heartless. Skepticism is also not mindless, it is heartless. Neither of them are our friends. Have you ever been in a supermarket or bank where there is no queue, no people standing in line, yet the teller demands that you pull out the waiting ticket with a number? That's someone who knows the *gramma* or letter of the rule, but not the *logos* or logic behind the rule.

The written word, the *gramma*, is the product of the thoughts and intents of God the *Logos*. We can see things, even believe things, without understanding the reason behind them. I am not speaking about intellectual reasoning; I'm speaking about discovering the *spirit* of the speaker. As we mature spiritually, God wants us to know Him as the *Logos*. Without a tender heart to understand the personal *Logos*, you cannot *logistically* walk out what you've heard.

I believe that it was the Greek's fascination with science, numbers, and the *logic* behind them that prepared them for the Gospel that would arrive through Christians. Today, the Church has forgotten logic or even put it down. Some well-meaning Christians tell their skeptical friends to "just believe" without giving any logical reason.

This book is about the *logos* of numbers. It's about the splendid evidence God intends for us to see. Once you catch the logic, you will also get the logistics of how to apply His wisdom in your life.

NOTES TO THE READERS

We will leave aside the usual convention of writing out numbers (one, two, three) as we have many numbers in this book which will be easier to read as 1, 2, 3, and so on.

I will sometimes refer to the numeric value of a word or its *gematria*. Turning words into "geometry" was once common among Jewish interpreters and is approved by the New Testament in Revelation 13, which advises us to calculate the number of the Beast's name or 666. How can names be turned into numbers? It is possible only in an alphanumeric system such as Hebrew and Greek.

Jews use 22 letters (all consonants) in their alphabet and ancient Greeks used 27 letters (both consonants and vowels), but neither had separate symbols for numbers. So the ancient Hebrews and Greeks assigned a numerical value to every letter in their alphabet (like A = 1, B = 2, C = 3). By replacing the letters of a word with its numeric equivalent, you can calculate its *gematria*.

Adding these numbers has preoccupied some people to the extreme. Yet there is no denying researchers have found some curious "coincidences" by calculating the numeric value of Biblical words. For instance, the gematria of the Hebrew word *pregnancy* is 271. The average length of pregnancy from fertilization to delivery is also 271 days.[2]

The Biblical study of numbers cannot be separated from the Biblical study of words because God chose to use two languages which did not separate their linguistic symbols from their mathematical symbols. In other words, their letters were their numbers and sometimes their words created interesting sums.

The Hebrew gematria of the name "Emperor Nero" (the burner of Christians) is 666. The numeric value of the Greek name "Jesus" is 888. Profound? Read this book and decide for yourself.

INTRODUCTION

THE PURPOSE OF NUMBERS

NUMBERS MAKE US HUMAN. Life would be impersonal without numbers. Numbers tell us our age, height, size, address, phone details, health, income, portfolio performance, track record, anniversaries, appointments—overall some very personal things. Yet reducing everything to numbers makes it all so…ah, impersonal. Yes, we seem to have a love-hate relationship with numbers!

We memorize numbers, quote numbers, and calculate numbers. But we also want to run away from numbers on our bills, race against numbers on our clocks, fight against numbers of passing years on our calendars, and sometimes ignore numbers on our evaluations or report cards. But I want to tell you why we cannot ignore numbers for too long. Creatures in the animal kingdom can do it. But we can't—for one simple reason.

Numbers make us divine. We are the unique part of God's creation that is innately preoccupied with the future. My dog does not think about his future. Yes, beavers may build dams for future winters and bears may eat up before they hibernate, but these behaviors are followed out of mechanical necessity. We, on the other hand, long for the future. Given a moment of solitude, our thoughts soon turn to the prospects of tomorrow. You can put a man in prison by robbing him of his future. You can set a man free from prison by giving him hope of a better tomorrow. When we don't get to ponder or plan our future, we literally feel stuck and shackled—burdened by our past regrets or stressed out about our present situation. When the future cannot be predicted, we feel a sense of uncertainty. We *want* to know the future. We *need* to know our future. And numbers open a divine door into that future!

NUMBERS TELL US THE FUTURE

There are "prophets" in nearly every field of work and knowledge. Many people are highly sought after and highly paid to make some sort of educated *prediction* about the future. Nearly all of them do it by numbers.

Political analysts use polling numbers to calculate popularity and project an election result. Meteorologists plug numbers into computer models to forecast the weather days, weeks, and months ahead of time. Actuaries are employed to calculate the risk of possible events that could impact insurance claims.

Watch the financial pundits on TV. Little do they report the present. Most of the time they are speculating about the future. Investors analyze the history of price patterns to project potential returns on investments.

Listen to sports commentators. Have you noticed how much of their commentary is *not* about the actual game? How often it's about future games, future outcomes, and future champions. Sports analysts use statistics to rank a player's or team's past performance and project who will enter the finals and win.

Numbers have a way of opening a portal into the future for humans. In 1927 W. D. Gann published a book that correctly predicted Japan's attack on America. He also predicted the stock market crash of 1929. He predicted the Great Depression would end in 1932. No one knew exactly how he did it, but two things are certain: (1) he used numbers, and (2) he prospered when many others did not, either because they did not know about numbers or did not believe the numbers.

There is no mysticism about it. No man, including Gann, knows everything. "For we know in part and we prophesy in part" (1 Cor. 13:9), Paul wrote two thousand years ago. Only when the Perfect comes will our imperfect knowledge be done away with. Meanwhile the "prophets" of the world can study probability. We don't "know" what a single coin toss will yield, but we "know" that if you flipped a coin 100 times, 50 percent of the time it will turn out to be heads, 50 percent tails.

King Solomon tells us the value of studying probability, "That which *has been* is what *will be*, that which is *done* is what *will be done*, and there is nothing new under the sun" (Eccles. 1:9, emphasis added). I'm sure W. D. Gann, as a Christian, thought about these Biblical words many times as he sought to forecast the probability of the world's markets turning up or down. In the vernacular, we say it this way: "History repeats itself." If it didn't, there wouldn't be any value to studying history!

This leads me to the uniqueness of the God of the Bible. Our God invented numbers, repeats beautiful patterns, and likes to work in cycles. God is into patterns and prophecy. His Book is the premier book about numbers and the future. Many numbers recorded in the Bible are only beginning to make sense now. Many things recorded in the Bible are repeating themselves. Much of the public doesn't even know about this numeric aspect of God's Word. Patterns are prophetic. History is prophecy. God is far from mythical, He's mathematical. God counts!

NUMBERS KEEP US HONEST

One piece of evidence that tells me the Bible is not intended to be myth is the preponderance of specific numbers and numerical patterns contained in it. There is nothing mythical about a population or military census taken by tribes, clans, and families. Anyone who asks, "Isn't the Bible a collection of myths?" can find his answer by studying the numbers in the Bible. Numbers tells us concrete facts about reality in a countable way.

Numbers keep us honest. We may say we are watching our weight, but the number of kilograms on the scale doesn't lie. We may feel we put a lot of effort at work and deserve that promotion, but our sales figures show our true performance. We may assume that the Bible has been changed by copyists' errors, but numbers tell a different story.

Every handwritten Torah scroll contains 79,847 words or 304,805 Hebrew letters. Yes, they count the number of words and the letters before sanctioning every copy! Not only were Jewish scribes meticulous in counting the total number of words and letters, they also counted the number of each individual letter of their *alephbet*. The first letter *aleph* appears 27,057 times in the Torah. The second letter *bet* appears 16,344 times. And so on. The last letter, *tav*, appears 17,949 times.[1]

On a purely mathematical basis, allegations of textual corruption are untenable and were proven so by the Dead Sea Scrolls. Discovered from 1946 to 1956, this treasure of 972 documents is so called because they were found in clay jars hidden in 11 caves at Qumran near the Dead Sea. Why is it considered one of the greatest archeological findings of modern times? Let me give you three reasons.

First, fragments of every book of the Hebrew canon were found except for the Book of Esther. Second, out of twenty-two copies of the Book of Isaiah found, one copy was so well preserved you could read it from Isaiah 16 through Isaiah 66. Third, this "Isaiah Scroll" is one thousand years older than any previously known copy of Isaiah, and much to scholars' surprise, it reads virtually the same as our 1611 King James Bible! The minor differences were in spelling and tense errors, but no change to the overall message was found. Counting those 304,805 letters ensured the Bible was transmitted precisely to us!

NUMBERS LEAD US TO TRUTH

By simple math, anyone with a Bible could have calculated or predicted the exact day the Messiah was to come! There are many amazing prophecies in the Bible, but the most startling is the one in Daniel chapter 9. It is the most mathematically precise prophecy ever recorded both in Scripture and in all world literature. Who knew about this mathematical prophecy?

Those who read the Bible did! Their knowledge of numbers is the reason they came to see the Messiah when He was a baby. How else did Simeon the devout man and Anna the prophetess show up at the right time to worship Jesus, whereas Joseph and Mary still hadn't fully grasped what Child was this who was born to them! These believers came and started worshiping the Savior before He ever preached a sermon. How did they know? Undoubtedly they had read Daniel chapter 9.

Who else in the first century knew the Savior was coming to Earth? The magis of Persia! How did they know? Daniel was in captivity in Babylon-Persia for seventy years, during which time this Jewish prophet became the highest advisor to the various kings. His prophecies became well-known and studied among the educated, who were called *magis* (a Persian word from which we get "magistrates"). By trusting in Daniel's math, these Persians arrived in Bethlehem at the right time to see the Child Jesus. Can you imagine that…math lead educated people to the Savior of the world!

Skeptics who claim the Gospel of Jesus Christ was made up by Paul or a collusion of fourth-century Christians not only fail to understand the Old Testament prophecies, but they are also unaware of the most basic math contained in it.

Can numbers help you find meaning in life and reveal more about the divine plan of God? Can the knowledge or ignorance of numbers affect your future? You're about to find out! This short guide to divine numbers will open up to you the meaning of the most significant numbers.

DECODING NUMBERS

Let him who has understanding calculate the number …
REVELATION 13:18

THE MEANING OF NUMBERS

A book about numbers is necessarily also a book about the future and end times. In this chapter I will explain some viewpoints on end times, and more importantly how we derive meaning from numbers.

People are fascinated by numbers because they are inherently futuristic. Listen to any expert on the news and pay attention to how much they talk about the past and present versus the future. The most highly paid and sought after personalities speak about the future. The sports commentator does not merely go over past games, but makes predictions about future games. The financial gurus don't sit and describe past prices and performance, but make predictions about interest rates and the direction of the market. The weatherman does not talk about the rain that fell last month, but predicts future weather patterns. And no matter how many times the weatherman and the business pundits get it wrong, we go back to TV and stay tuned in, because we crave the future. *Numbers tell us the future!*

But different people have different ideas about what numbers mean. You only have to look at the stock market to realize how many experts contradict each other even though technically they are all staring at the same numbers. Is there an objective source of meaning for numbers? I believe there is and I'm not alone. That's why you're reading this book.

HOW TO DECODE THE MEANING OF NUMBERS

The clearest explanation of numbers comes from the Creator of numbers. Dr. Peter Plitcha explained it this way in *God's Secret Formula*: "It was a decisive mistake that science began to interpret numbers as a human invention approximately one hundred years ago, just so that mysticism could be expelled from science and mathematics. In this way God was also expelled from nature.... There is a divine structural plan behind this world."[1]

God created numbers and He built nature in harmony with numerical patterns. When He blessed us with a written record of His thoughts (the Bible), that record must also be in harmony with the numbers we see in the universe. Or more profoundly, our entire universe must be in harmony with His Word! It's the other way round because His Word preceded the universe.

To understand numbers, we must understand that God made numbers and the numbers are about Him. God is the beginning and the end of numbers. He is the source and the goal of understanding numbers. *Numbers teach us about God!*

Christian theologians have come to realize that numbers in the Bible have divine meaning. For instance, most agree that 7 represents rest, completion, and perfection. As we study the Bible, we discover it is the only book in the world with intricate patterns of 7's that are unlikely to be there by mere accident or human contrivance.

If we start with God's Word instead of God's universe, we will get the meaning of numbers and also be able to forecast the unknown. For instance, we start with the knowledge that God's Word tells us that man was created on the 6th day, then we compare it to our knowledge that mankind lives on 6 continents and no written history of him can be found beyond 6,000 years.* Even when most of humanity lived on only three continents (Africa, Asia and Europe), a Bible reader could have made a reliable prediction that there should be another three inhabitable continents (North America, South America, and Australia), and there are probably seven continents in total (Antarctica is reserved for the Millennium, when the ice will melt and humans will enjoy living on one continent not completely ravaged by sin and crime). Before modern scientists understood atoms and atomic numbers, a Bible reader could have made an accurate prediction that whatever element man was made of, it should be linked to the number 6. As it turns out, scientists now understand from the periodic table of chemical elements that man is made up of mainly carbon; and its atomic number is....wouldn't you know it, 6! Can you see how numerical patterns are both meaningful and predictive?

---

* China, Japan, Greece, Bahrain, and the Inuits are all celebrating 5,000 years of history around the year 2010. Why do skeptics insist that man has been on Earth for unknown millions of years despite the obvious fact that the oldest civilizations *known* to mankind can trace their written history no further than 5,000 years—which coincides with the time of Noah's Flood? The oldest known words, spoken by Adam and Eve and recorded in the Bible, are about 6,000 years old.

NUMBERS DIVIDE US

Numbers divide people into two camps: those who count, and those who don't count. There are those on one side who say, "Nowhere in the Bible are we told to be interested in numbers." This side is wary that studying numbers can lead to superstition or sidetrack our interpretation of the plain text of the Bible. There is validity to this claim that some people have become so mystified by the numbers in the Bible that they have neglected to pay attention to the main message of the Bible.

Yet those who deny the importance of numbers must come to terms with a Biblical instruction from God, "Let him who has understanding *calculate*" (Rev. 13:18, emphasis added). People on the other side say, "We are commanded by God to look at numbers with spiritual eyes and discern their divine messages."

The appropriate warning is not that *no one* should calculate. It's that people who don't *understand* the Bible's plain text (words) should not venture into the subtext (numbers and codes). The subtext exists only to authenticate, confirm, and magnify the main message of the text, which is Christ!

Christ said, "[I am] Lord of the Sabbath" (Luke 6:5). In other words, "I am Lord of the 7th day." Had Jesus said, "I am Lord of Thursday," that would not have had as much meaning. Thursday is not related to Jesus' core mission of salvation. The number 7, on the other hand, represents rest, perfection, and completion, all of which are found in Jesus! The number hinted at and supports the overt claim that Jesus is the true Savior and there is neither rest nor salvation outside of Him. 7 was loaded with such meaning while it waited to find its fulfillment in Him. Numbers support and authenticate the claims of the God of the Bible.

We want to be among those who count, because God counts. God wrote an entire book in the Bible called "Numbers"! Throughout the Bible, God told priests to count offerings, tradesmen to measure the dimensions of the Temple, generals to count the troops, and spiritual leaders to take a census of the tribes. Daniel the prophet said, "I, Daniel, understood by the books the *number*" (Dan. 9:2, emphasis added). God gave the prophet Daniel a precise mathematical 70-week prophecy which counts down Israel's prophetic timetable. (We will get to that later.)

DIFFERENT VIEWS ON THE LAST DAYS

If you want to know the future, you have to know numbers. If you want to know the projected population of your country, you can by knowing her birth rate, migration rate, and mortality rate. If you want to forecast the weather in May, you can by searching the historical temperatures and precipitation in previous Mays. If you want to know how a business will perform long term, you can make a sound projection based on the company's fundamentals, the bank's interest rates, the government's tax rates, and the nation's growth rate. If you want to make an educated guess which sports team will most likely win the championship, you need to keep its scores from previous games and seasons.

If you want to know the future of God's plan, you will have to know God's numbers—the divine codes. If everyone can see the divine codes, why are there so many different views of the end times? Given the same prices on the stock market, everyone does not all buy and sell the same shares. It is subject to interpretation.

When it comes to end-time interpretation, there are three main schools of thought. Let's summarize them:

1. The **preterist** (from Latin *praeter* or past) holds that Biblical end-time prophecies were fulfilled in the first century. This is generally the view of the Catholic Church.

2. The **historicist** holds that Biblical end-time prophecies are being fulfilled throughout Church history, from the first century till now. This is generally the view of the Protestant Church.

3. The **futurist** holds that most Biblical end-time prophecies are yet to be fulfilled in the future. This is generally the view of the modern Pentecostal and charismatic Churches.

Which one is true? The surprising truth we may find when we get to Heaven is all of them were true to a certain extent! For instance, to the preterist Roman Emperor Nero was the Anti-Christ, not only because he burned Jews and Christians, but also because the Greek gemetria of his name, *Neron Kaisar*, is 666.

To the historicist, the Roman papacy was the Anti-Christ, because no organization has done more to suppress the translation of the Bible and to persecute Jews and Christians. This was the dominant view of Protestant Reformers such as Martin Luther and John Calvin. They saw Roman Church history as one filled with apostasy, bloodshed, and corruption. Roman Popes started the Crusades, persecuted Jews, killed Huguenot Christians, branded Bible translators heretics, and burned born-again Christians at the stake. To Protestant Christians, they were experiencing the Tribulation! Adding to their case, they calculated the Latin gematria of a title of the Pope *Vicarius Fililii Dei* (the Vicar of the Son of God) and found it to be 666.

To the futurist, the Anti-Christ is an Anti-Christian, anti-Semite leader who is yet to come.* He has yet to walk into the Third Temple to defile it because it is yet to be built on the Temple Mount in Jerusalem. He has yet to behead many Christians and Jews in modern times. His gematria is yet to be revealed (or only recently revealed according to some numericists).

You may ask, "Which one is true?" My question is, why not all three? A great paradox about God's Word is that it practically pays no attention to debates about Christian denominational traditions, but pays a lot of attention to answering the pre-Christians' main questions: "Is the Bible true? Can I trust the Bible?" While Christian denominational leaders are debating over their favorite theological positions, ignoring the real questions posed by their increasingly skeptical children and flock, the Bible is focused on answering the pre-Christians' questions and ignoring the debate between Christian denominations.

Not only does God prove that the Bible is true, He shows the Bible is true on multiple levels and in multiple time frames. Many Anti-Christs fulfill Bible prophecies in the short-term, medium-term, and long-term. This is startling because there is no anti-Buddha or anti-Krishna in any place in any time frame. The Bible is true over and over again.

CAN THE BIBLE BE TAKEN LITERALLY?

It should be noted that all 3 schools of interpretation—preterist, historicist, and futurist—arrive at their conclusions through some kind of literal interpretation of the Bible. The preterist believes Christians suffered tribulation in the first century, the historicist believes Christians have been suffering throughout Church history and are called to suffer persecution right now, the futurist believes the ultimate Tribulation is a well-defined, 7-year period that is yet to come (some would argue has already started). Why could not all of them be right at some level? The main point is that all Christians for all centuries in all major denominations have tried their best to interpret the Bible literally. To be literally true means the Bible finds its fulfillment in objective reality.

There are many levels of application following the literal interpretation of the Bible. It is not a narrow-minded way of which anti-Theists accuse Christians. Literalists are open-minded enough to that see different perspectives can add value to how we interpret the Bible (whether preterist, historicist, or futurist). The narrow-minded person is the one who insists the Bible is only myth,

---

* This doesn't mean futurists are more favorable to the Pope than historicists. Though most futurists do not think the Pope can be the Anti-Christ, they see the Roman Church featured prominently in the Bible as "Mystery Babylon" or a spiritual entity following the Babylonian pagan system. Futurists like Dave Hunt make the argument that while the Anti-Christ is the Beast, the Roman Church is the "woman who rides the beast."

allegory, or symbolism (a viewpoint called "idealism"). Such a person wants to believe that there is only one layer of meaning to the Bible.

We know that the idealist view is too shallow because of the numbers. The Bible contains intricate numerical patterns that could not have been contrived because the writers themselves would not have known they were there until after the compilation of the Bible was finished, that is, after the writers' deaths. To say the Bible is myth is too superficial.

While Christians are regaining the understanding that the Bible has many layers of meaning, the Jews apparently never lost it. From the early days of their theological training, future Jewish leaders are taught 4 layers of Bible interpretation, summarized in the acronym PRDS (pronounced "pardes").

HOW DO JEWS INTERPRET THE BIBLE?

Jewish rabbis are trained to interpret the Bible on 4 levels:

1. *Pashat* (simple, literal meaning). This means that God uses words in much the same way we do, so we must start with the most normal, natural, commonly accepted meaning of a word. The Talmud warns, "No passage loses its Pashat." For instance, if "Babylon" means Rome or the Vatican, as some claim, then the word "Babylon" has no objective meaning. The allegorical can stretch or enhance but not replace the literal meaning.

2. *Remez* (hinted, implied meaning). Many truths are hinted at by the literal text. Without hinted meaning, the Bible would have to be a much bigger book. Here are examples of *remez*: Paul said in 2 Corinthians 12:2 that he was caught up to the "third Heaven." That implies there is a first Heaven and second Heaven (our atmosphere is called Heaven, the first level; outer space is the second level). In Revelation 1:5 Jesus is called the "firstborn from the dead." That implies He will not be the last; there will be a 2nd, 3rd, 4th, and in fact many more persons who will be resurrected from the dead. In Revelation 11:1–2, John is told to measure the Temple of God on Earth, which implies that there has to be a physical temple rebuilt on the Temple Mount in Jerusalem. It cannot be a spiritual reference, for how can one "measure" a spiritual temple?

3. *Drash* (searched out, drawn out, metaphorical or homiletical meaning). All students of literature are trained to look for

metaphors used by great writers and to understand the "sub-text." Most Protestants now accept this level of interpretation and call the Biblical metaphors "types" and "shadows." The Exodus of the Jews from Egypt is an object lesson of the deliverance of Christians from sin. In Luke 17:26 (NIV), Jesus applied the *drash* to understand a passage in Genesis, "Just as it was in the days of Noah, so also will it be in the days of the Son of Man." In other words, the days of Noah were a preview to the end times. The *drash* also tells us that the first dictator of the world Nimrod should be a model of the future Anti-Christ. The *drash* includes the "day-year" theory, which can be drawn out from many refer-ences, including 2 Peter 3:8 (NIV), "With the Lord a day is like a thousand years." We will find this a principle helpful for us to understand many numbers. It does not mean that every day in the Bible refers to a thousand years. The context should show prophetic or eschatological intention. For example, Genesis is prophetic of Revelation (the beginning hints at the end), so we can draw many prophetic meanings out of Genesis.

4. *Sod* (secret or mystical meaning). This may involve turning letters into numbers and numbers into letters. Revelation 13:18 tells us the identity of the Anti-Christ will be revealed by calculating the number 666. *Sod* may also involve dissecting a word into its indi-vidual component letters, each of which has its own meaning in the Hebrew language. For instance, Jesus said He is the Truth. The Hebrew word for truth, *amet*, is a 3-letter word consisting of "aleph," "mem," and "tav." Truth starts with the first letter of Hebrew, *aleph*, and ends with the last letter of Hebrew, *tav*. In other words, the *sod* is telling us that Jesus is the Aleph-Tav, the Alpha and Omega, or God Himself. Furthermore, the pictorial of *aleph* is an ox, and the pictorial of ancient *tav* is a cross. The Aleph-Tav is a word picture pointing to an ox (servant or sacri-fice) on a cross! (The sod will be particularly helpful for us as we decipher the divine codes on future dates.)

Unlike some Christian ministers, Jewish rabbis seem comfortable with the thought that the Bible has many layers of meaning and God's Word can be understood on many levels. To Christians, this can be a scary thought. What if we get far out? What if we misinterpret the Bible? Valid concerns, I would agree.

HOW TO STAY BALANCED

How do we stay balanced in our approach to God's Word in general and to God's numbers specifically? The safest rule I can offer you is this (and it's the one I offer my students in international Bible schools): regardless of what level of interpretation you may come across, the deeper message must never contradict the simple text. Or else the Holy Spirit would be contradicting Himself and that would make Him a liar! By definition, God will not contradict Himself. Numbers 23:19 tells us, "God is not a man, that he should lie." So regardless of what dream, revelation, vision, or visitation you get, if the "deep" message contradicts the plain message of the Bible, reject it at once! Lay it aside and put it out of your mind. The purpose of studying God's Word is to think His thoughts, not replace them with spiritual-sounding opinions.

Reading the Bible is always a fresh and new experience for me because I do not close my mind to possibilities unless the interpretation contradicts the plain message of Scripture. This means that Christians must get a solid handle of the basic message of Scripture before venturing to other levels we may study.

I would venture to say that in eternity, we will find the Bible has meaning and messages on an *infinite* number of levels. It is the Supreme product of the Supreme Mind of God. I believe we will be studying God's Word forever!

Specifically, how do we stay balanced when it comes to studying numbers? How can we avoid falling into the one ditch of ignoring numbers and the other ditch of being more engrossed with numbers than the Creator of numbers? Here is the balance: the study of numbers is useful so long as it centers on Christ, who made the numbers and assigned to them meaning. But when numerology centers on man and his attempts to make predictions about himself, then it becomes like astrology, a perversion of something good God made. God made the stars to reflect His glory and tell His Son's story.

STUDYING THE STARS IS ASTRONOMY, BUT FOLLOWING THE STARS IS ASTROLOGY.

STUDYING NUMBERS IS BIBLICAL NUMEROLOGY, BUT FOLLOWING NUMBERS IS IDOLATRY.

With that in mind, I pray that these studies on commonly repeated numbers will enrich your understanding of the Bible and help you see the beauty of the life God gave us.

1

---

1 IS THE NUMBER OF UNITY. God is one. "I and the Father are *one*," Jesus said in John 10:30 (NAS, emphasis added). There are two words for "one" in Hebrew: *echad* meaning a composite unity and *yachid* an absolute singular.

The *shema* or the Jew's daily prayer based on Deuteronomy 6:4–9 starts with, "Hear (*shema*), O Israel, the Lord our God, the Lord is one!" In this prayer, the Hebrew uses the word *echad*, not *yachid*. The Lord is "one" in a similar way a married man and woman become "one flesh"—they become *echad* (Gen. 2:24). This composite unity of God is not made up by the apostle Paul as anti-Trinitarians accuse, but is taught since the first page of the Bible.

Jewish rabbis have long been puzzled by a grammatical "error" found throughout Scripture. All nouns ending in "im" or "in" are plural in Hebrew, like *seraphim* and *cherubim* (angels); *nephillim* and *rephaim* (giants); and *Elohim* (plural of *Eloah*, God). *Elohim* is a plural noun that is always used with a singular verb! Genesis 1:1 begins with, "In the beginning, God [*Elohim*, plural] created [singular] the Heavens and the earth." So is God a singular God or a plural God?

The answer is obvious in the Shema: *Shema Yisrael Adonai Eloheinu Adonai Echad*, which literally says, "Hear Israel God Lord God One." Since *Adonai*, Lord, is a divine title of God, it would be no contradiction to say, "Hear Israel God God God One." The people who deny the Trinity (tri-unity of God) don't understand this concept is not made up by Christians, but revealed by God from the very first words of the Torah.

Another important Scripture to Judaism is the Aaronic or priestly benediction in Numbers 6:24–26:

> The LORD [1] bless you and keep you;
>
> The LORD [2] make His face to shine upon you,
> And be gracious to you;
>
> The LORD [3] lift up His countenance upon you,
> And give you peace.

The use of Lord 3 times corresponds with God the Father, God the Son, and God the Holy Spirit.

The first Lord who "blesses and keeps us" corresponds with God the Father. Ephesians 1:3 says, "The God and Father of our Lord Jesus Christ, who has blessed us with all spiritual blessing in heavenly places in Christ."

The second Lord who "makes His face to shine upon us and is gracious to us" corresponds with Christ, who is "the image of God" (2 Cor. 4:4; Col. 1:15). No human has looked into God the Father's face, but Jesus claimed, "He who has seen Me has seen the Father" (John 14:9). No one was ever so gracious as Jesus, for "grace and truth came through Jesus Christ" (John 1:17).

The third Lord who "lifts up His countenance upon us and gives us peace" corresponds with the Holy Spirit. He was sent to lift up Jesus. Speaking of the Holy Spirit's ministry, Jesus taught, "He will glorify Me, for He will take of what is Mine and declare it to you" (John 16:14). The fruit of the Holy Spirit is "Love, joy, *peace*" (Gal. 5:22, emphasis added). "The kingdom of God is…righteousness and *peace* and joy in the Holy Spirit" (Rom. 14:7, emphasis added). The Holy Spirit lives in us and keeps us in perfect peace!

Is it a coincidence that the 3 most important Scriptures of the Torah— Genesis 1:1, Numbers 6:24–27, and Deuteronomy 6:4-9 —all allude to the Trinity? No doubt this is by design.

The Bible is "progressive revelation" which means as we continue to read through the Bible, concepts that begin in seed form grow clearer to the learner. How many persons do you think King David was referring to in his last words: "The Spirit of the Lord [1] spoke by me, and His word was on my tongue. The God of Israel [2] said, The Rock of Israel [3] spoke to me: 'He who rules over men must be just, ruling in the fear of God'" (2 Sam. 23:2–3)? Clearly David had a revelation of 3 divine persons in the Godhead.

There are other Scriptures which show God talking to God and God acting in conjunction with God. In Genesis 19:24, God had come down to Earth to judge Sodom and Gomorrah, but another person in the Godhead was still up in Heaven: "Then the Lord [1] rained brimstone and fire on Sodom and Gomorrah, from the Lord [2] out of the heavens." David recorded this conversation between God and Himself in Psalm 110:1, "The Lord [1] said to my Lord [2], Sit at My right hand, Till I make Your enemies Your footstool."

IS THE TRINITY NECESSARY?

What philosophers have failed to understand is that a God who is not a Trinity *cannot* be God. One reason is that a lone God would have no understanding of love, apart from His creation. He would *need* His creation to experience love, relationship, trust, community, giving, receiving, authority, submission, and countless other virtues which mortal men know and partake of. If God *needs* His creation, He would cease to be Supreme. A God who is alone is no God at all.

Our God is the God of Community. He has known love and relationship since eternity past, without us and without His creation. God the Father, God the Son, and God the Holy Spirit existed in a harmonious community from the very beginning and didn't need us. He created us out of His overflowing love.

ONLY THE TRINITY CAN BE GOD

An attribute of God is that He must be "all in all" (1 Cor. 15:28). Humans cannot be "all in all" because we live within limitations. To be "all in all" means to *understand* human limitations while at the same time *transcend* all human limitations.

There are Scriptures which indicate that no man has seen God at any time; yet there are many Scriptures in which believers claimed they had seen God face-to-face and not died. These Scriptures seem contradictory. How can both be true?

Only the Trinity can remain unseen on the Father's throne and yet seen face-to-face in the Son. Only the Trinity can exist outside of time through the Father and inside of time through the Son. Only the Trinity can be unknowable and intimately knowable at the same time. Only the Trinity can be *above* humans in the Father, *among* humans in the Son, and *within* humans by the Holy Spirit. Only the Trinity can simultaneously be all in all. Logic affirms the Trinity is the true God.

WHAT DO CULTS THINK OF THE TRINITY?

All "Christian" cults* deny the Trinity because the central issue to salvation is Christ's deity. The Bible is clear that man is a sinner and *God* is the Savior. If Jesus is not God, He is also not our Savior.

A Scripture often quoted by cults is Colossians 1:15: "He is the image of the invisible God, the firstborn over all creation." Cults don't know what the term "firstborn" refers to. They think it means Jesus was *firstborn* of creation or first created. The argument goes like this: if Jesus were created, then He could not be eternal; if He were not eternal, then He could not be God. This is a cultic

---

* "Christian" cults are typically cults whose leaders came out of a Christian Church background. All Christian cults claim to believe Jesus while denying His deity and claim to believe the Bible while promoting other religious books (such as the Book of Mormon, the Pearl of Great Price, Watchtower Literature, Awake Magazine).

attempt to deny the divinity of Christ. The solution to such misinterpretation is to "let the Bible interpret the Bible." In other words, read the Bible in context.

First we should look at the immediate context. Paul wrote a few verses later, "For in Him dwells all the *fullness* of the *Godhead* bodily" (Col. 2:9, emphasis added). In other words, Paul believed Jesus is "God in a body." He would not deny the divinity of Christ in one sentence then assert the divinity of Christ a few sentences later.

Next we should look at the broader context; that is, other Scriptures on the same topic. The New Testament explains that Jesus was not called the "firstborn" at the Genesis Creation nor at the Incarnation, but at His mighty Resurrection! Luke recorded this in Acts 13:33 (KJV), "God hath fulfilled the same unto us their children, in that he hath *raised up* Jesus again; as it is also written in the second Psalm, Thou art my Son, *this day* have I *begotten thee*" (emphasis added). "This day" refers not to the day Jesus was born in Bethlehem, but to the day Jesus resurrected from the dead.

Finally we see in Revelation 1:5 that Jesus is called the "firstborn from the dead." Jesus is called the firstborn because He was the *first* to be resurrected. He's not the firstborn of creation, but the first born of the resurrection. As God, Christ had no beginning. As man, Jesus had a beginning both at birth and at the Resurrection when He became the *firstborn* from the dead. Nothing is more certain in the Bible than the divinity of Christ.

IS THE TRINITY LOGICAL?

A skeptic once challenged me on the Trinity by asking, "How can $1 + 1 + 1 = 1$? Doesn't $1 + 1 + 1 = 3$? You Christians believe in 3 Gods!"

No, in fact, Christians do not believe in 3 separate Gods (called *polytheism*). Nor do Christians believe in 1 God who is merely perceived as 3 different persons (called *oneness*). The Trinity transcends both: God is simultaneously 3 and 1.

I answered this person by saying, "You understand simple math. But this is complex math. It's not $1 + 1 + 1 = 1$, which is wrong. It's more like $\infty + \infty + \infty = \infty$ (infinity + infinity + infinity = infinity), which is right." God the Father is infinite, God the Son is infinite, and God the Holy Spirit is infinite. Together they are not 3 Gods, but 1 infinite God.

This kind of unity is hard for our finite minds to grasp; but make no mistake about it: the Tri-unity of God is mathematically sound and perfectly rational. The Hebrew word *echad* or "one" describes this transcendent unity.

MORE ON 1

1 represents the 1st of the 10 Commandments: "You shall have no other gods before Me" (Exod. 20:3). Jesus says it positively: "And you shall love the LORD your God with all your heart, with all your soul, with all your mind, and with all your strength. This is the first commandment" (Mark 12:30). The question we can ask ourselves to see if we keep the 1st commandment is, "Who do I put before God?" The Bible says Eli honored his sons "more than Me" (1 Sam. 2:29). That was Eli's downfall. God removed His blessing from Eli's family, which was done in all fairness: "For those who honor Me I will honor, and those who despise Me shall be lightly esteemed" (v. 30). The number 1 reminds us we should put God first.

1 is also the atomic number of hydrogen, the smallest element in the universe. It simply is made up of 1 proton and 1 electron. The fusion of 2 hydrogen atoms forming 1 helium atom releases the greatest power known to mankind—the solar energy that makes life possible on Earth.

In this age of energy crisis, most people have heard of nuclear power. But there are 2 kinds of nuclear energy: fission and fusion. On Earth, nuclear power is achieved by *fission* or *splitting* the atoms of the heaviest naturally occurring element—uranium (atomic number 92). In Heaven* nuclear power is sustained by *fusion* or *joining* two hydrogen atoms together. There are at least 2 great lessons from God's design of nuclear energy.

First, the greatest power on Earth comes from *splitting* big elements; whereas the greatest power in Heaven comes from *uniting* the smallest elements. To become more heavenly, we need to do more uniting than splitting!

Second, coal and oil are millions of times larger than a hydrogen or uranium atom, but a little atom can release millions of time greater power. One of men's great mistakes is to underestimate the power of things he does not see and to be impressed with things he does.

God, though invisible to us, is the One constant who made all life on Earth. He does not have to be seen to be felt or known.

A single individual, though seemingly powerless alone, can work in a team to accomplish great things! A few people coming together have won great victories, built great enterprises, and solved great problems. Don't ever underestimate the power of small things or invisible things. The greatest secrets are locked away in them.

---

* The Bible speaks of 3 Heavens. The first Heaven is our atmospheric Heaven, the second Heaven is outer space, and the third Heaven is the home of Christ, His holy angels, and His saints. Our sun and all stars are in the second Heaven. Paul said he "was caught up to the third Heaven" (2 Cor. 12:2).

1.618

1.618 IS CALLED "PHI" (pronounced "fi") in Greek or the golden ratio. It is the number of wisdom or design. Phi appears throughout nature, classical architectural and Biblical architecture.

Noah's ark, the ark of the covenant, and the golden altar all happened to be golden rectangles. Noah's ark was 300 cubits long, 50 cubits wide, and 50 cubits tall (Gen. 6:15)—*the* ideal proportion for stability. The ratio of 5 to 3 is 1.666, as close to phi as you can get with such simple numbers. Visually speaking, the difference between 1.618 and 1.666 is imperceptible to the eye.

The Mosaic ark of the covenant was 2.5 cubits long, 1.5 cubits wide and 1.5 cubits high (Exod. 25:10). The ratio of 2.5 to 1.5 is 1.666.

The Mosaic altar was 3 cubits high, 5 cubits long and 5 cubits wide (Exod. 27:1). The ratio of 5 to 3 is again 1.666.

Phi is a fitting number to represent God's wisdom as it is a number that can *never be written* or *completely known*, its decimals extending out into *infinity*. We may think we know a lot, but phi teaches us we don't even know phi! Humbling indeed.

2

2 IS THE NUMBER OF UNION. Jesus has 2 natures—divine and human; light has 2 natures—wave and particle; the Bible has 2 Testaments—Old and New; humanity needs 2 members—male and female.

2 is also the number of division. Jesus spoke of 2 classes of people—sheep and goats; Paul spoke of 2 kinds of vessels—one for honor, one for dishonor; James spoke of the double-minded man wavering between 2 opinions. When our thoughts are split between 2 options, we become "unstable in all [our] ways" (James 1:8).

2 is the atomic number of helium, the 2nd most common element in the universe, comprising nearly 25 percent of all matter. Hydrogen is the most abundant element in the universe, compromising 75 percent of all matter. Hydrogen and helium together comprise nearly 100 percent of all elements in the universe.[1] That tells us, despite all the alien watchers out there, that the elements on Earth which make life possible are extremely rare. We live on a favored planet. We should be in awe of how God made us special and grateful He formed the earth to be inhabited! (See Isaiah 45:18.)

2 bases are needed for a binary number system, the language of computers. Computers reduce all information—whether word, photo, music, or movie—to 2 numbers: 0 and 1. Computers use binary numbers to represent everything. Something as simple as capital "A" is rendered 01000001. Small letter "a" is 01100001. The binary number system is the foundation of the technological revolution that has swept the world. It would be impossible to grow a modern economy without computers. 2 is all it takes to change the world!

2 is the number of the second person of the Trinity: Jesus Christ. Jesus is both God and man. Jesus has 2 Advents. Jesus multiplied bread twice. Jesus sent His disciples out 2 by 2. Jesus was crucified between 2 thieves. Jesus offers 2 kinds of baptisms: water and fire.

The first letter of the Bible is not "aleph," but "bet" in the word "bereshit" (beginning). In other words, the very first revelation of God was the letter "bet"! Jewish sages have puzzled over why this should be the case, since "aleph" with a numeric value of 1 seems a more obvious choice. "Bet" has a numeric value of 2. It should be no surprise to Christians that the first thing God wanted to reveal was His Number 2—representing Jesus Christ! The Hebrew word "create" or *bara* starts with "bet." One of Jesus' titles, "Son of God" or *Ben Elohim*, also starts with "bet." 2 is the number of Jesus, the first revelation of God, the Creator, the Son of God; He is our Savior who loved us since the beginning.

God gave the Hebrews 2 calendars: the Genesis calendar (starting on the 1st of Tishri) and the Exodus calendar (starting on the 1st of Nisan—the Passover month when the innocent Lamb was slain and Israel delivered from bondage). The first calendar is considered civil or secular. The second calendar is considered religious or spiritual. I am not aware of any other major culture or civilization that was given 2 calendars. What could these 2 calendars represent?

No doubt they represent our old life in sin and our new life in Christ! Every Christian has 2 birthdays: the first is natural, none of us chose to be born physically; the second is spiritual, we all have a choice to be born again spiritually. As the saying goes, "Born once, die twice (spiritually, then naturally). Born twice (naturally, then spiritually), die once."

The new birth is what Jesus referred to when He said, "I am the resurrection and the life. He who believes in Me, though he may die [be separated from his body], he shall live. And whoever lives and believes in Me shall never die [be cut off from God the Author of Life]" (John 11:25–26). When we're born again, it's as if the clock of our life starts again. The calendar turns over to a new year. Truly everything seems new when we repent of our sins and take Christ for our salvation! (See 2 Corinthians 5:17.)

THE 2ND COMMANDMENT

2 represents the 2nd of the 10 Commandments: "You shall not make for yourself a carved image—any likeness of anything that is in Heaven above, or that is in the earth beneath, or that is in the water under the earth; you shall not bow down to them nor serve them" (Exod. 20:4–5).

Idolatry is simply making a god to suit yourself. This can be carved in wood, in stone, or in our hearts. Idolatry usually begins with this statement, "*To me*, God is like this…." So often I've heard people say, "*To me*, God wouldn't judge anyone," or "*To me*, God wouldn't send anyone to hell." Of course, *that* god wouldn't, because *that* god doesn't exist. A god who turns a blind eye to crime, sin, and injustice is not God at all. The true God says He will hold every sinner responsible for his or her sins. In the meantime, He's giving sinners a grace period to repent, believe His Son, and be changed by His Holy Spirit. To avoid idolatry, we must not make a god of our own imagination, but find out who God really is according to His own words.

2 is the number of twins. How many sets of twins were there in the Bible? Just 2: Jacob and Esau, and Pharez and Zerah (Gen. 25:24–26; 38:27–30). Thomas was called "the Twin" (John 11:16; 20:24; 21:2) but we don't know who his twin brother or sister was. Tryphena and Tryphosa (Rom. 16:12), two female ministers in the Church at Rome, may have been twins; this theory is based solely on the similarity of their names.

There are also spiritual twins in the Bible: the twins of faith and patience; and the twins of fear and doubt. Hebrews 6:12 says through "faith and patience" the saints inherited the promises. (See also 2 Thessalonians 1:4; Revelation 13:10.) If we ask and instantly received every time, where would the faith be? We wouldn't need to believe, instead we would *know* by our physical senses that we have received something we wanted. But if we ask and there is a time lag before receiving, then we are trusting God with our hearts and exercising Biblical faith with patience.

Those who truly are in faith will always be calm, in peace, and at rest on the inside, though storms may rage on the outside. (See Hebrews 4:1–10; 3:11–19.) Jesus could sleep during the middle of the storm (Mark 4:38) because He was in faith that nothing could kill Him before the time His mission was completed. Once I pray about something, I refuse to think about it anymore. If the thought or burden tries to come on me, I just remind God, "It's not my concern even though it concerns me." You can be strong in faith and patience by saying, "I cast my care upon You, Lord. It's in Your hands now." Then rejoice and don't worry about it anymore. Just praise God for faith and patience inherit the promises!

THE JEWISH THEORY OF 2 MESSIAHS

Rabbis have tried to reconcile the apparent "contradiction" of one set of Scriptures claiming the Messiah will be a mighty King and another set of Scriptures claiming the Messiah will be a suffering Servant (such as Isaiah 53 vs. Zechariah 12:10). They came up with the theory of "2 Messiahs": one is *Messiah ben Yosef* (Son of Joseph); the other is *Messiah ben David* (Son of David).

The Talmud (Oral Tradition) unnecessarily adds to Scripture by claiming that Messiah ben Yosef will precede Messiah ben David. Messiah ben Yosef will lead the armies of Israel against the nations and die at the battle of Gog and Magog. Messiah ben David will then ask God to resurrect Messiah ben Yosef.[2]

This makes Messiah ben Yoseph the forerunner of Messiah ben David, which is unscriptural since Elijah is the real forerunner. (See Malachi 4:5; Matthew 17:10.) One error breeds more error. Rabbis add more unfounded speculation that there will be a 45-day period[3] between the death of Messiah ben Yosef and the appearance of Messiah ben David, during which time Elijah, the forerunner of the Messiah (uh, which one again?), will come. This type of human speculation is an illustration of Jesus' point to the Pharisees: "Thus you nullify the word of God by your tradition that you have handed down" (Mark 7:13, NIV).

The theory of 2 Messiahs can be discarded when one realizes that all Scriptures get fulfilled in 1 Messiah who has come once and is coming a second time. He came the first time as a suffering Servant to die for the sins of the world; He will come a second time as a glorious King to rule all the earth. Jesus fulfills all Scriptures by His 2 comings and His 2 natures: He is fully God and fully man. Who can save us from our sins? Only God or a perfectly sinless man can. Jesus qualifies on both counts to be the world's Savior.

2

DOUBLES

2 IS THE NUMBER OF DOUBLING. The doubling of anything is an interesting numerical milestone.

Elisha asked Elijah for a *double* portion of his anointing (2 Kings 2:9). On a simple count, Elisha did perform double the miracles that Elijah did. Elijah resurrected one person from the dead. Elisha resurrected two people from the dead! (For a more complete count of miracles in their ministries, read chapter 16.)

Paul said ministers who teach God's Word should be "counted worth of *double* honor" (1 Tim. 5:17) or double pay.

Doubling is an important concept in finance. Any investor knows the *power* of compound interest. Conversely, any debtor feels the *pain* of it! Compound interest is a two-edged sword that can work *against* the borrower, but *for* the lenders and investors.

An interesting question to ask yourself is, "At what rate of interest would I need to invest to double my money every twenty years?" The figure is a surprisingly low 3.49 percent.

Before you get too excited and deposit your money at a local bank paying 3 percent, do you know the average rate of inflation in your nation? In America and Australia, it ranges between 2.5 percent and 4.5 percent.

Inflation is a result of the government printing more money, thus devaluing money and our purchasing power. The more politically correct way to measure inflation these days is by the CPI (consumer price index) which tracks the change (rise) in prices of goods and services.

Inflation is the reason the first Model T Ford produced in 1913 sold for $575, but a Ford sedan today sells for $15,000. That's over 2,000 percent inflation in a lifetime! At an average rate of 3.4 percent inflation compounded, we are losing half our wealth every 20 years simply by doing nothing but holding cash.[1]

Understanding the inflation rate and the power of compound interest helps us to appreciate the wisdom of God. This may be one reason why the God was so adamant that Israel acquire her own land! When God promised to make Israel wealthy (see Deuteronomy 28), He did not give them money. He gave them land

> However, there will be *no poor* among you, since the Lord will surely bless you *in the land* which the Lord your God is giving you as an inheritance to possess.
>
> —Deuteronomy 15:4, nas

Land tends to rise in value while money loses its value. In Australia, land historically doubles its value every 7 years. This certainly is one way to beat inflation!

Many people are counting the rate at which human population *doubles*. The current global growth rate is 1.17 percent. (In parts of Africa, Arabia, and Latin America it exceeds 3 percent.) At this rate the world's population doubles every 40 or so years.

Here are the milestones of human population numbers:[2]

Year	Population
950 A.D.	250 million
1600	500 million
1804	1 billion
1927	2 billion
1960	3 billion
1974	4 billion
1987	5 billion
1999	6 billion
2012	7 billion (projected)

What this is showing is the speed of compound growth. It took 650 years to double 250 million to 500 million, 204 years to double 500 million to 1 billion, 123 years to double 1 billion to 2 billion, and only 47 years to double 2 billion to 4 billion.

What does the speed of compound growth in population tell us? It begs a question for evolutionists: "How many people in total have ever existed if humans have been around for at least half a million years (as evolutionists claim)?" Creationists question the very assumption of millions of years. How can we settle this debate?

Mathematician John Heffner proposed a simple way that any person with a calculator can lay aside all evolutionary and creationist bias and calculate for themselves how long humans have most likely been on this planet.

Let's start with the evolutionary timeline that *Homo sapiens* appeared 500,000 years ago. Start with only 2 people and multiply that by a conservative growth rate of 0.456 percent per year.* What should the current population be after 500,000 years? 2.45×10^{990} people.[3]

To put it in perspective, that's 2 with 990 zeros after it. That's more people than *all* the electrons in the universe! There are 10^{130} electrons. That's also more people than *all* atoms on the earth! 10^{48} is the estimated number of all atoms on the earth.[4] Clearly something is wrong with the evolutionary timeline.

Let's go with a shorter timeline that humans appeared 100,000 years ago (short in evolutionary terms—what's a hundred thousand years when evolutionists talk in terms of *millions* of years?). Let's also drop the population growth rate to 0.1 percent (near extinction level, lower than any in recorded history). If the first human pair appeared 100,000 years ago and the growth rate were just 0.1 percent per year, what should the current population be after 100,000 years? 5.38×10^{43} people.[5] That's 5 with 43 zeros after it. To put it in perspective, 10^{21} is the estimated number of stars in the universe.

This is obviously wrong. Numbers simply don't lie. We currently have 6.5×10^9 or 6.5 billion people.

If Homo sapiens have been around for as long as a million years, there should be billions upon billions of human remains. *Where are all the people?* Archaeology shows humans have buried their dead from the earliest times (cremation being recent). *Where are all the graves?* All of our cities should be built upon piles of human bones! *Where are all the bones?*

To be fair, everyone with a calculator should test the Biblical scenario. God's account of human history records 4 couples survived a worldwide flood some 4,500 years ago. Start with 8 people and multiply by the average growth rate of 0.456 percent, what should the current population be after 4,500 years? 6.5×10^9.

In gaming language, we call that a "bull's eye." The mathematical proof for the Biblical timeline and against the evolutionary timeline is irrefutable. No scientist can challenge this. It doesn't require any twisting and manipulating of

---

* Growth rates are not constant, but fluctuate. For instance, most couples had more children in the past than now and there are now 80 more autoimmune diseases than even as recently as the 1970s. So growth rate should have been higher in the past, but let's assume there were endless wars and constant incurable diseases. Therefore, we use a low figure of less than half the current grow th rate.

data. 2 + 2 = 4 for everybody. The evolution of ape to man never happened and can be disproven by simple crunching of numbers.

As Henry Morris says, "It begins to be glaringly evident that the human race cannot be very old! The traditional Biblical chronology is infinitely more realistic than the million year history of mankind assumed by evolutionists."[6]

There is a counterargument that current growth rates cannot be compared to past growth rates, which is true. If anything, past growth rates should be significantly *higher* than now. In all agricultural societies, couples had more children.

The Bible tells us that people lived longer and had more children in the past. Abraham lived to 175, Isaac 180, Jacob 147, Joseph 110, Moses 120, Aaron 123, and Joshua 110. Three of my great-grandparents lived to 104, 99, and 96. How many children could such long-lived people have?

After the Flood, God told Noah's sons to "be fruitful, and multiply, and replenish the earth" (Gen. 9:1, KJV). Japheth had 7 sons, Shem had 5, and Ham had 4. If we assume the same number of daughters (usually more females born than males), then they had an average of 10.7 children per couple. In the next generation, Japheth had 23 grandsons, Shem had 14, and Ham had 28. The Biblical average after the Flood was 8 to 8.5 children per couple. My own grandmother had 8 children. So did her grandmother.

This represents a population growth rate of 3.7 percent per year or a doubling time of about 19 years.[7] At that more realistic rate, it would be mathematically impossible for man to have existed for millions of years.

Another counterargument says modern growth rate should be *higher* with the advent of modern medicine and sanitation. However, evidence tells us the contrary. "First world" nations with modern medicine are experiencing a decline in growth rate, while "developing world" nations like India and China have outstripped the West in population growth. These objections simply do not stand. Facts confirm the Bible.

Humans re-populated the earth after a worldwide Flood about 4,500 years ago.

I have studied world history and evolution in well-respected schools with anti-Bible professors. I know how ingrained the mantra of millions of years is. Yet, as I was studying, certain questions kept popping up which were unanswerable by the professors.

Why is there no record of human reading or writing beyond 5,000 years ago? In evolutionary terms, the human brain did not develop 5,000 years ago. That is genetically impossible. Why did man suddenly read and write about 5,000 years ago? Linguists are baffled by the *sudden* appearance of languages with complex grammatical rules. Older languages such as Latin and Sanskrit are not "less evolved" than modern languages, they were *more complex!*

No known civilization (Chinese, Mesopotamian, European, or Aztec) dates back more than 5,000 years. Why the absence of evidence if humans have been around for millions of years?

Both Sumerian and Egyptian civilization began abruptly with *no development.* That means at one moment, no one was there; at the next moment (around 5,000 years ago), a society appeared with an advanced form of government, complete written language, legal code, sanitation system, art and music, and complex architecture. It only sounds like a mystery to those who do not believe the Bible.

Within the first few generations after Adam, the Bible names Jabal as a cattle rancher and inventor of tents; Jubal a teacher of musical instruments; and Tubal-Cain a teacher of metal workers (Gen. 4:20–22). Noah and his 8 sons were extremely intelligent people who built an ark, kept a record of God's Word, and repopulated the entire earth. Their descendants built cities and towers with precise engineering that would outlast today's constructions.

2 is the number of doubling. Our human population doubled from 3 billion in 1959 to 6 billion in 1999, a period of only 40 years. Doubling reminds us that evolution is impossible and its timeline incredible. Contrary to the mantra on TV documentaries, math disproves mankind has been around for millions of years. The TV producers have never crunched the numbers. The Bible and math agree.

2

DREAMS

2 IS A NUMBER ASSOCIATED WITH DREAMS. Pharaoh was given 2 dreams. Pharaoh's first dream was of 7 fat cows eaten up by 7 lean cows. Pharaoh's second dream was of 7 plump heads of grain devoured by 7 thin heads of grain. Joseph trusted God for understanding and interpreted the 2 dreams to Pharaoh, "The dreams of Pharaoh are one; God has shown Pharaoh what He is about to do" (Gen. 41:25). The 2 dreams were about the same thing: 7 years of prosperity to be followed by 7 years of famine. Then Joseph explained why the same dream was given twice, "And the dream was repeated to Pharaoh twice because the thing is established by God, and God will shortly bring it to pass" (v. 32). Repetition meant confirmation.

The Book of Daniel records 2 dreams about the same future events. In chapter 2 it tells how Nebuchadnezzar dreamt of a statue with a head of gold, chest and arms of silver, belly and thighs of bronze, legs of iron, and feet of part iron part clay. Finally a stone cut without hands hit the feet of the statue, destroyed it, and filled the whole earth. Daniel trusted God to interpret this dream to Pharaoh. He explained the statue represented successive empires which would deteriorate in glory but increase in strength till the last one.

1. The golden head was Babylon;
2. The silver arms were Medo-Persia (a dual kingdom congruent with the 2 arms) which would defeat Babylon.
3. The bronze belly was Greece which would defeat Medo-Persia.
4. The iron legs was Rome (2 parts again because the Roman Empire would be divided into Eastern Byzantium and Western Rome in A.D. 1054).
5. The feet of clay and iron would be the weakest world kingdom, predicting a revived Greco-Roman Empire, which the European Union (EU) partially fulfills.

All of these empires have one thing in common: they all hated and persecuted Israel. They will finally be struck down together by the Messiah, the "stone cut without hands" (Dan. 2:34) whose kingdom will grow and surpass all other kingdoms.

There is, of course, no way that Daniel could have known which world kingdoms would rise up to oppress Israel. Most political pundits cannot even predict the outcome of the next election. But a wonderful, omniscient God wants us to know that He knows the end from the beginning. His Word is supernatural and reliable. This dream of future empires was so important, God repeated it to Daniel.

In chapter 7, Daniel saw 4 great beasts coming up out of the sea (the sea typifies Gentile nations): first was a lion with eagle's wings; second a bear; third was a leopard with 4 wings; last was a composite beast with 4 heads, iron teeth, 10 horns, and a little horn. Then Daniel saw the last beast and its little horn destroyed by the "Ancient of Days…[and] the Son of Man coming with the clouds of Heaven…His kingdom [is] the one Which shall not be destroyed" (Dan. 7:9, 13–14).

The interpretation of Daniel's dream was the same as Nebuchadnezzar's.

1. The lion was Babylon.

2. The bear was Medo-Persia.

3. The leopard was Greece—with 4 wings because after the death of Alexander the Great, his kingdom was divided among his 4 generals into Thrace (east), Macedonia (west), Syria (north) and Egypt (south).

4. The composite beast represented both ancient Rome and the end-time Greco-Roman Empire (EU) which shall contain all the elements of the first 4 empires.

The reason I said the EU does not yet completely fulfill the prophetic picture is we are waiting for Iraq (Babylon), Iran (Persia), Syria, and Egypt (the northern and southern divisions of ancient Greece) to come into play. The 2 Gulf Wars have certainly put Iraq back on the prophetic map. Iran's nuclear ambitions put her back on world center stage. We are now waiting for Syria and Egypt to be back in geopolitical prominence. Then the picture of the composite anti-Semitic beast would be complete.

Remember it is a loose confederacy, not as united as the previous gold, silver, bronze, or iron kingdoms, but mixed of iron and clay—substances that do not stick well together. The little horn of this mixed up beast will be the Anti-Christ.

All of these worldly kingdoms which share a hatred for Israel will pass away when one like the "Son of Man" will rule an eternal kingdom in their stead. This is a prophetic description of Jesus Christ the King.

2 is the number of confirmation. "By the mouth of two or three witnesses every word shall be established" (2 Cor. 13:1; Matt. 18:16; Deut. 19:15).

It a court of law, a minimum of 2 to 3 witnesses is required to establish a truth. In theology, a minimum of 2 to 3 Scriptures are needed to establish a doctrine. Peter saw the vision of God calling unclean animals clean three times (Acts 10:16). This was to *confirm* to Peter that God was indeed calling Gentiles to become part of the body of Christ.

I have found that when a leading is of the Lord, it doesn't tend to go away. Jonah knew he was called to Nineveh no matter how he ran from the call. Paul knew he would suffer by going to Jerusalem, "The Holy Spirit testifies in every city, saying that chains and tribulations await me" (Acts 20:23). Because the Lord's voice is persistent, I do not interpret every passing whim and feeling as the leading of the Lord. If it is God's will, it will be confirmed by the Scriptures, in my spirit, and often through spiritual people whom I trust (like my wife). I do not demand confirmation from God, and I never ask for signs, which are very dangerous for believers to ask. As a New Testament believer, I trust that God's leading will be so clear in my born-again spirit, I will never be in confusion. When God speaks, I have only 2 options: obey or disobey. When it's not so clear, it's not time to act.

2 is a number associated with holy dreams. I read a newspaper article about one Australian minister who claimed he had a dream of the great Australian bush fire of February 2009 about 3 months before it happened; but another leader rejected his dream. The leader of an old mainline denomination said he doubted that God spoke to anyone in dreams anymore and quoted Hebrews 1:1–2 as his justification, "God, who at various times and in various ways spoke in time past to the fathers by the prophets, has in these last days spoken to us by His Son."

It is true that we must be careful not to accept every dream or vision. Mohammed and Joseph Smith both claimed to have seen an angel and out of those visions came two new religions that deny Jesus Christ as God—Islam and Mormonism.

On the other hand, we should not throw the baby out with the bath water. If Hebrews 1 (written ca. A.D. 68) meant God would no longer communicate to us in dreams and visions, then that would strike out the entire Book of Revelation (written ca. A.D. 90). John received the message of Revelation entirely through dreams and visions *after* the writing of the Book of Hebrews.

To say that God no longer communicates in dreams and visions would contradict Acts 2:17, quoting Joel 2:28, which promise, "And it shall come to pass in the last days, says God, That I will pour out of My Spirit on all flesh; Your sons and your daughters shall prophesy, Your young men shall *see visions*, Your old men shall *dream dreams*" (emphasis added). Not only should we believe God can speak in dreams, the Bible predicts there will be an *increase* in dreams and visions in the last days. Many stories of modern conversions in countries where Christians are heavily persecuted began in dreams that led the seekers to a Bible or personal contact with a Christian who shared the Gospel.

The way to stay Biblically balanced is not to dismiss dreams, but to test every dream and vision by the litmus of God's Word. No holy dream or vision can ever contradict God's written Word. Even Peter, who witnessed Jesus' transfiguration before his very eyes and heard God the Father's audible voice declare, "This is My Beloved Son, in whom I am well pleased. Hear Him!" (Matt. 17:5), admitted, "We have also a *more sure* word of prophecy; whereunto ye do well that ye take heed" (2 Pet. 1:19, KJV, emphasis added). According to Peter, what is more sure than what his eyes saw and his ears heard? God's written Word!

I have had several dreams from God. I always checked them against God's Word, and the meanings of the dreams were immediately apparent to me. God does not speak to us in dreams to confuse us. He is trying to get our attention.

Members of my Church have also reported unusual dreams and visions. As long as the interpretation lined up with the Word of God, I believed the dreams could be legitimate. In repeated instances, a Church member who cannot read or write was told by an angel, "Go back to Church!" That command certainly agrees with Hebrews 10:25, doesn't it? "Not forsaking the assembling of ourselves together."

Some Christians get caught up with dreams and visions and ignore God's Word. This is a mistake that will derail them off course. Even Paul, who was caught up to the third Heaven where he heard things unspeakable, acknowledged in 2 Timothy 3:16, "All Scripture is given by inspiration of God, and is profitable for doctrine, for reproof, for correction, for instruction in righteousness." Paul knew to put God's Word above his own visions. Every true minister of God will elevate the Word of God above his dreams and visions. The clearest leadings and confirmations I have ever received have come from God's Word!

3

3 IS GOD'S NUMERICAL SIGNATURE, the number of the Divinity. There are 3 persons in the Trinity. The very title "Lord Jesus Christ" contains the Trinity—Lord refers to the Father, Jesus refers to the Son, and Christ refers to the anointing of the Holy Spirit.[1] There are 3 parts of man—spirit, soul, and body; 3 time periods we know—past, present, and future; 3 physical dimensions we live in—width, depth, and height; 3 atoms to the molecule of life H_2O; 3 states of water which makes life possible on Earth. We are the only planet known in the universe where water exists simultaneously as liquid, vapor, and solid ice. We live on 30 percent of the surface area of the 3rd planet in the solar system.

The Trinity made all the elements in the universe out of 3 subatomic particles: protons, neutrons, and electrons. Protons and neutrons form the nucleus of every atom (except the hydrogen nucleus made of a single proton), and electrons revolve around the nucleus. Protons and neutrons are now known to be each made up of quarks, which are even smaller subatomic particles. (See chapter 12 or 24.) A proton is made of 3 quarks (2 up, 1 down). A neutron is also made of 3 quarks (2 down, 1 up). Electrons are responsible for the energy on which human civilization depends: electricity. Electricity produces 3 things we need: light, heat, and power. Like God's power, electricity cannot be seen, yet its benefits can be felt by all, described by some, and harnessed by few. Treat it carelessly, and you will be destroyed by it. Treat it with respect, and you will enjoy life much more abundantly. Most people are unaware of electricity, just as they are unaware of God, but treat God with respect, and He will give light to your mind, a warm glow to your spirit, and healing power to your body.

In chemistry there are 3 types of bonds: single, double, and triple. Only 3 elements can form all 3 types of bonds: carbon, nitrogen, and oxygen. Our genetic library—the DNA—is made up of 3 chemical building blocks: phosphates, sugars, and nitrogen bases (A, T, C and G). 3 types of alleles (A, B, O) make up the 4 human blood types (A, B, AB, and O)

First John 1:5 says "God is light" and 2 Corinthians 4:4 calls the Gospel "light." The speed of light is 300,000 kilometers per second. When the Human

Genome Project (1990–2003) was completed, guess how many DNA base pairs they counted in humans? 3 billion!

The Levites, chosen for divine service in God's house, represented the 3rd tribe of Israel. The Book of Leviticus outlines 3 types of laws: moral, sacrificial, and ceremonial (about diet, hygiene, sanitation). Most religious people are aware of the moral rules of do's and don'ts, but if they were sufficient to save us, why is ⅓ of the Law about the need for blood sacrifices to wash away sins? The ceremonial laws were both practical advice and a prophetic picture of our need to be fed and cleansed daily by God's Word.

There were 3 items in the ark of the covenant: the 10 Commandments written in stone; Aaron's rod that budded; and a golden pot of manna or heavenly bread. If the Law were sufficient for us to approach God, why were the other 2 items in the ark, which represents the presence of God? The Law only leads us to Aaron's rod that budded—something dead that gives life—a perfect picture of the Cross and Resurrection of Christ. The manna represents the Word, which daily renews our mind after getting saved at the cross.

The Hebrew Bible or Tanakh is made of 3 parts: the Torah (Law), Nevi'im (Prophets) and Ketuvim (Writing or Psalms). The first letter of each division spells the acronym T-N-K. Since ancient Hebrews did not write vowels, the 3 consonants T-N-K can be vocalized as TaNaKh.*

There are 3 types of mitochondria DNA (mtDNA) which are distributed throughout the world's population. Named M, N, and R, these 3 mtDNA provide stunning validation of Noah's Flood and the 4 couples on board. Why? Just as the Y chromosome is inherited only from fathers, mitochondria DNA is inherited only from our mothers. Noah's wife would have passed her mtDNA to her 3 surviving sons. However, their children would have inherited their mtDNA from the 3 wives of Noah's sons. There are other mtDNA which are very closely related to each other but isolated to sub-Sahara Africa. Named L0, L1, L2, and L3, Dr. Rob Carter reasons that these may be accounted for by post-Flood genetic mutations in mtDNA N.** Advances in human genome studies are disappointing to evolutionary theory because it shows all humans are genetically 99 percent the same! Where is the genetic diversity after "millions of years"? Where is the mitochondrial diversity? All males have nearly the same Y chromosome and all humans have only 3 lineages of mtDNA. Genetics is

* Similarly, the covenant name of God is made of 4 consonants YHWH which can be vocalized as YaHWeH or JeHoVaH.
** The entire "out of Africa" theory of human origins rests on the assumption that L0 is the first mtDNA, whereas Dr. Carter statistically shows that mtDNA "R" was more likely Eve's mtDNA. The difference is not in evidence, but how the evidence is explained, i.e. the stories scientists tell. See Carter, Dr Robert, *Mitochondrial Eve and the 3 "Daughters" of Noah*, DVD, at www.creation.com.

adding evidence there had to be 1 Y-chromosome "Adam" and 1 mitochondrial "Eve."

There are 3 types of languages on the earth: isolating languages (e.g., Chinese, Tibetan, most Southeast Asian languages except Malay); fusional or inflected languages (e.g., Latin, Greek, most European languages); and agglutinative languages (Korean, Japanese, Turkish, Finnish, Hungarian, Basque).

Interestingly, the Third Commandments is a prohibition on language or the wrong use of our tongue. The 3rd Commandment reads: "You shall not take the name of the LORD your God in vain, for the LORD will not hold him guiltless who takes His name in vain" (Exod. 20:7). This sin is called blasphemy. In an age of increasing disrespect, we tend to make light of blasphemy, but it is the third worst sin in the Bible.

In January 2009, the Australian public was shocked that novelist Harry Nicolaides was sentenced to 3 years of jail by the Thai court for "insulting the King of Thailand." Many people today don't understand the gravity of the crime, but in older times, such a loose mouth would be executed! (See 1 Kings 21:10.) The Thais understand the crime and accept the sentence as proportionate to the offense, because they have such a love and respect for their king. He has, after all, ruled the nation benevolently for 62 years. He deserves some respect.

What about God? He has ruled long before anyone else ruled. He is loved by billions of angels and saints. Does He deserve respect? But He says, "My name is blasphemed continually every day" (Isa. 52:5).

What is blasphemy? It is using God's name in vain. That includes using the name of Jesus as an expression of disgust. Could anyone get away with it if, in a moment of disgust, they shouted the king of Thailand's name in vain? No! If such honor is paid an earthly king, how much more should be paid to Jesus, Heaven's King!

There is a lot more blasphemy going on than we care to admit. God would not have made it His number 3 otherwise. In the New Testament, it is the only unpardonable sin. Jesus said: "Therefore I say to you, every sin and blasphemy will be forgiven men, but the blasphemy against the Spirit will not be forgiven men. Anyone who speaks a word against the Son of Man, it will be forgiven him; but whoever speaks against the Holy Spirit, it will not be forgiven him, either in this age or in the age to come" (Matt.12:31–32).

What was Jesus' definition of blasphemy? In this context, he healed a blind and mute man, but the religious Pharisees said the devil healed the man. The Pharisees had blasphemed the Holy Spirit. In other words, blasphemy is crediting the work of God to Satan, and the work of Satan to God.

Things that should not be blasphemed are: God, God's name, God's Word,

3

God's servants, God's people, and God's tabernacle. (See Titus 2:5; Acts 6:11, 13:45, 18:6; Revelation 2:9, 13:6.)

The 3rd commandment is one of the most violated commandments in Scripture. The Bible predicts a rise of blasphemers in the end times: "But know this, that *in the last days* perilous times will come: For men will be lovers of themselves, lovers of money, boasters, proud, blasphemers, disobedient to parents, unthankful, unholy" (2 Timothy 3:1–2).

Have you ever heard a person mocking one of God's servants: "That evangelist is just out to get money"? When the Jews accused Jesus as being a counterfeit and an imposter, He replied, "I do not have a demon; but I honor My Father, and you dishonor Me" (John 8:49). He was saying, "You are blaspheming Me, because I am a true Servant of God." A critical person must have real evidence before he accuses a servant of God, or else he will be liable for blasphemy.

Unfortunately Paul had to instruct some Christians to stop blaspheming: "But now you yourselves are to put off all these: anger, wrath, malice, blasphemy, filthy language out of your mouth" (Col. 3:8). No Christian I know would like to think he or she could possibly be guilty of blasphemy, but if none blaspheme, to whom was Paul talking?

Have you ever heard a Christian say, "Speaking in tongues is of the devil"? According to 1 Corinthians 12:10, it is a gift of the Holy Spirit! How believers can say such things without fear of breaking the 3rd commandment is beyond me. They may not understand it, but the Holy Spirit deserves respect nonetheless. To call God's gift demonic—what is that if not blasphemy?

Have you ever heard a Christian say: "God made me sick to teach me a lesson"? Some Christians do not think there's anything wrong with accusing God of making them sick. Yet Scriptures point to Satan as the source of sickness and God as the source of healing.

> The *thief* [Satan] does not come except to steal, and to kill, and to destroy. I [Jesus] have come that they may have *life*, and that they may have it more *abundantly*.
>
> —JOHN 10:10, EMPHASIS ADDED

Anything that steals, kills, and destroys is from Satan. Sickness robs people of their health and destroys their bodies. Jesus never once made anybody sick. He made people well. He came to give us abundant life.

> So ought not this woman, being a daughter of Abraham, whom *Satan has bound*—think of it—for eighteen years, be loosed from this bond on the Sabbath?
>
> —Luke 13:16, emphasis added

Jesus called sickness satanic bondage. Satan bound, Jesus loosed. They never switch roles!

> So *went Satan forth* from the presence of the Lord, and *smote* Job with sore boils from the sole of his foot unto his crown.
>
> —Job 2:7, emphasis added

> And the Lord turned the *captivity* of Job, when he prayed for his friends: also the Lord gave Job twice as much as he had before.
>
> —Job 42:10, emphasis added

The Book of Job calls sickness satanic captivity. One thing is clear: Satan held Job captive, but God set Job free. Don't let any religious argument or experience alter the plain teaching of God's Word: Satan struck Job, God healed Job.

> How God anointed Jesus of Nazareth with the Holy Spirit and with power, who went about *doing good* and *healing* all who were *oppressed by the devil*, for God was with Him.
>
> —Acts 10:38, emphasis added

Luke the physician called sickness demonic oppression. Jesus was anointed to do *good* and *heal* the sick. Healing is called good.

"Woe to those who call *evil good*, and *good evil*" (Isaiah 5:20, emphasis added). Despite all these Scriptures calling sickness bad and healing good, some Christians insist on calling sickness "good" or a "blessing in disguise." Though some Christians do not think anything wrong of it, is it not blasphemy? It is crediting the work of Satan to God.

Everyone who blasphemes feels justified in doing it, even the novelist who was jailed for insulting the king. But the Bible tells Christians to not blaspheme. 3 reminds us of blasphemy.

When we humbly obey God's Word, God promises healing and long life!

> And ye shall serve the Lord your God, and he shall bless thy bread, and thy water; and I will take sickness away from the midst of thee.

There shall nothing cast their young, nor be barren, in thy land: the *number* of thy *days* I will fulfil.

—Exodus 23:25–26, KJV, EMPHASIS ADDED

Healing and longevity are God's promises to the obedient. Here is the same promise in another translation.

You must serve only the LORD your God. If you do, I will bless you with food and water, and I will protect you from illness. There will be no miscarriages or infertility in your land, and I will give you long, full lives.

—Exodus 23:25–26, NLT

It takes 3 witnesses to confirm a truth in the Bible or in a court of law. I have cited 5 witnesses which say Satan makes sick and God makes well. We may praise God through times of sickness or even use a period of hospitalization to witness to other sick folks about God. However, I do not have to be sick to witness in a hospital. I have intentionally gone to many hospitals to witness to and pray for the sick, their visitors, nurses, and doctors. God does not use sickness to teach us a lesson. God uses His Word to teach us. We may decide to obey God during times of sickness, but His Word should be enough to cause us to obey.

Our God, being a Trinity, does not need a man, an angel, or any other witness to confirm His testimony. He is His own perfect witness.

3.1415

3.1415 IS CALLED "PI" not to be confused with "phi" (1.618). Pi is the ratio of a circle's circumference to its diameter. Like phi, it is a constant whose decimal value never repeats and never ends. 3.1415 is only an estimate.

There is a common complaint by Bible skeptics based on the value of pi. They say that the Bible gives the wrong value of pi in 1 Kings 7:23 and 2 Chronicles 4:2 (NIV):

> He [Hiram the metal worker in Solomon's Temple] made the Sea of cast metal, circular in shape, measuring ten cubits from rim to rim and five cubits high. It took a line of thirty cubits to measure around it.

Ignore the height of 5 cubits; the skeptics are only worried about the 30 cubits circumference divided by 10 cubits diameter. 30 divided by 10 equals 3. Such dimensions, say they, give the wrong ratio for pi; therefore the Bible must not be the Word of God!

Truly this proves nothing but nitpicking. Any math student knows that 3.1 can be rounded off as 3. Any Bible student knows that the Bible doesn't give any decimal for any number. Any history student knows that the decimal point was not in common use at the time of Solomon. Many ancient cultures did not even have a symbol to notate "0," never mind digits to the right of 0.

The Jewish sage Maimonides (1135–1204) commented on 1 Kings 7:23, "The ratio [which Greeks called pi] cannot be known. Since it is impossible to arrive at a perfectly accurate ratio, they assumed a round number."[1] Maimonides is revealing advanced mathematical knowledge based on his knowledge of God. He made this statement in the 12th century, long before Johann Lambert proved pi is irrational (cannot end) in 1761 and Ferdinand von Lindemann proved pi is transcendental (cannot have repeating patterns) in 1882. God's people should have more wisdom that the world's.

Would Bible skeptics repent of their sins and embrace a life of obedience had the writer of 1 Kings 7:23 written, "Solomon's bowl actually measured 9.64866 cubits in diameter and 30.31213 cubits in circumference"? I seriously doubt it.

Perhaps the ancient writer hated fractions, like many students do, and thought any reasonable person would accept 10 and 30 cubits as rounded figures!

But to prove to any sincere skeptic that God always anticipates their questions, I will give a more precise solution.

Whenever someone attacks the Scriptures or misinterprets a Scripture, the answer is often found right there in the context. In other words, most answers to big Bible conundrums have been found by simply reading the verses *before* or *after* the verse in question. In this case the skeptics have omitted to read the following verses:

> He made the *Sea* of *cast metal*, circular in shape, measuring *ten cubits from rim to rim* and *five cubits* high. It took a line of *thirty cubits* to measure around it. [What does "it" refer to? The cast metal of the inner bowl.] *Below the rim*, gourds [KJV, knops] encircled it— ten to a cubit. The gourds were cast in two rows in one piece with the Sea....*It* [the extra outer rim, an addition to the inner bowl] was a *handbreath* in *thickness*, and its *rim* was like the *rim* of a cup, like a lily blossom. It held two thousand baths.
> —1 KINGS 7:23–24, 26, NIV, EMPHASIS ADDED

John Boatwright pointed out that the brim in verse 23 was an attribute of the bowl, but *not* that the brim itself was 30 cubits in circumference or 5 cubits tall (making the bowl a cylinder).[2] The measurement of the diameter included this thick brim as a finished bowl; but for the purpose of metal casting, Hiram only needed the circumference of the inner bowl, without the extra thick brim to hang the knops. A handbreadth being approximately 0.225 cubit or 4.5 inches, we would have to subtract 0.45 (0.225 x 2 sides of the brim) from the diameter, which gives us a circumference to diameter ratio of 30 to 9.55. What then is the Bible's value for pi? 3.14!

Our estimate of a handbreadth being 4.5 inches could well be slightly off. It would not surprise me that with precise knowledge of a cubit and handbreadth, the Bible's pi value would be exact.

If the skeptics were honest, they should admit God is perfectly wise and His Word perfectly accurate. Accusing God of being wrong in math is a smokescreen for a proud heart. We should settle it in our hearts that no accusation will ever stick to God. When we feel like complaining against God, realize that we have incomplete knowledge. When we think His Word is wrong, we can safely assume the Word is not wrong. We should exercise enough humility to admit our understanding may be wrong.

Numbers can teach us about God! Let's see if any skeptic will become a believer after reading this. "Don't let the pi hit you in the eye!"

One last note on pi: The ratio of the 22 letters of the Hebrew alphabet to its 7 vowels is 22/7 or pi (3.14). Jewish rabbis claim that Hebrew was the original language of mankind before the Tower of Babel. Perhaps we will be reading and writing Hebrew in Heaven.

3.5

3.5 IS HALF OF 7. It is the number of preparation (half way to completion). Jesus' ministry lasted 3.5 years; the disciples' training under Jesus lasted 3.5 years; the Tribulation and Great Tribulation are 2 periods each lasting 3.5 years or 42 months or 1,260 days. The smallest unit of time in the Hebrew calendar is 1 *helek* or 3 ⅓ seconds, which means there are 1080 *halakim** in an hour. It takes 3–4 years to graduate most Bible schools. It takes 3–4 years to obtain a university degree. It takes 3–4 years to complete an apprenticeship in a trade. I suppose 3.5 years should be the ideal length of time for a season of preparation.

There is a distinction between calling and separation. Paul knew this when he introduced his letter to the Romans, "Paul, a bondservant of Jesus Christ, *called* to be an apostle, *separated* to the gospel of God" (Rom. 1:1, emphasis added). Paul was called in Acts 9, but he was not separated until Acts 13, "As they ministered to the Lord and fasted, the Holy Spirit said, 'Now *separate* to Me Barnabas and Saul for the work to which I have *called* them'" (v. 2, emphasis added). Calling comes before separation. Between calling and separation is preparation.

In Paul's case, he sensed his calling since he was young. Paul was schooled under one of the most famous Jewish rabbis named Gamaliel (see Acts 22:3), yet he was not ready to serve the Lord. On the contrary he worked *against* the Lord by persecuting Christians. When Paul was miraculously saved on the road to Damascus, he learned the true nature of his calling—to preach Christ among the Gentiles—yet he was not ready to jump into ministry. Paul had to be retrained in the "School of the Spirit."

In Galatians 1:16–18, Paul described God's call on his life and his preparation: "To reveal His Son in me, that I might preach Him among the Gentiles, I did not immediately confer with flesh and blood, nor did I go up to Jerusalem to those who were apostles before me; but I went to Arabia, and returned again to Damascus. Then *after three years* I went up to Jerusalem to see Peter, and remained with him fifteen days" (emphasis added). How long did his preparation take? About three years!

It was probably in Arabia and Damascus that Paul received most of his

---

* *Halakim* is plural of *helek*, much as seraphim and cherubim are plurals of seraph and cherub.

revelations. Then he went to double-check his doctrine with Peter and James, the Lord's brother. These were the respected Christian leaders in Jerusalem. Even though Paul received visions and revelations directly from Jesus, he did not get into pride and think he was above accountability. Instead, after 3 years of preparing, he submitted all his teachings to Peter and James. This attitude of humble submission is the mark of all true ministers of God.

Paul expected the Corinthian Christians to have grown up spiritually by the time he wrote the book of 1 Corinthians. That letter came 3–4 years after he had established that Church.

> And I, brethren, could not speak to you as to spiritual people but as to *carnal*, as to *babes* in Christ. I fed you with milk and not with solid food; for until now you were not able to receive it, and even now you are still not able; for you are *still carnal*. For where there are envy, strife, and divisions among you, are you not *carnal* and behaving like mere [unspiritual] men?
>
> —1 Corinthians 3:1–3, emphasis added

One can detect a note of disappointment in the apostle's tone. Paul was disappointed that they were still carnal, as evidenced by their envy, strife, and division, after 3–4 years of learning God's Word. That tells me it is possible to mature spiritually within 3-4 years, if we set our hearts to study God's Word and pray.

I believe it takes at least 3 years to know anyone truly. Judas' heart was not revealed till the end of 3.5 years. Evidently he had fooled everyone for 3 years, as none of the other disciples suspected he was the betrayer; but he could not fool everyone after 3.5 years.

I dated my wife a little over 3 years before I married her. I'm glad we took the time to date and really get to know each other. Too many young people rush when time is on their side. 3.5 years is not long compared to being married for a lifetime. Let time prove people's attitudes and motives. Time is your friend!

4

4 IS THE NUMBER OF THE GOSPEL, which is the story of how man can be restored to right relationship with God. By extension, 4 is also the number of relationship. 4 (3 + 1) = Gospel (God + man). That is why there are 4 Gospels (Matthew, Mark, Luke, and John); 4 major prophets (Isaiah, Jeremiah, Ezekiel, and Daniel); 4 gates into the tabernacle (representing the way to God); 4 languages used in the Bible (Hebrew, Chaldean, Greek, Aramaic); 4 women named in Jesus' genealogy (Rahab, Ruth, Tamar, Bathsheba)*; 4 forces governing the relationship between every matter in the universe (strong, weak, electromagnetic, and gravitational); 4 nucleotides in the DNA (adenine, thymine, guanine, and cytosine); 4 personality types (choleric, melancholy, sanguine, phlegmatic); 4 blood types (A, B, AB, O)**; 4 kinds of soil of the human heart (wayside, rocky, thorny, or good); and 4 "months till harvest" (John 4:35). Judah, the Messianic tribe from which David and Jesus descended, is the 4th tribe of Israel. The first 4 of 10 Commandments deal with our relationship to God (the last 6 deal with our relationship to fellow man, hardly a coincidence since 6 is the number of man).

Jesus told His disciples to spread the Gospel in 4 places: "But you shall receive power when the Holy Spirit has come upon you; and you shall be witnesses to Me in Jerusalem, and in all Judea and Samaria, and the end of the earth" (Acts 1:8). Literally this took place as the Church first grew within Jerusalem and Judea; then was forced out by persecution to Samaria, then to the rest of the world. (See Acts 8; 11:19.)

---

* In Matthew 1, not counting Mary. Other than the royal mother, women ancestors are not usually named in ancient royal family trees. The mention of these 4 women—a prostitute from Canaan, a Gentile from Moab, an incestuous woman in Israel, and an adulteress in Israel—is purely redemptive. It tells us God is able to restore anyone no matter how dark their past.

** Human blood types can also be + or −. People with type O− are considered universal donors because they can give blood to any human. People with type AB+ are considered universal recipients because they can receive any blood type. Blood types have nothing to do with personality, but the legend that it does is so popular among the Japanese that they often ask, "What is your blood type?" 99 percent of the Chinese have + blood types, yet no one would claim 99 percent of the Chinese have similar personalities. Cats have 11 blood types, yet no one would claim cats have 11 personalities (9 lives, maybe). The 4 blood types of humans are by God's design, pointing to the Gospel. He wrote 4 Gospels for every type of person. It would not surprise me that the 4 Gospel writers also had 4 different blood types. We won't know till we get to Heaven.

Personally this means Jesus wants Christians to preach about Him in 4 places: our home [our Jerusalem]; our neighborhood [Judea]; places we don't like to go to [Samaria]; and distant lands [the uttermost part of the earth].

In the Book of Acts, we find that the Apostle Paul went on 4 missionary journeys to spread the Gospel and establish some of the first Churches.

1. Acts 13–14
2. Acts 15:36–18:22
3. Acts 18:23–20:38
4. Acts 23:11–28:31

By reading the Book of Acts one can see how the local Church holds a special place in God's heart and Gospel plan.

A key Gospel verse, "The just shall live by faith," appears 4 times in the Bible (Hab. 2:4; Rom. 1:17; Gal. 3:11; Heb. 10:38). Martin Luther rediscovered this verse while reading the Book of Romans and the world has never been the same since! The Protestant Reformation exploded from this revelation. If the just shall live (be saved eternally) by faith, then we should not depend our own good works, religious merits, or any other form of *self-salvation*. This key verse distinguishes the Christian message from every other religion in the world. God's wisdom says we must be saved by trusting in Someone greater than ourselves; man's pride says I hope to be saved by depending on *no one* greater than myself.

4 is the number of good news, even before Jesus came. The pre-Flood warning was preached to 4 generations: those of Enoch, Methuselah, Lamech, and Noah. Enoch obviously knew about the Flood because he named his son Methuselah, meaning "when he is dead it [the Flood] shall come." What a strange name to call your son. I'm sure every believer was concerned about Methuselah's health every time he sneezed! The number of years each of these 4 men lived all have a unique number. Enoch never saw death or the Flood because he was translated to Heaven at the age of 365. Methuselah lived the longest life on record and died on the year of the Flood at the age of 969. Lamech died before the Flood at the age of 777. Noah died after the Flood at the age of 950.

After the Exodus, the Jews traveled through the wilderness with God's tabernacle (holy tent of meeting) at the center. As they journeyed from Egypt to the Promised Land, the 12 tribes were regimented into 4 camps of 3 tribes each, each camp being positioned according to cardinal compass points: the camp of

Dan to the north of the tabernacle; the camp of Reuben due south; the camp of Ephraim due west; and the camp of Judah due east.

Everything God does has significance; and thanks to Chuck Missler's calculations, we now know have a vivid picture of what these 4 camps represented (see chart, "The Camp of Israel").[1]

Since God's instruction to the tribes was not to *encircle* the tabernacle, but to *spread out* due north, south, east, and west of the tent, the 4 camps actually formed a cross marching through the desert. Based on the number of people in each camp, we can see that the north and south camps had roughly the same number of people, the west camp had the least, and the east camp had the most. By drawing the 4 camps directly north, south, east, and west of the tabernacle, we discover a picture of the cross on which Jesus would be hung.

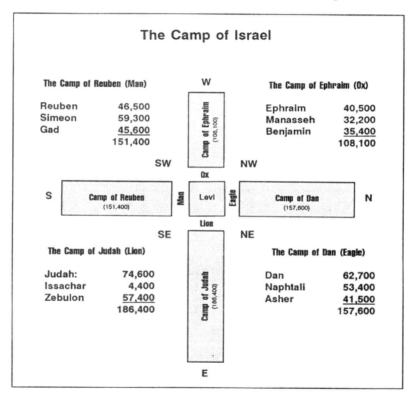

When the prophet Balaam looked down on the approaching Israeli army, he did not see a swarm of soldiers around the tabernacle, but 4 distinct, tightly-organized camps in symbolic order. Balaam asked, "Who can count the dust of

Jacob, and the number of the *fourth part* of Israel? Let me die the death of the righteous, and let my last end be like his!" (Num. 23:10, KJV, emphasis added). When Balaam looked down on God's marching people, he actually saw the cross moving through the desert! 4 is the number of the Gospel, in object lesson form!

4 is the number of restoration. David told Nathan that whoever stole the lamb, "he shall restore *fourfold* for the lamb, because he did this thing and because he had no pity" (2 Sam, 12:6, emphasis added). He didn't know that in this case the lamb was Bathsheba and the thief was himself! The day Zacchaeus got saved he said, "Look, Lord, I give half of my goods to the poor; and if I have taken anything from anyone by false accusation, I restore *fourfold*" (Luke 19:8, emphasis added). The Gospel is the news that restores a sinner back to his original position with God.

Jews celebrate the Passover with 4 cups based on the 4 "I will's" of God in Exodus 6:6–7. "*I will* bring you out from under the burdens of the Egyptians, *I will* rescue you from their bondage, and *I will* redeem you with an outstretched arm and with great judgments. *I will* take you as My people" (emphasis added).

1. The 1st cup is the cup of bringing out.
2. The 2nd cup is the cup of deliverance.
3. The 3rd cup is the cup of redemption or blessing.
4. The 4th cup is the cup of taking out.

Every detail of the Passover feast points to Christ. Each of these 4 cups speaks of the 4 phases of Jesus' work in the believer's life.

First, Jesus *brings* our spirits *out* of Satan's kingdom. By faith in Christ, we are saved from sin and given a brand-new spirit.

Second, Jesus *delivers* our minds through His Word. Moses may have been the first preacher to make this statement, "You can take Israel out of Egypt, but you can't take Egypt out of Israel!" It means Israel was physically removed out of Egypt, but they were still mentally held captive by their past in Egypt. Like Israel, we too may be saved spiritually but not delivered mentally from our old patterns of thinking. Romans 12:2 tells us to renew our minds by studying and obeying the Bible. The Lord wants to deliver us from our old mental bondage and emotional strongholds. The right way to think is to think in line with His Word.

Third, we begin to experience the fullness of God's *blessings* physically here on Earth. Can we really expect blessings here on Earth? Jesus told us to pray that God's will be done "on earth as it is in Heaven" (Matt. 6:10). Is there any sickness or poverty in Heaven? No! So it's not God's will that there be sickness or lack on Earth. Is there any curse in Heaven? No! So it's not God's will that we live under any curse. We can receive physical healing now for "Christ has *redeemed* us from the curse of the law, being made a curse for us" (Gal. 3:13, KJV, emphasis added).

It is the third cup of blessing which Jesus instituted for the New Testament Church at the Last Supper, yet it is probably the most misunderstood one. (See 1 Corinthians 10:16.) Too many Christians are still at the first cup, or at best the second cup, but they have not taken the third cup of blessing. Being blessed does not mean we will never suffer persecution from men, but it does mean that we have power over the devil and he should no longer take advantage of us. We have been *brought out* spiritually, *delivered* mentally and emotionally, and *blessed* physically and socially.

Fourth, we await to be "taken out." We long for Jesus, whom we will see either at our death or at the Rapture. At the Rapture, we who believe and are alive at His Coming will be literally taken up, out and away. The Rapture is nothing new. Enoch was raptured or taken up without seeing death 5,000 years ago. Isaiah 57:1 (NIV) records a 2,700-year-old description of the Rapture, "The righteous perish, and no one ponders it in his heart, devout men are *taken away*, and *no one understands* that the righteous are *taken away* to be spared from evil" (emphasis added). The righteous will disappear in an instant but it will not bring understanding to those who reject the truth. They will be confused. They will not realize that a terrible period of time the Bible calls the Tribulation is about to come on Earth. Perhaps they will feel so overwhelmed with their own problems or so deceived by the Anti-Christ that they will not care Jesus has taken away the righteous "to be spared from evil."

God loves us and never wants us to suffer as the world suffers, God does not call us to suffer sin, sickness, or poverty; but He does call us to suffer righteously for preaching the Gospel and teaching His Word. If you teach His Word, some people will not like it, because it doesn't agree with their theology. Then you will find out how much you can suffer for Jesus!

Amazingly, the 4 cups of Passover point to Jesus and are symbolic of the entire Gospel plan mapped out in 4 stages!

When Nebuchadnezzar threw Shadrach, Meshach, and Abed-Nego into the fiery furnace, intending to kill them, the Bible records that he rose in haste and spoke to his counselors, saying, "'Did we not cast three men bound into the midst of the fire?' They answered and said to the king, 'True, O king.' 'Look!' he answered, 'I see four [4] men loose, walking in the midst of the fire; and they are not hurt, and the form of the fourth is like the Son of God" (Dan. 3:24-25). Who was the 4th man who brought protection from fire to the 3 Hebrew faithfuls? He is the Savior, of course. This is called a theophany or an appearance of Christ before His Incarnation. Since 4 refers to salvation, we can be sure of our salvation once we trust in the 4th man.

God wrote 4 Gospel accounts, 1 for every personality type. Your favorite Gospel may have something to do with your personality.

+ The Gospel of Matthew is logical, methodical, and detailed— perfect for melancholies.

+ The Gospel of Mark is short, fast-paced, and exciting—fun for sanguines.

+ The Gospel of Luke is compassionate and contains more healing than any other Gospel—it tugs the heartstring of phlegmatics.

+ The Gospel of John is unique (different from the other 3 synoptic Gospels) and visionary (John paints big pictures)—it motivates the big thinkers or the cholerics.

No other religious book in the world is crafted to suit all 4 major personalities. God knows our make up well because He crafted each personality type to represent a part of Him. Through the Gospel, He wants to reach every personality type so that everybody may return to Him.

4 is the master time factor. Earth times are often divided or multiplied by a factor of 4. There are 4 seasons in a year; 4 financial quarters annually; 4 phases of the moon; a new month about every 4 weeks; a leap year or extra day every 4 years. Is it a surprise that Jesus appeared 4,000 years after the fall of Adam? Ancient rabbis believed that the Messiah was due to come during the 4th millennium because the "Great Light" appeared on the 4th day of Creation. They should have known that Christ had come. Jesus, the Light of the world, appeared at the end of the 4th millennium. He will come again to rule and reign at the start of the 7th millennium.

4 has another special meaning, to which we will dedicate the next chapter.

4

ANGELS

4 IS THE NUMBER OF ANGELS. There are 4 living creatures near God's throne; 4 faces on each living creature (lion, calf, man, and eagle); 4 wings on the 4 living creatures*; 4 angels bound in the river Euphrates; 4 angels named in Scripture (Michael, Gabriel, Lucifer, Abaddon or Apollyon); 4 archangels named by Hebrew sources; and 4 ranks of angels in the Bible.

THE NATURE OF ANGELS

The word *angel* simply means "messenger" in both Hebrew (*malak*) and Greek (*angelos*). There are good angels, but there are also fallen angels or demons. Before we explain about both, let's clear up some common misconceptions.

People tend to either worship angels or fear demons. The Bible tells us to neither worship them nor fear them. Angels are not to be worshiped because Christ is greater than angels and we will one day judge and rule over angels. (See Hebrews 1:5–14; 1 Corinthians 6:3.) All holy angels in Scripture are male. They are never babies, female, or sexless (as some speculate from Luke 20:36). Demons may appear as a man, woman, child, or even animal (remember the serpent in the Garden of Eden). Most angels do not have wings, or else they would be recognized as angels. On the contrary, Hebrews 13:2 tells us that if you met an angel, it is unlikely that you were aware of it; therefore, "do not forget to entertain strangers, for by so doing some have unwittingly entertained angels."

All angels are created beings. They are not equal to God. They are not omnipresent, omnipotent, or omniscient. They cannot read our minds, but they do listen to our words. That's why thoughts unspoken die unborn. Our words are vitally important. Jesus said in Matthew 12:37, "For by your words you will be justified, and by your words you will be condemned." Angels and demons cannot act on our thoughts, but they can act on our words. Gabriel

---

* See Ezekiel 1:6, 8; 10:21. The only angels with wings are the Cherubim, Seraphim, and Zoas or "living creatures."

said to Daniel, "From the first day that you set your heart to understand, and to humble yourself before your God, your words were heard; and I have come because of your words" (Dan. 10:12). Daniel did not pray silently. His words, not merely his thoughts, were heard. The archangel was sent in response to Daniel's spoken words, not his unspoken thoughts. Jesus spoke to demons to command them to leave. He did not just think the thought, "Please leave." He commanded vocally. Anointed words spoken in Jesus' name can always defeat the devil.

One third of angels fell in a rebellion against God led by Lucifer, now called the devil or Satan. (See Revelation 12:3–4.) Demons, ghosts, and evil spirits are not the spirits of deceased humans. When humans die, they are not in limbo or suspension, but depart Earth for Heaven or descend to where hell is.

A common ploy of the devil is to impersonate people we once knew. If you have ever seen a dead relative, a common experience among people in the occult, the Bible says you have encountered a "familiar spirit."* That is a spirit that is familiar with the history of your family. Remember angels and demons are not omniscient, they do not know everything; but they have been around before you were born, your parents were born, your grandparents were born, so they do know some intimate details of your life. They know, for instance, what sins work well in your family history. For some families, alcohol destroys male after male. For others, it may be adultery, violence, gambling, or money. Demons are not omnipotent; they are limited in power and numbers, so they follow the path of least effort and resistance. They habitually deploy the same spiritual tactics against you that worked on previous generations in your family.

Do not be afraid of them! They are afraid of you, if you are Christian and know your rights to use the name of Jesus. If you suffer recurring nightmares or suicidal thoughts, that is the devil pushing his lies on you. You can end them by believing in Jesus to forgive your sins and then say, "Satan, I rebuke you in the name of the Lord Jesus Christ!" The visions, apparitions, or nightmares will end. I have seen people set free many times.

I have also seen a few people who, unfortunately, did not want to be set free, but felt "spiritual" because they saw these familiar spirits. It made them feel special. In reality it is a common experience that deceives you in the end. Read the Bible often to clear your mind. Better to follow truth as the "truth will set you free" (John 8:32, NIV).

Now let's explore more details about the good and the bad angels.

---

* See Leviticus 19:21; 20:6, 27. In 1 Samuel 28 Saul was consulting a medium who calls up a spirit pretending to be the deceased prophet Samuel.

THE GOOD ANGELS

Jews believe in 4 classes of good angels. According to a commentary on Genesis dated around 150 B.C., the *Book of Jubilees*, there are: angels of the presence, angels of sanctification, angels over natural phenomena, and guardian angels over individuals.

Jews believe in 4 archangels, 2 named in Scripture, and 2 named in extra-Biblical Jewish sources: Michael, Gabriel, Uriel, and Raphael.[1] Each supposedly correspond to the 4 divisions of the armies of Israel and 4 directions of the camp: "Michael on my right, Gabriel on my left, Uriel before me, Raphael behind me, and above my head the Shekinah [glory] of God."[2]

- Michael means "Who is like God" (*mi* who, *ke* as, *El* God)

- Gabriel means "Strength of God."

- Uriel means "Light of God" or "Fire of God."

- Raphael means "Healing of God."

Gabriel's name appears 4 times in Scripture: Daniel 8:16, Daniel 9:21, Luke 1:19, and Luke 1:26. Gabriel is known as the messenger of God. Michael is the leader of the Lord's hosts and the prince (guardian angel) of Israel.

In Genesis 18:2 "three men" appeared to Abraham after his circumcision. Abraham recognized one of them as the Lord, a pre-incarnate appearance of Jesus Christ. The other two are not identified by name, but Genesis 19:1 calls them "angels." Jews believe Michael and Gabriel accompanied the Lord on His visit. They destroyed Sodom and Gomorrah. The Bible confirms that they work together: when Gabriel was detained by the demonic prince of Persia, Michael came to Gabriel's aid and released him on his mission to help the prophet Daniel understand (2,500 years ago) the end times.

> But the prince of the kingdom of Persia withstood me twenty-one days; and behold, Michael, one of the chief princes, came to help me, for I had been left alone there with the kings of Persia. Now I have come to make you understand what will happen to your people in the latter days, for the vision refers to many days yet to come.
>
> —DANIEL 10:13–14

The Midrash, Genesis Rabbah 63.24, says that Michael and Gabriel together recorded Esau's selling his birthright to Jacob. Did you know that all your words, attitudes, and actions are being recorded? That there are books in Heaven is proven by Scriptures.

> Then those who feared the LORD spoke to one another, and the LORD gave attention and heard it, and a *book* of remembrance was written before Him for those who fear the LORD and who esteem His name.
> —MALACHI 3:16, NAS, EMPHASIS ADDED

If our conversations about God are being recorded "before Him," then God is not the One writing. Who is writing them? Some angels are employed in the task of recording the details of our lives.

> A river of fire was flowing And coming out from before Him; Thousands upon thousands were attending Him, And myriads upon myriads were standing before Him; The *court* sat, And the *books* were opened.
> —DANIEL 7:10, NAS, EMPHASIS ADDED

> And I saw the dead, great and small, standing before the throne, and *books* were opened. Another *book* was opened, which is the *book* of life. The dead were judged according to what they had done as recorded in the *books*.
> —REVELATION 20:12, NIV, EMPHASIS ADDED

We cannot confirm from Scripture the Midrash's account that Michael and Gabriel recorded Esau's decision to dishonor his birthright. But it would not be against Scripture. We know according to the New Testament that angels witness men's decisions. Luke 15:10 says they watch our activities: "Likewise, I say to you, there is joy in the presence of the angels of God over one sinner who repents." And we know that our decisions are being recorded in books for Heaven's purposes. If the task does not belong to God Himself, then it is safe to say angels are busy recording the evidence that will be used on the Day of Judgment for eternal rewards and punishments.

My rule is simple: I pick only stories from the Midrash that are not in conflict with Scripture and reject all stories that are anti-Scripture. All spiritual information should pass the Bible test. If it doesn't line up with the Bible, we should not accept it.

The Midrash says Michael refused to take Moses' soul when he was supposed to die. The New Testament sheds better light this incident, "Yet Michael the archangel, in contending with the devil, when he disputed about the *body* of Moses, dared not bring against him a reviling accusation, but said, 'The Lord rebuke you!'" (Jude 1:9). The dispute was over Moses' body, not Moses' soul, which ascended to Heaven.

The Book of Enoch claims that Uriel asked God to destroy the Nephilim (giants of Genesis 6:1–4) and that along with other angels Uriel served as Enoch's guide to Heaven when he was translated. Again, we cannot confirm from Scripture that it was Uriel, but we do know from Scripture that angels accompany righteous saints when they die. Evidently unrighteous souls go alone.

> So it was that the beggar died, and was carried by the angels to Abraham's bosom. The rich man also died and was buried.
>
> —LUKE 16:22

The believing beggar was never alone in death but had a triumphant parade to glory. The unbelieving rich man did not get the same treatment. Jesus simply said his body was buried.

The Midrash, Exodus Rabbah 1.24, claims that Gabriel made baby Moses cry so that Pharaoh's daughter would have compassion on him and adopt him as her son. We know from Scripture that angels surround children.

> And he said: "I tell you the truth, unless you change and become like little children, you will never enter the kingdom of Heaven....See that you do not look down on one of these little ones. For I tell you that their angels in Heaven always see the face of my Father in Heaven."
>
> —MATTHEW 18:3, 10, NIV

By Jewish tradition, Raphael is considered to be involved with healing. Although we do not believe in angels to heal us, it is interesting to note that the New Testament mentions an unnamed angel who "went down at a certain season into the pool, and troubled the water: whosoever then first after the troubling of the water stepped in was made whole of whatsoever disease he had" (John 5:4, KJV). An impotent man who met Jesus complained that whenever the angel troubled the water, he was too late to get in and always missed his healing. Jesus ignored the angel and the man's complaint and healed him on the spot! When we have Jesus, we do not need to wait for an angel who was limited in ability and could not heal everybody. By His stripes, we should declare, we were healed.

THE BAD ANGELS

Now concerning the fallen angels: There are 4 ranks of fallen angels according to Ephesians 6:12:

1. *principalities*—low-level devils, then

2. *powers,* then

3. *rulers of darkness,* and lastly

4. *spiritual wickedness in high places*—Satan's highest henchmen.

In day-to-day spiritual life and prayer, Christians only have to deal with low-level devils, hence the New Testament's emphasis on *principalities* and *powers.* (See Romans 8:38; Ephesians 3:10; Colossians 1:16, 2:15.) We have authority over these devils in the name of Jesus (Mark 16:17). When we bind the low-level devils on Earth, the higher-ranking devils will also be bound in the heavens. Jesus said so:

> Assuredly, I say to you, whatever you bind on earth will be bound in Heaven and whatever you loose on earth will be loosed in Heaven.
> —MATTHEW 18:18

We are supposed to bind some things on the earth and let the Lord and His army deal with some things in the heavens. That means some devils are on Earth, while other devils are in the heavens—the atmospheric heavens above the earth, not the Heaven God lives in, for there are no devils there. Satan is called the "prince of the power of the *air*" in Ephesians 2:2 (emphasis added). The fact that believers only need to deal with low-level devils and God's army will automatically deal with higher-ranking devils is clear from Jesus' words:

> Behold, I give you the authority to trample on serpents and scorpions, and over all the power of the enemy, and nothing shall by any means hurt you.
> —LUKE 10:19

Firstly, Jesus compares the devils we face to serpents and scorpions, low-level, belly-crawling enemies.

Secondly, the picture Jesus gives the Church is that we are in a *superior* position *above* those enemies. Our stance is to *stomp on, step on,* or *trample down* these low-level devils in the name of Jesus!

> And these signs will follow those who believe: In My name [the name of Jesus] they will cast out demons.
>
> —MARK 16:17

Never does Jesus paint a picture of the Church being underneath the devil and having to "pull them down" from above us. No, no, no! The Church is the body of Christ. We are *above* the fallen demons and they are trodden underneath our feet. (See Ephesians 1:22–23; Romans 16:20.)

A much misunderstood Scripture is the one in which the Holy Spirit admonishes us to "pull down strongholds." What are these strongholds? Read the Scripture in context as Paul defines these "strongholds."

> For the weapons of our *warfare* are not carnal but mighty in God for pulling down *strongholds*, casting down *arguments* and every high thing that exalts itself against the *knowledge* of God, bringing every *thought* into captivity to the obedience of Christ.
>
> —2 CORINTHIANS 10:4–5, EMPHASIS ADDED

What is the warfare the Holy Spirit is referring to? A battle of the *mind.* What are the strongholds the Holy Spirit is referring to? The strongholds are synonymous with *arguments* against God's Word, *higher criticism* of God's Word, and *disobedient thoughts* to Christ.

We need to understand something basic about our makeup. Humans are made up of 3 parts—spirit, soul, and body (1 Thess. 5:23). Once our spirits are saved by faith in Jesus, we have a mind or soul that needs to be renewed (Rom. 12:2) and a body whose appetites need to be controlled by the Spirit (Rom. 8:13–14). The main battle of the believer is the battle of the mind.

Too many Bible preachers have made the strongholds out to be something *outside* the believer or even *above* the believer, misleading Christians into unproductive hours of praying against "spiritual" or "demonic" strongholds. I've been in such meetings; and other than the benefit of coming together to be with each other and the Lord, I didn't see much good or lasting deliverance come out of those shouting meetings.

Actually the strongholds are *mental.* The battle is not *outside* of us, but *within* the mind of each believer. Strongholds include religious traditions, rationalizations, and prejudices that cloud our understanding of God's Word. The religious Pharisees had a lot of mental strongholds that kept them from being saved and healed by Jesus.

The main tool of the enemy is the power of *mental suggestions*. The devil merely introduced a wrong thought to Eve, "Is God's Word really true? If you disobey God, nothing bad will happen to you. In fact, you'll be better off to reject God's Word!" That's my paraphrase but it sums up what the devil continues to successfully do to people's minds as soon as they hear God's Word. "Don't believe it. Don't act on it. It doesn't work. God isn't good. God doesn't help. God didn't answer your prayer. Listen to your feelings instead." These are variations of thoughts that regularly come into people's heads, which need to be pulled down by a decision to believe and speak the truth. Just opening the Bible and speaking it can defeat the devil.

The devil knows that the worst thing he can do to you is to make you reject God's Word and believe a lie instead. It is no overstatement to say that every sorrow in the world comes from believing a lie. Every divorce is the result of someone in the marriage believing a lie. Every drug or sexual addiction is the result of someone believing a lie. Every lost soul is lost because someone believed a lie about God or about themselves. That is why Jesus calls Satan "a *liar* and the father of it" (John 8:44, emphasis added), and the Bible summarizes Satan's activity on Earth as *deceiving* the nations (Rev. 18:23; 20:3, 8).

We must pull down strongholds of wrong thought patterns, lies, and deception. We can do this by studying and embracing God's Word for ourselves, no matter what others around us may think. Jesus promised us victory over every stronghold, not by praying against devils, but by putting God's Word first: "If you abide in My word, you are My disciples indeed. And you shall know the truth, and the truth shall make you free" (John 8:31–32).

There are spiritual forces to contend with but they are underneath our feet. There are low-level devils that bring sickness, lies, or mental suggestions; but Jesus and the disciples simply cast them out. There is really nothing for the believer to worry once he or she knows his or her authority in Christ and uses the name of Jesus in prayer. The devils are afraid of the name of Jesus!

5

5 FOR GRACE

5 IS THE NUMBER OF GRACE. Grace is what distinguishes Christianity from every religion in the world. All religion asks man to try harder; Christianity tells man to give up and ask for help. By grace, not by self-centered effort, we must be saved. All religion asks man to save himself by acting good; Christianity alone tells us to depend on the only Savior. Grace is a uniquely Christian doctrine. No wonder 5 appears so often in the Bible.

Gabriel told Mary, "Do not be afraid, Mary, for you have found favor with God." The Douay-Rheims translation of Luke 1:30 says, "For thou hast found *grace* with God" (emphasis added). The same Greek word *charis* means grace and favor. Mary then had 5 sons: Jesus (when she was a virgin), James, Joseph, Simon, and Judas (author of Jude). (See Matthew 13:55; Mark 6:3; Luke 8:19-21; John 2:12; Galatians 1:19.)

Some people misunderstand the Trinity and think it means God the Father, Mary the mother of God, and Jesus the Son. Then they profanely assume that God had sexual intercourse with Mary to produce Jesus. This is *not* a Christian belief. The Trinity is God the Father, God the Son, and God the Holy Spirit. They conceived a plan to redeem man by being born on Earth to take his punishment for him. God borrowed Mary's womb just as a couple can borrow a surrogate's mother womb. The surrogate mother does not have intimate relation with the couple and does not share DNA with the baby. Mary is not divine, is not omniscient, for she was not privy to the plan of redemption until Gabriel announced she had found grace. Mary is not God, but a human vessel of grace.

Noah's name first appears in Genesis 5 and on the 5th appearance, the Bible records that "Noah found grace" (Gen. 6:8). There was nothing Noah could do to save himself. Noah could only be saved by believing God and going into the ark for safety. The wooden ark (like many wooden typologies in the Old Testament) represented the cross of Christ. The ark had only one door located on the second floor of the triple-decker boat, representing the second person in the Trinity.

In the flood of sin, we cannot save ourselves by treading water. We can only be saved by accepting rescue on board the Ark of Jesus.

Noah was 500 years old when he began fathering the only 3 sons who survived the Flood. (See Genesis 5:32.) The ark of Noah rested on Mount Ararat, which is 5 kilometers above sea level, truly a pinnacle of grace. The Jews who wrote the Bible did not live in Ararat, work in Ararat, and as far as we can tell, never went near Ararat for any reason. Yet they recorded that Ararat was the resting place of the ark. As it turns out, Ararat is higher than the highest peak of Europe and one of the highest in Asia. The highest mountain in the European Alps is Mont Blanc, at 4,810 meters. Ararat stands at 5,137 meters (this includes a thick layer of ice cap that would not have been there at Noah's time).

Compare the Bible with mythology. Both the Greeks and Romans claimed survivors of a flood landed on Mount Parnassus in central Greece, whose peak is 2,457 meters above sea level. The Gilgamesh Epics claimed a flood survivor named Utnapishtim landed in the Zagros Mountains in western Iran. The highest peak of the Zagros stands at 4,548 meters. Neither of these mountains is ideal for a realistic landing, as they would prolong the survivors' wait in the boat, while humans and animals run out of food, water, and supplies. But Ararat, towering over 5,100 meters, is the most plausible site of a resting ark.

Mount Ararat is part of historical Armenia (now eastern Turkey). The Armenians believe they are descendants of the great-great grandson of Noah through Japheth, Gomer, and Togarmah—a man named Hayk (not found in the Bible). In other words, Armenians claim to descend from a 5th generation patriarch after the Flood. The 5th century historian Moses Khorenatsi recorded in the *History of Armenia*: "Hayk and his people, from the time of their forefathers Noah and Japheth, had migrated south toward the warmer lands near Babylon. In that land there ruled a wicked giant, Bel [or Nimrod by other accounts]. Bel tried to impose his tyranny upon Hayk's people. But proud Hayk refused to submit to Bel. As soon as his son Aramaneak was born, Hayk rose up, and led his people back to the land of his forefathers, the land of Ararat."[1] Two of the original 12 apostles—Bartholomew and Judas Thaddeus (not Judas Iscariot)—are said to have preached in Armenia and founded the Armenian Apostolic Church, at about A.D. 50. Armenia is considered the first Christian country in the world. The number 5 is associated with grace.

The name change from *Abram* (a barren man) to *Abraham* (the father of many nations) was simply made by inserting the 5th letter of the Hebrew alphabet "*heh*" into his name. The same 5th letter changed *Sarai* (contentious) to *Sarah* (princess).

Benjamin, Joseph's younger brother, was given 5 times as much meal as his elder brothers and 5 changes of garments as opposed to his other brothers' one (Gen, 43:34; 45:22). Benjamin had done nothing to deserve this. He was the object of his older brother's favor.

God forbade Israel from eating the fruit of a tree until the 5th year after its planting (Lev. 19:23–25). God wanted to give Israel "vineyards and olive tress which [they] did not plant" (Deut. 6:11) as a symbol that God's promise is by grace. Once Israel entered the land, they were allowed to plant fruit trees, but not forget God's grace.

David had faith he could defeat Goliath with only 5 smooth stones. It was grace, not David's aim, that brought the little shepherd boy victory and saved the nation. Some ask why did David bother to bring 4 other stones? To kill Goliath's 4 other brothers, but they all ran away. (See 2 Samuel 21:16–22; 1 Chronicles 20:4–8.)

The angel Gabriel said Mary had found grace with God (Luke 1:30). Mary was the 5th woman mentioned in Jesus' genealogy (Matt. 1:16). Mary bore 5 sons: Jesus (while she was a virgin), James, Joseph, Simon, Judas (Jesus' 4 half-brothers, 2 of which became early apostles and writers of New Testament books). (See Matthew 13:55; Mark 6:3; Luke 8:19–21; John 2:12; Galatians 1:19.)

John is sometimes called the "Apostle of Love" as he understood God's grace and emphasized it more than any other apostle. (See John 1:16; 1 John 4:19.) How many books did God use John to write? Exactly 5!

1. The Gospel of John
2. The Epistle of 1 John
3. The Epistle 2 John
4. The Epistle 3 John
5. The Book of Revelation. What a privilege it must have been for John to close the canon of Scripture!

Moses also wrote 5 books of the Bible, collectively called the *Torah* in Hebrew or *Pentateuch* in Greek:

1. Genesis
2. Exodus
3. Leviticus
4. Numbers
5. Deuteronomy

These first 5 books of the Bible are sometimes called "The Law." But law and grace are inseparable. An understanding of the strict requirements of the law leads to a deep appreciation of grace. No one can truly understand the solution Jesus brings without first understanding the problem Moses described.

Since none of us can perfectly keep all 613 holy laws contained in the 5 books of Moses, we are in violation of the law. The law requires the guilty party to pay; but the law will also accept an innocent party to step in and bail the guilty out. The person who doesn't understand law won't embrace the grace of Jesus Christ. Jesus bailed us out at a Supreme cost to Himself. 5 reminds us that God had hidden grace as the solution to broken law from the very start.

There are 5 "days of grace" between Yom Kippur (the Day of Repentance) on the 10th of Tishri and Feast of Tabernacles (symbolic of the Millennium) on the 15th of Tishri.

5 virgins valued grace and were prepared to accept the undeserved invitation to our Lord's wedding; 5 virgins were foolish and squandered grace by being careless.

5 represents the 5th of the 10 Commandments: "Honor your father and your mother, that your days may be long upon the land which the LORD your God is giving you" (Exod. 20:12). The New Testament reiterates this commandment as the first commandment with a promise. Paul quotes the 5th commandment in the book of Ephesians:

> Children, obey your parents in the Lord, for this is right. "Honor your father and mother," which is the first commandment with *promise*: "that it may be *well with you* and you may *live long* on the earth."
> —EPHESIANS 6:1–3, EMPHASIS ADDED

How many children's lives would be prospered and lengthened if parents taught them the 5th commandment? Explain to your children why this Scripture is so important to their future.

5 IN SCIENCE

We have 5 physical senses; what a grace it is to be able to see, hear, touch, taste, and smell! It's difficult to put to words how we can taste a taste or smell a smell, yet tasting and smelling are part of God's amazing gifts to us. God could have made the universe duller and the earth less colorful, but by His grace, life is full of 5 physical sensations.

In an octave, the 5th and 3rd notes create the basic foundation of all chords.

God's grace (5) from the Trinity (3) always creates a beautiful sound and perfect harmony.

According to Astronomy.com, nearly all meteors burn up before they reach an altitude of 50 miles over our heads. Considering at least 6 meteors enter the earth's atmosphere per hour (on an ordinary "non-shower" day) and an estimated 100 to 1,000 tons of meteoric material fall into our atmosphere per day, it is by grace that our homes, cars, and heads are not peppered with meteor showers. Thank God there is an invisible barrier protecting us at 50 miles above.

5 FOR GRACE OVERFLOWING TO GENTILES

One of the great expressions of God's grace is the inclusion of Gentile believers in the family of God. The Jews were originally given the Bible, the covenants, and the promises; the Gentiles were by and large excluded. However, hints of God's grace overflowing to the Gentiles were always in the Old Testament. (See Genesis 17:4, 18:18, 22:18, 26:4; Psalm 72:11, 117:1; Isaiah 2:2–4, 42:1–6; 2 Chronicles 6:32; Micah 4:2–5.)

The word *Greece* or *Greek* (*Javan* in Hebrew) is mentioned 5 times in the Old Testament (Dan. 8:21, 10:20, 11:2; Joel 3:6; Zech. 9:130). *Greek* was synonymous with *Gentile* to the ancient Jews. Since 5 is associated with Greeks, is it a coincidence that more Gentiles have become recipients of God's saving grace than Jews? "Through their fall [unbelief]," Paul wrote, "salvation has come to the Gentiles" (Rom. 11:11).

There are 5 books in the Jewish Bible that are *not* specifically about Jews. Why would the ancient Jews, who looked down upon Gentiles, include 5 "Gentile" books in their Bible? The inclusion was by God's design and is intended to show that His eternal plan of redemption included the Gentiles also. Which are the 5 Old Testament books specifically about Gentiles?

1. Job—a Gentile believer. The Book of Job is considered the oldest book of the Bible, evidenced by the fact that there is no mention of Israel, the Mosaic Law, or the tabernacle. Job was a Gentile who lived before the nation of Israel was birthed, before the Laws of Moses were written, and before the tabernacle was built. Though Job didn't have a Bible to read, he had a personal relationship with God. We who have easy access to Bibles have no excuse to be far from God.

2. Ruth—a Gentile widow from Moab who married a Jewish kinsman redeemer named Boaz. Ruth accepted the God of the

Bible and God accepted her. She became an ancestor of both King David and the Lord Jesus.

3. Jonah—an unwilling prophet to the Gentile city of Nineveh, Assyria. One of the greatest miracles of the Old Testament is the repentance and salvation of an entire Gentile city through this reluctant man's preaching.

4. Obadiah—"an ambassador…sent among the heathen" (1:1, KJV). Obadiah had a vision about Edom (present-day Jordan). Because Edom gloated over Judah's downfall, Edom would be destroyed. Much of Edom lays waste and deserted today.

5. Nahum—a prophet who followed up Jonah's ministry to the city of Nineveh about 100 years later. After the short-lived revival a century earlier, the inhabitants of Nineveh forgot about God and excelled in murder, lies, robbery, wanton wars, whoredoms, witchcraft, and drunkenness (3:1–11). Nahum's message? God spared Nineveh because it repented, but now He will not delay their judgment.

These messages to Gentiles or other nations make the Bible unique. Most nations have their own gods. The Canaanites worshiped Canaanite gods. The Egyptians had Egyptian gods. The Vikings had Viking gods. Till today, many religious people will say they follow a certain religion because they were born in a certain country. I've heard people proud to be "orthodox Christian" because they were born in Armenia, Egypt, Ethiopia, Syria, Greece, or Russia. Being born in a particular country does not give us access to Heaven; rather it's being born again by faith in the Blood of Jesus that truly makes us Christian. Biblical faith differs from all traditional faiths in the world because it is not bound to a nation or ethnic group. The God of the Bible does not see Himself as God of the Jews only. Whereas other religions appeal mainly to a specific people group, the God of the Bible sees Himself as the universal Owner of all nations.

Whenever God wanted to highlight people who believed and served Him outside of the Jewish family, He did so. Job from Uz, Melchizedek from Salem, Rahab from Jericho, and Ruth from Moab, these were 4 outstanding examples of Gentile believers. Rahab was a Canaanite prostitute and Ruth was a Moabite widow, yet God accepted both Gentile women into the Davidic or Messianic line. Why? To show that the Messiah is the Savior of the world—both Jews and Gentiles.

Whenever God wanted to send His message to country outside of Israel, He did so. He sent Jonah and Nahum to Nineveh. He sent Obadiah's prophecy to Edom. Other prophets wrote inspired prophecies about Lebanon, Syria, Egypt, Iraq, Iran, etc. The God of the Bible felt He had as much right to call them to repentance and judge them for their sins as He did the Jews. The 5 Gentile books of the Old Testament affirm that God's grace is international and it extends to every person! This is why it's called amazing grace!

There are only 5 nations in the world that have never been under the West's imperial rule: Afghanistan, China, Iran, Japan and Thailand. On the one hand, we can say only 5 nations have experienced the grace of not being colonialized. On the other hand, these 5 nations represent some of the proudest people and fiercest fighters, and God would that there be more humility. There is a grace on those who were colonialized, because they received the benefit of learning English or another European language (which now gives them a market advantage) and they were often introduced to the Gospel which stopped many ills such as cannibalism, child sacrifice, female circumcision, etc.

According to author Richard Maybury, except for these 5 countries, nearly all national boundaries and political structures we see today "are either creations of the Europeans or outgrowths of those creations."[2] Is it any wonder that there is now a reaction from the rest of the world against Western power and interference? I do not believe all things Western are evil, but I can also sympathize with people's desire to direct their own national affairs. National sovereignty was God's idea. Globalization was Nimrod's idea, and tends to be the aspiration of every dictator since (they are consumed with the delusion of 'taking over the world!'). Globalization centralizes power and hence evil. National sovereignty protects people when things go bad across the border (e.g., the British sterling was protected when the Euro was in crisis). When America's subprime mortgage crisis and uncontrolled debt threatened to destabilize the whole world, China's and India's growing economies saved the world from sinking into another Depression. In an age of rapid globalization and the good things it may bring, we should remember that the idea of national sovereignty is God's idea and God kept 5 nations on earth from ever being dominated by Western powers.

5 STANDS FOR VARIOUS GIFTS

The anointing oil was made of 5 parts: olive oil, myrrh, cinnamon, calamus, and cassia. God's anointing upon our lives is always a gift. In the secular world, someone who is naturally talented is called a "gifted" child. Did you ever ask, "Gifted by whom?" In 1 Corinthians 15:10, Paul said of his own call: "But by the *grace* of God I am what I am, and His *grace* toward me was not in vain; but

I labored more abundantly than they all, yet not I, but the *grace* of God which was with me" (emphasis added).

When we discover God's call on our lives, we will also discover the supernatural grace, gifting, and anointing to help us accomplish that call. We will succeed "not by might nor by power, but by My Spirit, Says the LORD of hosts" (Zech. 4:6).

5 individuals in Scripture resurrected others from the dead: Elijah, Elisha, our Lord Jesus, Peter, and Paul. (See 1 Kings 17:17–24; 2 Kings 4:18–37, 13:20–25; Matthew 10:18–26; Luke 7:11–16; John 11; Acts 9:40, 20:10.) It takes the gifts of special faith, working of miracles, and healing to resurrect someone from the dead and keep them alive. This doesn't mean resurrections from the dead no longer happen, they do. A bunch of unnamed disciples (not specially anointed apostles) resurrected Paul from the dead in Acts 14. As long as someone is young and did not wish to die, they are candidates for being resurrected from premature death. Don't go around praying for old people to resurrect—they want to go to Heaven, which is far better. God wants the young to live out their full potential and serve Him on Earth.

God entrusted the message of grace to 5 ministry gifts. Listed in Ephesians 4:11, they are:

1. Apostles
2. Prophets
3. Evangelists
4. Pastors
5. Teachers

While the Lord Jesus is the head of the body of Christ, the Holy Spirit is often called the hand of the Lord; the 5-fold ministers act like 5 fingers on the hand. They are at the forefront of the work of reaching humanity with the gift of salvation.

Under the Old Testament, there were only 3 main ministry offices: prophet, priest, and king. Today, the Lord has blessed humanity with more ministers of God. Whereas the Law gave the Jews 3, grace gives the Church 5. It should be noted that *no one* has been or ever will be called to stand in all 5-fold ministries except Jesus! (See chapter on 8 Ministries of Christ.)

Finally, there are 5 instances of people being filled with the Holy Spirit in the Book of Acts. They are contained in Acts chapters 2, 8, 9, 10, and 19. The number 5 is by design. The gift of the Holy Spirit, like the gift of salvation, is not something we can try to earn on our merits.

Too many people delay receiving Christ's new birth or the Holy Spirit's baptism because they are too ashamed to come just as they are. They sincerely want to "clean up their lives first." But if you could clean up your life without Jesus, you wouldn't need Him! You would be the Savior, not Jesus. But the fact is there is only one Savior.

Come to Jesus with all your warts and flaws, hiding nothing from Him. He knows everything about you anyway. I know this will upset some religious people, but you should come to Jesus with a pack of cigarettes in your shirt pocket and a booze bottle in your bottom drawers. Come without trying to quit your addiction first, and then let God fill you with the power to kick bad habits!

God will do it. I know because I used to smoke and drink. I came to Jesus with all my problems and addictions. I humbled myself and asked Jesus for His help. Oh, how He's helped me! He's been the Helper by my side ever since.

I've seen drug addicts completely set free by receiving Christ in their hearts and the power of the Holy Spirit in their tongues. What seems hard for you to do is *easy* for God to do. He filled 5 groups of people with the Holy Spirit in the Book of Acts. Why not you?

The only condition to receive grace is humility. James said:

> God resists the proud, But gives grace to the humble.
>
> —JAMES 4:6

Peter reiterated this key to obtaining undeserved gifts from God:

> God resists the proud, But gives grace to the humble.
>
> —1 PETER 5:5

Be humble enough to admit you need help, and then ask God for His grace to get you out of sin, chronic pain, and recurring problems. Ask in Jesus' name and receive with joy. By grace through faith we can all receive His provisions!

6

6 IS THE NUMBER OF MAN. Adam was created on the 6th day; 6 days a week a man is to work; the atomic weight of the building block of life carbon is 6; 99 percent of human mass is made up of just 6 elements (oxygen, carbon, hydrogen, nitrogen, calcium, and phosphorus); it takes 6 seconds for a man in a strangle hold to pass out; peak performance coaches know that an athlete cannot maintain his maximum speed for longer than 6 seconds; every able man in the ancient Greek ecclesia* was given 6 minutes to speak, there are 66 books in the Bible containing the only plan for man's salvation.

There are 6 continents man inhabits. 6 feet is the average height of man. As a rule of thumb, the temperature of the earth increases 1 ¼° F for every 60 feet in depth. The distance to the earth's core is about 6,000 kilometers. The temperature of the earth's core is about 6,600 ¼° C. The weight of the earth is 6 x 10²⁴ kilograms (6 with 24 zeros after it). The Greek gematria for the word *world* (*cosmos*) is 600. The world's population hit 6 billion about the same time Israel's population hit 6 million about the same time Jerusalem's population was 600,000. The 6 billion people alive are communicating in about 6,000 known languages. Their collective life expectancy is 66 years.[1] Turkey, an often overlooked key player in the end times, has a GDP of $660 million. World War II, humanity's worst war which introduced 2 atomic bombs, killed about 60 million people.[2] When the Human Genome Project (1990–2003) was completed, guess how many nucleotides (letters of the DNA) they counted in every human cell? 6 billion! What are the chances of such repetitive patterns occurring by chance?

Genesis records 6 of Adam's descendants lived in excess of 900 years: Seth, Enos, Cainan, Jared, Methuselah, and Noah. Jewish sages believe that the idea of 6,000 years from Adam till the Messiah's rule is hidden in the very first verse of the Bible, Genesis 1:1, which has 6 Alephs in it. As the first letter of the Hebrew language, Aleph has a numerical value of both 1 and 1000. Therefore the 6 alephs allude to both the 6 days of Creation and the 6,000 years of *Olam Hazeh* (the

---

* *Ecclesia*, from which we get the French *eglise*, Spanish *iglesia*, and English *ecclesiastes* (preacher) or *ecclesiastic* (clergyman). The original meaning of this word was the "assembly" or "called out ones," comprised of all men over 30 who owned property. They had to prove themselves by speaking for 6 minutes on the *bema* stone or speaker's platform. They formed the heart of Athenian democracy. God used this Greek concept and applied it directly to His Church, calling it the *ecclesia*.

present world). Both ancient rabbis and early Church fathers believed Adam's family was given 6,000 years to rule the earth. In other words, Adam's lease on earth is about to run out, and we are to expect Jesus' Second Coming soon!

The number of soldiers when Israel left Egypt was 600,000 (Exod. 12:37).

6 of the 10 Commandments deal with our relationship with fellow man (the rest deal with our relationship to God). The 6th commandment is such an interesting subject, it warrants treatment in its own chapter to come.

6 times in the Sermon on the Mount Jesus contrasted man's misinterpretation of the Law with God's true meaning of the Law. While God gave the Jews the *Torah* (the Laws of Moses) to prepare their hearts to be convicted of sin and search to the Savior; rabbis added their own interpretations and oral laws (called the *Mishna*) to skirt the Law and justify themselves. In the Sermon on the Mount, Jesus exalted God's holy laws above the rabbi's oral laws. When Jesus quoted the Bible, He said, "It is written." When Jesus addressed the rabbis' misinterpretation or oral traditions, He said, "It is said." Jesus repeated 6 times, "You have heard that it was said" (once in the form of "it has been said"). Here's an example:

> You have heard that it was said, 'You shall love your neighbor and hate your enemy.' [The rabbis agreed with this; and by their own standard, they were righteous and worthy of Heaven.] *But* I say to you, love your enemies [this they could not keep; the rabbis hated the Romans, the Greeks, the Samaritans, the Christians], bless those who curse you, do good to those who hate you, and pray for those who spitefully use you and persecute you, that you may be sons of your Father in Heaven; for He makes His sun rise on the evil and on the good, and sends rain on the just and on the unjust. For if you love those who love you, what reward have you? Do not even the tax collectors do the same? And if you greet your brethren only, what do you do more than others? Do not even the tax collectors do so? Therefore you shall be perfect, just as your Father in Heaven is perfect.
>
> —Matthew 5:43–48, emphasis added
> (See also Matthew 5:21, 27, 31, 33, and 38.)

By God's standard, anyone who does not love in this way is a sinner. None who refuse to love his or her enemy is worthy of Heaven. Jesus set the standard higher than the Pharisees. Why? To produce honesty and humility in the hearers' heart. 6 represents us trying to justify ourselves with "what we have said" and "what we have heard" and "what we think"; whereas Jesus came to tell us "what is written" by God! We must be perfect, or else we must repent and trust in the perfect Savior Jesus Christ!

6 is the number of man's incomplete theories instead of God's perfect truth. Jesus often taught against the teachings of the Pharisees because they twisted or complicated the Word of God till it was "of no effect" (Mark 7:13). These rabbinic discussions, dating from 536 B.C. till A.D. 70, were first written down in the *Mishna*. Interestingly, rabbis divide their own *Mishna*, or first written record of their Oral Tradition compiled around A.D. 200, into 6 orders:

1. *sera'im* (seeds—about agricultural rules and blessings)
2. *mo'ed* (seasons or festivals—about ceremonial rules)
3. *nashim* (women—about marital and sexual rules)
4. *neziqin* (damages—about commercial and criminal laws)
5. *qodashim* (sacred things—about the Temple and its sacrifices)
6. *tohorot* (purifications—about sanitation rules)

Another name for the *Mishna* is the *shas*, an abbreviation of *shisha sedarim*, meaning the "six orders." From A.D. 300 to A.D. 500, rabbis compiled more discussions about the *Mishna* into the *Gemara*. Together, the *Mishna* and *Gemara* form the Jewish *Talmud*, or oral teachings not inspired by God. This doesn't mean the *Talmud* is completely wrong (some rabbis have wise things to teach us), but it does mean that it should not be revered nor put on the same level as God's written Word.

6 is the number of the devil. Nebuchadnezzar's idolatrous image stood 60 cubits high and 6 cubits broad. Goliath was 6 cubits tall and his spearhead weighed 600 shekels of iron. The Bible names 6 kinds of giants who were a crossbreed of devils and humans: Nephilim, Anakim, Emim, Zamzummim, Amorites, and Rephaim. Goliath, whom David slew, was a Rephaim who lived among the Philistines. Goliath was not just an abnormally large human, but half human, half demon.*

Accounts of giants are not only in the Bible, but throughout various cultures. The Greeks named at least 2 races of giants, the Cyclops and Titans, of which Atlas was one. Homer's Odyssey mentioned a race of giants and cannibals called Laestrygones who lived in the far north. Scandinavian folklore speaks of many giants among Norse gods, the most famous one called Thor. King Arthur slew one giant named Rhitta Gawr. The Knights of the Round Table slew or were slain by other giants. The Hindu epic of Ramayana credits King Rama with slaying the

---

* Both 2 Peter 2:4–5 and Jude 1:6–7 confirm that some fallen angels sinned by having illicit intercourse with women, and for this cause God has cast them into fire. The fact that a class of angels is not loosed on the earth with Satan, but is now in confinement, proves they committed a sin besides that of the original rebellion with Satan. Jude 1:7 compares their sin to that of "Sodom and Gomorrah," clearly referring to sexual immorality.

evil giants of Sri Lanka. Thais and Laotians still have many statues of mythical giants called "Yak," in front of which modern tourists like to take photos.

The traditions of ancient people all over the world are unanimous in asserting that in an earlier time there lived a race of giants on the earth. Who were the giants? Only the Bible explains. Genesis 6:4 (emphasis added) makes it clear:

> There were giants [nephilim] on the earth in those days [before the Flood], and also afterward [after the Flood], when the sons of God [fallen angels] came in to the daughters of men and they bore children to them. Those were the *mighty men* who were *of old, men of renown.*

Do not the mythological figures, such as Atlas and Thor, qualify as "mighty men of old" and "men of renown"? The ancients called them gods and worshiped them. Although this is a corruption of the facts, there is still a seed of truth in mythology. Because they were partly of supernatural original, giants were easily mistaken for gods. The Ante-Nicene (early Church) Fathers agreed that poets and mythologists, not knowing demons begot giants, called them "gods." "On the earth," wrote Greek poet Homer in 400 B.C., "there once were giants."

6 times man dared to accuse the Savior of having a devil (Matt. 12:24 or Mark 3:22; Luke 11:15; John 7:20, 8:48, 8:52, 10:20). 6 times people asked the Lord for a sign (Matt. 12:38 or Mark 8:11; Matt. 16:1; Matt. 24:3 or Mark 13:4; Luke 11:16; John 2:18; John 6:30).

The greatest apostasy in Jesus' ministry is recorded in John 6:66, "From that time many of His disciples went back and walked with Him no more." Is it a wonder the number of the Anti-Christ, a leader who exalts man above God, is 666?

6 is the number of death. There were 6 instances of unassisted suicide in the Bible: Samson, Saul, Saul's armor bearer, Ahithophel, Zimri, and Judas. (See Judges 16:29–30; 1 Samuel 31:4–5; 2 Samuel 17:23; 1 Kings 16:18; Matthew 27:5; Acts 1:18.) Judas was the last case of suicide in the Bible, which suggests to me that the Cross stopped the curse. There was a case of assisted suicide in Judges 9:54, where Abimelech was hit in the head by a millstone and asked his armor bearer to kill him. In my estimate this incident qualifies more as a murder. There was one attempted suicide by the Philippian jailer who thought an earthquake had set all his prisoners free, so despaired for his career and life. Paul stopped him from taking his life, which tells me the voice of a minister of God can prevent suicide (Acts 16:26–29). Before I came to Christ, I nearly took my own life, but I turned to the Cross and the Holy Spirit stopped me. Then the voice of a man of God brought me back to life.*

---

* Steve's near death experience with a full teaching on the 6 suicides of the Bible are recorded on the DVD "Don't Give Up!" available at www.discover.org.au.

6

EMPIRES

6 IS THE NUMBER OF GENTILE EMPIRES that oppressed Israel in the Bible:

1. Egypt
2. Assyria
3. Babylon
4. Medo-Persia
5. Greece
6. Rome

Satan has always tried to rule over what God has reserved for Himself!

6 is also the number of regime changes during the intertestament period between Malachi (end of Old Testament) and Matthew (beginning of New Testament). Far too few Christians understand the events leading up to the first coming of our Savior. The reason we should know about these 6 intertestament regimes is "history repeats itself" and "those who do not know history are doomed to repeat it." After the Babylonian captivity ended, the Jews were governed by these 6 successive regimes:

1. **Persian.** Their most notable king was Cyrus the Great, named by Isaiah 150 years before he was born (Isaiah 44:28, 45:1). Cyrus fulfilled prophecy by issuing the decree to allow Jews to return to Israel in 537 B.C. The rise of the Persia Empire was also predicted by Daniel's interpretation of the writing on the wall in 5:28 and the vision of the bear in 7:5.

2. **Greek.** The meteoric rise of Alexander the Great was predicted by Gabriel's interpretation of the he-goat in Daniel 8:21 and again by the angel Gabriel in Daniel 10:20. Following

Alexander the Great's premature death at the age of 32, his
Greek empire was divided up to his 4 generals: Cassander over
Macedon (modern Greece or west); Lysimachus over Thrace
(modern Turkey or east); Ptolemy over Egypt (south); Seleucid
over Syria (north).

3. **Egyptian**. Hellenistic Egypt came under the rule of the
   Ptolemies, or the kings of the South, as predicted by Daniel 11.
   Israel was caught in between the power struggle between the
   Seleucids to the north and the Ptolemies to the south. From
   323 B.C. to 198 B.C., the Ptolemies ruled Israel. Ptolemy I Soter
   (a Greek) founded the Ptolemy dynasty. His son Ptolemy II
   Philadelphus founded the Alexandrian Library. The Ptolemies
   were benevolent rulers and their promotion of religious freedom
   and scholarly education resulted in the completion of the
   Septuagint—the Greek translation of the Bible and the Bible of
   choice for early Christians.

4. **Syrian**. Hellenistic Syria came under the rule of the Seleucids,
   or the king of the North, as predicted by Daniel 11. Seleucid
   I Nicator founded the dynasty. His son Antiochus I Soter
   made Antioch capital of their empire. In 198 B.C. Antiochus
   II seized Judah from Egypt. From 198 B.C. to 167 B.C., the
   Syrians spread heathen altars and heathen festivals all over
   Israel; and outlawed reading the Torah, observing the Sabbath
   and circumcision. Ironically, Antioch became the headquarters
   of Christianity and the missionary base from which Paul con-
   ducted his missionary journeys. Christ is able to redeem the vile
   and turn all things for good!

Antiochus IV Epiphanes ordered a pig to be offered in every Jewish village
and one in the Temple of God on his birthday—the 25th of Kislev (our
December) 167 B.C. This prompted the Maccabean revolt.

5. **Maccabean**. When Antiochus' agents arrived in the village of Modein to carry out the pig sacrifice, an aged priest
   named Mattathias Maccabeus killed both the first Jew who
   approached the pagan altar and the royal officer. This sparked
   a spontaneous revolt throughout Israel. After his death, his 5
   sons carried on the struggle. Through guerrilla warfare, Judas

Maccabeus (the "Hammer") defeated the Seleucid army and restored Temple worship 3 years later, on the 25th of Kislev 164 B.C. This victory is commemorated at Hanukkah or the Feast of Dedication, which Jesus attended in John 10:22. Judas died in battle and his brother Jonathan became leader and high priest. Thus the Hasmonean Dynasty of priests/civil leaders began. After Jonathan was killed, his brother Simon became commander and high priest. After Simon was murdered, his son John Hyrcanus ruled for 30 years. John conquered Idumea or Edom (southern Israel or Jordan) around 140 B.C. and required all Idumeans to obey Jewish laws or leave; most Idumeans converted to Judaism. From here came Herod's family, who, although they were Edomites or descendants of Esau, claimed they were Jewish. John Hyrcanus' great-great granddaughter married Herod the Great.

6. **Roman**. The 6th regime brought in the reign of the Herodian Dynasty. In 47 B.C. Julius Caesar appointed Antipater II, an Idumean or Edomite, procurator over Judea. Antipater appointed his son Herod governor of Galilee when he was 25. Although not a Jew, Herod tried to court the Jews' favor by marrying a Hasmonean princess; he was circumcised and adopted into the Jewish religion. In 40 B.C. Rome appointed Herod "King of the Jews." This is "Herod the Great," called *great* mainly for his colossal construction projects such as expanding the Temple for 46 years (John 2:20), building the fortress of Masada, and developing Caesarea as a coastal tourist destination. Herod the Great tried to kill Jesus at the time of His birth. After his own death, his son Herod Antipas became tetrarch of Galilee, beheaded John the Baptist, and presided a mock trial of Jesus in which he "arrayed Him in a gorgeous robe" (Luke 23:11). Herod Agrippa I, nephew of Herod Antipas and grandson of Herod the Great, ordered the execution of James the brother of John (Acts 12:2) and arrested Peter (Acts 12:3). His son, Herod Agrippa II, was the king before whom Paul spoke in Acts 25 and 26. He said, "You almost persuade me to become a Christian" (Acts 26:28). Herodians became a term for Jewish agents of Rome. The rise of the Roman Empire was predicted in both Nebuchadnezzar's vision

of the irons legs (Dan. 2:40) and Daniel's vision of the fourth beast with iron teeth (7:7).

7. **Jesus**. We add Jesus' rule here because His victory over Satan demarcates the greatest regime change of all! Man's 6 imperfect regimes and empires serve as a contrast to Christ's perfect leadership and kingdom.

Ecclesiastes 1:9 makes this end-time prediction, "that which *has been* is what *will be*, That which *is done* is what *will be done*, And there is nothing new under the sun" (emphasis added). In other words, there is a high probability of a very similar power struggle between these 6 groups leading up to the Second Coming of Jesus Christ.

It is easy to identify the parallels between ancient history and modern history so far. Just as the Ptolomies were friendly to the Jews, so too modern Egypt became the first Arab country to sign a peace treaty with Israel in 1979. For that peace agreement, Egyptian President Anwar El Sadat was gunned down in 1981. Just as the Seleucids instigated a reign of terror over Jews, so too Syria and Iran (territories of the Seleucids) are avowed enemies of the nation of Israel today. How accurate and predictive is the Bible! Just as Rome did not directly rule over Israel, but appointed an Idumean governor over the province of Judea, so too Western Europe is not likely to meddle directly with Israel, but may appoint an Arab diplomat to broker its will over the Middle East.

We should be on the lookout for a future Antiochus or Herod, a Middle Easterner figure popular among the Europeans, because he may well be the forerunner to the Anti-Christ, or even the Anti-Christ himself (see the number 666).

By association with fallen man, 6 signifies imperfection. Perfect 7 minus 1 equals imperfect 6. Triple the number—666—and you get total depravity and imperfection.

7

THE NUMBER 7 IS THE HEARTBEAT OF SCRIPTURE. 7 represents perfection or completeness. The conjunctions of 7s in Scripture, nature, history, and prophecy are beyond random.

7 IN NATURE AND HISTORY

There were 7 days of Creation and there are still 7 days to complete a week. Apart from the Genesis account of the 7-day Creation, there is no reason for a week to equal 7 days. The universally accepted 7-day week has no correlation to any movement of the earth, moon, sun, or other astronomical body. We have 24 hours in a day because the earth rotates on its axis in 24 hours. We have 365 days in a year because the earth revolves around the sun in 365.25 days. But why do we have 7 days in a week? Why not 10 days? Why not 5? Only the Book of Beginnings—Genesis—explains this! God created the world in 6 days and rested on the 7th.

The fact that every culture and nation recognizes the 7-day week attests to the plain truth that the God of the Bible is the original God all cultures once knew and His Word is the oldest revelation of God.

There are 7 continents (Africa, Antarctica, Asia, Australia, Europe, North America, and South America); 7 seas or largest bodies of water (the Arctic, Atlantic, Caribbean, Gulf of Mexico, Indian, Mediterranean, Pacific); 7 full notes on a music scale. There can only be 7 eclipses per year: 5 solar and 2 lunar; 4 solar and 3 lunar; or 3 solar and 4 lunar. There cannot be more than 7. Since the Protestant Reformation (1517), there have been 7 years with 7 non-penumbra eclipses.[1] Twice in the 20th century, a year with 7 eclipses of any kind fell on milestones in Israel's history:

- 1917 coinciding with the Balfour Declaration (Britain's recognition of the need for the state of Israel) and

- 1973 coinciding with the Yom Kippur War (the 4th time Arab nations invaded Israel, whose resounding victory led Egypt to concede she could never win a war against Israel and to become the first Arab state to sign a peace treaty with Israel in 1979).

7 IN SCRIPTURE AND PROPHECY

In his book *God Counts*, W. E. Filmer revealed the unusual patterns of 7 God concealed in His Word. The very first sentence of the Bible—"In the beginning God created the heavens and the earth"—contains 7 Hebrew words. Of these 7 words:

- The total number of letters is 28 (4 x 7).
- The first 3 words contain 14 letters (2 x 7).
- The remaining 4 words contain 14 letters.
- The 3 nouns—God, heavens, and earth—together have 14 letters.
- The gematria of these 3 nouns is 777 (111 x 7).
- The gematria of the verb "created" is 203 (29 x 7).
- The gematria of the first, middle and last letters of the verse is 133 (19 x 7).
- The gematria of the first and last letters of the first and last words is 497 (71 x 7).
- The gematria of the first and last letters of all 7 words is 1392 (199 x 7).

No wonder Filmer made this challenge, "I defy anyone to construct another sentence which incorporates such an amazing set of numerics. I should never have believed that such a sentence could exist if it were not for the fact that it is there."[2] This is only the first sentence of the Bible! Such supernatural patterns are replete throughout the Scriptures.

Russian born mathematician Ivan Panin (1855–1942) discovered patterns of 7 that are beyond chance in the first pages of the New Testament. The first 17 verses of Matthew outline the genealogy of Jesus. In this section:

- The number of generations (42) is divisible by 7.
- The number of vocabulary words (72) is divisible by 7.

- The number of nouns (56) is divisible by 7.
- The frequency of "the" (56) is divisible by 7.
- The gematria of all 72 vocabulary words (42,364) is divisible by 7.

From verse 1 to 11 is Jesus' genealogy up to the Babylonian Captivity. In this section, the number of vocabulary words (49) is divisible by 7. Of these 49 words:

- The number of letters (266) is divisible by 7.
- The number of vowels (140) is divisible by 7.
- The number of words beginning with a consonant (21) is divisible by 7.
- The number of words beginning with a vowel (28) is divisible by 7.
- The number of words appearing more than once (35) is divisible by 7.
- The number of words appearing only once (14) is divisible by 7.
- The number of nouns (42) is divisible by 7.
- The number of proper names (35) is divisible by 7.
- These 35 names are used 63 times (9 x 7).
- The number of male names (28) is divisible by 7.
- These male names occur 56 times (8 x 7).
- The number of words which are not nouns is 7.
- The only city named—Babylon—contains 7 Greek letters.

The rest of Matthew chapter 1 from verse 18 to 25 tells the history of Christ's birth. In this section:

- The number of words (161) is divisible by 7.
- The number of vocabulary words (77) is divisible by 7.
- The gematria of vocabulary words (52,605) is divisible by 7.

- The number of unique words used in this passage and never again in Matthew is 6—these 6 words contain 56 letters (8 x 7).

- The number of proper nouns is 7.

- The number of words spoken by the angel to Joseph (28) is divisible by 7.

The second chapter of Matthew tells the history of Jesus' childhood. In this section:

- The number of vocabulary words (161) is divisible by 7.

- The number of letters (896) is divisible by 7.

- The gematria of vocabulary words (123,529) is divisible by 7.

There are more patterns of 7 in Matthew chapter 2 than we can include. These heptadic patterns appear in the next book Mark. The more you get into it, the more mind-boggling it gets!

If these patterns appeared in only 1 book or by 1 writer, it would be astonishing enough. But they also appear in coordinated fashion among different writers who did not know each other and could not know whose writings would be included in the Bible.

The Hebrew word "seven" occurs 287 times in the Old Testament (41 x 7). The word "seventh" occurs 98 times (14 x 7). The word "sevenfold" occurs 7 times. "Seventy" occurs 56 times (8 x 7). "Seventy" in combination with any other number occurs 35 times (5 x 7).

Vocabulary unique to Matthew is used 42 times (6 x 7) and contains 126 letters (18 x 7). How is this possible? One possibility is that Matthew contrived this by getting all other 7 writers of the New Testament to agree not to use those words. That doesn't seem likely. Another possibility is that Matthew was the last writer of the Bible, thereby he knew exactly what words the other 7 New Testament writers did not use. The only one problem with this argument is all 8 writers of the New Testament used unique vocabulary not used by any other writer and the occurrence of unique words are in multiples of 7 for every writer: Mark, Luke, John, Paul, James, Peter, and Jude. No wonder Psalm 12:6 tells us, "The words of the LORD are pure words, like silver tried in a furnace of earth, purified *seven* times" (emphasis added).

7 times the God of the Bible says He is the "first and last" (Isa. 41:4; 44:6; 48:12; Rev. 1:11, 17; 2:8; 22:13). There is no one else before or after Him.

7 people are called a "man of God" in the Old Testament: Moses, David, Samuel, Shemaiah, Elijah, Elisha, and Igdaliah.

7 Old Testament writers are named in the New Testament: Moses, David, Isaiah, Jeremiah, Daniel, Hosea, and Joel. The numeric values of these names is 1,554 (222 x 7). David's name is found 1,134 times (7 x 162).[3]

There are 7 named prophetesses in the Bible: Miriam; Deborah; Huldah; Noadiah; Elizabeth, the mother of John; Mary, the mother of Jesus; Anna the prophetess. (See Exodus 15:20, Judges 4:4, 2 Kings 22:14, Nehemiah 6:14, Luke 1:41–45, Luke 1:46–55, Luke 2:36–38.) Add to these 5 unnamed prophetesses (Isaiah's wife in 8:3 and Philip's 4 daughters in Acts 21) and there were 12 female prophets in total.

Psalm 69 is quoted 7 times in the New Testament: twice by Matthew (23:29–38, 27:34, 38); twice by John (2:13-17, 15:18–25) and three times by Paul (Rom. 11:7–10, 15:3; 1 Thess. 2:15, 16).

THE MYSTERY OF SYMMETRY

All of these patterns of 7s throughout the Bible are breathtaking. Could they be contrived by humans? The reason the writers could not "stage-manage" the Word of God was that God used at least 33 different authors living in different places and at different times over a period of 1,600 years, writing in different languages (Hebrew, Chaldean, Greek, and Aramaic). They did not all know each other. They also did not know whose writing and which of their own writings would be included in the canon of Scriptures. That decision was made independently of the writers by independent councils. God used so many people to remove the possibility of human engineering. All this precaution which God took silences every false accusation of human contrivance.

God wants people to know His Word is His Word. He went to great lengths to prove it. Some skeptics cast doubt on the Bible, claiming it's not original, not pure, or not true. They insinuate that perhaps the Bible has been doctored or changed since its original form. If that were really the case, it would destroy all the symmetry we find in it. Notice that if we changed even a single letter in the first sentence of the Bible, we would not find the heptadic symmetry or patterns of 7s.

APPLYING 7 TO YOUR LIFE

When Joshua led Israel into the Promised Land, Jericho was the first city they had to conquer. In this first "battle," 7 priests carried 7 trumpets while the Jewish men marched around Jericho once for 7 days and 7 times on the 7th day.

At the end of the silent march, the people gave a loud shout and the walls of their enemy came tumbling down!

God wanted to make sure that His people learned that victory came by His grace and not by their own works. God ensured they understood this in a number of ways: He told all the soldiers to be circumcised 4 days before, which would have made them weak and sore; He told them to march silently for 7 days, so they were not allowed to taunt the enemy; He told them to march 7 times on the 7th day. Even if Jericho was a small city of 7 kilometers circumference, circling such a city 7 times would have required a 50 kilometers march and depleted most soldiers of energy before a fight. Sometimes God has to wait until we are depleted of all our own devices and strength before He can show us His grace.

Elisha told Naaman the Syrian leper to go wash in the Jordan 7 times. The funny thing was the Jordan was not a wide or a spectacular river. It didn't have the fertility of the Nile, the religious fame of the Ganges, or the commercial value of the Mississippi. In fact Naaman disdained it, "Are not Abanah and Pharpar, the rivers of Damascus, better than all the waters of Israel? Could I not wash in them and be clean?" (2 Kings 5:12). But he yielded to the prophet's word and dipped 7 times, and his flesh was restored like the flesh of a little child. God may ask us to do things that don't seem to bring us closer to the solution we want, but 7 dips remind us His ways are perfect. Don't give up on only the 5th dip or 6th dip. Do what God says and do it fully the way He says it.

There is a relationship rule based on the number 7. Though there may be exceptions, it is customary for women to prefer older men and men to prefer younger women. So how young is too young? It is widely reported that the older a man gets, the younger he prefers his wife to be. At what point does the age gap get "creepy"?

There is a "creepiness rule" which states: "never date anyone under half your age plus seven."[4] For instance, a 50-year-old should not date anyone under the age of 32. A 40-year-old should not date anyone under the age of 27. A 24-year-old should find someone aged 19 and up. Anything less is creepy…not to mention illegal under many jurisdictions. If one is mature, one should desire someone who is commensurate to oneself. It is not natural to desire a minor or a partner who is separated from oneself by too much of an age gap! The creepy standard—"half your age plus 7"—implies no one under the age of 14 should date at all. 14 is the minimum threshold because 7 (14/2) + 7 = 14.

Back in the old days when young people were more mature and demonstrated more responsibility, teenagers sometimes married. However, I do not think it wise for teenagers to rush into marriage or sex today. Until one is ready to financially support a family and raise a child, one should focus on growing spiritually in God, learning from a mentor in Church, and becoming emotionally intelligent and socially well-adjusted. These days, the minimum threshold for a relationship may be 7 + 7 + 7 or 7 x 3 or 21. That happens to be the age when most students graduate university. Again, 7 is the perfect number for relationships.

7 THE NUMBER OF JESUS

If 3 is the number of God the Father, then 7 is the number of God the Son. As the number of perfection, 7 befits Jesus who alone lived a perfect life, finished a perfect work, and is the perfect Savior. There are 7 feasts in Israel, each pointing to events in Jesus' first and Second Coming. Jesus spoke 7 kingdom parables in Matthew 13. Jesus sent 7 letters to 7 Churches in the Book of Revelation. The 7 letters to 7 Churches represent both 7 historical Churches and 7 prophetic ages or stages of the Church since the first century. The 7 letters contain 7 basic elements: region, role of Christ, recognition, rebuke, recommendation, wrap up, reassurance.* In the Book of Revelation, there are 7 seals opened by the Lord and 7 angels blowing 7 trumpets and releasing 7 vials of judgment poured on rebellious earth.

7 people are named before birth: Ishmael, Isaac, Solomon, Josiah (325 years before birth), Cyrus (175 years before birth), John the Baptist, and Jesus (1,500 years before birth). While no one knew for certain the Messiah's name, a big clue was given long ago. Before completing his ministry, Moses prophesied about the Messiah.

> The Lord thy God will raise up unto thee a *Prophet* from the midst of thee [born in Israel], of thy brethren [a Jew], *like unto me*; unto *him* [not unto Moses] ye shall hearken.
> —Deuteronomy 18:15, kjv, emphasis added

When Moses said this, there were two applications to his prophecy: one immediate and one in the distant future. His listeners were obviously not looking for the Messiah to come thousands of years later. They were looking for Moses' successor to fulfill this prophecy. Who was Moses' successor? What was his name? *Jesus* in Greek or *Joshua* in Hebrew.

Joshua's name was prophetic of the One who was to be a prophet like unto

---

* Smyrna and Philadelphia received no rebuke or condemnation. Sardis and Laodicea received no recognition or commendation. See Steve's DVD on Revelation, available at www.discover.org.au.

Moses, a title of Messiah. (See Deuteronomy 18:15–19, John 1:21, John 6:14.) Joshua historically was the prophet like unto Moses, succeeding directly after him, whereas Jesus was prophetically the Prophet like unto Moses, arriving about 1,500 years later. They both shared the same name. The Messiah's name was revealed in type first, and then revealed in person by Gabriel to Mary. (See Matthew 1:21; Luke 1:31.)

How was Jesus a prophet like unto Moses? The most glaring similarity is that both came *twice* to their own people. The first time they arrived to help, they were rejected. The second time Moses returned (after 40 years of being away), the Jews accepted him but with much grumbling. The second time Jesus will return (after 2,000 years of being away), one-third of the Jews will accept Him with much repentance. Zechariah 12:10, written 500 years before Christ, predicts this event, "Then they will look on Me whom they pierced. Yes, they will mourn for Him as one mourns for his only son, and grieve for Him as one grieves for a firstborn."

The Savior was named before birth, if only we have eyes to see it. Every instance of the Hebrew word *Yeshua, Jehoshua,* or *Joshua*—meaning *God is Salvation*—was a clue that God would be the Messiah and He would be named *Jesus*—the Greek form of *Yeshua*. Try inserting *Yeshua* where the word *salvation* appears in these Scriptures and see if you can see the Savior prophetically: Genesis 49:18, Exodus 14:13, 15:2, Deuteronomy 32:15, 1 Samuel 2:1, Psalm 20:5, 21:1, 85:9, 91:16, 96:2, 118:14. For example:

> With long life I will satisfy him, and show him My [Yeshua].
> —PSALM 91:16

Salvation is a person. His name is Yeshua. At the end of a life of faith, we will get to see Him.

> Sing to the LORD, bless His name; proclaim the good news of His [Yeshua] from day to day.
> —PSALM 96:2

Good news was always about Yeshua from the beginning.

> The LORD is my strength and song, and He has become my [Yeshua].
> —PSALM 118:14

When God was born in the flesh, He became Yeshua—God is my Savior.

Jesus called Himself Lord of the Sabbath or Lord of the 7th day. Jesus intentionally performed 7 miracles on a Sabbath, irritating the Pharisees, but delivering 7 individuals from oppression:

1. A man with an unclean spirit (Mark 1:21–25)
2. Peter's mother-in-law (Mark 1:21, 29–31)
3. A man with the withered hand (Mark 3:1–5)
4. A woman bent over for 18 years (Luke 13:10–17)
5. A man with dropsy (Luke 14:1–6)
6. A man paralyzed for 38 years (John 5:1–10)
7. A man born blind (John 9:14)

7 times Jesus said for Christians to pray, command, and cast out devils "in His name." That means Jesus has given the believer His own authority to use on Earth.

1. "In My name [the name of Jesus]...cast out demons...speak with new tongues...lay hands on the sick" (Mark 16:17–18).
2. "Whatever you ask in My name, that I will do" (John 14:13).
3. "If you ask anything in My name, I will do it" (John 14:14).
4. "Whatever you ask the Father in My name He may give you" (John 15:16)
5. "Whatever you ask the Father in My name He will give you" (John 16:23).
6. "Until now [under the old covenant] you have asked nothing in My name. Ask, and you will receive, that your joy may be full" (John 16:24).
7. "In that day [when the new covenant has been established] you will ask in My name" (John 16:26).

Most of the time, the sick approached Jesus for healing. In a minority of instances, the Lord approached the sick first. How many individuals did Jesus approach to heal? You guessed it—exactly 7! You can read about them in chapter 19 Healings.

Jesus described the torments of hell 7 times. (See Matthew 8:12, 13:42, 13:50, 22:13, 24:15, 25:30; Luke 13:28.)

There will be weeping, wailing, and gnashing of teeth. Anyone who disbelieves in hell has to assume they know something Jesus didn't. It's safer to assume Jesus knew what He was talking about and was preparing us to not go there.

Jesus was crucified on a hill called *Golgotha* in Aramaic or *Calvary* in Latin. Calvary is 777 meters above sea level.

7 IS PERFECT

All these patterns of 7s are breathtaking because they transcend the frame of reference of the individual writers. As many Bible critics have been quick to note, the 4 Gospel accounts do not match in timeline and detail. The stories are not presented in the same chronological order and the words are not always quoted the same way. Uncoached eyewitnesses do not tend to give the exact same account of the same events, simply because they have not colluded and naturally come from different perspectives.

Clearly God intended the Gospel accounts to be this way precisely to meet the skepticism of prebelievers. What the minor differences prove is that the 4 Gospel writers did not collaborate. That means Luke wasn't saying to Matthew, "You put 6 references to weeping in hell and I'll put 1—that will make a nice, neat 7." Matthew could not say to Mark, "You write about 2 healings on the Sabbath, I'll write about 1, hopefully Luke and John will have enough sense to put together 4 Sabbath miracles and no more." They didn't know what each other was writing. John could not say to Matthew, "You quote Psalm 69 twice, I'll quote it twice, and we'll leave Paul to quote it 3 times to make a perfect 7." The heptadic structure constantly found in Scripture happened beyond the frame of reference of the writers. In other words, the patterns were not contrived by man but superimposed by divine sanction.

This simply is another proof of the inspiration of God's Word. To those who ask, "How do I know which book is truly God's Word?" the answer is: "The Book with His signature of 7 on it."

When voices come to cast doubt on the authority of God's Word, the 7-day week reminds me that the God who created the world in 7 days also commanded us to believe in His Word which is full of 7s. The 7-day week points to no other person but Jesus—the Lord of 7. When we meet Him, we will be without excuse because every week of our lives pointed to Him as the Creator God.

7

SACRED OBJECTS

THERE WERE ONLY SEVEN DIVINELY ORDAINED OBJECTS in Moses' tabernacle and Solomon's Temple, all pointing to Christ. Every Christian should have them committed to memory as they are object lessons about our relationship with God. The first two objects are in the courtyard, the next three objects are in the holy place, and the final two objects are in the innermost holy of holies.

1. Brazen (bronze) altar—on which sacrifice was made. This was the first object any worshiper of God saw upon approaching the presence of God. The blood and fire remind us of Jesus' blood and His suffering in hell for three days. Bronze is a type of judgment. The way to God is through Jesus Christ, who was judged and sacrificed for our sins.

2. Brazen laver or water basin (also called "the sea")—where servants of God washed. This was the second object any worshiper of God saw. After we are saved by the blood sacrifice of the Messiah, we must be baptized.

3. Table of showbread—bread representing the Word of God. Once saved and water baptized, we are to get into God's Word and feed on it. We must hear God for ourselves, not just through someone else. Daily devotion to God's Word is so important to every believer. This is our daily bread.

4. Golden lampstand (the "menorah")—continually lit and filled with olive oil, representing the Holy Spirit. No believer or minister is equipped without the anointing of the Holy Spirit.

5. Altar of incense—incense represents the prayer of the saints. (See Psalm 141:2; Luke 1:10; Revelation 8:3–4.) No one can successfully approach God in prayer until he has passed the altar of sacrifice, the water basin, the table of showbread, and the lampstand. This is a vivid metaphor of how many people fail in prayer because they have not accepted the sacrifice of Christ, been baptized, and been filled with the Word and the Spirit. But our prayers become successful when no sin separates us from God, we live in obedience, we love His Word, and we seek His presence; then, and only then, are we guaranteed of a higher prayer life. Now, we are invited into the holy of holies.

6. Ark of the covenant—a wooden box overlaid with gold, containing 3 things: the original 10 Commandments; Aaron's rod that budded; and manna (bread from Heaven). What do these objects represent? The 10 Commandments represent the holiness of God. When we open the ark of the covenant, we find God is holy. We are undone. To what shall we turn? Next we find Aaron's rod. Like most wooden objects in the Old Testament, it represents the cross of Christ. The budding of Aaron's rod is a picture of the resurrection of Christ. God is able to bring life from the dead. Manna represents God's provision. He wants to give us the Bread of Life. He provides salvation.

7. Mercy seat—a lid of solid gold with 2 cherubim above it, which closes the ark of the covenant. Once a year blood is sprinkled on the mercy seat by the high priest. The mercy seat covers God's judgment. We do not need to fear the God's holiness because Christ's blood has been sprinkled over the mercy seat. We can come boldly into the presence of God, where once only the high priest could approach once a year.

These 7 objects are an excellent illustration of the progression of our relationship with God. No one can be saved without first passing the altar of sacrifice and brazen laver. No one can pray successfully without being filled with the Word and the Spirit. No one can dwell in God's holy of holies without a correct estimation of God's holiness and dependence on the mercy and protective covering of Jesus' blood. The blood is the first and the last thing we see when we enter God's house of worship. Clearly everything in the Temple and tabernacle point to God's Son. Our relationship with Jesus Christ was described by a 4,000-year-old metaphor or object lesson.

7

FEASTS

GOD REVEALED TO ISRAEL that there are certain *moeds* or "appointed times" in which He will do certain things. These *moeds* divide up time and help us to commemorate as well as anticipate a major event in God's prophetic plan. There are 12 months in a Hebrew non-leap year with 7 feasts of Israel on the following months:

1. Nisan*
   Nisan 14: Passover (*Pesach*)
   Nisan 15–21: Feast of Unleavened Bread (*Chol Moed Matza*)
   Nisan 17: Feast of Firstfruits (*Yom Bikkerim*)

2. Iyyar

3. Sivan
   Sivan 6: Pentecost or Feast of Weeks (*Hag Ha Shavout*) or Feast of Harvest (*Hag Ha Kazir*).

4. Tammuz

5. Av

6. Elul

7. Tishri**
   Tishri 1: Feast of Trumpets (*Yom Teruah*) or the Civil New Year (Rosh *Hashanan*).
   Tishri 10: Day of Atonement (*Yom Kippur*)
   Tishri 15–21: Feast of tabernacles or Booths or Ingathering (*Sukkot*)

8. Heshvan

---

* Nisan is the same month as Abib (Exod. 34:18). Both are the 1st month of the sacred calendar and 7th month of the civil calendar. Abib was called Nisan after the Babylonian captivity (Neh. 2:1).
** Tishri is the same month as Ethanim. Both are the 7th month of the sacred calendar (1 Kings 8:2) and 1st month of the civil calendar.

9. Kislev

10. Tebet

11. Shebat

12. Adar

A leap year adds a 13th month called Adar II, which has 1 day less than Adar I (i.e. 29 days instead of the usual 30).

It's readily apparent to us that there are 2 groups of 3 feasts separated by a long gap of nearly 6 months. The first 3 feasts are concentrated in the first month of the religious calendar (Nisan), followed shortly by Pentecost in the third month (Siva), then a long gap of nearly 4 months till the last 3 feasts in the seventh month (Tishri). Why such grouping?

Agriculturally speaking, the first 3 feasts coincide with the spring harvest of barley, Pentecost with the summer harvest of wheat, and the last 3 feasts with the fall harvest of grapes. But surely God's "appointed times" refer to more than barley, wheat, and grapes.

Spiritually speaking, the first 3 feasts foreshadow Jesus at His first coming; the last 3 feasts foreshadow Christ at His Second Coming. Many Jewish rabbis have struggled with 2 apparently contradictory sets of Scriptures about the Messiah. One set seems to show Him as a suffering servant, another set as a victorious ruler. Some of the ancients concluded that there must be 2 Messiahs. They named the first one *Messiah ben Yosef* after Joseph who suffered much because of his brothers. They named the second one *Messiah ben David* after Israel's greatest king. The truth is the contradiction is resolved in Christ. The first 3 feasts point to Christ's first coming as a suffering Servant; the last 3 feasts point to Christ's Second Coming as a conquering King.

The 4th feast represents the harvest of the nations into the Church, which began on the Day of Pentecost in the 4th millennium. The early feasts have thus had their fulfillment, the gap corresponds to the present Church age, and the last feasts await their fulfillment in the latter days.

Let's highlight the meaning of each feast, which is God's annual object lesson pointing to the Messiah:

1. Passover (*Pesach*)

The blood sacrifice of an innocent lamb represents the crucifixion of the sinless Son of God, which occurred precisely on Passover day.

2. Feast of Unleavened Bread (*Chol Moed Matza*)

Leaven represents sin, false doctrine, and religious self-righteousness. Jesus dubbed it the "leaven of the Pharisees" (Matt. 16:11–12). Unleavened bread or *matza* was flat bread that was stripped, perforated, and slightly burned. Without doubt the *matza* points to Jesus Christ. Like bread without leaven, Jesus was sinless. Like bread with stripes, Jesus was whipped 39 times and "by His stripes we are healed" (Isa. 53:5; 1 Pet. 2:24). Like bread pierced with holes, Jesus' hands and feet were pierced by nails and His side by a spear. Finally the burn marks on the *matza* reminds us Jesus went to hell for 3 days and 3 nights, the place of burning (Acts 2:27; Prov. 23:14).

During a traditional Passover meal, Jewish adults remove the 2nd *matza* out of 3, wrap it in cloth, and hide it for the children to find. This game amazingly speaks about Jesus, who is the 2nd person of the Trinity; He came down to Earth to die for us; His body was wrapped in graveclothes and hidden in a tomb for 3 days and 3 nights; but He has risen in victory. If we seek Him like little children seek the 2nd *matza*, we will find eternal life. The Messiah is a great discovery and great reward.

3. Feast of Firstfruits (*Yom Bikkerim*)

Historically the Red Sea parted on the Day of Firstfruits. Israel's "baptism" through the Red Sea is a great type of New Testament baptism, because it left their Egyptian enemies forever. (See Exodus 14.) Prophetically firstfruits represent resurrection. Christ was the first one to rise from the dead precisely on the Day of Firstfruits. He is called *the* firstfruits (1 Cor. 15:20–23).

The Bible states that Noah's ark rested on Mount Ararat on the 17th of 7th month of the Genesis calendar, which is the 1st month of the Exodus calendar—the Day of Firstfruits. Just as the old world had a new beginning on the Feast of Firstfruits, so too we can experience a new beginning because of the resurrection of Jesus Christ.

4. Pentecost or Feast of Weeks (*Hag Ha Shavout*) or Feast of Harvest (*Hag Ha Kazir*)

Pentecost celebrates the wheat harvest, which represent the first wave of mainly Gentile believers swept into the kingdom of God since the first century.

This is the only feast which *allows* leavened bread, giving it a distinct "Gentile" flavor. Pentecost always falls on a Sunday, being the "morrow after the Sabbath" (Lev. 23:15, KJV). The Law was given on the Day of Pentecost. The Holy Spirit was given on the Day of Pentecost. And the Church was birthed on the Day of Pentecost.

5. Feast of Trumpets (*Yom Teruah*) or the Head of the Year (*Rosh Hashanah*)

Occurring on the 1st of Tishri, this is a special day for many reasons.

Firstly, ancient rabbis believe the birthday of the world is on *Rosh Hashanah*.

Secondly, there is scholarly consensus that Jesus was not likely born on the 25th of December. When was the most likely month of Jesus' birth? The month of Tishri (our September). Commentators' estimates vary from the 1st of Tishri (coinciding with the Feast of Trumpets) to the 15th of Tishri (Feast of Tabernacles). Chuck Missler believes a possible date for the birth of Christ is September 29, 2 b.c. (1st of Tishri 3758 Jewish year).[1] Roy Reinhold believes a possible date is September 11, 3 b.c. (1st of Tishri 3759).[2] If the latter were true, it might explain why Satan wanted to defile the date 9/11 with his most audacious act of terrorism so far. Satan only perverts what is good.

If Jesus was in fact born on the Feast of Trumpets, then ancient Israel would have unknowingly been blasting the trumpets while Jesus was being born. God had commanded the nation to announce the birth of her king. We may never know the exact date of Jesus' birth till we see Jesus face-to-face and ask Him, so I will not linger on speculations and let the interested reader pursue his or her own further study.

Thirdly, the Feast of Trumpets may symbolize the blast that raptures the Church. We know that a trumpet will sound when the dead in Christ shall be raised and the living saints will be raptured to meet the Lord in the air. Two New Testament Scriptures fit well with this feast:

> "For the Lord Himself will descend from Heaven with a shout [*teruah*], with the voice of an archangel, and with the *trumpet* of God [shofar of Yahweh]. And the dead in Christ will rise first. Then we who are alive and remain shall be caught up together with them in the clouds to meet the Lord in the air. And thus we shall always be with the Lord.
> —1 Thessalonians 4:16–17, emphasis added

> Behold, I tell you a mystery: We shall not all sleep, but we shall all be changed— in a moment, in the twinkling of an eye, at the last *trumpet* (shofar). For the *trumpet* will sound, and the dead will be raised incorruptible, and we shall be changed.
> —1 Corinthians 15:51–52

The Feast of Trumpets is known by many alternative names, all of which support it being prophetic of the Church's Rapture:

- *Yom HaKeseh*—the Hidden Day, when the raptured saints will be hidden from tribulation

- *Yomim Noraim*—Days of Affliction, when Israel's main friend, the Christians, will have disappeared, leaving the Jews without ally in the world

- *Yom HaDin*—the Day of Judgment, when the 7 seals of judgment will be opened and 7-year Tribulation will occur

- *Ha Kiddushin* or *Nesuin*—the Wedding of the Messiah. While the earth suffers tribulation, Revelation 19:7 says the Church will be in Heaven celebrating the Messiah's wedding feast. This once again indicates the Church has been raptured.

- *Ha Melech*—the coronation of the Messiah. While the earth suffers tribulation, the saints will be before His throne casting our crowns before Him (Rev. 4:10). The Messiah will be adored as King of kings and Lord of lords!

In ancient Israel, Yom Teruah was also known as the Unknown Day because the population would wait for the rabbis to announce when Yom Teruah would occur. One of the complications of the Hebrew solar-lunar calendar meant that an extra month (second Adar) was added 6 times every 19 years. Imagine how hard it would be for the average person to figure out when New Year's Day would be. The Rapture may occur on a future Yom Teruah; certainly it qualifies as an Unknown Day the general population will not anticipate.

6. Day of Atonement (*Yom Kippur*)

This day occurs 10 days after *Rosh Hashanah*, 10 representing the Tribulation. (See Revelation 2:10.) *Yom Kippur* symbolizes Israel's National Day of Repentance, predicted in Hosea 5:15 and Isaiah 53. On that day, Israel as a nation will finally recognize her Messiah.

Then Hosea 5:15 will be fulfilled, "I will return again to My place [meaning Messiah has already come once] Till they acknowledge their offense [of rejecting Messiah]. Then they will seek My face; In their affliction [the Tribulation] they will earnestly seek Me."

This will be when the Jewish survivors of the Tribulation will finally read and understand Isaiah 53, which is currently forbidden in the synagogues. The Tribulation will be a time of Jacob's Trouble, yet the end of it will be a time of great salvation for the Jews who choose their Messiah. Revelation says Jesus will tread the "winepress of the fierceness and wrath of Almighty God" (Rev. 19:15). This is Hebraism indicating the fall season in Israel, or the harvest of grapes, when these judgments may begin.

While Jesus' first coming was tied to Passover, Jesus' Second Coming will be tied to Yom Kippur. Some prophecy teachers believe Jesus' feet will touch down on the Mount of Olives on Yom Kippur. (See Zechariah 14:4.)

7. Feast of Tabernacles or Booths (*Sukkot*)

This is a joyful feast 5 days after Yom Kippur, during which Jews built tents and temporarily lived in them for 7 days. The Transfiguration of Jesus into His glorious form likely occurred on the Feast of Tabernacles, because of Peter's reference of building tents for Moses and Elijah (Matt. 17:4). Peter was not making an unusual offer since the law required everyone to stay in tents.

This feast is the Sabbath of Sabbaths, for it is the 7th of 7 feasts celebrated on the 7th day of the 7th month for 7 days. After the 7 days, they were to leave the temporary for the permanent. Solomon's Temple was dedicated on the Feast of Tabernacles. Whereas Moses' tabernacle was a portable place of worship, Solomon's Temple represented a permanent place of worship. This idea of moving into the permanent leads us to believe this final feast represents the Millennium (1,000 years of Sabbath rest) and the Messianic kingdom (a permanent kingdom that will never end).

There is another Scripture that connects the Millennium with the Feast of Tabernacles. Revelation 7:9 says: "After these things I looked, and behold, a great multitude which no one could number, of all nations, tribes, peoples, and tongues, standing before the throne and before the Lamb, clothed with white robes, with palm branches in their hands." Why palm branches? An orthodox Jew should know, but a Gentile would miss the clue. These are the building materials to celebrate Tabernacles.

According to Zechariah 14, Sukkot is the only feast all nations are required to attend in the Millennium. If Jesus proclaims the start of the Millennium 5 days after His Second Coming on Yom Kippur, then Sukkot shall be remembered as the feast that ushered in the Messianic kingdom. Just as we look back to the Last Supper and the sacrifice of Jesus Christ through communion, the nations will look back to the start of the Millennium and the Messianic kingdom through the Feast of Tabernacles.

The 7 feasts of Israel are God's way of illustrating the Messiah to our sight, sound, touch, taste, and smell. The feasts are audio-visual, multisensory object lessons about what Christ did in the past and what He's about to do in the near future.

How could Christ have contrived to be born into a society that had 7 feasts about Him? Even the coincidence of one feast like the Passover would be an outstanding miracle. Could Jesus have orchestrated His own birth into a society that killed innocent lambs to atone for sins, or His own death on the very day they killed that lamb to atone for sins, or the nation's cessation of lamb sacrifice shortly after His resurrection? For nearly 2,000 years, the Jews have not killed a Passover lamb. Why not? Because the true Passover Lamb has already been slain. How could Jesus have accomplished all this unless He were truly God— the very One who instituted the 7 feasts prior to His own coming.

The more we study the Bible in detail, the more absurd the claim appears that Jesus was nothing more than a good teacher or nice person. Jesus was definitely something quite far beyond. He was, is, and will be the Eternal One.

8

8 IS THE FIRST CUBE, the cube of two (2^3 or 2 x 2 x 2). It is the number of new life, new beginning, or the resurrection. A day is divided into 3 periods of 8 hours (8 x 3 = 24). Most people work 8 hours, have 8 hours of free time, and sleep 8 hours, after which they are ready to start a new day.

8 people wrote the New Testament divided into 3 parts: Gospels, Acts, and Epistles. Noah was the 8th person from Adam and he had 3 sons (Gen. 9:18; 2 Pet. 2:5); there were 8 people who survived the global Flood; the world had a new beginning starting with these 3 couples (Gen. 7:13, 1 Pet. 3:20). Elijah performed 8 miracles, the 3rd one being a resurrection of a widow's son (1 Kings 17:17–23). The words *sun* and *earth* appear together 8 times in Scripture; it takes 8.33 minutes for the sun's light to reach the earth. (See Genesis 19:23; 2 Samuel 23:4; Psalm 19:4; Psalm 50:1; Jeremiah 8:2; Joel 2:10; Amos 8:9; Luke 21:25.) 8 is the atomic number of oxygen, a 3-atom molecule that gives fuel to fire and life to us as we breathe it. Jesus was resurrected on the 8th day (Sunday), after spending 3 days in hell. The Holy Spirit descended on the 8th day (Sunday), after 3 years of Jesus' earthly ministry.

8 is the number of new beginning. Most people require 8 hours of sleep before they wake up refreshed and ready to start a new life. All the universe points to the fact that our biological clock was wound up by the Creator of the universe who said the earth will have a new beginning in the 8th millennium. God will create a new Heaven and new earth after the millennial reign of Christ, starting the 8th millennium.

These patterns of 8 are found in Scripture and nature, which makes them also appear in history. Some economists, such as Martin Armstrong, have observed an 8.6 year cycle to the financial markets.* Every 3 cycles of 8.6 years, 25.8 years, there also happens to be a major earthquake. These patterns may be interrelated. For instance, the 1906 San Francisco earthquake led to the Panic of 1907 as capital flowed from insurance companies on the east coast

---

* In Biblical times, there was a 7-year cycle of boom and bust which led to the meteoric rise of a man of God named Joseph, who believed God, believed in cycles, and prepared accordingly. The Dust Bowl of the 1930s was also a 7-year drought. The 7-year cycle may have lengthened to 8.6 in more modern times.

to pay for damages on the west, sparking a shortage of cash on the east that rationalized the creation of Federal Reserve System in 1913.[1] The 8.6 year cycle in earthquakes and climate changes may influence new economic policies far more than governments and politicians.

The 2010 Haitian earthquake which killed 230,000 people and left a million homeless came on time: 4 cycles of 25.8 years after the San Francisco earthquake, or 12 cycles of 8.6 years. I suspect, however, that the interval between major earthquakes will shorten as the earth goes into what Jesus called "birth pangs" or labor contractions before the Messiah arrives.

Male circumcision—a sign of new relationship with God—was commanded on the 8th day. (See Genesis 17:12; Genesis 21:4; Leviticus 12:3; Luke 1:59; Luke 2:21.) The timing of circumcision varies in other cultures from the 1st day to the 13th year. Is there any reason the God of the Bible specifically commanded it to be on the 8th day? Scientific studies have shown that babies do not produce optimal levels of prothrombin, a blood clotting glycoprotein that helps healing, until the 8th day of life.[2] How did the writer of the Bible know that before modern medicine, while other cultures had no idea?

There are 8 glyco carbohydrates or biological sugars which spell out the language of life. These 8 sugars on cell surfaces are responsible for the sperm finding the egg and the immune system identifying friends from foes. They are involved in nearly all cell-to-cell communication and most healing of the human body. These sugars also determine our blood type. Whereas there are 4 letters (nucleotides) in our DNA, there are 8 letters (sugars) on our cells. These 8 letters create a vastly more complex combination of codes than the DNA codes. God chose 8 nutrients to spell out the cellular language of life. 8 is the number for new life.

There are 8 cases of infertility in the Bible: Sarah, Rebekah, Rachel, Manoah's wife, Hannah, Michal, a Shunammite who fed Elisha, and Elizabeth. All were healed by prayer except: (1) the Shunammite who honored the man of God and was rewarded by being told she would have a son, and (2) Michal who despised David's love for God and cared more about outward appearance than inward obedience. She remained infertile for the rest of her life. There is no record of her praying.

8 women (7 barren and 1 virgin) had miraculous conceptions and gave supernatural childbirth: Sarah, Rebekah, Rachel, Manoah's wife, Hannah, a Shunammite, Elizabeth, and Mary. All 8 sons became great men of God: Isaac, Israel, Joseph, Samson, Samuel, the Shunammite's son, John the Baptist, and our Lord Jesus. We don't know much about the life of the Shunammite's son

other than he became a type of Christ by becoming the 2ⁿᵈ person in Scripture to be raised from the dead. (See 2 Kings 4:18–37.)

If you have had problems conceiving a child, be encouraged that God has given life where it seemed impossible before. Instead of focusing on a doctor's report, believe the Great Physician's report. He who made the womb can fill it for you! Bring these 8 cases of infertility and 8 cases of miraculous conceptions to God, and humbly ask Him to do the same for you in Jesus' name. Be willing to give your first child to God, as Hannah, Elizabeth, and Mary did.

8 THE NUMBER OF THE RESURRECTED ONE

Both 7 and 8 are numbers associated with Jesus Christ. 7 represents His perfection; 8 His Resurrection. Jesus called Himself the Lord of the Sabbath—the 7ᵗʰ day; Jesus resurrected on Sunday—the 8ᵗʰ day. David, a type of Christ, is called both the 7ᵗʰ and 8ᵗʰ son of Jesse. (See 1 Samuel 16:10–11, 17:12; 1 Chronicles 2:15.) How can both be true? The death of a previous son would explain why both figures are linked to David. These kinds of preconceived patterns in the Old Testament truly magnify Christ because they only make sense after Christ is revealed to us. There is no reason for the Old Testament writers to contrive such details. Only God knew ahead of time they would find meaning in Christ.

Not surprisingly, the gematria of Jesus' Greek name is 888:

I	H	S	O	U	S	TOTAL
10	8	200	70	400	200	888

All 7 of Jesus' divine titles all have gematria that are multiples of 8.[3]

TITLE	GEMATRIA	MULTIPLE
Lord	800	100 x 8
Christ	1480	185 x 8
Our Lord	1768	221 x 8
Savior	1408	176 x 8
Immanuel	25,600	3200 x 8
Messiah	656	82 x 8
Son	880	110 x 8

What is the probability of that occurring by chance!

8 IN CULTURE

The ancient Chinese were very interested in the study of numbers. (Perhaps that's what made so many of them the merchants of the old world and the business owners of today.) The Chinese especially liked the number 8 as it represented "luck" or "prosperity" to them. Where did this belief come from?

The 8th letter of the Hebrew alphabet is "heh," which symbolizes God's life. When Abram's name was given the 8th letter, "heh," his name became "Abraham"—the father of many nations. Sarai's name was also given a "heh" in the middle, and she became "Sarah"—princess and mother of nations. Through God's breath of life this century-old couple received power to supernaturally give birth to Isaac.

It seems likely to me that the origin of some Chinese myths could have been passed down from the original believers of *El Shaddai*. Even the Chinese word for God *Shan-ti* sounds a lot like the Hebrew word for the Almighty—*El Shaddai*.

All Asians can trace their common ancestry to Shem, one of Noah's 3 sons who migrated to the East after the global Flood. Shem was a godly man and an ancestor of the Messiah. His name is the origin of the Asiatic term "Semite" and "Semitic."

Asians traditionally have a high respect for their ancestors and sometimes cite ancestral worship as a reason to not become Christian. Yet what would our ancestors want of us? They would want us to be good people, live a good life, and find the truth. Asians should look to Shem to credit many of their traditions and godly wisdom. No Asian originally descended from a God hater. All Asians descended from the first Asian, who was God-fearing Shem. He in turn was the son of a God believer, Noah, the 8th from Adam. And all humanity ultimately descended from God-believers Adam and Eve. When we find Christ, we please all of our ancestors.

A FINAL WORD

Many people have wondered how long Adam and Eve lived in innocence before the Fall. It may not be the most pressing question to our spiritual life, but there is at least one ancient Jewish source from 150 B.C. which proffers an exact date to this question.

The Book of Jubilees 3:17 claims that Adam and Eve lived 7 full years in the Garden of Eden; then on the 8th year of creation, in the 2nd month, on the 17th day, Satan came as a serpent to tempt Eve. On that day, they turned their backs on God and were expelled from the Garden of Eden to the land of Elda, the land of their creation. Also the mouths of all animals were closed, so that all animals ceased to communicate with mankind.

Some people speculate whether or not Adam and Eve had children before the Fall. Romans 5 indicates that sin entered the world through one representative man, therefore we, who were unborn but in Adam, "inherited" sin and death through him. The Book of Jubilee agrees and says that Adam and Eve had no son till the 8th year of Creation.

Although these dates cannot be verified by Scripture, they are congruent with the numerical patterns we observe. It should come to us as no surprise that Adam and Eve lived in perfection for 7 years or 1 week of years. Then in the 2nd week or 8th year of Creation, mankind had an unfortunate "new" beginning of deception and disobedience, of suffering and death, which had not existed before the Fall. New life, a newborn son, also came in the 8th year.

Jesus resurrected to new life on the 8th day. Through Christ, God wants to reverse this curse in our lives first, then in the earth, then in the entire universe. Christianity is the only religion in the world which says that God can come to live inside of man. 8 times in Scripture believers are called the "Temple of God": 1 Corinthians 3:9, 16, 17; 1 Corinthians 6:19; 2 Corinthians 6:16; Ephesians 2:22; Hebrews 3:6; 1 Peter 2:5. When seven thousand years are complete, in the eighth millennium, we who believe in Christ will enjoy a new Heaven and new earth.

9

9 IS THE MAXIMUM NUMBER (single digit). It is associated with spiritual activity and supernatural power. The Jewish 9th hour (our 3:00 p.m.) was the time Jesus died on the cross. The 9th hour is a Biblical time of prayer. In Acts 3, Peter and John went to the Temple to pray at the 9th hour. At that time a man crippled from birth got healed. In Acts 10, God sent an angel to meet Cornelius at the 9th hour. He and his family were the first Gentiles to become Christian! Jews celebrate 3 feasts around the 9th month of September: Rosh Hashanah (New Year), Yom Kippur (Day of Atonement) and Sukkot (Feast of Tabernacles).

9 is associated with truth. The Hebrew word for truth is *amet* composed of 3 letters with the following values: aleph (1), mem (40), tav (400). The gematria of aleph, mem, tav: 1 + 40 + 400 = 441 (49 x 9). The reduced gematria of 441 is 4 + 4 + 1 = 9. Both the gematria and reduced gematria of "truth" is a multiple of 9. The sum of all 22 letters in the Hebrew alphabet is 4995 or 555 x 9 (grace x truth). The Hebrew language is shouting God's Truth about Grace, Grace, Grace! The 9th Commandment tells us it's a sin to lie; in other words, tell the truth, the whole truth, and nothing but the truth!

9 is the number of the Holy Spirit. There are:

> 9 fruits of the Spirit—love, joy, peace, longsuffering, gentleness, goodness, meekness, faithfulness and temperance (Gal. 5:22–23). These 9 character traits of the born again believer are listed in the 9th book of the New Testament.

> 9 gifts of the Spirit—word of wisdom, word of knowledge, gift of special faith, gifts of healings, miracles, prophecy, discerning of spirits, tongues and interpretation of tongues (1 Cor. 12:7–11)

> 9 months from conception till a child is born

9 planets in our solar system*

9 demon-possessed cases delivered by the power of the Holy
Spirit:

DELIVERANCE OF	MATT.	MARK	LUKE
A man with an unclean spirit		1:23–28	4:31–37
Mary Magdalene who had 7 spirits			8:2
2 men with unclean spirits who had a fetish for nudity, death and tattoos or mutilation of the flesh	8:28–43	5:1–21	8:26–39
A mute man	9:32–34		11:14
A blind and mute man	12:22–23		
A girl with an unclean spirit	15:21–28	7:31–37	
An epileptic boy with an unclean spirit	17:14–21	9:17–29	9:37–42
A woman with a spirit of infirmity 18 years			13:16–17
A fortune-telling girl with a spirit of divination			Acts 16:16–18

A common question is: "Did Jesus ever meet a homosexual?" The answer is, very likely, because the term "unclean"** (see Romans 1:24–27; Galatians 5:19; Ephesians 5:3–5; Colossians 3:5) is a Biblical euphemism for sexual immorality. Jesus met 4 types of spirits: spirits of infirmity (spirits that cause certain sicknesses); spirits of divination (occult spirits); seducing spirits (religious spirits impersonating Christianity or Christians); and unclean spirits (spirits of porno and perversion). Unclean spirits were the *most prevalent* spirits Jesus met. Sexual sins were as common then as they are today.

Notice the men at Gadarenes possessed with unclean spirits ran around naked and lost their sense of modesty. In Mark and Luke's accounts, the writers could not bring themselves to mention both men. But Matthew tells us

---

* At least until August 24, 2006, when the International Astronomical Union demoted Pluto to a dwarf planet; this was partially due to the 2005 discovery of the most distant known object in the solar system, another dwarf planet 27 percent larger than Pluto called Eris; both Pluto and Eris have one moon each.

** The Greek word for *uncleanness* is *akatharthos*, meaning impure in thought and action. The Bible is telling us homosexuality begins with an unchecked thought and unchecked desire. By becoming Christian, the Holy Spirit will empower us to self-control.

there were 2 men living together in a tomb, which strongly suggests they were homosexuals cast out of society.

What's interesting is Jesus met 2 children with unclean spirits, a boy and a girl. This tells us that sexual thoughts start at an earlier age than most of the Church is willing to accept or care to deal with. It also explains the *only* instance in the Bible where the disciples "could not" cast out a spirit. It was called an unclean spirit or likely a spirit of homosexuality. Notice the great agony it caused in the parents of both these children. Sins that violate sexual boundaries or confuse sexual identities cause the greatest pain in families. The Church has changed little today, as most Christian disciples would not know what to do about an unclean spirit. But through Jesus, deliverance is possible!

Please note it is wrong to be homophobic, that is to physically or verbally torment a homosexual. Jesus never did, even though it is likely He encountered homosexuals. He loved them as He did all sinners and helped those who wanted to be set free.

> 9 Feasts of Israel. There were originally 7 Feasts under the Mosaic covenant: the Feasts of: Passover, Unleavened Bread, Firstfruits, Weeks, Trumpets, Day of Atonement and Tabernacles.
> However, Jewish rabbis added 2 other non-Mosaic Feasts:
>
> *Purim* (Lots) celebrating Esther and the Jews' victory over Haman. Coincidentally, the last day of the first Gulf War in 1991 was on the Feast of *Purim*. Just as God had delivered Esther's people from Haman, so too God delivered the Jews from Saddam Hussein. He is still delivering those who dare to believe Him.
>
> *Hanukkah* (Feast of Dedication or Feast of Lights) celebrating the cleansing of the Temple from the "abomination of desolation" or the Greeks' pig-sacrifice in the Temple of God. Though not sanctioned by Moses, Jesus clearly recognized the Feast of Dedication and made a point of attending it in John 10:22–23. This feast happens in Israel's winter or around the month of December, often coinciding with our celebration of Christmas.

The 7 Mosaic Feasts speak of Jesus and His work in the plan of salvation. The addition of 2 other feasts takes the number of feasts from 7 to 9, which symbolizes the additional blessing of the Holy Spirit to the gift of salvation. The Temple menorah has 7 branches, representing the light of Jesus Christ in the world. The Hanukkah menorah has 9 branches, representing the supernatural provision of the Holy Spirit.

Being linked to the Holy Spirit, 9 is also the number of miracles. By the anointing of the Holy Spirit, Jesus performed 9 recorded miracles or interruptions in the normal course of nature:*

1. Turning water into wine, called the "beginning of miracles" in John 2:11 (KJV). This verse alone dispels all cults' claims that Jesus performed childhood miracles such as turning clay into birds or men into monkeys. Turning water into wine at a wedding was His *first* miracle.

All of His miracles shared the same tone and tenor: to bless mankind and to show us how to live above the dominion of Satan by trusting in Him. None of Jesus' miracles were gratuitous, showy, or done merely to prove His deity. He performed all of them as a Son of Man anointed by the Spirit of God. (See Luke 4:18; Acts 2:22, 10:38.)

2. Multiplication of 5 loaves and 2 fishes to feed 5,000 men, with leftovers filling 12 laundry-size baskets (Matt. 14:15–21).

3. Multiplication of 7 loaves and a few fishes to feed 4,000 men, with leftovers filling 8 laundry-size baskets (Matt. 15:32–38).

4. Causing a net-breaking, boat-sinking catch of fish when in the natural the professional fishermen could catch nothing all night (Luke 5:1–11).

5. Causing a second miraculous catch of 153 fish when in the natural the fishermen could catch nothing all night (John 21:1–11).

Notice 5 miracles are about providing food for people. Just as Jesus taught in Matthew 6, believers are not to worry about what we shall eat, what we shall drink or what we shall wear, because God clothes the lilies of the field and feeds the sparrows, and "you are of more value than many sparrows" (Matt. 6:26; 10:31). Jesus is revealing Himself as our gracious Provider. God provides by grace; we receive by faith with thanksgiving.

6. Walking on water (Matt. 14:22–32). This was an exceptional miracle— one done apparently for convenience to catch up with the disciples who had

---

* Besides innumerable healings, signs, and wonders not described specifically, such as those in John 2:23, 7:31, 11:47.

gone ahead of Him while He was praying alone. Lest anyone should accuse Jesus of acting showy to prove His deity, the Holy Spirit noted 2 details for us: (1) He "would have passed them by" (Mark 6:48), meaning He intended to go unnoticed; and (2) when the disciples saw Him walking on water, He invited any of them to come out and join Him. Only Peter had enough courage to follow Him. Walking on water does *not* prove someone is God. What makes Him God is His pre-existence before Creation. (See John 1:1–3, 8:51–58; Colossians 1:16–17.) Only God pre-existed everyone.

7. Resurrection of Jairus' daughter (Mark 5:21–43).

8. Resurrection of a widow's only son (Luke 7:11–17).

9. Resurrection of Lazarus (John 11:38–44).

Some may wonder why I do not count among the miracles Jesus' stilling the winds and the waves in Mark 4 or Jesus' cursing the fig tree in Mark 11. On both occasions Jesus indicated these were ordinary uses of faith and any believer could have done them.

Jesus could barely hide His disappointment that the disciples didn't do them instead of Him. In Mark 4:40 Jesus asked them, "Why are you so fearful? How is it that you have no faith?" If only Jesus could calm the storms, then the disciples had every right to be afraid. I have known several men of God who have stilled storms, tornadoes, and hurricanes coming their way. I know of one Church in Louisiana where not a single pane of glass was broken during Hurricane Katrina on August 29, 2005.

The pastor of the Church spoke to the storm just like Jesus did. He believed for protection over his property. Why, some may want to know, didn't he ask for all other properties to be protected? It wasn't his right to.

In the natural we have authority over our own property but not over other people's. It is the same in the spiritual. Unless someone gives us their key and asks us to guard their house, we cannot walk in and stay in their place. That's called "breaking and entering"! It's criminal. Likewise, unless someone asks us to pray protection over their property, we have no right to meddle spiritually. It's their right to believe God or other humans or themselves. We have a right to pray for people who are under our care and related to us. But we cannot pray for strangers against their will and volition. God respects everyone's personal right to ask for His assistance or reject His interference.

In Mark 11 Jesus cursed a fig tree and the next day the disciples "saw the fig tree dried up from the roots" (v. 20). Rather than saying, "Only I can do this miracle," Jesus used the occasion to teach them about ordinary faith in God.

> So Jesus answered and said to them, "Have faith in God. For assuredly, I say to you, whoever *says* to this mountain, 'Be removed and be cast into the sea,' and does not doubt in his heart, but believes that those things he *says* will be done, he will have whatever he *says*. Therefore I say to you, whatever things you ask when you pray, believe that you receive them, and you will have them.
> —Mark 11:22–24, emphasis added

Too many Christians have underestimated the power of their words. Yet we daily experience how words shape destinies and change futures. Have you ever had a teacher, a coach, or a role model lift you up with words of affirmation? You can soar on those words for days! Have you ever experienced a Christian praying over you in such a powerful way that all burdens simply seem to evaporate away? That's the power of faith-filled words!

It doesn't work just for adults; it works for children, too. Harsh words can scar a child's life. (Thank God Jesus can wash those past wounds away if we ask Him.) Scriptural words can encourage a child to see himself or herself as a champion. Positive words lift children up to believe that anything is possible. This is what Jesus wants every Christian to believe every day, "I say to you, if you have faith as a mustard seed, you will *say* to this mountain, 'Move from here to there,' and it will move; and nothing will be impossible for you" (Matt. 17:20, emphasis added).

9

AV

9 IS THE MAXIMUM NUMBER (single digit). It is associated with spiritual activity and supernatural power. The Jewish 9th hour (our 3pm) was the time Jesus died on the cross. The 9th hour is a Biblical time of prayer. In Acts 3, Peter and John went to the Temple to pray at the 9th hour. At that time a man crippled from birth got healed. In Acts 10, God sent an angel to meet Cornelius at the 9th hour. He and his family were the first Gentiles to become Christian! Jews annually celebrate 3 feasts - Rosh Hashanah (New Year), Yom Kippur (Day of Atonement) and Sukkot (Feast of Tabernacles) - around September or our 9th month.

The ninth of *Av* (fifth month of the Hebrew religious calendar) is considered the saddest day in Jewish history." It is one of 4 fasts which the Jews observe by tradition, not by commandment of the Torah. The fasts are:

1. *Shiva Asar Be Tamuz* or 17th of Tamuz (4th month): the day the city walls protecting Jerusalem were breached by Nebuchadnezzar in 587 B.C. The Talmud states that Roman General Titus also breached the walls of Jerusalem on the same day in A.D. 70. The Talmud claims that this was the day Moses descended Mount Sinai and found Israel worshiping a golden calf, upon which he broke the two tablets of stones containing the Ten Commandments.

2. *Tisha Be Av* or the 9th of Ave (5th month): the day the First Temple was destroyed by Nebuchadnezzar. The Second Temple was also destroyed on exactly the same day 656 years later by General Titus.

3. *Tzom Gedalia* or the Fast of Gedaliah on the 3rd of Tishri (7th month): the day Ishmael assassinated Gedaliah the Jewish governor appointed by Nebuchadnezzar, a final blow which ensured the scattering of the Jews under Babylonian rule. Jeremiah 40–41 recorded this tragedy and the Jews remember

it not only as a historic, but a prophetic event that may likely happen again in the end times.

Why would God allow a believer to be assassinated? This is a great lesson in leadership and in hearing the voice of God. Just as God warned Noah before the Flood and Lot before the destruction of Sodom, God sent Johanan (John) and other leaders to warn Gedaliah of Ishmael. Gedaliah failed to see the evil intentions of Ishmael and did not believe God's warning. Ignoring God's voice cost him his life, the lives of those with him, and the lives of 70 Jews who came up to worship God in Jerusalem (see Jeremiah 40:13–41:10).

In the end times, tragedies will occur, but God will always send forewarning. Amos 3:7 promises, "Surely the Lord God does nothing, unless He reveals His secret to His servants the prophets." The lesson from Gedaliah is we all need to get as *close to God* as possible and learn to listen to His voice—whether by the Word, by the Spirit, or through His leaders. We need to *hear God* in the end times and we will be safe.

4. *Asara Be Tevet* or 10ᵗʰ of Tevet (10ᵗʰ month): the beginning of Nebuchadnezzar's siege of Jerusalem. Today, this fast is also the occasion to remember the Jewish victims of the Holocaust whose day of death is unknown.

Though not instituted by Moses, God recognizes these 4 fast days in Zechariah, which indicates that they may be prophetic.

> Thus says the LORD of hosts: The *fast* of the fourth month, The *fast* of the fifth, The *fast* of the seventh, And the *fast* of the tenth, Shall be joy and gladness and cheerful feasts For the house of Judah. Therefore love truth and peace.
> —ZECHARIAH 8:19, EMPHASIS ADDED

The 9ᵗʰ of Av is the most significant fast as both Temples were destroyed on the same day. Traditionally it is also the day the 10 spies returned from Canaan with an evil report of unbelief. They doubted Israel could inherit the land God promised, whereas Joshua and Caleb brought the minority report of faith. They believed and 38 years later entered the Promised Land. The ten leaders who doubted, along with 3 million Israelites who believed them instead of Joshua, all died in the wilderness. *Joshua* in Hebrew is the same name as *Jesus* in Greek. How prophetic it was that millions of Jews perished unnecessarily for not believing in Jesus.

This story is also a lesson for the modern Church to learn from—the majority will doubt; only the minority will believe. It is the believer who receives. It is the believer who enters the Promised Land. It is the believer who obtains the provision, the healing, the baptism of the Holy Spirit, and the full blessing of God. When you choose to have faith when others try to cast doubt, you are following Joshua instead of the 10 spies.

The 9th of Av has proven to be prophetic. Jews (and Protestants) suffered the Spanish Inquisition and were expelled from Spain on the 9th of Av 1492. World War I started when Germany declared war on Russia on the 9th of Av 1914. Adolf Hitler began the extermination of Jews on the 9th of Av 1942. President Richard Nixon resigned from office after the Watergate scandal on the 9th of Av 1974.

According to Zechariah 8:19, God will turn the 4 fast days of Israel into occasions of joy and gladness. Therefore, we need not expect only bad things to happen on these dates. If we have faith in the Messiah, then every day can be a Sabbath rest, a celebration, and a good day.

10

10 IS THE NUMBER OF THESE RELATED THINGS: law, sin, test, judgment, and conscience (the moral seat of responsibility). Moses gave Israel the 10 Commandments; we have 10 fingers to remind ourselves of God's Commandments; if God had found only 10 righteous in Sodom and Gomorrah, He would have spared the wicked cities; both Rashi and Ramam say that Abraham was tested 10 times and found faithful and patient in spirit; Daniel asked the eunuch to test him and the other Hebrew servants on a kosher diet for 10 days (Dan. 1:12)*; God expects us to tithe a 10th to the Levites—that is, a 10th of our income should go to support ministry efforts.

10 times Pharaoh suffered 10 plagues for his idolatry and disobedience. 10 times Israel tempted God, mainly by murmuring and complaining. (See Numbers 14:22.) 10 times fire fell from Heaven upon:

1. Sodom and Gomorrah (Genesis 19:24)
2. The first offering (Leviticus 9:24)
3. The disobedient priests Nadab and Abihu (Leviticus 10:2)
4. The complainers at Taberah (Numbers 11:1)
5. The rebels Korah and his company (Numbers 16:35)
6. Elijah's offering at Mount Carmel (1 Kings 18:38)
7. Jezebel's first set of soldiers coming to arrest Elijah (2 Kings 1:10)
8. Jezebel's second set of soldiers (2 Kings 1:12)
9. David's offering (1 Chronicles 21:26)
10. Solomon's offering (2 Chronicles 7:1)

Leprosy was the most dreaded diseases of the ancient world as it was infectious and incurable. Lepers were ostracized from society and leprosy was as good as a death sentence. Consequently the Bible uses leprosy as a type of

---

* This was an act of faith with a supernatural outcome, because a period of 10 days is not long enough to see the results of a diet.

sin and lepers a type of sinners. Sin is also infectious, incurable, bars us from Heaven, and is a death sentence. Since sin is associated with the number 10, it is no surprise that God put 10 instances of leprosy in the Bible:

1. Moses twice—first time privately (Exodus 4:6–7)
2. Moses—second time publicly (Exodus 4:29–31)
3. Miriam (Numbers 12)
4. Naaman (2 Kings 5)
5. Gehazi (2 Kings 5)
6. The 4 lepers in the days of Elisha (2 Kings 7)
7. King Azariah (2 Kings 15)
8. A leper who asked if Jesus was willing to heal him (Matthew 8). Jesus said He was. He still is willing to heal you, since He never changes.
9. Simon the leper in Bethany (Matthew 26)
10. Another 10 lepers Jesus healed (Luke 17)

Sin is curable if we repent of our rebellion and accept God's way out of sin. There was only one sinless person in the world—Jesus Christ—and He willingly died for the sins of the world. His sacrifice becomes effective in our lives when we put our faith in Him for our salvation.

The worst result of judgment on sin is death. Because God's heart is not death but life, not judgment but mercy, there are 10 individual cases of temporary resurrection. (We say temporary to contrast with Christ's permanent resurrection—He is the first one, but more are to come.) The 10 cases of resurrection:

1. Widow's son in Zarephath, raised by Elijah (1 Kings 17:17–24)
2. Shunammites's son, raised by Elisha (2 Kings 4:18–37)
3. Moabite man, raised by Elisha's bones (2 Kings 13:20–21)
4. Jonah, raised by God (Jonah 2:1–10, Matthew 12:40)
5. Jairus' daughter, raised by Jesus (Matthew 10:18–26)
6. Widow's only son in Nain, raised by Jesus (Luke 7:11–16)
7. Lazarus, raised by Jesus (John 11)
8. Dorcas, raised by Peter (Acts 9)

9. Paul, raised by disciples (Acts 14)

10. Eutychus, raised by Paul (Acts 20)

10 times Israel gave rebellious answers to God in the last book of the Old Testament, Malachi:

1. "Yet you [the believer] say, 'In what way have You [God] loved us?'" (1:2).

2. "Yet you say, 'In what way have we despised Your name?'" (1:6).

3. "You offer defiled food on My altar, but say, 'In what way have we defiled You?'" (1:7).

4. "You say, 'The table of the LORD is defiled, and its fruit, its food, is contemptible.' You also say, 'Oh, what a weariness!' And you sneer at it [that is, sneered at serving and offering to God] (1:12–13).

5. "He does not regard the offering anymore, nor receive it with goodwill from your hands. Yet you say, 'For what reason?' Because the LORD has been witness between you and the wife of your youth, with whom you have dealt treacherously" (2:13–14).

6. "You have wearied the LORD with your words; Yet you say, 'In what way have we wearied Him?' In that you say, 'Everyone who does evil is good in the sight of the LORD, and He delights in them,' or, 'Where is the God of justice?'" (2:17).

7. "'From the days of your father you have gone away from My ordinances and have not kept them. Return to Me, and I will return to you, says the LORD of hosts.' But you said, 'In what way shall we return?'" (3:7).

8. "Will a man rob God? Yet you have robbed Me! But you say, 'In what way have we robbed You?' In tithes and offerings. You are cursed with a curse, for you have robbed Me" (3:8–9).

9. "'Your words have been harsh against Me,' says the LORD, Yet you say, 'What have we spoken against You?'" (3:13).

10. "You have said, 'It is useless to serve God'" (3:14).

Some Christians have misunderstood the Book of Malachi and removed tithes from these 10 rebellious acts which God will judge in the *future*. They claim since tithing is taught by Moses and Malachi, it is a relic of the Old Testament and unnecessary for Christians to obey.

A rule of Bible interpretation is to read verses in context: that is, we don't lift a single verse out of the Bible and understand it in isolation; we must read the verses before and after it, and compare our understanding with the rest of the Bible, too. Now the context of Malachi 3 shows that refusing to tithe and justifying it is 1 of 10 rebellious excuses God *will* judge on the Day of Judgment. The context is not about the past, but about the future.

Malachi 3:2–3, 6 sets up this future scene we will all see one day: "But who can endure the day of His coming? And who can stand when He appears? For He is like a refiner's fire And like launderers' soap. He will sit as a refiner and a purifier.... And I will come near you for judgment... Says the LORD of hosts." Now just in case anyone doubts that God will not change His mind on the tithe and He will judge these 10 rebellious statements in the future, God confirmed it with this assertion, "For I am the LORD, I change not."

Think about it: if doubt (1:2), blasphemy (1:6), and slothfulness (3:14) will be judged on the Day of Judgment, why should robbing God (by stealing tithes) be excluded on the Day of Judgment? Refusing to tithe is breaking the 8th Commandment, "Thou shalt not steal."

Unfortunately many pastors have not studied the subject of tithing enough to be bold in proclaiming its blessing to their people. My family and I have proven to ourselves and our Church that tithing works. Not only do we teach the Church to tithe, but we as pastors tithe all our income, and our Church tithes on all the offerings that enter the ministry. Our finances are always protected, our property is protected, and our lives are blessed. Tithing works because it's Biblical.

God showed me through His Word that tithing is not merely an Old Testament command to Israel, but an eternal principle. Did you ever ask yourself why Joshua was not allowed to take any of the spoils, the silver, gold and raiment, from Jericho, the first city they conquered? If you count the number of battles in Israel's first military campaign, you will find they fought 10 battles for 10 territories:

1. Jericho (Joshua 6)
2. Ai (Joshua 8)
3. Makkedah (10:28)
4. Libnah (9:29–30)
5. Lachish (9:31–32)

6. Gezer (10:33)

7. Eglon (10:34–35)

8. Hebron (10:36–37)

9. Debir (10:40–41)

10. "From Kadesh Barnea as far as Gaza" (10:40–43).

Jericho was one of 10 cities, in other words the tithe; therefore, Jericho belonged to the Lord. Israel was not supposed to touch its wealth because the tithe belongs to the Lord. One man named Achan refused to honor the Lord the tithe, and consequently the entire nation of Israel lost the next battle at Ai. It was the only battle Israel lost in the Book of Joshua. When Joshua found Achan withholding some of the clothes, silver, and gold from Jericho, he ordered Achan and his family to be punished. Achan's theft of the tithe had brought a curse on his entire family and nation.

The word *tithe* was never mentioned in the dedication of Jericho or the defeat at Ai. No specific law of Moses was invoked, yet the seriousness of withholding a tenth was understood by all. Jericho is evidence that Joshua's obedience to honor the Lord with a tenth was based on an eternal principle of God. We need to put God first, not only with our lips but with something so dear to our hearts—our material wealth. When we do, God can have all our hearts and He will lead us from victory to victory.

10

DAYS

10 IS A PERIOD OF TESTING. Human pregnancy lasts on average for 10 sidereal months (a sidereal month is 27.3 days long; an average female is pregnant for 273 days). Daniel the prophet asked the royal eunuch to test him for 10 days on a kosher (Biblical) diet. Jesus told His first disciples to wait 10 days in the Upper Room for the baptism of the Holy Spirit.

Since the Holy Spirit has come, we no longer have to wait for the Holy Spirit. We can believe and instantly receive. But we do patiently wait for other things, such as seeing justice served in an unjust world or seeing skeptics turn to Christ. Such things are difficult to wait for, but God promised, "Rest in the LORD, and *wait* patiently for Him; Do not fret because of him who prospers in his way, Because of the man who brings wicked schemes to pass...For evildoers shall be cut off; But those who *wait* on the LORD, They shall inherit the earth." (Ps. 37:7, 9, emphasis added).

The Seleucid king Antiochus Epiphanes IV erected a statue of Zeus in the Temple of God and 10 days later sacrificed a pig on the altar of God. This infamous event in Jewish history occurred on the 25th of December[1] 167 A.D. and was predicted by the prophet Daniel 400 years in advance. It is called the "transgression of desolation" in Daniel 8:13 and the "abomination [that] makes desolate" in Daniel 9:27. The "abomination of desolation" (11:31; 12:11) will be mimicked (or re-enacted) by the Anti-Christ according to Jesus (Matt. 24:15), Paul (2 Thess. 2:4), and John (Rev. 13:15).

Jesus told the Church of Smyrna she would be tested for 10 days. This could literally mean she would be tested for a very short period of time, 10 literal days. Or it could mean she would be tested by a period of 10 years of persecution under Emperor Diocletian. Or it could figuratively mean she was going to be tested during 10 periods of persecution by 10 Roman emperors. All of the above could be true as Biblical prophecy is often fulfilled multiple times. The last view was held by Eusebius the Bishop of Caesarea (A.D. 260–340), who identified 10 wicked emperors who persecuted Christians; he was an eyewitness of the persecution by the 10th emperor.

1. Nero (A.D. 54–68)—killed his own mother, burned Christians alive to light his garden (origin of the disc burning software called *Nero*), accused Christians of burning Rome in A.D. 64, beheaded Paul and crucified Peter upside down, and finally committed suicide in A.D. 68.

2. Domitian (81–96), brother of Titus who sacked Jerusalem in A.D. 70—exiled John on the Greek island of Patmos where he saw the vision of Revelation.

3. Trajan (98–117)—persecuted Christians including Ignatius the Bishop of Antioch.

4. Marcus Aurelius (161–180)—killed Polycarp the Bishop of Smyrna and the Christian martyrs of Lyon and Vienne, France.

5. Septimus Severus (193–211)—killed Origen's father, Leonides (Origen wanted to follow his father into martyrdom, but was prevented by his mother); Septimus extended persecution of Christians to north Africa.

6. Maximus (235–238)

7. Decius (249–251)—imprisoned and tortured Origen.

8. Valerian (253–260)

9. Aurelian (170–275)

10. Diocletian (*Gaius Aurelius Valeris Dicletianus* 284–305) and his co-regent, Maximian (285–305)—the Diocletian Persecution from 303–311 (10 years) was the largest and bloodiest official persecution of Christianity. He burned Christian books and Churches; outlawed Christian gatherings; denied Christians the right to fair trial; imprisoned, tortured, and killed multitudes of Christians.

However, Diocletian failed to destroy the Christian Church. Just as Jesus had promised the Church of Smyrna, early Christians would go through only 10 periods of testing. In 311 Diocletian committed suicide.

By 313, his successor, Constantine the Great (306–337), issued the Edit of Toleration (Milan), ending the persecution of Christianity and proclaiming religious tolerance throughout the empire. At this time half of the population of the Roman Empire professed Christ.[2] Constantine became the first Christian Roman Emperor, exempted Christian ministers from taxes and military service, and favored Christians in positions of leadership. He appointed Eusebius as his chief religious advisor. Slavery, gladiator fights, infanticides, and crucifixions were abolished.

Disturbed by the aristocratic and pagan influences in Rome, Constantine relocated his capital to the Greek city of Byzantium and renamed it Constantinople in A.D. 330. This would become the "New Rome" and capital of his new Christian empire.

Contrary to many teachings, Constantine did not make Christianity the official religion of the Roman Empire. It was his second successor, Theodosius II (379–395), who declared "Catholic Christianity" the official state religion on February 27, 380, thus marrying religious and political power. This was a tragic mistake because the Bible would be neglected, the Gospel would be forgotten, and so-called Christian leaders would be preoccupied with political struggles instead of the saving of souls. Western Christianity fell into idolatry, syncreticism, and religious dead works; out of which many Christians today still have not escaped. Penance replaced true repentance. Merits earning replaced God's grace. Medieval Christianity became a false religion of self-salvation like every other religion in the world.

With a strong arm, Theodosius II tried to stamp out paganism, destroying pagan temples and prohibiting pagan festivals. His persecution of pagans is reminiscent of his predecessors' persecution of Christians; his severe actions did not uphold freedom of religion nor exemplify Christ's love for sinners. Christianity cannot be legislated; it has to be chosen. Until the true Gospel is preached, the choice has never been presented to sinners who may or may not want to repent and receive Christ. To avoid persecution, masses of pagans called themselves Roman Christians. With good intentions, Theodosius II did much harm to the mission of Christ.

By exalting Catholic Christianity, Theodosius II prepared the way for 3 great schisms between East and West.

Politically, the Roman Empire was divided in A.D. 395 into Eastern and Western legs, just as Daniel's vision of the 2 iron legs had predicted.

Religiously, Christianity divided in 1054 into the Eastern Orthodox Church and the Roman Catholic Church, a landmark known as the Great Schism.

Spiritually, the last great schism occurred during the Protestant Reformation, which saw numerous Churches breaking away from papal authority to return to Biblical authority. In 1517 Martin Luther posted his 95 *Theses* on the door of Castle Church in Wittenberg, Germany, causing the break away Lutheran Church. In 1845 Henry VII rejected the Pope's authority to not grant him a divorce, causing the break away Anglican Church (Church of England and Episcopal Church in the USA).

Emperor Constantine built an Eastern "Byzantine Empire" that would outlast the Western "Holy Roman Empire" by 1,000 years. He also left a lasting legacy for Christianity—the Nicene Creed. Refuting the heresies that had crept up in the past 3 centuries, Constantine convened the first ecumenical council in the city of Nicea (modern Turkey) in A.D. 325 to write a Christian "statement of faith." The Council of Nicea reaffirmed what the Bible, the apostles, and the early Church fathers taught: the Trinity and the deity of Christ. This may well represent the last universal decision of the Church agreed upon by the Eastern Orthodox Church, the Roman Catholic Church, and even the Protestant Churches such as the Lutheran, Anglican, Presbyterian, and Methodist.

By the Edict of Toleration, Constantine fulfilled Jesus' words that the early Church would go through no more than 10 days of testing.

10 represents tests and trials. The persecution of early Christians by 10 evil emperors reminds us of Jesus' words in Mark 13:13, "And you will be hated by all for My name's sake. But he who *endures to the end* shall be saved" (emphasis added). It is a great day of victory when we can say, "No matter what comes, I will never abandon my faith in Jesus Christ!" and to say with all Christians the following declaration:

THE NICENE CREED

I believe in one God, the Father Almighty, Maker of Heaven and earth, and of all things visible and invisible;

And in one Lord Jesus Christ, the only-begotten Son of God, begotten of the Father before all worlds; God of God, Light of Light, very God of very God; begotten, not made, being of one substance with the Father, by whom all things were made;

Who, for us men and for our salvation, came down from Heaven, and was incarnate by the Holy Spirit of the virgin Mary, and was made man; and was crucified also for us under Pontius Pilate; He suffered and was buried; and the third day He rose again, according to the Scriptures; and ascended into Heaven, and sits on the right hand of the Father; and He shall come again, with glory, to judge the quick and the dead; whose kingdom shall have no end;

And I believe in the Holy Ghost, the Lord and Giver of Life; who proceeds from the Father and the Son; who with the Father and the Son together is worshiped and glorified; who spoke by the prophets.

And I believe one holy catholic and apostolic Church. I acknowledge one baptism for the remission of sins. And I look for the resurrection of the dead and the life of the world to come. Amen.[3]

10

COMMANDMENTS

GOD GAVE THE 10 COMMANDMENTS TO MOSES from the very early part of the Bible. Yet very few people can name the 10 Commandments and fewer still know *why* they were given.

Most people make the assumption that the 10 Commandments were given to us so that by them we might enter Heaven. Some even boast that they live by the 10 Commandments, although I have yet to meet one claimant who can so much as *name* all 10 Commandments.

Can you name the 10 Commandments? We have touched on the first 6 commandments in this book. Please take a look at the full list below and see how many of them you can keep every day of your life.

1. Love the Lord your God with all your heart, with all your soul, with your entire mind and with all your strength; or simply, always put God first!
2. Do not make or bow down to idols.
3. Do not blaspheme God's name.
4. Keep the Sabbath holy or dedicate one entire day a week to worship God.
5. Honor your father and your mother.
6. Do not murder.
7. Do not commit adultery.
8. Do not steal.
9. Do not lie.
10. Do not covet.[1]

Now we are not meant to use God's laws to judge others. I'm not your judge. You're not my judge. But we *are* to judge ourselves.

So how did you go judging yourself? Can you keep the 10 Commandments perfectly? These laws have been written into our hearts (see Romans 2:15) and our conscience will convict us whenever we break them. Everyone in the world, even people who have never read the Bible, knows that these laws are good and breaking them is bad.

The big trap of religion is to misuse rules and laws. The Pharisees read the same Bible and studied the same laws as we do, yet somehow they did not see themselves as sinners who needed a Savior. One weakness religious people tend to have is applying good laws on others but not on themselves. This habit comes from Adam and Eve eating the fruit of the "tree of the knowledge of good and evil" (Gen. 2:17). If we were to update the story in modern language, then we would say that the first humans became sinners when they ate the fruit of the "tree of religion." They immediately found fault with each other and the serpent, but no fault with themselves. This is what religion does to people. Those who think they can keep the 10 Commandments have probably never read Jesus' words: "Did not Moses give you the law, yet *none of you* keeps the law?" (John 7:19, emphasis added).

THE LOGIC OF LAW

The purpose of God's laws is to convict our own conscience of sin and bring us to our knees before the Savior. Paul understood this when he wrote, "Therefore by the deeds of the law no flesh will be justified in His sight, for *by the law* is the *knowledge* of *sin*" (Rom. 3:20, emphasis added).

In other words, the law is not the solution; the law is a diagnosis of the problem. Paul wrote further, "I would not have known sin except through the law. For I would not have known covetousness unless the law had said, "You shall not covet" (Rom. 7:7).

Once we realize the true function of the law and come to terms with our own immoralities, what should we do? Contrary to common assumption, God does *not* want us to try harder to be a sinless person.

A sinner trying to clean himself of his sin is like an insomniac trying to fall asleep. The more you think of falling asleep, the more awake you'll be. The more you try to cleanse yourself of sin without Christ's cleansing power, the more sin-conscious and sinful you will end up becoming. Just as we fall asleep by *surrendering*, so too we are saved by *surrendering* to Christ. God wants us to humble ourselves and depend on His Son's help.

Paul put it this way, "Wherefore the law was our schoolmaster to *bring us unto Christ*, that we might be justified *by faith*" (Gal. 3:24, KJV, emphasis added).

The reason Christ alone can save us is because Christ alone is without sin. By trusting in Jesus Christ, we are hanging our entire future on the only perfect person who ever lived. He came without sin, lived without sin, died for our sins, and resurrected to new life.

Our trying harder or resolving to become more religious does not lead to salvation. It only leads to self-centeredness and self-righteousness, all of which is really pride. To become honest about who we really are (expressing humility) and who Jesus really is (expressing faith), that's the open door to salvation. Job 22:29 says, "He will save the humble person."

10 is the number of law and sin. Is it any surprise the Bible records 10 people who said, "I have sinned"?

1. Job (7:20)
2. Pharaoh (Exodus 9:27, 10:16)
3. Balaam (Numbers 22:34)
4. Achan (Joshua 7:20)
5. Saul (1 Samuel 15:24, 30, 26:21)
6. David (2 Samuel 12:13, 24:10, 17; 1 Chronicles 21:8, 17; Psalm 41:4, 51:4)
7. Shimei (2 Samuel 19:20)
8. Hezekiah (2 Kings 18:14, rendered *I have done wrong* in KJV and NKJV. Young's Literal Translation correctly renders Hezekiah's words as "I have sinned.")
9. Nehemiah (1:6)
10. Micah (7:9)

Judges 10:10 records Israel half-heartedly admitting their guilt: "And the children of Israel cried out to the LORD, saying, "We have *sinned* against You, because we have both forsaken our God and *served* the Baals!" (emphasis added). True repentance would not go back to sinning and forgetting God.

God does not expect us to save ourselves from sin. He wants us to ask Him to change our hearts and impart a new nature in us so that we can live and be clean like Him.

11

11 IS THE NUMBER OF THE SUN. Every 11 years, solar activity* reaches a peak and the solar poles actually reverse. While it may seem strange to us, the sun's magnetic poles switch places—i.e. north becomes south and south becomes north—every 11 years.

The solar magnetic activity cycle (Schwabe cycle) is linked to changes in space weather, Earth's weather, and possibly Earth's current climate change. While pollution is certainly a terrible thing to dump into our environment, it may not be the most influential factor in our climate change. Two other factors that are even more important:

1. Solar activity. It is clear that the cyclical nature of solar activity influences our planet more than human activities. It's impossible to speak about climate and ignore the sun. The sun rules Earth's temperature. When it goes down, the earth is cooler. When it comes up, the earth is warmer. When there's an eclipse, there's an immediate drop in temperature. Solar activity overrides all other factors as the chief instigator of Earth's cyclical climate.

2. Man's sin. Sin is the worst environmental pollution to our planet, for without sin, moral decay, and spiritual pollution, there would be no toxic waste, chemical sludge, or industrial pollution. There would be no Chernobyl, Exxon Valdez oil spill, or BP Gulf oil spill.

An anti-scriptural idea that has been promoted through the secular media is that our planet is fragile. Since God made the earth to last forever, we must believe that the earth cannot be fragile. Did you know that one volcanic eruption (recall the 2010 eruption in Iceland) dumps more toxic chemicals into the earth's atmosphere than all the car exhausts in the world combined? The earth absorbs the volcanic plume and recycles it away naturally. It is not

---

* Refers to sunspots, irradiance, and short-wave radiation.

the earth that is fragile, but humans living under sinful conditions who are fragile.

The earth can also tolerate changes in temperature—it has been through an ice age before and it has experienced global warming before. That Greenland is called "green" is testament to the fact that global temperatures were once higher than they are now. Should we be worried about global warming? What would be the effect of the earth's temperature rising by a few degrees? While we have all heard of doom and gloom predictions, one report projects that if the earth warmed up a bit, northern European countries would benefit from an agricultural boom.[1]

When God made the sun, the sun was intended to play a central role to our planet. It is not us who control the seasons or cycles. The sun has more sway on Earth's weather than all of man's activities. While some are convinced that man's CO_2 emission is causing global warming, other scientists such as Piers Corbyn are calling it "green religion" with no scientific evidence. His organization, Weatheraction, predicted more accurately than anybody else a harsh winter of 2010–2011 in the UK and Europe, which has been proven correct.

Astrophysicist Piers Corbyn attributes his predictions to studying the sun's full 22-year cycle, not man's CO_2 emission. He believes that oil companies and governments love the CO_2 theory because it justifies their raising energy prices, taxing our "carbon footprint," and trading "green." Part of a one world government is a global tax, but the world will not accept the addition of a global tax, unless it was called a "green tax."

Other scientists are asking what is causing the apparent global warming of other planets. They observe at least 4 other planetary bodies—Mars, Jupiter, Triton (Neptune's largest moon), and Pluto—are experiencing global warming. Granted, solar activity may not be the only explanation for why these planetary bodies are warming, but one can safely say they are not warming because there are too many cars on Mars or too many capitalists opening new factories on Triton. We take ourselves too seriously if we think we are the saviors of the planet. The planet doesn't need saving as much as *we* do!

Salvation through Christ is the greatest clean-up action for this planet. Once Jesus cleanses our inward nature from sin and fills us with the presence of the Holy Spirit, we will automatically become better citizens of this planet and better stewards of God's resources. Solomon wrote in Proverbs 12:10, "A righteous man regards the life of his animal, But the tender mercies of the wicked are cruel." Nothing could be better for the welfare of plants, animals, and the ecosystem than for sinners to stop sinning, turn their lives over to Jesus, and live clean Christian lives on a planet we share.

11 is the number God assigned to solar activity. The next peak in the solar cycle and due date for a solar pole reversal is 2012. (For more related to the number 11 or solar activity, read chapters "2011," "2012," "2013–2014," and "2020 and Beyond.")

12

12 IS THE NUMBER OF GOVERNMENT. There are 12 tribes of Israel; 12 apostles of the Lamb; 12 months in a year; 12 hours in a day; 12 hours in a night; 12 constellations of stars; 12 musical notes in an octave; 12 foundations of heavenly Jerusalem, with 12 gates made of 12 pearls and 12 angels guarding those gates. Jesus said He could pray to the Father and He would send Him 12 legions of angels. The measurements of New Jerusalem are 12,000 stadia.

There are 12 minor prophets in the Old Testament: Hosea, Amos, Micah, Joel, Obadiah, Jonah, Nahum, Habakkuk, Zephaniah, Haggai, Zachariah, and Malachi.

Anyone who wants to understand the chronology of the Old Testament needs to read only 12 books in this order: Genesis, Exodus, Numbers, Joshua, Judges, 1 Samuel, 2 Samuel, 1 Kings, 2 Kings, Daniel, Ezra, and Nehemiah.

The rest of the Bible books are important and tell the stories within the main plot. For instance, Ruth lived during the time of the Judges and is a Gentile woman who would become an ancestor of Jesus. Most Psalms were written during the period of 2 Samuel. Nearly all major and minor prophets lived during the time of 2 Kings, with the notable exception of Haggai, Zechariah, and Malachi who lived during the time of Ezra.

There were 12 prophetesses in the Bible: 7 named (Miriam, Deborah, Huldah, Noadiah, Elizabeth, Mary, and Anna) and 5 unnamed (Isaiah's wife in 8:3 and Philip's 4 daughters in Acts 21:9).

There are 12 lay ministry gifts in the body of Christ.

There are 12 persons anointed with oil in the Bible: Aaron, Nadab, Abihu, Eleazar, Ithamar, Saul, David (anointed 3 times!), Absalom, Solomon, Jehu, Joash, and Johoahaz. The first 5 were anointed priests, the next 7 kings. 12 = 7 (perfect) + 5 (grace).

What about Christ—was He not anointed? Of course, the title "Christ" means the "Anointed One." But Jesus was not anointed by men with oil, but by God the Father with the Holy Spirit. And unlike other men in the Bible, Jesus was not anointed to stand in only one or two offices. He was and is the only Person to ever be anointed into all offices including King, Priest, Apostle, Prophet, Evangelist, Pastor, and Teacher. Jesus' first sermon was about His anointing or empowerment by the Holy Spirit (Luke 4). After His anointing, Jesus empowered 12 disciples to govern His Church and carry on His mission to preach the Gospel to the world.

If 12 means government in the Bible, we should also find 12 governing nature. That's exactly what we find! 12 fermions or fundamental matter particles make up matter in our universe: 6 quarks (up, down, charm, strange, top, bottom) and 6 leptons (electron neutrino, electron, muon nutrino, muon, tau neutrino, tau). Previously it was thought an atom was a fundamental (or indivisible) particle, but then scientists broke the atom down into 3 parts: proton, neutron and electron. These were thought to be fundamental particles until scientists broke the proton and neutron into 3 quarks each. The electron is a fundamental lepton. Only 12 fermions make up all the diversity of matter we see and don't see!

12 bosons or mediator particles govern the known forces of the universe: 8 kinds of gluon, 2 kinds of W boson, Z boson, and photon. Physicists cannot yet explain the origin of gravity, so theorize that there must be responsible particles called gravitons, but they have not yet been discovered. (Another theorized particle, the Higgs boson, is also unproven.) The "Standard Model" of subatomic particles does not even include gravity. It is amazing that the most obvious force to human experience, gravity, remains a mystery to scientists. At night we can observe a giant satellite called the moon revolving around the earth, and yet have no idea what is causing it to hang in the sky without flying away on the one hand or falling into the earth on the other. This type of counter-intuitive encounters in science point to the Kingdom of God. What seems obvious (gravity) is not obvious at all (no cause can be found). What seems big (gravity) is actually the weakest of all (out of the 4 forces). A true understanding of science shows us why it makes sense to believe not only the visible, but even more so the invisible. "By faith we understand that the universe was created by the word of God, so that what is seen was not made out of things that are visible" (Heb. 11:3, ESV). The more we understand science, the more we are sure that the small, and often the invisible, things of life are the most important of all!

13

13 HAS OFTEN BEEN ASSOCIATED WITH EVIL in the Bible.

Jesus taught 13 evils proceed from man's heart: "evil thoughts, adulteries, fornications, murders, thefts, covetousness, wickedness, deceit, lewdness, an evil eye [Hebrew idiom for stinginess], blasphemy, pride, foolishness" (Mark 7:21–23).

Nimrod the 13th man from Adam was the world's first dictator and founder of the rebellious city of Babel.

There were 13 famines (financial recessions) in the Bible. (See Genesis 12:10, 26:1, 41:45; Ruth 1:1; 2 Samuel 21:1; 1 Kings 18:1; 2 Kings 4:38, 7:4, 25:3; Nehemiah 5:3; Jeremiah 14:1; Luke 15:14; Acts 11:28.)

There were 13 civil wars in Israel. (See Judges 12 and 20; 2 Samuel 2:1–11; 2:12–3:1; 15–18; 20; 1 Kings 12; 15:7; 15:16–22; 16:8–20; 16:21–22; 2 Kings 9; 14.)

The noun *leaven* representing false doctrine (Matt. 16:11–12) occurs 13 times in the New Testament; the "dragon" representing the devil is mentioned 13 times in the Book of Revelation.

Revelation 13 is *the* premier chapter revealing the Anti-Christ. Actually, the term *Anti-Christ* is never once used in the Book of Revelation, because the word *Anti-Christ* is primarily a Gentile term referring to anyone who opposes Christ as the only way to be saved, whereas the Book of Revelation deals primarily with Israel and the Jews post-rapture.

Revelation instead uses the term *beast*. There are not one but *two* beasts the Jews are to look for during the time of "Jacob's Trouble." Revelation 13:1–10 describes the first beast "out of the sea." Revelation 13:11–18 describes the second beast "out of the earth." One interpretation is that the first beast is a Gentile (sea is a symbol for nations) whereas the second beast is Jewish (the geopolitical center of the earth is Israel).

The first beast is a political leader (perhaps a world leader); whereas the second beast is a false religious leader, belonging to an ecumenical religion of some sort for the masses will not accept any other kind of religion. The truth it calls "dogma" and rejects, a lie it calls "compromise" and accepts.

The second beast imitates John the Baptist while the first beast imitates

Christ. The false messiah, his false prophet, and Satan make an unholy trinity that will persuade the world to hate Israel and hate God. Considering opinion polls now, Satan doesn't have much more convincing to do. The world's media-driven, Bible-illiterate population is *ready* to embrace anti-Israel leaders. So far America, Australia, and England have not given them one. If a charismatic Middle Eastern leader rises with enough power to rival the pro-Israel Western leaders, the world will fall on its knees to follow him and his spokesperson. These two charismatic beasts of Revelation 13 will deceive many. That time doesn't seem far away.

13 is a prime or indivisible number. The series of prime numbers starts with 1, 3, 5, 7, 11, 13, 17, 19, etc. What is interesting is that 13 is the 6th of such numbers, 6 being significant of the Anti-Christ.

There were 13 judges in the Book of Judges, the 6th one being the worst one. One of the worst periods in Israel's history was the time of the judges. Israel was under anarchy (Judges 21:25), worshiped false gods (Judges 5:8, 10:10); public streets were not safe (Judges 5:6–7); homosexuality was common (Judges 19:22); one of the worst crimes in the Bible occurred when bisexuals from Gibeah[1] tried to rape a Levite, and then succeeded in raping his concubine. Israel asked for the sodomites to be handed over and punished according to the Law of Moses, but the tribe of Benjamin refused and protected them, contrary to the Law of Moses. In retaliation Israel nearly wiped out the tribe of Benjamin, killing 25,100 young men and leaving only 600 left.[2]

Without spiritual and national leadership, Israel was trapped in a cycle of sin,[3] suffering (usually oppression by their enemies), brief repentance, and being rescued by a deliverer (called judge at the time). After God sent each judge to save them, their repentance was short-lived and they returned to sinning. Here were the 13 judges in the Book of Judges:

1. Othniel of Judah saved Israel from the Mesopotamians and ruled 40 years (3:9–11).
2. Ehud of Benjamin saved Israel from the Moabites and ruled 80 years (3:15–30).
3. Shamgar (3:31).
4. Deborah of Ephraim, with Barak of Naphtali, saved Israel from the Canaanites and ruled 40 years (4:4–5:31).
5. Gideon of Manasseh, with a band of only 300 men, saved Israel from the Moabites and ruled 40 years (6:7–8:35).

6. Abimelech, the son of Gideon, ruled 3 years. He oppressed his own people, killing 70 sons of Gideon, except Jotham.[4] He created civil strife because he wanted to be king and evidently turn Shechem into his capital. He was killed by a woman of Thebez who threw a millstone on his head (Judges 9).

   If the 6th judge is a type of the devil or Anti-Christ, then the woman who threw a millstone was a type of the Church, who speaks Christ's Word which acts like a rock (see 1 Corinthians 10:4) and a hammer (see Jeremiah 23:29) on the devil's head.

7. Tola of Issachar ruled 23 years (Judges 10:1–2).

8. Jair of Gilead ruled 22 years (10:3–6).

9. Jephthah of Gilead saved Israel from the Ammonites and sadly enough from civil attack by the tribe of Ephraim. When Jephthah won victory over the Ephraimites, the survivors tried to cross the River Jordan back to their home territory. Jephthah's men were waiting at the river and identified disguised soldiers by asking them to say the word *shibboleth*. If they said "sibboleth" instead, their mispronunciation gave them away and they were killed.

This is the origin of the term *shibboleth* in English, meaning a linguistic, social, or cultural identifier, such as an accent from a particular region, or jargon used by a subculture, or a physical sign such as male circumcision. In Word War II, American soldiers used knowledge of baseball as a shibboleth to identify German infiltrators from real American troops. Till today, Thai police uses several shibboleths to identify refugees who cross the Thai border illegally and stay to work. The police may listen for a Burmese refugee to say a word with a Thai "b" in it; the Burmese confuse the Thai "b" with a "w." Sometimes policemen will make the Burmese pretending to be a Thai sing the Thai national anthem. If they can't sing it with the right words or accent, they are sent back to Burma.

Jephthah was the first to use the shibboleth and ruled Israel 6 years (Judges 10:10–12:7). He, Barak, Gideon, and Samson are among the great men of faith mentioned in Hebrews 11. Gideon, Barak, Jephthah, and Samuel also get honorable mention by the Lord in 1 Samuel 12:11.

10. Ibzan of Judah ruled 8 years (Judges 12:1–10).

11. Elon of Zebulun ruled 10 years (12:11–12).

12. Abdon of Ephraim ruled 7 years (12:13–15).

13. Samson of Dan saved Israel from the Philistines by his death; he ruled 20 years (13:2–16:31).

After recording the 13 judges, the writer of Judges ends with one of the worst indictments against the spiritual condition of Israel, "In those days there was no king in Israel; everyone did what was right in his own eyes" (21:25).

13 is the total number of the tribes in Israel, because Joseph's two sons, Ephraim and Manasseh, were adopted by Jacob and count as 2 tribes. These are the sons in birth order: Reuben, Simeon, Levi, Judah, Dan, Naphtali, Gad, Asher, Issachar, Zebulun, Manasseh, Ephraim, Benjamin. All Biblical lists show 12 tribes, which makes for interesting discussion as to why 1 tribe gets omitted and why the tribes are in the order they are.

Most lists give Reuben first place, being the firstborn of Jacob. However, Judah heads other lists because he was chosen to be an ancestor of the Messiah. Long ago Jacob prophesied about his son Judah,

> The sceptre [symbol of kingship] shall not depart from Judah, Nor a lawgiver from between his feet, Until Shiloh [a term for the Messiah] comes; And to Him shall be the obedience of the people.
> —GENESIS 49:10

All of Israel's godly kings came from Judah, including David, Solomon, Hezekiah, and Josiah. All of these kings were ancestors to Jesus. Most genealogy in the Bible ultimately exists to link Jesus Christ to David, Abraham, and Adam. No other book in the world presents a continuous account of history from Creation to the first century A.D. (omitting the 400 year intertestament period).

What about the omitted tribes? In several lists Levi is not mentioned because they are ministers not soldiers. In the Book of Revelation, the tribe of Dan is missing. Why? The omission may serve as a clue to Dan's future: the tribe may become so apostate that it will be rejected during this time, or it may be in cooperation with the Anti-Christ. In Deborah's time, Dan was guilty of cowardice.[5] (See Judges 5:16–17.) Deborah asked, after victory over the Canaanites, "Why did Dan remain in ships?" After Samson, Dan couldn't handle the Philistines and decided to move to the far north of Israel. (Dan is the only tribe with 2 disconnected pieces of land.) Those of us who study end times interpret Dan's absence from the 144,000 end-time ministers of God as a clue that the false messiah, or else his false prophet, may be a Jew from the tribe of Dan. The sign of the tribe of Dan is a serpent.[6] The word *dan* means "judgment."

13 is not a number we should be afraid of, because everything negative gives God an opportunity to show His power to overcome evil. The Anti-Christs of the world will not prevail. Many have come and gone, while the Gospel continues to advance and the Church grows.

Haman the Agagite (Amalakite) planned to kill the Jews on the 13th day of the 12th month, but God turned it for the Jews' good. Israel was delivered from her enemies on the 13th day of Adar and still celebrates the 13th–14th days in an extra-Biblical feast called *Purim* (meaning lots). (See Esther 3:12–13; 9:1–18.)

13 can be derived from adding 6 + 7, signifying man's evil overcome by God's perfection. 13 can also be derived from 5 + 8, signifying the grace to start a new beginning. 13 can even be derived from 4 + 9, signifying the power of the Gospel and the Holy Spirit combining to overcome all temptations.

There were originally 13 colonies on the East Coast of America, now the 13 states of New England.

13 cannot be all bad since it's the age boys become men in Jewish culture. At the age of 13, a boy becomes a *bar mitzvah* or "son of the commandment." It is the age at which a young man chooses to follow God and not turn back. Abraham's circumcision is mentioned 13 times in the Torah.[7]

Moses Maimonides (1135–1204) wrote 13 articles of faith summarizing the basic beliefs of Judaism:

1. The existence of God
2. The unity of God
3. God is Spirit
4. God is eternal
5. Worship God alone and not those that are below Him
6. Prophecy or revelation through prophets
7. The preeminence of Moses among the prophets
8. The Torah was given by God on Mount Sinai
9. The completeness of the Torah, i.e. it is not lacking
10. God knows man's actions and does not ignore them
11. God will punish those who break His commandments
12. The Messiah will come though he delays his coming

13. The Resurrection of the dead, conditional on the Messiah's coming.[8]

13 is the number of times Joshua's army marched around Jericho before it fell: 6 times on the first 6 days and 7 times on the 7th day.

Remember 13 is just a number. Let's stay positive and have faith in God, not numbers.

14

14 IS 7 X 2 which represents two weeks and may signify a waiting period. The number is most prominent in Jesus' genealogy. Matthew 1:1–17 records:

+ 14 generations from Abraham to David

+ 14 generations from David to the Babylonian Captivity

+ 14 generations from the Babylonian Captivity to Christ

What does the repetitive pattern of 14 in Jesus' family tree mean? Remember that the Hebrews used their letters as their numbers because they had no separate numeral system. Therefore when Jews wrote numbers, they could also mean words and names. Did Matthew know that 14 has a special connection to both David and the Messiah who is called the "Son of David"? The gematria for David's name is Dalet + Vav + Dalet = 4 + 6 + 4 = 14. Since 3 is the number of complete witness, it was as if Matthew were saying 3 times, "Jesus is the Messiah because He is the Son of David!" The plain lineage of Christ proves that He is related to David, but the symmetry of 14 added numerical proof: Jesus is the royal seed of David.

Luke's record shows:

+ 10 generations from Adam to Noah

+ 10 generations from Noah to Abraham

+ 14 generations from Abraham to David

+ 40 generations from David to Joseph

Much theological debate has raged over the differences between Matthew's genealogical account and Luke's. But all confusion is solved when one understands that Matthew records Jesus' paternal lineage whereas Luke records His maternal lineage.

Luke 3:23 contains *italicized words* which are additions by the translators of the King James Version. Usually the additions are meant to help us understand the passage better in English; but in case they didn't, the translators knew enough to let us know by *italicizing* the additional words:

> And Jesus himself began to be about thirty years of age, being (as was supposed) the son of Joseph, which was *the son* of Heli.

The words "the son" of Heli are *italicized* because they are not there in the original Greek. It would make much more sense to read the verse as "Joseph, which was *the son-in-law* of Heli [Mary's father]." Luke then traces Jesus' maternal lineage.

Typically ancient records only showed the paternal genealogy of a king or an important person. (Commoners kept no genealogy at all, as most of us can attest. I don't know too many commoners who can trace their family trees beyond 4 generations.) Why would the Gospel writers want to trace Jesus' family tree back through 42 paternal generations and 62 maternal generations?

Writing to the Jews, Matthew was concerned with proving that Jesus is the Jewish Messiah. The Messiah must be of royal descent, heir to the throne of David, descendant of the tribe of Judah, and the seed of Abraham. Nobody today can prove those qualifications, which precludes all other claims to the Messianic title. Jesus is the last person to completely trace His lineage to David and Abraham.

Luke was addressing the Gentiles. Both the Gospel of Luke and the Book of Acts are addressed to a Roman named "Theophilus," which may have been a real person or a code name for anyone of us who is a "lover of God." Therefore Luke was more concerned with proving Jesus is the Seed of the Woman (Gen. 3:15) or the Savior of the world promised to every generation since Adam. Accordingly Luke 3:23–38 traces Jesus' genealogy back to Adam.

Luke's record is the only complete genealogy of any man which can be traced back to Adam and Eve, clearly disproving evolution. Although some people may not realize it, redemption depends on humans descending from humans. The incarnation of Jesus as God in human form is proof that only a human descended from a human has the legal right to save mankind. God could not unilaterally intervene to save mankind and defeat Satan. God has given certain rights to humans; the first humans abdicated those rights to Satan, so it would only be just and legal for a human to redeem those rights and give them back to humans. This completely human lineage is necessary for redemption.

Luke's genealogy proves Jesus did not descend from apes, but from the fully human Adam and Eve. Over and over Jesus called Himself the "Son of Man." (Make no mistake about it: Jesus also called Himself the "Son of God.") Whether the Bible refers to Jesus' humanity or to His divinity, there is no reference to any ape in Jesus' genealogy. Jesus did not believe in evolution.

16

16 IS AN IMPORTANT RITE OF PASSAGE for young people. Girls celebrate their "sweet 16." Boys look forward to getting their drivers' permit or license, depending on the country they live in.

In Acts 2, the first disciples to be baptized with the Holy Spirit spoke in the tongues of 16 nationalities. The onlookers from 16 regions of the world thought they were drunk and asked, "And how is it that we hear, each in our own language in which we were born?" (v. 8)

16 is most prominent in the ministry of Elisha. Elisha performed 16 miracles, exactly double of Elijah's 8. This is a divine response to Elisha's request for a "double portion" of his mentor's anointing. Not only were Elisha's miracles greater numerically, they were sometimes greater qualitatively.

Below is a table of miracles performed by Elijah and Elisha. (We are not counting prophetic utterances as miracles, for then the number would be untold.) By the end of Elisha's ministry, he had only performed 15 miracles. So God granted his dead bones, no doubt saturated with the double anointing, to resurrect a dead man (2 Kings 13:20–21). This posthumous miracle made 16 miracles in total.

We should find comfort in this fact that the anointing can last beyond us. We can all dwell in God's presence to the point that His anointing saturates our being and bones and spills over into our shadows or clothes, like it did for Peter and Paul. (See Acts 5:15; 19:11–12.) No doubt we can pass our anointing on to our disciples and children who wish to follow us, as Moses did for Joshua, Elijah did for Elisha, and Paul did for Timothy.

16 is the number of the double portion of anointing.

Miracles of Elijah	OT Reference	Miracles of Elisha	OT Reference
1. Causing rain to stop for 3 1/2	1 Kings 17:1	1. Parting the Jordan River	2 Kings 2:13–15
2. Multiplying the barrel of meal and cruse of oil	1 Kings 17:4	2. Healing the water	2 Kings 2:19–22
3. Resurrecting the widow's son	1 Kings 17:22	3. Cursing 42 mockers who died by bear mauling	2 Kings 2:23–25
4. Calling fire from Heaven	1 Kings 18:20–40	4. Filling the valley with water without rain	2 Kings 3:16–20
5. Causing it to rain	1 Kings 18:45	5. Defeating the Moabites	2 Kings 3:21–23
6. Outrunning the king's chariot for 50 kilometers	1 Kings 18:46	6. Multiplying the widow's oil	2 Kings 4:1–7
7. Calling fire from Heaven on soldiers	2 Kings 1:9–12	7. Healing the Shunammite's infertility	2 Kings 4:16
8. Parting the Jordan River	2 Kings 2:7–8	8. Resurrecting the Shunammite's son	2 Kings 4:32–37
		9. Healing food poisoning	2 Kings 4:38–41
		10. Multiplying bread for 100 men	2 Kings 4:42–44
		11. Healing Naaman the leper	2 Kings 5:1–14
		12. Cursing Gehazi with leprosy	2 Kings 5:27
		13. Making an axe head float	2 Kings 6:1–7
		14. Blinding the Syrian Army	2 Kings 6:18–19
		15. Healing the Syrian's blindness	2 Kings 6:20–23
		16. Resurrecting the Moabite man	2 Kings 13:20–21

18

JEWS CONSIDER 18 TO BE THE NUMBER OF LIFE, as the numerical value of the Hebrew word *life* (*chai*) is 18. Man breathes an average of 18 breaths per minute. When man, 6, meets God, 3, man has life, 18. 6 x 3 = 18. Jesus healed a woman who was crippled for 18 years (Luke 13:11). 18 people were killed by the collapse of the tower in Siloam (Luke 13:4).

18 is a significant milestone for many young adults, being the age at which they can vote, go to war, or drive a car unaccompanied, depending in which country they live.

For Jewish children, learning how to pray starts with reciting the *Shema*[1] (which affirms monotheism) and the *Shemoneh Esre* ("The 18," or literally "8 + 10"), an originally 18-point prayer central to Judaism. Jews pray the *Shema* twice a day—evening and morning. Children say it before they go to bed. Observant Jews pray the *Shemoneh Esre* 3 times a day—evening, morning, and afternoon—standing up. For this reason it is also known as the *Amidah* (Standing) and *Tefilah* (The Prayer).

The 18-point prayer is made of 3 parts: 3 praises to God, 13 petitions of God, and 3 thanksgivings to God. 3 + 13 + 3 = 19. So why do the call it "The 18"? Because an extra, ungracious request against heretics was added in the second century in response to heresies, including what they perceived as the growing threat of Christianity.

Jesus taught against praying "vain repetitions" (Matt. 6:7), of which the Pharisees were fond. What Christians now call the "Lord's Prayer"[2] may be a concise version of the *Amida* as it follows the same basic structure of praise, petition, and thanksgiving. The Lord's Prayer is not technically a new covenant prayer, as Jesus had not yet paid the price for redemption. As He drew closer to the Cross, Jesus taught new covenant believers to pray in His name. (See John 14:13–14; 15:16; 16:23–24, 26; and Mark 16:17–18.)

19

19 IS A PRIME NUMBER that is of such importance to astronomy that I've included it here as the number of order or grand cycle. It is the number of the Metonic cycle. The Metonic cycle, or the time it takes for the phases of the moon to recur on the same dates, is 19 years. In other words, if one could take a snapshot of the earth, moon, and sun in relation to one another, the length of time it would take for us to see the exact same picture again is 19 years.

Our Western calendar is a solar calendar. The Islamic calendar is a lunar calendar. But the Hebrew calendar instituted by God is the only solar-lunar calendar: the months follow the moon; the years follow the sun. While we add a day to our Gentile calendar every 4 years, the Hebrews add a whole month to their calendar 7 times every 19 years.

According to rabbinical understanding, all time is divided into multiples of 7s, and every 7 x 7 years or 49 years marks a "jubilee." Adam lived for 19 jubilees or 930 years (19 x 49 = 931 -1 for no year "0" = 930). The *Book of Jubilees* makes 2 interesting comments: "And he lacked 70 years of 1,000 years; for 1,000 years are as 1 day in the testimony of the heavens and therefore was it written concerning the tree of knowledge: 'On the day that ye eat thereof ye shall die.' For this reason he did not complete the years of his day; for he died during it." And, "For the days of the forefathers of their life were 19 jubilees; and after the Flood they began to grew less than 19 jubilees, and to decrease in jubilees, and to grow old quickly, and to be full of their days by reason of manifold tribulation and the wickedness of their ways, with the exception of Abraham."[1]

King David had 19 sons, 6 born in Hebron, 4 in Jerusalem by Bathsheba, and 9 others in Jerusalem by other wives. According to 1 Chronicles 3:1–9, daughters and sons of concubines were omitted.

After the glorious days of King David and King Solomon, Israel was divided into north (called Israel, Samaria, or Ephraim) and south (called Judah), each with their own succession of kings.

There were 19 kings of Israel, all of them wicked: Jeroboam, Nadab, Baasha, Elah, Zimri, Omri (the 6th person—the one who established Samaria as capital of Israel and a rival religious center to Jerusalem; the woman at the well mentioned this rivalry during her conversation with Jesus in John 4; there was also a division in the northern kingdom during Omri's days with half wanting to follow Tibni and half Omri; Omri fathered a very wicked son named Ahab), Ahab (husband of idolatress Jezebel), Ahaziah, Joram, Jehu, Jehoahaz, Joash, Jeroboam II, Zechariah, Shallum, Menahem, Pekahiah, Pekah, and Hoshea.

There were 19 kings of Judah, all descendants of King David; 7 were good, most were bad: Rehaboam, Abijah, Jehoshphat, Jehoram, Ahaziah (Queen Athaliah—the 6th person was the wicked daughter of Ahab and Jezebel. The only ruling queen in Judah or Israel, she reigned for 6 years, but is usually excluded from the list of kings), Joash, Amaziah, Uzziah, Jotham, Ahaz, Hezekiah (revival in his days), Manasseh, Amon, Josiah (the last good king, he also saw revival), Jehoahaz, Jehoiakim, Jehoiachin, Matthaniah whose name was changed to Zedekiah by the king of Babylon.

Although there were 19 kings in both Israel and Judah, their reigns were not of equal length. The northern kings were all wicked, usually died young, and were replaced by conspiracy or were assassinated. The northern kingdom lasted only 207 years until the Assyrian Deportation in 722 B.C.* (See 2 Kings 17:23–29.)

Judah's kings were a mix of good and bad. Some of them chose to follow the example of their father David, others rejected it. Hezekiah avoided the Assyrian Captivity by turning to God and believing Isaiah's two prophecies. Because of godly leadership, Judah was saved by the miraculous defeat of Assyria's army when an angel slew 185,000 in one night. (See 2 Kings 19.) God could have and would have done the same thing for Israel, but she opted to worship idols and trust her own strength. The southern kingdom lasted for 393 years until the Babylonian Captivity and destruction of Solomon's Temple in 586 B.C. The survivors were deported to Babylon for 70 years, including Ezekiel and Daniel. Only Daniel survived the 70 years.

The stories of Israel and Judah's kings are recorded in the books of 1 and 2 Kings.** They show us how much God cares about families. God wanted fathers to teach their children the Bible because it would cause them to grow up into

---

* Assyria's policy of bringing foreigners into Samaria and encouraging them to intermarry with the inhabitants of Samaria is partly responsible for the Jews' hatred for the Samaritans. With intermarriage often came idolatry. See John 4:9 and 8:48 to see the Jews' racism against Samaritans. That is why Jesus' choice of making the "Good Samaritan" the hero of Luke 10 made it a very convicting parable. The Jews thought they were good and didn't need a Savior, but they failed to obey even the first commandment—love your neighbor. Only the new birth can end racism. Only faith in Christ makes loving our enemies possible.

** First and Second Chronicles record only the stories of the kings of Judah, because only they are relevant the Messianic line. Christ must descended from the Tribe of Judah and be related to all the kings of Judah. Jesus had such great ancestors as King David, Solomon, Jehoshaphat, Hezekiah and Josiah. He is not only King of Heaven, but also the rightful heir to the throne of his father David.

godly leaders for the nation. Israel failed miserably, and that failure started in the kings' homes. Judah did slightly better—the good kings show us both the blessings of the godly heritage David left his descendants; and also the opportunity some children who had bad parents have to *choose God* and redeem their families. Hezekiah and Josiah both had ungodly fathers, but both *chose God* despite of their upbringing and saw revival in their days.

The causes of failure of all kings can be summarized in two:

1. Allowing their children to do whatever they wanted without discipline and training. Children need involved parents who communicate why we believe what we believe and do what we do. The lessons of God and life are meant to be passed down by godly parents.

2. Allowing their children to marry unbelievers. Ahab of Israel was bad, but he got worse by marrying the manipulative and idolatrous Jezebel.

Jehoshaphat of Judah was a godly king, but for political advantage he married his son Jehoram to Ahab and Jezebel's daughter Athaliah. It cost him his son's life, who went with his grandfather Ahab to a war he shouldn't have been involved in. After his son's death at the tender age of only 23, Jehoshaphat's decision continued to cost Judah 6 years of wicked tyranny under Queen Athaliah who was not even part of the tribe of Judah. (See 2 Kings 11:1–3.)

Malachi 2:15 asked why God made man and woman one? "That He might seek a godly seed" (KJV). One of the purposes of marriage is to give children an opportunity to grow up in a God-centered environment. That is why the Holy Spirit commanded that Christians should not be "unequally yoked" with unbelievers (2 Cor. 6:14). One reason Christians should not marry unbelievers is because when it's time to raise children, it creates spiritual confusion. The children of Israel and Judah's kings are an example for us of what denying a godly heritage can do to a child's life. Sadly, I know Christian parents who are more concerned about their child marrying someone of a particular skin color than marrying a believer. Raising children is hard enough, you do not want to do your child a disservice by arguing with your spouse whether Jesus Christ is Lord or attending Church every week is right. Learn from the 19 kings of Israel and Judah.

19TH

BOOK

THE BOOK OF PSALMS IS THE 19TH BOOK OF THE BIBLE and may map out the prophetic destiny of Israel starting from the 19th century. For instance, book 19 Psalm 48 seems to allude to the rebirth of Israel in 1948, "Beautiful in elevation, The joy of the whole earth, Is Mount Zion [representing Israel]…The city of the great King.…The kings assembled, They passed by together. They saw it, and so they marveled [the world marveled that Israel returned to her homeland].…As we have heard, So we have seen In the city of the LORD of hosts, In the city of our God: God will establish it forever." (vv. 2, 4–5, 8).

The most important prophecy in the Bible, other than the coming of the Messiah, is the rebirth of Israel in 1948. It should not be surprising that God would predict it in plain words and in hidden codes. J. R. Church believes many of these codes are found in Israel's Psalms. Could Psalms be mapping out God's prophetic plan for Israel? Even the positioning of the book within the Bible may be a macro-clue to the year of Israel's rebirth. Psalms is 19 books from Genesis and 48 books from Revelation.

The notion that God speaks to us not only in plain words but also in hidden codes and prophetic models is unpopular among some Christian theologians, but not so among Jewish rabbis. They have always taught that there was more to the Bible than the surface text. They believe that the Bible is supernatural, every letter has a meaning, and when Messiah comes, He will reveal the meaning of every letter and even the spaces between the letters. Most Christians today understand that beyond the plain text of the Bible, God also speaks to us through object lessons and messianic metaphors called "types"—such as the Lamb of God, the Feasts of Israel, the story of Ruth and Boaz, which parallels Christ and the Gentile Church, etc.

I am not insisting that Psalms is definitely prophetic of Israel's modern events, but let us explore a few more examples before we dismiss the concept.

Book 19 Psalm 42 may correspond to the outbreak of World War II in 1942.

Three times the psalmist wrote that his soul was "cast down." Verse 9 sounds eerily like the cries of the Jews during World War II, "I will say to God my Rock, 'Why have You forgotten me? Why do I go mourning because of the oppression of the enemy?'"

Book 19 Psalm 43 may correspond to the Holocaust: "Vindicate me, O God, And plead my cause against an ungodly nation [Germany?]; Oh, deliver me from the deceitful and unjust man [Adolf Hitler?]" (v. 1). Adolf Hitler deceived the rest of the world while he killed 6 million Jews.

Book 19 Psalm 45 sounds like the end of World War II in 1945: "My heart is overflowing with a good theme.... Your arrows [bombs?] are sharp in the heart of the King's enemies; The peoples [axis powers of Germany, Italy, and Japan] fall under You.... Instead of Your fathers shall be Your sons [a new Jewish generation assured after the Holocaust], Whom You shall make princes in all the earth [many Jews have been among the top leaders of many fields in many countries]" (vv. 1, 5, 16).

Book 19 Psalm 46 may be prophetic of 1946, the first full year of peace since World War II: "He makes wars cease to the end of the earth" (v. 9).

Book 19 Psalm 91 is the definitive "psalm of protection," often carried and prayed by soldiers at war. It may be prophetic of First Gulf War in 1991, in which the United States won a crushing victory against Saddam Hussein and liberated Kuwait: "You shall not be afraid of the terror by night, Nor of the arrow that flies by day, Nor of the pestilence [i.e. disease—the U.S. military was very concerned that Saddam would unleashed poison gas or biological weapons on them, just as he did on the Kurds] that walks in darkness, Nor of the destruction that lays waste at noonday. A thousand may fall at your side, And ten thousand at your right hand; But it shall not come near you [U.S. forces overwhelmed the dictator's military with little casualty, praise the Lord!]" (vv. 5–7).

Since the 19th book ends on the 150th Psalm, an obvious question is, "Will the world come to an end in 2050 (1900 + 150 = 2050)?" Before we jump to rash conclusions, J. R. Church drew attention to the fact David and Solomon are credited with compiling Psalms 1 to 106, but Ezra is credited with compiling Psalms 107 to 150. Psalms 1 to 106 appear to correspond to prophetic events in chronological order; however, the chronology *may* break after Psalm 107. Ezra's Psalms, if we can call them that, look forward to an eternal kingdom under Messiah. No one can set the date when Messiah will come back. I am one who hopes it will be sooner than 2050. But we must work as if Christ may not come back for 100 years and live as if Christ may return tomorrow.

If the 19th book of the Bible is really prophetic of events starting from 1900, it would agree with the significance of the number 19 standing for the master time cycle. Whether or not the reader sees the prophetic nature of the 19ᵗʰ book, the Book of Psalms certainly has many unique features. It is the longest book of the Bible; contains the longest chapter of the Bible (119) and the shortest chapter of the Bible (117); and the middle verses of the Bible (103:1–2)*: "Bless the LORD, O my soul; And all that is within me, bless His holy name! Bless the LORD, O my soul, And forget not all His benefits." Charles Spurgeon once said: "The delightful study of the Psalms has yielded me boundless profit and ever-growing pleasure."[1]

---

* Contrary to popular misconception, the middle verse of the Bible is not Psalm 118:8. Since there is an even number of verses in the Bible (31,102 in KJV), there are 2 middle verses (verses 15,551 and 15,552). See Nic Kizzah, "King James Bible Statistics," http://www.biblebelievers.com/believers-org/kjv-stats.html (accessed October 25, 2010).

19

HEALINGS

AS I TEACH in Churches and seminars, a study of every individual case of sickness and healing in the Bible is extremely helpful to obtaining your own healing. Let me summarize the highlights of my research into healing for you.[1]

There are 19 individual healing stories in the 4 Gospel accounts, not counting all the multitudes of people Jesus healed.[2] (See Matthew 4:23; 9:35; 12:15; 14:14; 15:30; 19:2; Luke 5:15; 6:17–19; 9.) Given 19 instances of individual healings, it would be wise to ask, "How were the sick healed?" If we can find out how they got healed, we can find out how we can get healed, because "Jesus Christ is the same yesterday, today and forever" (Heb. 13:8), and God never changes (Mal. 3:6). God is still the same Healer today and He is still healing the same way.

2 CAMPS ON HEALING

When it comes to healing, there are basically 2 camps: the sovereignty camp and the faith camp. The sovereignty camp holds the view that God can heal, but it's up to Him if He wants to heal you. All you can do is wait and see. If you're healed, it means it was God's will. If you're not healed, it means it must not have been His will. God gets the credit for healing, and God gets the blame for lack of healing.

The faith camp holds the view that healing (like salvation) is always God's will, but whether or not you get healed (or saved) is partly up to you. If you are not healed, it is never God's fault. There's something you either don't know or didn't do. You have a role to play in obtaining forgiveness and healing. God should never be blamed. Your salvation and healing are not all up to God, or else everybody in the world would be saved and healed right now. Each person has a responsibility to cooperate with Him. Responsibility is not a word most people like to hear. Both sides can get very emotionally charged about this subject. Which side is right?

To some extent, both sides are right. They both have merit scripturally.

Sometimes God initiates healing without any faith on the part of the sick; this is called a manifestation or move or gift of the Holy Spirit. (See 1 Corinthians 12:1, 4, 7.) Other times the sick initiates healing on their own faith. What would add value to the discussion is counting how many times Jesus approached the sick versus the sick approached Jesus.

Numbers removes emotions out of the debate. We don't need to argue about doctrine if we can count how many times Jesus approached a sick person to heal them (points to the sovereignty camp) and how many times the sick approached Jesus for healing (points to the faith camp).

Before I reveal the numbers, I want to reveal the *logos* or logic of divine healing. God heals because sickness is an intruder, a curse of the Fall. Old-time preachers used to say that sickness is the offspring of its mother sin and its father Satan. When we see sickness attack someone, we should all be on the same side—the Healer's side. There is no record of Jesus turning a sick person away and saying what so many modern preachers claim, "Stay sick so that God can teach you a lesson," or "Remain sick for God's glory." On the contrary, people in the New Testament did not give glory to God until they saw the sick were healed. (See Matthew 9:8, 15:31; Mark 2:12; Luke 5:26, 13:13, 17:15; John 11:4; Acts 4:21.) Healing, rather than sickness, brought glory to God.

I believe both sides share more in common with each other than they see. Both sides believe in the sovereignty of God and the importance of faith. But it's a matter of definition. When we say "God is sovereign," we do not mean, "God does whatever He wants." That is not the definition of a sovereign. It is the definition of corruption, tyranny, and dictatorship. A sovereign is a ruler who abides by His own laws. God is sovereign because He always moves in line with His own Word. Once we understand His Word, we understand how God in His sovereignty has chosen to heal. So when we say "God healed sovereignly," we mean He healed by gifts of the Spirit which occur "as He wills." On the other side, when we say "faith," it should be clear we are not referring to "blind faith," which is the caricature of religion by Hollywood and anti-theists. No, we are referring to Biblical faith founded upon evidence and knowledge of a good God.

JESUS APPROACHING THE SICK

Out of 19 cases of healing, 7 of them were initiated by Jesus. In other words, Jesus walked up to the sick and healed them without any discernible faith on their part.

HEALING INITIATED BY JESUS/ THE SPIRIT	MATT.	MARK	LUKE	JOHN
1. Peter's mother-in-law	8:14–15	1:29–31	4:38–39	
2. Man with withered hand	12:9–13	3:1–5	6:6–10	
3. Deaf and dubm (mute)		7:31–37		
4. Lame man at Pool of Bethesda				5:2–15
5. Man born blind				9:1–7
6. Woman with spirit of infirmity for 18 years			13:10–17	
7. Man with dropsy			14:1–6	

Why did Jesus sovereignly choose to heal these 7 people without faith on their part? By studying we can usually find good reasons why Jesus initiated the healing process.

In the case of the deaf man, he could not hear Jesus. Since faith comes by hearing, this man could not have had any faith. So Jesus approached the deaf man, led by the Spirit of God. We can say that most deaf cases must be healed by gifts of the Spirit or the initiation of the Spirit. If the deaf cannot hear, they cannot approach Jesus based on their own faith. I have seen 3 deaf children instantly healed in Africa and can tell you that none of them could have heard or understood a word I preached. They were healed by a sovereign move of the Spirit.

Jesus had good reasons to approach others. Peter's mother-in-law was sick in bed and unable to meet Jesus. The lame man in Bethesda was unable to walk. The Lord has compassion on the bed-ridden. I have heard several stories of bed-ridden Christians being visited and healed by the Lord. The lesson seems to be: if you're able-bodied enough to walk and to move, you should not delay to come to Jesus and obtain healing on your own faith!

In the remaining 4 cases where Jesus approached the sick—the man with the withered hand, the man born blind, the crippled woman and the man with dropsy (edema or swollen legs)—we find one commonality in their stories. Jesus deliberately performed these 4 healings *all on the Sabbath!* The sovereign moves of the Spirit seem to be a divine challenge to the religious attitude of the Pharisees who didn't want Jesus to heal on the Sabbath. He simply ignored religion and proved the religious wrong. Now you don't have to wait till the Sabbath to get healed! You can get healed any day of the week.

Healing Initiated by the Sick	Matt.	Mark	Luke	John
1. Leper	8:1–4	1:40–45	5:12–15	
2. Centurion's servant	8:5–13		7:1–10	
3. Nobleman's Son				4:46–54
4. Paralytic lowered through roof	9:2–8	2:1–12	5:17–26	
5. Two blind men	9:27–31			
6. Jairus' daughter	9:18–19, 23–26	5:22–24, 35–43	8:41–42, 49–56	
7. Woman with issue of blood 12 years	9:20–22	5:25–34	8:43–48	
8. Syrophoenician's daughter	15:21–28	7:24–30		
9. Blind man at Bethesaida		8:22–26		
10. Lunatic son	17:14–21	9:14–29	9:37–42	
11. Ten lepers			17:11–19	
12. Blind Bartimaeus	20:29–34	10:46–52	18:35–43	

70 PERCENT VERSUS 30 PERCENT

A number of facts become obvious upon glancing at these tables. The majority of sick people were healed through their own faith; the minority of people were healed by waiting for a sovereign move of the Spirit. The ratio of those healed by approaching Jesus versus those waiting for Jesus to approach them is 12:7, or 63 percent by faith versus 37 percent by gifts of the Spirit.

Since the deaf cannot have faith, the healing of the deaf inflates the 37 percent of cases healed sovereignly by the Lord. Had he the ability to operate on his own faith, he could also have received healing by faith like the majority did. Removing the deaf case brings the ratio of faith to gifts of the Spirit to 12:6, or 67 percent healed by faith, and only 33 percent healed by gifts of the Spirit operating "as He wills" (1 Cor. 12:11).

In simple terms, 7 out of 10 Christians will be healed by their own faith. Using rounded numbers, we can say that in 70 percent of cases, the recipient initiated the healing process, while 30 percent of the recipients waited for God to approach them with healing.

WHAT THE MAJORITY DID TO GET HEALED

You need to understand this: it wasn't all up to Jesus. Your salvation is not all up to Jesus, is it? Salvation requires you to hear the Gospel, choose to believe it, and decide to receive it verbally. Romans 10:9 says, "If you confess with your mouth the Lord Jesus and believe in your heart that God has raised Him from the dead, you will be saved."

Your healing is not all up to Jesus. Once you hear the truth about Christ the Healer, you need to believe it, speak it, and act on it in order for it to work. Jesus wasn't walking around picking whom He would heal. In the case of the woman with the issue of blood for 12 years, Jesus actually turned to the crowd and asked, "Who touched Me?" (Mark 5:31). The woman got healed before Jesus could identify her. Who decided her healing?

There is another insight I want to draw out of the 19 healing cases. It will help you obtain your healing. Out of 12 cases of people who approached Jesus first, the word *faith* is either specifically mentioned or implied in all 12 instances.

To the woman with the issue of blood Jesus said, "*Your faith* has made you well. Go in peace, and be healed of your affliction" (v. 33, emphasis added).

To Jairus Jesus said, "Do not be afraid, only *believe*" (v. 36, emphasis added).

To the centurion Jesus said, "I have not found so great *faith*, not even in Israel....Go your way, and as you have *believed*, so be it done unto you" (Matt. 8:10, 13, emphasis added). Isn't it interesting Jesus did not say, "As God wills, so be it done unto you" or "I, the Son of God, sovereignly choose to heal you"? He could have said that, but Jesus specifically credited the healing to the centurion's own faith.

To two blind men, Jesus asked, "Do you *believe* that I am able to do this?" They said to Him, "Yes, Lord." Then He touched their eyes, saying, "According to *your faith* let it be to you" (9:28–29, emphasis added). Notice Jesus did not say, "According to *My* faith be it done unto you," or, "According to the apostles Peter, James, and John's faith, may you be healed." No, your faith matters.

To the Syrophoenician woman Jesus said, "O woman, great is *your faith*! Let it be to you as *you* desire" (15:28, emphasis added). Why didn't Jesus say, "Let it be to you as *God* desires"? Obviously our desire and our faith have something to do with our healing.

In 12 out of 19 cases, Jesus attributed healing to the recipient's faith. Faith is a key to receiving healing. Too many think they will be healed if they really need it, or if they beg God enough, or because they serve God they deserve to get healed. But healing, like salvation, is a gift *by grace through faith.* You cannot deserve to be healed. You cannot beg enough to be healed. You cannot wish to be healed. You cannot say, "But I need it so bad, why hasn't God done anything?" or "O Lord, You know I've served You at Church, why don't You heal me?"

It's up to us to study God's Word on healing, trust God is true to His Word, and act according to the Word. I have never failed to receive healing for myself or for my family in this way. Do not trust in your own religious tradition or put it above God's Word. Do not assume you already know everything there is to know about God's Word. It is vital to study what the Bible says before accepting other people's opinions, even if they have degrees and PhDs. It's not their body or their health that's on the line; it's mine and my family's, so I cannot trust the best of men's opinions.

LET THE NUMBERS SPEAK HEALING!

What is God trying to teach us through these 19 healing cases? God is clearly showing that in the *majority* of cases (70 percent), you're going to have to do something about your own healing. Your volition and your cooperation have much to do with your obtaining a blessing from Jesus. Those who sat passively were *not* healed. Sick people like the woman with the issue of blood and blind Bartimaeus cried and pushed their way through crowds to get to Jesus. They were healed. Despite religious and personal opposition, they believed Jesus, acted on their belief, and obtained their healing.

The statistics tell us: 70 percent of individuals received healing by approaching Jesus. The remaining 30 percent waited for God to approach them.

However, we should put now this 30 percent figure in perspective. The reality is that healing by gifts of the Spirit was *rare* compared to healing by faith. In 3 ½ years of healing, only 7 cases were reported as initiated by the Lord. In contrast, there are multitudes of cases where innumerable people approached Jesus first for healing.

> Then the blind and the lame *came to Him* in the temple, and He healed them.
>
> —MATTHEW 21:14, EMPHASIS ADDED

And when the men of that place recognized Him, they sent out into all that surrounding region, *brought to Him* all who were sick, and begged[*] Him that they might only touch the hem of His garment. And as many as touched it were made perfectly well.

—MATTHEW 14:35–36, EMPHASIS ADDED

For he had healed many, so that those with diseases were *pushing* forward to touch him.

—MARK 3:10, NIV, EMPHASIS ADDED

Multitudes of people came to Jesus to obtain healing, and they got it. Not one failed to receive healing. If these multitudes could be counted in our equation, then the percentage of those healed by faith would rise higher than 70 percent. It would be safe to say that 80 percent to as high as 99 percent of those who got healed did so on their own initiative. So why be part of the minority (possibly 1 percent) who are passive about healing? Isn't it better to be part of the majority who get healed by actively pursuing God? That means reading your Bible, studying healing, and going to a Church where the Word of God is demonstrated, not just talked about.

SOVEREIGN MANIFESTATIONS

We have established that in the minority of cases, healing can occur without much knowledge or faith. In such cases where the sick did not approach Jesus or didn't even know who Jesus was, gifts of the Spirit were operating. If a sick person gets healed without knowing who Jesus is or without understanding the Word, then their healing could not be based on their own faith. It was a sovereign act of God.

When healing occurs without any faith involved, the Bible calls this a manifestation of 1 of the 9 "gifts of the Spirit" (listed in 1 Cor. 12:1–11). These supernatural gifts operate through an anointed minister, but are not controlled by the minister, as taught in 1 Corinthians 12:11. Paul said, "But one and the same Spirit works all these things [these 9 gifts], distributing to each one individually *as He wills*" (emphasis added).

No minister can make the gifts of the Spirit operate at his or her own will.

---

* Greek *parakaleo*, "to urge or implore," not *prosaiteo*, "to ask repeatedly," or *epaiteo*, "to beg." *Parakaleo* shares the same root as *Parakletos*, a title of the Holy Spirit meaning Helper. The Holy Spirit is not a beggar, but One who encourages, urges, and implores. The word *begged* should have been translated "requested," but old English used "beg" in the same sense that we still say I "beg your pardon," meaning "I ask you to say it again."

They operate as He wills. A minister simply needs to be open for the Holy Spirit to move. In revival meetings we often see many people get healed without much Bible knowledge or Bible faith. This clearly is a sovereign manifestation of the Holy Spirit. We also find many of those same people who get healed in revivals will tend to lose their healing shortly after the revival meetings. It's a truism that "if you don't know how you got it, you won't know how to keep it."

When the devil counterattacks and symptoms recur, those who did not fortify their faith in the Word of God will concede defeat and give up their faith by saying things like, "I guess the Lord didn't heal me." Then of course they're sick again and don't understand why. They *were* healed by gifts of the Spirit, but they had a responsibility to grow up spiritually. God expects us His children to take hold of His promises based on our own relationship with God, not based on a preacher's relationship with God. The preacher only helps advertise that God is real and His power is real. But then it's up to us to check in with God and get His Word directly into our hearts and minds.

No sick person can force any miracle or gift of the Spirit to operate at their own will. They occur sovereignly "as He wills." But every sick person can come to Jesus on their own initiative and by faith to receive healing. 12 out of 19 New Testament cases prove it.

If you need healing right now, have faith in Christ the Healer, and then declare to God:

> *I receive my healing from Christ my Healer. I won't wait or worry about it anymore. I will be part of the majority who get healed by approaching Jesus. I will not be the exception. God's Word will not fail. Thank You, Father, for Your Word! Thank You, Jesus, for making me well!*

Make sure you tell others how God healed you. 19 tells us God wants to heal! It is God's will to heal you!

20

20 IS A NUMBER ASSOCIATED WITH WAR. There are 20 potential opening moves in a chess game, though most of them are not taken because they would quickly lead to the opponent's advantage and your defeat.

20 is the age at which young men were enlisted into Israel's military. In Numbers 1, the minimum age requirement was repeated fourteen times in a single chapter. Many parents may have noticed a significant maturity gap between teenagers and those who hit 20 years of age. Feldhann and Rice offer a scientific explanation: "Science demonstrates that the frontal lobe of the brain—the area that allows judgment for consequences and control of impulses—doesn't fully develop until after the teen years. So in the absence of a fully functioning frontal lobe, teenage brains rely more on the centers that control emotions—which in effect means they give in much more easily to impulses."[1] The Bible was way ahead of science: "Take a census of all the congregation of the children of Israel....from twenty years old and above—all who are able to go to war in Israel" (Num. 1:2–3).

Deuteronomy 20 is *the* Torah's chapter on war. Within are instructions for every believer who is facing a test, trial, or battle on how to win. Second Chronicles 20 is *the* Old Testament chapter on how to conduct a successful war campaign. King Jehoshaphat faced an enemy that outnumbered him, but he followed God's strategy for war to victory.

God wants every believer to know that we are all called to battle. Yes, Paul told Timothy we are called to "fight the good fight of faith" (1 Tim. 6:12). Eight times in the Book of Revelation we are called to be overcomers. (See Revelation 2:7, 11, 17, 26; 3:5, 12, 21; 21:7.) If we are called to be "overcomers," it means we are going to have to "come over" some things. The Bible shows that every time a believer overcomes something, there is always reward waiting. Often when Israel won a victory, they took days to collect all the "spoils." Great victories are produced out of great battles.

It would behoove every believer to study Deuteronomy 20 and 2 Chronicles 20 to understand how to win a war. Let me list some keys to help you get started.

WAR STRATEGIES FROM DEUTERONOMY 20

1. The priest (minister) shall speak to the people God's Word (v. 2).
2. God's Word will eliminate fear (v. 3–4). The teaching of God's Word will always be the foundation of every victory.
3. The officers (leaders) shall speak to the people (v. 5).
4. The fearful must be eliminated out of the camp (v. 8). Doubt is destructive and contagious. There is no strength in numbers, only in faith. See Gideon's army of 32,000 reduced to 300 by God in Judges 7. Gideon asked all the fearful to leave and 22,000 departed. Victory did not depend on numbers, but on the fearless faith of a few.
5. When praying over an important matter, I never ask just anybody to pray with me. I only ask people I can trust—true believers who know their Bibles and are not afraid. I take no comfort in great numbers of people praying, but in the faith of a few believers. "This is the victory that has overcome the world, even our faith [not our numbers]" (1 John 5:4, NIV).
6. Offers of peace should be extended to human enemies (not to demons who are not subject to negotiation, and must be bound or cast out in the name of Jesus) (v. 10–12).
7. Victory and spoils are assured (v. 13–15).

WAR STRATEGIES FROM 2 CHRONICLES 20

1. Jehoshaphat sought God's face in prayer (v. 3–5).
2. Jehoshaphat spoke God's Word to the people (v.5–17).
3. God's Word eliminated fear and birthed faith (v. 6–7, 15–17).
4. Jehoshaphat worshiped and appointed worshipers to lead the battle (v. 18–22). Don't face the devil till you first face God.
5. The enemies were so confused they began to attack each other (v. 22–24).

6. Jehoshaphat and his people took 3 days to collect all the spoils (v. 25).

7. The fear of the Lord came upon all their enemies after the victory (v. 29).

21

21 IS AN IMPORTANT RITE OF PASSAGE in many people's lives. In America it is the age at which young adults can legally drink. In Australia many 21 year olds graduate a 3-year course with a degree and start a career. Isaac, Abraham's son of promise, was the 21st from Adam.

The demonic "prince of the kingdom of Persia" (Dan 10:13) withstood the angel Gabriel for 21 days, until Michael the archangel came to help him. Then Gabriel was able to deliver the prophetic end-time message to Daniel.

It would be no contradiction to extrapolate there is a demonic prince over America, Russia, Europe, China, India, etc., trying to influence the minds of the power brokers of each territory. Believers have the power to pray for our nations in Jesus' name. The good news is that under the new covenant, we no longer have to wait 21 days to get our prayers answered. No, Colossians 2:15 tells us about Jesus: "Having *disarmed* principalities and powers, He made a public spectacle of them, triumphing over them in it" (emphasis added).

The Cross made all the difference! Satan has been dethroned and his powers disarmed. He may roar like a lion, but he has been defanged and declawed. His main power and activity now is to deceive people, but he has no power to hinder our prayer life. Demons are afraid of Christians! James 4:7 says, "Resist the devil and he will *flee* from you" (emphasis added). To *flee* means he will run as fast as he can when he hears a Christian speak God's Word and use the name of Jesus. Christians need to understand the authority Jesus gave us in His name (see Mark 16:17).

21 is the 8th Fibonacci number. The Fibonacci series was discovered by an Italian mathematician *Leonardo* of *Pisa*, the *son* of *Bonaccio* (*Filius Bonaccio* was contracted to *Fibonacci*). The sequence starts with 1 and 1 and continues by adding the last two numbers to get the next number: 1, 1, 2, 3, 5, 8, 13, 21, 34, 55, 89, 144, 233, 377, 610, 987, etc. These numbers are frequently recurring in biology, physics, astronomy, art, and the stock market. Most technical analysts of stock charts are aware of the Fibonacci retracements, though they may not know an intelligent God designed those numbers to reflect His order and have meaning. (See the next Fibonacci number 34 for more on the stock market.)

22

22 IS CONSIDERED BY THE JEWS to be a very important number. There were 22 generations from Adam to Israel (Jacob) and 22 generations from Israel to David. The human head is made of 22 bones: 8 cranial bones and 14 facial bones.[1] There were 22 heads of mankind from Adam to Jacob: Israel was the 22nd one. There are 22 letters in the Hebrew alphabet. When God says that He created the world by speaking, rabbis hold the view that God literally created using the 22 letters of the Hebrew alphabet. Don't ask me how!

22 may be significant to worship. The ancient Hebrews had 2 stringed instruments translated in English as the lyre (Hebrew *kinnor*) and harp (*nevel*). The lyre had 10 strings and the harp 12 strings, giving a combination of 22 possible musical notes, thus corresponding to the 22 letters of the Hebrew alphabet. If each note corresponds to a Hebrew letter, then playing the right notes in the right sequence can actually be the musical equivalent of speaking out the Scriptures or prophesying!

The Bible indicates that there may be far more going on with music than we naturally understand. In 2 Kings 3:15, the prophet Elisha called for a harpist and "while the harpist was playing, the hand of the Lord came upon Elisha." The right kind of music brought the anointing upon the prophet and enabled him to minister. 1 Chronicles 25:1 tells us that King David and the army captains chose the sons of Asaph, Heman, and Jeduthun to "prophesy with harps, stringed instruments, and cymbals." How can one "prophesy" on a musical instrument? Apparently our vocal cords are not the only means of speaking God's Words. Inspired worship, to the angels' and devils' ears, may sound like Scriptures, sermons and prophecies being declared in the spiritual realm! No wonder worship is so powerful!

Immediately after the 7-day Feast of Tabernacles there is a special 1-day celebration called *Simchat Torah* or *Rejoicing in the Torah* on the 22nd of Tishri. On this day Jews who do not normally get to touch the Torah scroll are given the honor of embracing and dancing with the Torah scroll. It is customary to stay awake all night to read and learn the Torah. Though God did not command this celebration, it is a beautiful picture of the love for God's Word.

There is an interesting pattern of 22 in the Bible.

- 5 Books of the Law + 12 Books of Old Testament History + 5 Books of Wisdom = 22.

- 5 Major Prophets + 12 Minor Prophets + 5 New Testament History = 22.

- All the epistles or Christian Letters in the New Testament from Romans to Revelation total 22.

- If we categorized the books of the Bible into 3 parts, each division would contain 22 books. (66 ÷ 3 = 22.) Psalms 119 is an acrostic poem divided into 22 sections. There are 22 chapters in the Book of Revelation.

There are 22 autosome pairs or non-sex-determining chromosome pairs in the human genome. The final sex chromosome pair determines whether we are born a girl (XX) or a boy (XY).

The sun's magnetic poles reverse about every 11 years, therefore they return to the same place every 22 years (called the Hale cycle; see chapter 11).

23

23 IS THE TOTAL NUMBER OF CHROMOSOME PAIRS in a human cell.

24 is the number of chromosome pairs in apes, such as gorillas and chimpanzees. This is a big problem to evolutionists who claim that humans evolved from apes. If we did, what happened to the extra chromosome?

Evolutionists frequently get on secular TV to explain the flaws of their theories. Evolutionists now surmise that since apes have 24 chromosome pairs and humans have 23 pairs, then 1 chromosome pair must have fused. They claimed that ape chromosome number 11 and 12 probably fused into human chromosome number 2. What do they base their assertion on?

Before we examine their hypothesis, we first need to know that at the end of each chromosome is a series of repetitive DNA that protects the end of the chromosome from destruction. These protective caps are called *telomeres*. Every chromosome has 2 telomeres, one on each end. So if 2 chromosomes were to fuse (join end-on-end), we would expect to see 3 telomeres, one on each end and one in the middle. Evolutionists viewed human chromosome 2 under a microscope and saw what appeared to be 3 telomeres, two on each end and one in the middle. Voila, they claimed, that proves evolution!

The purveyors of evolution know that the majority of the public has not studied biology. They employ the media in a similar way marketing advertisers do, sending short sound bytes and stimulating pictures while leaving out crucial and opposing facts.

The first omission in the telomere argument is that ape telomeres are 24 kilobases long (a kilobase is 1,000 base pairs of DNA), whereas human telomeres are 10 kilobases long. Our telomeres differ on *every single* DNA strand, including chromosome number 2. Their argument proved nothing but the old adage, "When you're looking for something, you'll see it everywhere." They are seeing what they *want* to see.

The second omission is the known result of observed fusions, which is reduced fitness. Biochemist and neuroscientist Dr. David DeWitt summarized it best when he wrote: "Chromosome fusions can occur but are particularly messy and typically thought to reduce reproductive success due to the resulting monosomy and trisomy in the zygotes [the fertilized eggs] produced by the mating of a normal genotype [the individual with normal genes] and an individual with the fused chromosomes. Many of these types of chromosomal defects are associated with mental retardation."[1]

The third omission is the transmission problem: how would such a fusion (which tends to reduce fitness) get passed on to the entire human population? Dr. DeWitt wrote: "With no known selective advantage it is difficult to see how this fusion would become exclusively characteristic of man.... The chance of the same chromosome fusion occurring in two individuals at the same time in the same place such that they just happened to mate with one another to produce viable male and female offspring stretches credulity to breaking point."[2]

Another common argument from evolutionists is that the human genome is nearly the same as the chimpanzee genome. "We are 98 percent the same," evolutionists have cited. There are 2 major problems with this claim.

The first problem is best stated by evolutionist Steve Jones who said, "Bananas share 50 percent of our genes, but that doesn't make them half-human."[3] We should expect all of God's creation to share some of similar design because they come from the same Designer. All of Van Gogh's paintings share similar qualities, not because one painting evolved from another, but because they are all from Van Gogh.

A roller-skate and a car both have 4 wheels, but it hardly proves that a car evolved from a roller skate. They share 4 wheels because it's efficient engineering and good design. We may not know the identity of the manufacturer, but we can be certain the 4 wheels could not have arisen by chance or mindless accident. They need an intelligent designer.

Scientists have beliefs just like you and I do. Evolutionary scientists *believe* similarities prove common ancestry. Creation scientists *believe* similarities prove common Creator. What do the most recent DNA studies show? They are, in fact, overturning evolutionary assumptions that organisms with similar features are related.

In 2006 scientists discovered that *bats* and horses share a higher degree of DNA similarity than do *cows* and horses, a finding that was once again contrary to evolutionary thinking.

In 2007 the staunchly evolutionist magazine, *The New Scientist*, had to admit some key evolutionary ideas are flat wrong: "Don't bother looking at any textbook that's more than a few years old. Chances are that the tree of life you find there will be wrong.... These are turbulent times in the world of phylogeny [the study of "evolutionary relatedness" among organisms], yet there has been one rule that evolutionary biologists felt they could cling to: the amount of complexity in the living world has been on the increase. Now even that is in doubt.... The whole concept of a gradualist tree…is wrong…. Some evolutionary biologists now suggest that loss…is the key to understanding evolution…. We need to rethink the process of evolution itself."[4]

No matter how many times facts prove them wrong, few evolutionists will abandon their *belief* in evolution because evolution is a worldview. It is the dogma of a religion. Atheism is the religion and evolution is the prophet. Atheism denies God and evolution denies questioning atheism. Evolution works on children, atheism becomes lord over adults. Evolution indoctrinates atheism into children's minds with imaginary pictures, wishful tales, and computer-generated graphics. Without the artists' renditions of still missing "missing links" and fictitious life on other planets, atheism would collapse under the absurdity of its basic tenets of faith: spontaneous universe, spontaneous life, spontaneous improvement, and spontaneous intelligence,[5] none of which has ever been observed. All of these evolutionary dogmas violate observable facts in nature and in our lives, not to mention the Second Law of Thermodynamics (entropy).

The more scientific explanation is that life was created by Life, design is evidence of a Designer, intelligence was produced by an Intelligence who is communicating with us today through His Son and His written Word—the Bible.

The second problem with the 98 percent similarity claim is that the figure is highly disputed. You don't need to know much science, just enough math to know this figure is an exaggeration. Since chimpanzees have 2 extra chromosomes compared to ours, how could we be 98 percent the same genetically? The chimp genome is about 12 percent larger than the human genome. This would indicate a *maximum* of 88 percent DNA similarity from the outset, even if all other genes were identical (but we know they are not; for instance, the human Y chromosome is larger than and extremely different from the chimp's). How was 12 percent difference accounted for or ignored?

Don't let the evolutionist's use of percentages obscure the magnitude of differences. Let's assume humans and chimps differ by "only" 2 percent. That may not sound like much until you realize that it represents 60 million mutations (base pair alterations). If humans and chimps differ by at least 12 percent, that represents 360 million mutations, all of which have to *add* useful information that gives some evolutionary advantage.

Yet not 1 single genetic mutation has been proven to *add* information to the genome. All known mutations (e.g., superbug mutations) and natural selection (e.g., population shifts towards light or dark color, big beak or small beak) involves a *loss* of pre-existing information. Let me repeat: there has not been 1 observable instance of new information being added to the genome, a major problem for evolutionists. This fact has not been denied even by Richard Dawkins.[6] Evolutionists would require that something that has never been observed once to occur at least 60 million times flawlessly. Nothing but unholy imagination can bridge the gap between chimps and humans.

The truth is no matter how wide the gap between humans and chimps is found to be—whether 2 percent, 12 percent, or 20 percent—most evolutionists will not change their mind because they are emotionally committed to a *belief* that evolution is true. Even if humans were 20 percent different from chimps, most evolutionists will still shout a victory for Darwin and say, "But we are 80 percent the same!" The objective question remains: how were millions of new genetic codes added to the genome? Evolutionists have no answer. Creationists have a logical answer.

Humans did not evolve from apes. God created us with 23 chromosomes.

24

24 IS A DOUBLING OF 12. If 12 is the number of earthly government, 24 is the number of heavenly government. There are 24 elders seated around God's throne. There are 24 apostles named in the New Testament (listed below). The 12 tribes of Israel are listed 24 times in the Bible, sometimes by birth order, marching order, inheritance order, prophetic order, etc. (See chapter 13.)

There are 24 books in the Hebrew Bible. They are exactly the same books as the Christian Old Testament, but the Hebrew *Tanakh* combines Samuel I and II, Kings I and II, Chronicles I and II, Ezra, Nehemiah, and all 12 Minor Prophets into one book respectively.

Earth weighs 6×10^{24} kilograms (1 followed by 24 zeros). Thank God no matter how much we eat, the earth does not gain any weight.

There are 24 fundamental particles that cannot be broken down into smaller particles. 12 are fermions or particles associated with matter. 12 are bosons or particles that govern force. The fermions are: 6 quarks (up, down, charm, strange, top, bottom) and 6 leptons (electron neutrino, electron, muon nutrino, muon, tau neutrino, tau). Each quark and lepton also has a corresponding antiparticle but is not counted as a separate fundamental particle. The 12 bosons are: 8 kinds of gluon, 2 kinds of W boson, Z boson, and photon. All atoms are either fermions or bosons. Out of these 24 subatomic particles all of the universe is made.

We all have 24 ribs. Yes, both male and female have the same number of ribs. Even though God took Eve out of Adam's rib (Gen. 2:21–22), the rib is the *only* bone in the human body that regrows. Had Eve been taken out of any other bone in Adam's body, Adam would be missing a bone. God is not only wise, but also courteous to pick the right bone. The Bible is amazing in its scientific accuracy.

We have 24 vertebrae, divided into three sections of 7 cervical, 12 thoracic, and 5 lumbar vertebrae.

There are 24 apostles named in the New Testament. Most likely there were many more unnamed (see Romans 16:7). Some of them functioned in other offices such as that of prophet or teacher (Acts 13:1). Paul said he was "a preacher, an apostle, and a teacher of the Gentiles" (2 Tim. 1:11). Certainly all the New Testament writers qualify as both apostles and prophets (Eph. 2:20, 3:5). The original 12 apostles:

1. Simon Peter
2. Andrew, his brother
3. James, the son of Zebedee
4. John, his brother
5. Philip
6. Bartholomew, his brother
7. James, the son of Alphaeus
8. Judas, his brother
9. Matthew, the tax collector (also a son of Alphaeus, perhaps brother to James and Judas)
10. Simon Zelotes (tradition says he's also the brother of James and Judas, making possibly 4 brothers from a single family called to be apostles. Alphaeus must have been a very godly father.)[1]
11. Thomas Didymus, the twin (his twin was not an apostle)
12. Judas Iscariot (the one who betrayed Jesus)

Some theologians teach that the age of healing and miracles has been done away with the last of the 12 apostles. However, God continued to call and anoint apostles after the first 12. These continued the Gospel program of preaching, healing, and performing miracles in Jesus' name. God will not take away apostles because He gave the 5-fold ministers as "gifts to men" (Eph. 4:8–11) and "the gifts and the calling of God are irrevocable" (Rom. 11:29). The following lesser known apostles are proof that neither apostles nor healings and miracles have been done away with:

13. James, the Lord's half-brother who was head of the Church in Jerusalem, *not* Peter! (See Galatians 1:19, 2:9; James 1:1.)
14. Barnabas (See Acts 13:1–3, 14:14; 1 Corinthians 9:5–6; Galatians 2:9.)
15. Paul (See Galatians 1:1, 2:8; 1 Timothy 2:7; 2 Timothy 1:11.)
16. Andronicus, a relative of Paul saved before he was (See Romans 16:7.)
17. Junia, a relative of Paul saved before he was (See Romans 16:7.)

18. Apollos, an eloquent and well-read teacher and apostle (See 1 Corinthians 4:6–9.)

19. Silas (See 1 Thessalonians 1:1, 2:6.)

20. Timothy, Paul's son in the faith (See 1 Thessalonians 1:1, 2:6.)

21. Titus (See 2 Corinthians 8:23.)

22. Epaphroditus (See Philippians 2:25.)

23. Matthias (See Acts 1:26.)

24. Jesus, of course, is and will always be the greatest Apostle or "Sent One" (Heb. 3:1).

Though you may not know them as "apostles" by their titles, most missionaries and multiple Church planters are functioning as living apostles. Since Jesus is the same yesterday, today, and forever, since He has not changed, there is at least one apostle who continues to heal the sick and work miracles in believers' lives.

25

---

25 IS THE SQUARE OF 5 (5^2) or 5 x 5. It is a variation on 5, the number of grace. Joshua ruled Israel 25 years according to Josephus' *Antiquities 5.1.29*.

In the Parable of the Sower, Jesus compares Himself to a sower, the Word of God to a seed, and the listeners to 4 different soils. When the seed of the Word is sown into the human heart, it meets 4 types of soil: the wayside, the stony, the thorny, and the good ground. Only the good ground receives the Word of God and bears fruit. 25 is the percentage of hearers who are good ground for the Word of God.

25 percent helps us have a realistic expectation. People who expect 100 percent success are setting themselves up for disappointment. Babe Ruth, one of the greatest baseball players in history, had a batting average of .342. That meant for every 10 balls pitched, Babe Ruth swung the bat 7 times and completely missed. But he only had to hit it those 3 other times to become one of the great sports legends in the world.

Jesus' parable applies to daily life. If a baseball player hits 2.5 out of every 10 balls pitched, his batting average would be a terrific .250. A salesperson who closes 2.5 out of every 10 sales pitches would be one of the top in his or her company. (1 out of 10 would be more realistic!) A Christian who leads 2.5 out of every 10 persons to the Lord would have a level of success matching Jesus'. (Again 1 out of 10 would be superb!)

Jesus told 500 disciples to go wait for the baptism of the Holy Spirit (1 Cor. 15:6), but only 120 obeyed and got filled with the Spirit (Acts 1:15, 2:4). 120 out of 500 represents 24 percent—just shy of 25 percent.

We sometimes saddle ourselves with unrealistic expectations that only guarantee failure. Then we never step out and take a swing at life because of fear of failure.

Even if the best preacher preached, only ¼ or 25 percent will respond well to God's Word; ¾ or 75 percent will not respond. We do not need a perfect score to be a tremendous success in life!

26

26 IS THE GEMATRIA OR NUMERIC VALUE OF GOD'S NAME
YHWH. This unpronounceable Name has a special designation: the
Tetragrammaton or "4 letter word" in Greek. The 4 letters are the Hebrew
consonants *yud, hay, vav, hay.*

Gentiles add vowels in between these letters to get the Names *Yahweh* or
Jehovah. This does not mean that it is the correct pronunciation, though a
cult called Jehovah's Witnesses published that "Yahweh" is the "most likely
pronunciation."[1] The Jehovah's Witnesses are probably right in this respect,
because the letter "J" does not exist in Hebrew. So to be accurate they should be
called Yahweh's Witnesses instead. Though they do not follow their own advice,
they accuse all Christians of mispronouncing God's name as "Lord" instead of
saying "Jehovah."

Ordinary Jews would never pronounce the Tetragrammaton. They would
substitute it with *Adonai* (Lord) or *Ha Shem* (The Name). When the Temple in
Jerusalem was standing, the high priest once a year—on the Day of Atonement
(*Yom Kippur*)—pronounced the name inside the Temple. How he said it,
nobody knows.

Y	H	W	H	TOTAL
10	5	6	5	26

According to Perry Stone, the original acreage of the Temple Mount was
about 26 acres, matching God's name. No wonder it is called the Mountain of
the Lord![2]

Moses, the 26th generation from Adam, was given the *Torah* which revealed
God's covenant name *YHWH.*

27

3 X 3 X 3 = 27. There are 27 books in the New Testament, written by 8 different authors. Most of the authors were perceived as "uneducated and untrained men" (Acts 4:13) by the Pharisees, yet their writings are better preserved, more influential, and more widely read than any Jewish scholars or Greek philosophers.

Paul, the most educated of the apostles and schooled "at the feet of rabbi Gamaliel" (Acts 22:3), was the most prolific writer. God inspired him to write more New Testament epistles than anyone—14 in all if we count the Book of Hebrews (see chapter 33).

- John, the apostle of love and grace, wrote 5 of the 27 books.
- Peter wrote 2.
- Luke wrote 2.
- Matthew, Mark, James and Jude each contributed 1.

28

28 IS THE NUMBER OF THE MOON OR THE WOMAN. The moon's rotation on its axis (lunar day) and revolution around the earth (*sidereal* lunar month) are equally 27.3 days long. However, the moon takes 29.5 days to return to the same lunar phase (called *synodic* or *tropical* lunar month). The moon is as complicated as a woman to figure out!

One way to say it is it takes the moon 27.3 days to return to the same point on the sky as observed from the earth, but the moon takes 29.5 days to return to the same point on the earth as observed from the sun. So we just say the average lunar month is 28 days, which happens to be the average length of a woman's cycle.

- 28 = 7 (complete) x 4 (relationship)—signifying a completing or complementary relationship.

First Corinthians 11:11–12 says, "Neither is man independent of woman, nor woman independent of man.... For as woman came from man, even so man also comes through woman; but all things are from God."

- 280 days (40 weeks) is the length of a woman's gestation period.

30

30 IS THE NUMBER OF DEDICATION OR START OF MINISTRY. Joseph became second in command of Egypt at the age of 30 (Gen. 41:46); David became king at 30 (2 Sam. 5:4); Ezekiel became a prophet at 30 (Ezek. 1:1–2); Levites started serving at 30 (Num. 4:3, 23, 47; 1 Chron. 23:3); Jesus started ministry at 30 (Luke 3:23).

The Jews did not consider a man ready for the Sanhedrin (council of the elders) until he was 30. The height of Noah's ark was 30 cubits (Gen. 6:15). There are 30 days in a lunar month. Every month presents a new beginning to rededicate our lives and work for God afresh.

30 is the gematria of the name "Judah," the royal tribe from which Jesus' earthly parents descended. The Messiah is called the Lion of the Tribe of Judah (Rev. 5:5; Gen. 49:9–10).

30 is also the price of redemption. Judas sold Jesus for 30 pieces of silver, fulfilling a 500-year-old prophecy before Christ's death on the cross (Zech. 11:12–13; Matt. 26:15; 27:3, 9). Coincidentally, the prices of commodities (of which silver is an important one) peaks every 30 years.

Why did Jesus wait till 30 to start His ministry? There is widespread misconception that Jesus performed miracles to prove that He was God. There are 3 problems with this theory. First, why didn't He perform them at the age of 8, 18, or even 29? He could have proved He was God at any age, for He was always God even at the age of 8.

Secondly, Jesus in His earthly ministry did not display omniscience, but limited knowledge. When the woman with the issue of blood touched the hem of His garment and took healing from Him, He asked, "Who touched me?" Not only did Jesus not know who touched him, He did not even know whom He had just healed. Apparently anybody could have come to receive healing from Him. If Jesus was ministering as God, or to prove His deity, He should have displayed omniscience. He didn't. Again, Jesus displayed His humanity, not His deity, when He preached about His own Second Coming, "But of that day and hour no one knows, not even the angels in Heaven, nor the Son, but only the Father" (Mark 13:2). Why didn't Jesus know? Philippians 2:7 is a key verse to understanding so much about Jesus while He was on Earth. Here are several different translations of the same verse:

> But [Jesus] emptied Himself, taking the form of a bond-servant, and being made in the likeness of men.
> —PHILIPPIANS 2:7, NAS

> Instead, he gave up his divine privileges; he took the humble position of a slave and was born as a human being.
> —PHILIPPIANS 2:7, NLT

> But made himself nothing, taking the very nature of a servant, being made in human likeness.
> —PHILIPPIANS 2:7, NIV

> Nay, He stripped Himself of His glory, and took on Him the nature of a bondservant by becoming a man like other men.
> —PHILIPPIANS 2:7, WEYMOUTH

Jesus for 33 years lived as a man and for 3 ½ years ministered as a man. That is why He said He did not know the time of His own Second Coming. It would be wrong to assume Jesus still does not know when He now sits as the glorified Lord at the right hand of God the Father. Jesus is no longer emptied or stripped of His divine glory!

Thirdly, if Jesus performed miracles and healings to prove He was God, then Jesus failed to prove it to Nazareth. Mark 6:5 is a very important Scripture to understand, "Now He could do no mighty work there, except that He laid His hands on a few sick people and healed them." It doesn't say Jesus *would* not do mighty works. It says Jesus *could* not! Surely as God, He should be able to do whatever He wanted. But in Nazareth, He *couldn't*.

The truth is that Jesus waited till the age of 30 to perform miracles and healings because He ministered as a *man* anointed by the Spirit of God. Though He is God, His favorite title for Himself while on Earth was the "Son of Man." Why? Because, as Philippians 2:7 explains, Jesus laid aside His divine privileges and glory when He came to us.

Jesus' ministry did not prove what *God* can do. His ministry proved what a *man* anointed by the Spirit of God can do. That's why Jesus said, "He who believes in Me, the works that I do he will do also; and greater works than these he will do, because I go to My Father" (John 14:12). If Jesus ministered as God, it would be wrong for Him to say we could do the same works He did, because we are not God.

Wrong theology has stripped us of our true potential and power. God does not consider us weaklings with no ability to do defeat sin, sickness and Satan. God says the works that Jesus did, He wishes we would do also. What's our qualification? Faith in Christ and the baptism of the Holy Spirit.

Make no mistake about it, Jesus as a divine person stands in a class of His own. No one else can be like Him. Yet as a servant or a minister of the Gospel, He was not in a class by Himself. He expected His disciples to be able to do what He did and was disappointed when they underestimated their usefulness and ability. (See Matthew 8:26, 17:20, 21:21; Luke 17:6.) As a person, Jesus is to be worshiped and adored. As a minister, Jesus is to be copied and followed.

Whether at 3 years old or 30 years old, Jesus has always been God. The proof of His divinity was His words: "I and the Father are one" and "when you have seen Me you've seen the Father" and "Before Abraham was, I am" (John 10:30, 14:9, 8:58). His words are sufficient proof that He considered Himself equal with God the Father.

His healings and miracles, however, were not proofs but *examples* to us of what any believer should be able to do. As a minister, Jesus came to prove what a sinless man baptized in the power of the Holy Spirit can do. Such a believer who is filled with the Holy Spirit can defeat sin, sickness, and Satan!

30 reminds us that Jesus did not minister as God, but as a human. If you're a human, you can minister like Jesus. All you need is to believe in His blood to wash your sins away and then receive the help and power of Holy Spirit. Jesus did this at 30, but you can receive forgiveness of sins and the baptism of the Spirit any time.

33

---

33 IS THE NUMBER FOR COMPLETE WORK.

Jesus completed His earthly work at the age of 33; that's when our Lord died on the cross and rose again from the dead. He finished His life's work at a relatively young age, yet had more impact than any other person in history.

Jesus was never lost, therefore He never had to search for a way. He is *the* Way! He never searched for truth because He is the Truth. He never was sick because He is the Life. His public ministry lasted only 3 ½ years, yet no one's words are more widely known or quoted than His. Jesus privately taught religious elders at the age of 12 and saved the world at the age of 33. No life was more amazing than this!

David, as a type of Christ, reigned over the entire nation of Israel for 33 years (1 Chron. 29:27).

33 is the number of confirmed authors of the Bible. Christians often quote 40 authors of the Bible. And this may not be wrong if one counted all the visions and prophecies of Iddo, Ahijah, Shemaiah, and Jehu, which may have been used to compile Kings and Chronicles (see 2 Chronicles 9:29, 12:15, 20:34); and all the Psalms by Asaph, Heman, Ethan, and the sons of Korah. However, I can count only 33 authors who wrote whole books, not small portions of a book. These are the 33 major authors of the Bible:

1. Moses (Genesis, Exodus, Leviticus, Numbers, Deuteronomy, Job, and Psalms 90 and 91.)

2. Joshua (Joshua, the last chapter about his death could have been added by Eleazar, Phinehas, or Samuel.)

3. Samuel (Judges, Ruth, and 1 Samuel 1–24, i.e. up to his death.) Rabbis say Samuel wrote the Book of 1 Samuel chapters 1–24, while Gad continued the story of David and Nathan finished it.

4. Gad (1 Samuel 25–31 and 2 Samuel.) (See 1 Chronicles 29:25, 29.) According to 1 Samuel 22:5, Gad was a close advisor to David while he was fleeing Saul. In 2 Samuel 24, Gad remained his close advisor to the end of his life, when he bought the

threshing floor of Araunah or the present site of the Temple Mount.

5. Nathan (2 Samuel.) (See 1 Chronicles 29:29; 2 Chronicles 9:29.) According to 2 Samuel 7, Nathan was a close friend of David while he was king. David confided to Nathan his desire to build God a house. In 2 Samuel 12, Nathan was the only one who could confront David with his sin in the matter of Uriah and Bathsheba. In 1 Kings 1, Nathan was the one who encouraged Bathsheba to make sure Solomon was crowned successor. David actually named one of his sons Nathan (2 Sam. 5:14)* surely after the prophet. Nathan's two sons, Azariah and Zabud, became Solomon's closest friends (1 Kings 1:44).

6. Ezra (1 Chronicles, 2 Chronicles, Ezra, and Esther.) Ezra most likely compiled 1 Chronicles, 2 Chronicles, and either all or at least the fifth division of the Book of Psalms (i.e. no. 107–150) from public records and other authors. He may have written the post-exilic Psalms 107, 126, and 147. Ezra presided over the Great Synagogue of 120 sages who finalized the canon of the Old Testament.)

7. Nehemiah

8. David (Psalms, mostly by David; some Psalms attributed to Moses, Solomon, Asaph, Heman, Ethan, and the sons of Korah; many Psalms are "orphan" or anonymous; post-exilic Psalms could have been written by Ezra, Haggai, or Zechariah)

9. Solomon (Proverbs, Ecclesiastes, Song of Solomon, and Psalm 127.)

10. Isaiah (Isaiah, perhaps Isaiah assisted Ezra in compiling 1 Chronicles and 2 Chronicles.) (See 2 Chronicles 26:22; 32:32.)

11. Jeremiah (Jeremiah and Lamentations; 1 Kings and 2 Kings according to Jewish scholars; and probably Psalm 137 about the Exile in Babylon.)

12. Ezekiel

13. Daniel

---

* This Nathan—Solomon's older brother—is also the ancestor of Mary the Mother of Jesus (see Luke 3:31).

14. Hosea

15. Joel

16. Amos

17. Obadiah

18. Jonah

19. Micah

20. Nahum

21. Habakkuk

22. Zephaniah

23. Haggai

24. Zechariah (Zechariah, and probably Psalm 147 about the return from Exile.)

25. Malachi

26. Matthew

27. Mark

28. Luke (Luke and Acts.)

29. John (John, 1 John, 2 John, 3 John, and Revelation.)

30. Paul (Romans, 1 Corinthians, 2 Corinthians, Galatians, Ephesians, Philippians, Colossians, 1 Thessalonians, 2 Thessalonians, 1 Timothy, 2 Timothy, Titus, Philemon, and Hebrews.)

Modern theologians disagree with each other on who authored the Book of Hebrews. However, over 100 ancient writers ascribe the epistle to Paul. Typical of Paul's writing, Hebrews' message is the abolishment of the old covenant and the superiority of the new covenant. We know Paul was imprisoned in Italy (Acts 27–28); Hebrews was written from Italy (13:24). No other New Testament writer asked for prayer except Paul; the writer of Hebrews asked for prayer (13:18). No other NT writer mentioned Timothy; Hebrews mentioned Timothy (13:23). It sounds to me like Paul. And having examined the evidence, I personally have no doubt that it was Paul. Paul is considered the greatest apostle not only by virtue of his missionary activities, but also by virtue of penning 14 books of the Bible—more than any other author. Though Paul called himself the chief of sinners (1 Tim. 1:15), "one born out of due time," (1 Cor. 15:8), and the "least of the apostles" (1 Cor. 15:9), he may be a perfect example of Jesus' words, "But many who are first will be last, and the last first" (Matt. 19:30, 20:16).

(31) James

(32) Peter (1 Peter and 2 Peter)

(33) Jude

38

38 IS SIMILAR TO 40, it is the number of wandering.

Our time on this earth is called a wandering (Heb. 11:38). There are 38 individuals in the Bible whose time of wandering or natural lifespan was recorded—that is, we know their age at death and their cause of death was natural (not violent).[1]

Israel wandered an unnecessary 38 years in the desert; because by the end of the first 2 years after the Exodus, God was ready to bring them into the Promised Land. At Kadesh Barnea they sent out 12 spies and 10 came back with an evil report that made the hearts of the Israelites fearful. Only Joshua and Caleb brought back a faith report. The people sided with the majority of spies and all adults over the age of 20 perished over the next 38 years. Only Joshua and Caleb, leading a new generation, finally entered the Promised Land.

The impotent man at the pool of Bethesda was lame for 38 years (John 5:5). He was a picture of the spiritually lame nation of Israel, which was immobile in their faith and refused to follow the Messiah when He had arrived. Israel has been wandering needlessly since her Messiah has come.

There is another 38 year period not recorded in the Bible but prophesied by Jesus Christ. The Lord said because Israel failed to recognize the time of the Messiah's arrival, their enemies (the Romans) would surround them and destroy both the Temple and the city of Jerusalem.

> Now as He drew near, He saw the city [of Jerusalem] and wept over it, saying, "If you had known, even you, especially in this your day, the things that make for your peace! But now they are hidden from your eyes. For days will come upon you when your enemies will build an embankment around you, surround you and close you in on every side, and level you, and your children within you, to the ground; and they will not leave in you one stone upon another, because you *did not know the time* of your visitation.
>
> — LUKE 19:41–44, EMPHASIS ADDED

Jesus predicted Jerusalem's destruction in A.D. 32. Roman General Titus invaded and razed the city in A.D. 70, exactly 38 years after the prediction. If the Bible is merely a collection of myths penned by ordinary men, how could such men manipulate world events to fulfill prophecy and fulfill it in such a way as to fit the divine code in the Old Testament?

The Jews of Moses' day died 38 years after disbelieving his sermon that it was time for them to possess the Promised Land.

The Jews of Jesus' day perished or were deported 38 years after disbelieving His word that it was time for them to believe the Messiah. How could Jesus have manipulated the Roman invasion to occur 38 years after He died and rose again? Because such events are outside of the writers' frame of reference, we are sure that the writers were inspired by God, who knows the end from the beginning.

2 years from the Exodus was God's original and ideal waiting period before Israel entered the Promised Land. These 2 years may be prophetic. First Corinthians 10:11 tells us, "Now all these things happened to them as examples [types], and they were written for our admonition, upon whom the ends of the ages have come."

If Exodus pointed to the coming of a literal Savior (it did), and the Promised Land points to national Israel's literal salvation (it will), and the 2 years from Exodus to the Promised Land points to the waiting period for Israel to recognize her Messiah, then 2,000 years after Christ is a likely time for national Israel to be saved.

Two thousand years since Christ (our spiritual Exodus) should also mark the ideal time for the Church age (our spiritual wandering) to end and for the Millennium (our spiritual Promised Land) to begin.

39

THERE ARE 39 BOOKS IN THE OLD TESTAMENT.

Romans soldiers laid 39 stripes (lashes) on Jesus' back. Some preachers claim that there are 39 categories of diseases, in which case Jesus bore a stripe for every type of disease.

Some skeptics deny the death of Christ on the cross. They compare His crucifixion to the Filipino mock crucifixion which occurs around every Easter. These misguided souls who seem to genuinely want to get rid of their own sins do not understand that there is no penance to pay and no use of torturing the body when Jesus is our perfect substitute and only Savior. If we could save ourselves by torturing our flesh, then Jesus would not need to die for our sins. Nevertheless, the skeptics cite these Filipino examples as proof people can be "crucified" and not die.

However, the skeptics are omitting the fact that Jesus took 39 stripes on his body. The Bible tells us that His flesh was ripped off to the point that He could see some of His own bones (Ps. 22:17). History tells us that many criminals never made it to the crucifixion after such a beating. Many died on the spot. Jesus was beaten till His beard was ripped off. Jesus was severely tortured before the cross, to the degree that the soldiers had to make Simon from Cyrene carry the cross for Him so He could arrive at the crucifixion location (Mat. 27:32).

The place, date, and manner of Jesus' death were all prophesied in Scripture long ago and deliberately orchestrated to the last detail. There is no doubt that "Christ died for our sins according to the Scriptures" (1 Cor. 15:3).

The shedding of Jesus' blood was for our sins, and the beating of His body was for our sicknesses. Whenever we see the number 39, we should remember, "By whose stripes you were healed" (1 Pet. 2:24).

40

40 IS THE NUMBER OF PROBATION, TRIAL, OR TESTING. It rained for 40 days and 40 nights (Gen. 7:4, 12, 17) while Noah and his family remained safe in the ark. Moses spent the first 40 years of his life in Egypt, the next 40 years of his life in the desert of Midian, and the last 40 years of his life leading the people of Israel to the Promised Land. Moses was on Mount Sinai for 40 days. The 12 spies searched the Promised Land for 40 days (Num. 13:25); for their lack of faith Israel wandered the desert for 40 years. There are 40 chapters in the Book of Exodus; a human's gestation period is very long compared to that of most animals at 40 weeks; midlife crisis is often said to occur at 40; the U.S. economy peaks every 40 years like clockwork.[1] The Philistines controlled Israel for 40 years before God raised up Samson. Eli judged Israel for 40 years (1 Sam. 4:15–18); Goliath taunted the armies of Israel for 40 days before God sent David to accept his challenge; Saul, David, Solomon, and Joash each ruled for 40 years; Elijah's flight from Jezebel to Mount Horeb took 40 days (1 Kings 19:8); Jonah gave Nineveh 40 days to repent before their destruction (they repented!). Jesus was tempted 40 days by the devil; Jesus' post-resurrection ministry (a period of time non-Christians know little about) lasted for 40 days (Acts 1:3). These 40 days of meeting with the doubters (Mark 16:14) and showing proof to the skeptics (Luke 24:25–27) were probably some of the toughest ministry Jesus had to do. But these 40 days of mighty proofs turned both cowards and cynics into world-changing believers!

Only 3 men in Scripture are confirmed to have fasted for 40 days: Moses, Elijah, and Jesus. Only Jesus' fast can be truly counted as a complete 40-day fast, since Moses survived on the strength of God's glory and Elijah went on the strength of angels' food. Some say Joshua was a fourth person who completed a 40-day fast, because Joshua accompanied Moses up the mountain as his helper, but Joshua could have brought food. No evidence proves whether he did or didn't. If he did fast, then he would be a perfect type of Christ, sharing the exact same name (*Joshua* being Hebrew for *Jesus*), fasting the exact same period of time, and bringing victory after Moses (*Moses* representing the *Law*). Joshua came after Moses, because Moses could not bring Israel into the Promised Land. Jesus came after the Law, for the Law could not bring humanity into salvation.

"For the law was given through Moses, but grace and truth came through Jesus Christ" (John 1:17).

To the skeptic, all of these patterns of 40 could have been contrived in the sense that the Bible writers decided to use the number 40 whenever there was a test or trial. But could the writers contrive something that happened *after* their writing? Jesus warned that because of her rejection of the Messiah, Jerusalem will be sacked and her Temple leveled. 40 years passed from Jesus' warning to the time Roman General Titus destroyed Jerusalem in A.D. 70. The Temple was not spared, even though it was one of the great wonders of the ancient world, the center of Yahweh worship, and the symbol of Jewish religion. Clearly God had departed and Jesus' words were coming to pass posthumously. Could Jesus have contrived the destruction of Jerusalem and the ensuing Diaspora 40 years later?

Today a visit to Israel would confirm that the Temple was indeed destroyed, leaving only the western retaining wall or "wailing" wall where Jews continue to pray and lament God's departure from them. For nearly 2,000 years the Jews as a people have been dispersed throughout the world. Why had God forsaken them? According to the predicted cycle of judgment in Leviticus 26:14–45, Israel would be driven out of the Promised Land and dispersed among the nations as God's judgment on their rebellion. What was their act of rebellion that angered God so 2,000 years ago?

What key event happened 2,000 years ago? Everyone knows the arrival of the Messiah was so significant He literally split time in two (B.C. and A.D.) 2,000 years ago. the Messiah arrived and many of His own people rejected Him. Isaiah predicted the Jews' rejection, "He is despised and rejected by men.... We [Jews] hid, as it were, our faces from Him; He was despised, and we [Jews] did not esteem Him" (Isa. 53:3). But the Bible also predicts the national salvation of the Jews, thank God! She will one day soon recognize her own Messiah. "And one shall say unto him [Messiah], What are these wounds in thine hands? Then he shall answer, Those with which I was wounded in the house of my friends" (Zech. 13:6, KJV). In preparation for this national salvation, the nation of Israel was "reborn" in 1948, according to Ezekiel 37's "dry bone" prophecy. Exciting days are ahead of us and God's chosen people!

There is no other explanation why God's people were forsaken 2,000 years ago. When they forsook the Messiah and declared, "His blood be on us and on our children" (Matt. 27:25), they sealed their own fate. Now that they are back in the Promised Land, they must not be proud to think it was their own doing or that God has made light of their rejection of Messiah.

> Therefore say to the house of Israel, "Thus says the Lord GOD: 'I do
> *not* do this *for your sake*, O house of Israel, but *for My holy name's*
> *sake*, which you have profaned among the nations wherever you
> went. And I will sanctify My great name, which has been profaned
> among the nations, which you have profaned in their midst; and the
> nations shall know that I am the LORD,' says the Lord GOD, 'when
> I am hallowed in you before their eyes. For I will take you from
> among the nations, gather you out of all countries, and bring you
> into your own land.
> — EZEKIEL 36:22–24, EMPHASIS ADDED

Israel's return to their homeland in 1948 was not for their sake, but for God's sake. God had to keep His Word to all the prophets who had spoken in advance of this event. Despite the unfaithfulness of Israel, God remained faithful. "Let God be true and every man a liar" (Rom. 3:4).

Some Christians have mistakenly suggested the idea that the end of the world was to come in 1988, a figure they derived by adding 40 to Israel's rebirth in 1948 (1948 + 40 = 1988). 40 was supposed to represent either a generation (which is incorrect) or a period of trial (which is correct, but has no bearing on end-time prophecies).

This is certainly not the way to use God's numbers. It's an example of focusing on numbers while ignoring God's plain words, "And this gospel of the kingdom will be preached in all the world as a witness to all the nations, and then the end will come" (Matt. 24:14). The end will not come until every people group has had an opportunity to hear the Gospel in their own language. This work is nearing completion and every Christian should take the opportunity to be a part of it!

42

42 IS THE TOTAL NUMBER OF GENERATIONS from Abraham to Jesus (see Matthew 1:1–17), which was given in 3 sets of 14. 3 x 14 = 42.

6 x 7 = 42. Both 6 and 7 are significant to Jesus' first coming, as man (6) had to wait for the Messiah (7) for a period of 6 x 7 generations.

Jesus ministered on Earth for 42 months or 3 ½ years.

The Beast will blaspheme God for 42 months (Rev. 13:5).

Elijah prayed that it would not rain and it did not rain for 42 months. (See 1 Kings 17:1; Luke 4:25; James 5:17.) This period of time was given for Ahab and Jezebel to humble themselves before God and heed His prophet Elijah, but they refused to their own destruction.

46

---

46 IS THE GEMATRIA OF THE GREEK WORD FOR "MAN."

It seems more than coincidental as 46 is also the number of chromosomes in every human cell. (See chapter 23 for more.) In His wisdom God chose Greek and Hebrew for the languages of Scripture. Hidden in both these languages are mathematical codes that no one could have known at the time the Bible was written. No one can claim that Greek gematria was doctored by ancient writers because there were no geneticists in their time. Only God could have known the number of human chromosomes, and He chose Greek to be a vehicle of communicating His advanced knowledge, so that we in modern times with many modern ideas would have no reason to doubt His Word. The Bible is God speaking to us!

Just as we are constructed from 46 chromosomes, so too the Temple was constructed in 46 years. (See John 2:20.)

50

50 REPRESENTS THE HOLY SPIRIT OR PENTECOST. Pentecost is the Greek word for 50. There are 50 days between the Passover and the Feast of Weeks (Pentecost). There were 50 days between Jesus' crucifixion and the Church's baptism of fire with the Holy Spirit. There is a 50 year cycle in Jewish history, marked by a significant event in the 50th year. For instance, from the father of the State of Israel, Theodor Herzl's, first visit to Jerusalem in 1898 to the establishment of the State of Israel in 1948 was 50 years. From the British mandate to establish a national homeland of the Jews in 1917 to the capture of Jerusalem in 1967 was 50 years. According to this cycle, the next significant event is due in 2017.

There are 50 chapters in the first book of the Bible, inspired by the Holy Spirit. The Law was given on Pentecost, 50 days after the Jews were delivered out of Egypt.* (See Exodus 19.) The Church was born on Pentecost, 50 days after Jesus rose again. Note that Pentecost *always* falls on a Sunday, being "fifty days to the day *after* the seventh Sabbath" (Lev. 23:15–16, emphasis added). Therefore, the Torah was given on a Sunday, the Lord Jesus rose again on a Sunday, and the Church was birthed on a Sunday. In light of all this, Sabbatarians should not assume the majority of Christians are out of sync with God for gathering in worship on Sunday. God chose Sunday over Saturday for some very key events in His plan.

There is a teaching among Sabbatarians that worshiping on Sunday is actually the mark of the beast, which mark will condemn anyone to hell according to Revelation 14:11. This teaching persists despite Paul's injunction, "So let no one judge you in food or in drink, or regarding a festival or a new moon or *sabbaths*, which are a *shadow* of things to come, but the substance is of *Christ*" (Col. 2:16–17, emphasis added).

Contrary to Sabbatarian indoctrination, Sunday was not instituted by a Roman Emperor or Roman Pope; it was instituted by God who chose to give the Torah on a Sunday, resurrect His Son on a Sunday, and baptize the

---

* Israel left Egypt on the 14th of Nisan (the new 1st month on the religious calendar) and arrived at Sinai on the 1st day of the 3rd month. Moses was then given 3 days to prepare for meeting God and receiving the Torah, hence 50 days.

Church with Holy Spirit power on a Sunday. At the very least Sabbatarians should respect the ample Scriptural grounds on which some Christian choose to worship on a different day than they do.

There are 50 states in the United States. Trends analyst George Friedman noticed a 50-year cycle in U.S. history: "Every 50 years, roughly, the United States has been confronted with a defining economic and social crisis."[1] For example, the Great Depression of the 1930s, stagflation in 1970s, a major global shift in the 2020s. It would not surprise me if there will be a total of 50 presidents in American history, though it's not required by Scripture. Currently Barack Hussein Obama is the 44th president serving the 56th term of this office. Both founding fathers and former presidents Thomas Jefferson and John Adams died on the 50th anniversary of the signing of the Declaration of Independence, on July 4, 1826. Jefferson asked on his deathbed, "This is the Fourth?" Upon confirmation that it was, he passed away peacefully.

50 seems to be the number of the United States, possibly the most Pentecostal country in the world. Several modern Pentecostal movements trace their history back to the Azusa Street Revival of 1906 in Los Angeles, California, during which the baptism of the Holy Spirit and the Scriptural basis for praying in tongues were emphasized once again.

50 reminds us that we all need a personal Pentecost in our lives. We all need the Holy Spirit to descend on us! Let's look at some examples of Holy Ghost power on believers.

The Virgin Mary had a personal Pentecost when the Holy Spirit descended upon her and the Word of God was made flesh (Luke 1:35). She had a Pentecostal experience again when she obeyed Jesus and was among the first 120 believers to be filled with the Spirit and speak in unknown tongues.

Elizabeth, her cousin, had a personal Pentecost when Mary walked into her house and the child John the Baptist leaped in her womb and she was filled with the Holy Spirit (Luke 1:41).

The first 120 disciples had a great Pentecostal experience when "cloven tongues like as of fire…sat upon each of them. And they were all *filled* with the Holy Ghost, and began to *speak* with other tongues, as the Spirit gave them utterance" (Acts 2:3–4, KJV, emphasis added).

After Philip preached revival in Samaria, the apostles sent Peter and John to lay hands on the new born-again believers to receive the Holy Spirit. (See Acts 8.) There was such a dramatic transformation that Simon the sorcerer offered Peter and John money for the same power.

Paul had a personal Pentecost on the road to Damascus. After he was struck off his horse by blinding light, a disciple named Ananias came and laid hands on him. Apparently every Christian, not just the apostles, was able to lay hands to heal and fill others with the Holy Spirit. This ordinary disciple said, "Brother Saul, the Lord Jesus, who appeared to you on the road as you came, has sent me that you may receive your sight and be *filled* with the Holy Spirit" (Acts 9:17, emphasis added). Subsequent to Ananias' ministry through the laying on of hands, Paul was able to write, "I thank my God I *speak* with tongues *more* than you all" (1 Cor. 14:18, emphasis added). The context of chapter 14 shows Paul was *not* talking about speaking in "foreign languages" more than they did. He was talking about praying in the Spirit or praying in unknown tongues more than they did. Considering how spiritually "on fire" the Corinthian bunch was, that was a lot of praying in tongues.

Cornelius and his household were the first Gentiles to receive the Pentecostal experience. Although Peter and his men at first doubted whether Gentiles could be born again or baptized with the Spirit, they knew how to recognize the evidence of the infilling of the Holy Spirit, "For they *heard* them *speak with tongues* and magnify God" (Acts 10:46, emphasis added). With that evidence Peter was convinced!

Twelve disciples had an encounter with Paul in Ephesus. It is interesting to see how this great teacher of the Word ministered to people. Besides asking them about their salvation, Paul thought the second most important question to ask any disciple is this: "Did you receive the Holy Spirit when you believed?" (Acts 19:2). Obviously, there is a second and subsequent experience with the Holy Spirit after believing and being saved. These disciples were not sure who the Holy Spirit was, so Paul "laid hands on them, the Holy Spirit came upon them, and they *spoke with tongues* and prophesied" (v. 6, emphasis added).

Pentecost is a vital experience to intimacy with God and power over the devil. Jesus commanded the first 500 disciples to not even enter ministry until they had experienced their own Pentecost (Luke 24:49). Only 120 were obedient to show up to the Upper Room on the Day of Pentecost; but by obeying Jesus their lives and human history were changed forever.

66

6 BEING THE NUMBER OF MAN (1 less than the perfect 7), 66 is a double reminder of man's imperfection. The word *curse* appears 66 times in the Old Testament. Jacob's family fled the curse of famine and went to Egypt. How many lives were saved? Genesis 46:26 says, "All the persons who went with Jacob to Egypt, who came from his body, besides Jacobs' sons' wives, were sixty-six persons in all." 66 is the average life expectancy globally,[1] a tragically short time compared to what God originally intended for us. The Bible, God's message to man, contains 66 books: 39 in the Old and 27 in the New Testament.

The Book of Isaiah contains 66 chapters. Bible scholars have noticed that chapters 1–39 seem to differ greatly from chapters 40–66, leading some to suggest two different authors wrote the book. Such a conclusion is unwarranted because the New Testament frequently quotes Isaiah and 22 times confirms Isaiah is the author of both portions of the book.

Finnis Dake noticed this numeric symmetry and summarized it best: "Isaiah is a miniature of the Bible, having 66 chapters corresponding with the 66 books; 39 chapters in the first section dealing with law and judgment corresponding with the message of the 39 books of the OT; 27 chapters in the second section, corresponding with the 27 books of the NT both in number and message of comfort and salvation through Christst.... The theme of the last section is one of mercy, comfort, and eternal restoration under the Messiah."[2]

This kind of symmetry is yet another proof the Bible is divinely inspired. The finalization of both the Old Testament and the New Testament laid outside of Isaiah's frame of reference (he could not know there would be 39 books of the OT and 27 in the NT). Only God knew. The Jewish and Christian councils which finalized each canon were also unlikely to collude (agree to put 39 books in the Septuagint and let the Christians put 27 in the NT for prophecy's sake). God anticipated the New Testament in the Old Testament. The Book of Isaiah so powerfully points to Jesus Christ that it is sometimes known as "The Fifth Gospel."

69

PSALM 69 IS QUOTED 7 TIMES IN the New Testament by Matthew (27:34, 38), John (2:13–17; 15:18–25), and Paul (Rom. 11:7–10, 15:3; 1 Thess. 2:15–16).

69 is the number of "weeks" fulfilled so far in Daniel's 70-week prophecy. 69 weeks (69 x 7), 483 Hebrew years, 476 Gregorian years, or 173,880 days passed from Artaxerxes' command to rebuild the city Jerusalem to the arrival of the *Mashiyach Nagid* (Messiah the King). 1 more week of years remains for God to deal with the nation of Israel. This 7-year period is known by various names in the Old Testament, notably the "time of Jacob's trouble"; it is better known as the "Tribulation" in the New Testament. As Chuck Missler provocatively says, there is more written about this period of time than any other in the Bible. Please see the chapter 70 Sevens for more understanding.

70

70 IS 7 (perfection) x 10 (law) or the number of full responsibility. There were 70 elders of Israel (see Exodus 24; Numbers 11); 70 days of mourning for Jacob's death (Gen. 50:3); 70 years of Babylonian Captivity (Jer. 25:11–12; 29:10; Dan. 9:2); 70 weeks of Daniel (9:24–27); 70 parables Jesus told;[1] 70 disciples of Christ whom He sent out two by two. Genesis 10 (called The Table of Nations) lists 70 names from which sprung 70 nations (14 from Japheth, 26 from Shem, 30 from Ham). The Midrash *Tanchuma 26c* assumes there were also 70 languages at the Tower of Babel.

70 or LXX is the number of the Septuagint, the Greek translation of the Old Testament completed in 246 B.C. Legend says that 70 rabbis were locked in 70 separate rooms and came out with identical translations.

A more plausible version of the account is that Ptolemy II requested a Greek translation of the Bible. In response 72 Jewish scholars (6 from each of the 12 tribes) were sent to Alexandria, Egypt, to complete the translation. The work took about 40 years from 285–246 B.C.

The translation of the Bible into many languages is a great responsibility and was undertaken by the Church since its founding. The fact that early Bible versions in different languages match each other verifies that the Bible has not been doctored, but faithfully passed down.

70 is a very special number for Israel because Daniel was given Israel's future mapped out in 70 weeks of years (to be explained in the next chapter, "70 Sevens").

The Great Sanhedrin or the Supreme court of ancient Israel was made up of 70 members (plus 1 high priest): 24 chief priests + 24 elders of the people + 22 scribes. The first-century Sanhedrin conspired to murder Jesus and paid Judas Iscariot for help in His arrest. One of the last decisions of the Sanhedrin was the unjust trial and condemnation of Jesus. Their last binding decision was the adoption of the Hebrew calendar in A.D. 358. The Sanhedrin completely dissolved by the 5th century.

Roman General Titus burned the city of Jerusalem and destroyed the Temple in A.D. 70—the year Israel had to take full responsibility for rejecting

Messiah. Over a million Jews perished. History records not one Christian died, for believers heeded Jesus' prophecy in Luke 21.

> But when you see Jerusalem surrounded by armies [of Titus], then know that its desolation is near. Then let those who are in Judea flee to the mountains [of Edom or present-day Jordan], let those who are in the midst of her depart, and let not those who are in the country enter her [avoid Jerusalem!]. For these are the days of vengeance, that all things which are written may be fulfilled....And they will fall by the edge of the sword, and be led away captive into all nations. And Jerusalem will be trampled by Gentiles *until* the times of the Gentiles are fulfilled.
>
> —LUKE 21:20–22, 24, EMPHASIS ADDED

Jesus' words could have been easily disproven by:

1. failure of the destruction of Jerusalem;
2. failure of dispersion of the Jews;
3. failure of the Gentiles to trample on Jerusalem;
4. success of the Jews to regain full control of Jerusalem from the Gentiles.

Any of these would make Jesus' prophecy a sham. Yet the veracity of Jesus' words is unimpeachable after 2,000 years! Till now most Jews are dispersed abroad and till now Jerusalem has not been under full Jewish control. It will never be until the Jews repent of breaking the Mosaic covenant and recognize *Yeshua* as their Messiah.

70 is the number of appointed feasts the Jews were responsible to keep before the Lord. Referencing Leviticus 23, we can calculate the Lord's *Hamoyadim* or the "Appointed Times":

NUMBER OF	APPOINTED TIMES
52	Weekly Sabbaths
8	Days of Passover, Unleavened Bread and Firstfruits
1	Day of Pentecost
1	Day of Feast of Trumpets

NUMBER OF	APPOINTED TIMES
1	Day of Atonement
7	Days of Feast of Tabernacles
70 Total	Appointed Time

What's more intriguing for Bible code searchers is that if we look for the word *Hamoyadim* in equidistant letter sequencing, the word appears only once in hidden form, and on that one occasion its equidistant letter interval is exactly 70.[2]

70 is not only a special number to the Jews, but also to Christians. Jesus sent 70 disciples out with power to cast out devils and to heal (Luke 10:1–17). The Gospel program to be confirmed by God's power remains the greatest responsibility of every true disciple of Christ.

70 is a special number for the Church. Jesus taught us to forgive anyone who offends us 70 x 7 or 490 times (Matt. 18:21–22). By comparing Matthew 18 to the parallel passage in Luke 17, we find Jesus was telling Christians to forgive offenders 490 times *a day* (Luke 17:4), representing our full obligation to forgive. And why shouldn't we? God has forgiven us of our own long list of sins!

We may not feel like doing it, but we can do it by faith. That means we just say out of our mouths,

> Lord,
> I release that person. I refuse to hold a grudge or ill will against anyone. I choose to be a blessing and an example of grace. I forgive even as You forgave me. Amen!

This standard of offering forgiveness lavishly assures me of my own forgiveness in God's sight. If God expects me to forgive that much, can I not expect He will also forgive me to the same degree? According to 1 John 1:9, whenever we take full responsibility for our actions and sincerely repent for our wrongs, God is "faithful and just to forgive us our sins and to cleanse us of all unrighteousness." Since God expects us to lavishly forgive our offenders, we can be assured that God will also lavishly forgive our offenses when we repent and trust in Christ.

70

SEVENS

THE FUTURE IS BIG BUSINESS. A lot of people claim to know the future. But the world is misinformed to think that accurate prophecy is common. So I want to compare the Bible to the world's best known "prophet," Nostradamus. Born in 1503, this French astrologer published his collection of prophecies in 1555. He wrote in "quatrains," or 4-line verses, and grouped them into "centuries" or sets of 100. They purportedly foretold world events.

Nostradamus is big business. In Japan, Nostradamus has been a household name for over 2 decades. Every economic crisis seems to spawn another Nostradamus boom. Let's look at some examples:

> In the City of God there will be a great thunder,
> Two brothers torn apart by Chaos,
> While the fortress endures, the great leader will succumb,
> The third big war will begin when the big city is burning.

After the 9/11 attacks, the above quatrain was circulated on the Internet as an example of Nostradamus' foresight. Let's dispel this right off the bat. This was a hoax written by college student, Neil Marshall, to prove that the writings of Nostradamus were so cryptic that they could be shoehorned to fit almost any event.

Now let's look at a real quatrain, considered one of the best by Nostradamus believers.

> From the human flock 9 will be sent away,
> Separated from judgment and counsel:
> Their fate will be sealed on departure
> Kappa, Thita, Lambda the banished err. (I.81)

What is this about? Some claim this quatrain predicted the Challenger space shuttle disaster on January 28, 1986. How do they explain this? Thiokol, the company that manufactured the defective O-ring that is blamed for the disaster, contains the letters "TH," "K," and "L." But we have a couple of unresolved problems: there were 7 who died, not 9, and the rest is so vague as to have nothing to do with the Challenger. This is considered one of his "best."

Nostradamus' writings are full of obscure references that could mean anything. You have to work very hard to make his prophecies fit into real events. So why is he still popular? People relish Nostradamus because they are anxious to know the future and would like to have a sense of spirituality without any sense of moral accountability to a personal God. But remember this, the purpose of prophecy isn't to tantalize us, it's to prepare us for the future.

This is exactly what Bible prophecy does. By some account, one-third of the Bible is prophecy. More than half has already been fulfilled, which assures us that the rest of it will be also. No other book in the world has ever predicted the future with such accuracy. It's easy to prove the Bible is the Word of God! The greatest proof of the Bible is fulfilled prophecy.

To be fair to Nostradamus, we will pick a quatrain from the Bible—4 verses. This may be Jesus' favorite prophecy since in the Olivet Discourse (Matthew 24:15, Mark 13:14), Jesus quoted Daniel 9 and referred to the "abomination of desolation, spoken of by Daniel the prophet," as a key event to look for. Jesus quoted Daniel 9 again when he predicted the destruction of Jerusalem, 38 years before it occurred (Luke 19:41–44). This prophecy includes exact numbers which cannot be fudged and require studious calculation.

> *Seventy weeks* are determined For your people and or your holy city, To finish the transgression, To make an end of sins, To make reconciliation for iniquity, To bring in everlasting righteousness, To seal up vision and prophecy, And to anoint the Most Holy. Know therefore and understand, That from the going forth of the command To restore and build Jerusalem Until Messiah the Prince, There shall be *seven weeks* and *sixty-two weeks*; The street shall be built again, and the wall, Even in troublesome times. And after the *sixty-two weeks* Messiah shall be cut off, but not for Himself; And the people of the prince who is to come Shall destroy the city and the sanctuary. The end of it shall be with a flood, And till the end of the war desolations are determined. Then he shall confirm a covenant with many for one week; But in the middle of the week

He shall bring an end to sacrifice and offering. And on the wing
of abominations shall be one who makes desolate, Even until the
consummation, which is determined, Is poured out on the desolate.
—DANIEL 9:24–27, EMPHASIS ADDED

This little snippet of Daniel contains so many fulfilled prophecies it's mind-boggling—from God's plan to save the world from sin, to the Messiah's first coming, to the Messiah's execution, to the Romans' destruction of Jerusalem. It also contains unfulfilled prophecies such as the future rise of the Anti-Christ.

For the purpose of this chapter, we will concentrate on one facet of this prophecy: the timing of the first coming of Christ. God told Daniel exactly how many "week of years" till God would come to Earth and save mankind from sin.

The Bible tells us, "Let him who has understanding calculate" (Rev. 13:18). Let us who have understanding of God's plain words calculate the numbers God gave us in this prophecy.

First, you may be confused about the term "week of years" or 7 years. Don't be! While it may seem strange to our ears, to Jewish ears a week may mean 7 days, 7 months, 7 years, or even 7 thousand years. God has a right to use the term week in this way since He's the One who invented it! A *shavua* in Hebrew simply means a unit of "seven."

TYPES OF WEEK	BIBLICAL REFERENCES
Week of days	Genesis 29:27, Leviticus 23:16, 25
Week of months	Exodus 12:2, Leviticus 23:24 Nisan to Tishri is a week of months
Week of years	Leviticus 25:4–5, 26:34, Deuteronomy 15, Exodus 23:10–11, 2 Chronicles 36:19–21, Jeremiah 25:9–12, 29:10

The context tells us what kind of "week" is referred to. At the start of Daniel chapter 9, Daniel was praying about the 70-year-long captivity in Babylon. Leviticus 26:33–35, written about a thousand years before Daniel's time, predicted that if the Jews did not rest the land for 1 year out of every week of years (every 7 years), they would be exiled so that the land could enjoy its yearly sabbaths. The Jews had neglected to obey this command since the time of King David till the time of Jeremiah or for 70 weeks of years (490 years).

Therefore how much backdated rest did the Jews owe God? 490 years ÷ 7 years = 70 years. That's a major reason why God had removed the Jews out of the land of Israel for 70 years—to give the land rest while they were captives in

Babylon. When the 70-year period was up, Daniel prayed about going home to the Promised Land.

In Daniel's mind, when this cycle of 490 years was up, and the 70 years of rest were paid for, they would be free from Gentile oppression and the end would come. The Messiah would arrive. In this context, the angel Gabriel was sent to Daniel to give him good news and "bad" news: the 70 years of rest owing on the 70 weeks of disobedience were up, and the Jews would be allowed to go home. However, the Messiah was not coming yet. There would be another cycle of "70 sevens" or 490 years in which God would further deal with Israel. Clearly the context proves that all of Daniel 9 was speaking of weeks of years, not days.

Daniel 9 so accurately pinpointed the first coming of Christ that Jewish rabbis are prohibited from calculating this prophecy, lest they find out Messiah has come and overthrow the faith of some. Now with more light, let's review this prophecy.

> *Seventy weeks* [490 years] are determined for your people [the Jews] and for your holy city [Jerusalem], to finish the transgression, to make an end of sins [a magnificent claim...has Someone come to end sins?], to make reconciliation for iniquity [has Someone reconciled the world to God?], to bring in everlasting righteousness [has Someone come to make us the righteousness of God?], to seal up vision and prophecy, and to anoint the Most Holy [referring to the holy of holies in the rebuilt temple, which will be anointed by the Messiah in His Second Coming]. Know therefore and understand, that from the going forth of the command to restore and build Jerusalem until Messiah the Prince, there shall be *seven weeks* and *sixty-two weeks* [69 weeks or 483 years]; the street shall be built again, and the wall, even in troublesome times [Nehemiah rebuilt the wall in troublesome times]. And after the *sixty-two weeks* Messiah shall be cut off [Messiah will be executed. Something most Jews have yet to understand], but not for Himself [not for His own crime or sin, but for our crimes and sins]; and the people of the prince who is to come [Roman General Titus] shall destroy the city [Jerusalem] and the sanctuary [the temple was destined to be destroyed after the Messiah *had come*. In other words, the Messiah must come before the temple was destroyed. When was the temple destroyed? In A.D. 70! This authenticates Jesus' claim to be Messiah and invalidates all other claims by 19th, 20th, and 21st-century

charlatans who call themselves the Messiah.] The end of it shall be with a flood, and till the end of the war desolations are determined. [Western humanists have predicted global peace without God, through science or philosophy or politics, but the Bible predicted an increase of wars until the end. God knows human nature and unless it is changed through the new birth, it is violent.] Then he [the Anti-Christ] shall confirm a covenant [a treaty or resolution about Israel] with many for one week [7 years]; but in the middle of the week [3 ½ years into the treaty] he shall bring an end to sacrifice and offering [he will break his word, turn against the Jews, and end their temple sacrifices]. And on the wing of abominations shall be one who makes desolate, even until the consummation, which is determined, is poured out on the desolate.

—Daniel 9:24–27, emphasis added

Again the term "abomination of desolation" may be unfamiliar to our ears, but familiar to Jesus' audience and to Jews today. It refers to an event that is recounted every year to Jewish children at the Feast of Hanukkah. It refers to the act of a Greek king, Antiochus Epiphanes IV, offering a pig on the altar of God and erecting the statue of Zeus in the Temple of God on his birthday in 167 B.C. This vile act, which occurred once in history, is due to occur again in the middle of the Tribulation. This prophecy, by the way, assumes a Jewish temple will be rebuilt on the Temple Mount, where the Dome of the Rock currently stands. This is a temple the Anti-Christ will consent to be rebuilt. This will not be the millennial Temple Ezekiel prophesied of and Jesus will commission and oversee.

Let's now focus on the math in verses 24 and 25: "Know therefore and understand, that from the going forth of the command to restore and build Jerusalem until Messiah the Prince, there shall be seven weeks and sixty-two weeks [69 weeks]; the street shall be built again, and the wall, even in troublesome times. And after the [period of] sixty-two weeks Messiah shall be cut off, but not for Himself."

These words were written 500 years before Christ. Even before calculating the math, we can tell this is going to be one of the most exciting predictions. By it, if we had lived 2,500 years ago, we could have anticipated: (1) the Messiah would come soon, (2) He would die, and (3) He would die not for Himself or for His own sins, but He would die for the sins of the world!

If it were us living during that time, we would naturally ask, "When will the Messiah come?" This was a matter of simple calculation.

Daniel said counting from the decree to rebuild Jerusalem to the time the Messiah shall be cut off (crucified), there would be 69 weeks of years or 69 x 7 years or 483 Hebrew years. A Hebrew year has 12 equal months of 30 days or 360 days in a year. Here is the math: 69 weeks x 7 years = 483 lunar years; 483 lunar years x 360 days = 173,880 days until the Messiah would come.

The starting date from which to count down God's prophetic clock was the decree to rebuild the ruined city of Jerusalem (not the Temple as some Bible teachers mistakenly suppose). 4 decrees are recorded in the Bible.

DECREE BY	DATE	REFERENCE
Cyrus the Persian	537 B.C.	Ezra 1:2–4
Darius the Mede	515 B.C.	Ezra 6:1–12
Artaxerxes Longimanus	458 B.C.	Ezra 7:11–26
Artaxerxes Longimanus	445 B.C.	Nehemiah 2:5–18

Ezra, being a priest, was interested in the decrees to rebuild the Temple. Nehemiah, being a government official, was interested in the decree to rebuild the city walls. This is the decree which triggered the countdown to Christ's coming. Sir Robert Anderson, once head of Scotland Yard and knighted by Queen Victoria, documented in his book *The Coming Prince* (1894) that the decree was given by Artaxerxes on the 14th of March 445 B.C.[3] Starting from this date and counting 173,880 days brings us to the 6th of April A.D. 32, the very day of the Jewish Passover for that year and the exact date Jesus was executed.

March 14, 445 B.C. + 173,880 days = April 6 or 10 Nisan A.D. 32

10 Nisan A.D. 32 was the day Jesus entered Jerusalem as her humble King riding on a donkey. It happened to be the day when the rabbis inspected the lamb that would be sacrificed 4 days later. Jesus also happened to be crucified 4 days later on 14 Nisan A.D. 32. There was no margin of error in God's prophecy. For those who knew math, there was no question Jesus was due to appear at the time that He did, 483 lunar years after 445 B.C.

Daniel's 70-week prophecy is not finished. Since the 69 weeks have been fulfilled, there has been a 2,000-year pause for the Church age. Just like the clock in a basketball game can pause for substitution or half-time, God's prophetic clock has paused to let the nations come into the kingdom. When the fullness of the Gentiles has come in, God will restart the clock to count down 1 last week or 7 years, during which He will deal with His chosen people the

Jews. We know God is preparing to deal with Israel because He "rebirthed" the nation on May 14, 1948. Never before has any nation disappeared off the face of the earth and re-appeared 2,000 years later with its religion, culture, and language intact! We know based on this and other signs that the 70th week of Daniel is approaching. We are witnesses of Bible prophecy unfolding before our very eyes!

THE LAW OF DOUBLE REFERENCE

Daniel's 70-week prophecy accurately foretold the timing of Christ's first coming. This explains why the first-century magis came from Persia to offer gifts to the child Jesus. How did they know? Daniel used to live in Persia and was one of the most powerful statesmen in the empire; therefore his prophecies and teachings would have been well circulated. As a prophet he would have been interested in teaching others. These magis came at the right time because they must have studied and calculated Daniel's prophecy. The irony is while the Gentiles came looking for a Jewish king as a result of a Jewish prophecy, so many Jews were oblivious to the arrival of their own Messiah.

Can Daniel's 70-week prophecy tell modern Jews the timing of the Tribulation or the Second Coming of Messiah? Can Daniel's prophecy be applied twice?

There is a rule of Bible interpretation called the "law of double reference." It states that Biblical prophecy will not only be fulfilled, but it may be fulfilled twice or even multiple times. Examples are replete in the Bible. For instance:

Scriptures about the "abomination of desolation" (Dan. 9:27, 11:31, 12:11) will have been fulfilled twice: once by Antiochus Epiphanes IV in 167 B.C.; a second time by the Anti-Christ (Matt. 24:15).

Scriptures about the forerunner to the Messiah (Isa. 40:3; Mal. 4:5) will have been fulfilled twice: once by John the Baptist who came in the spirit and power of Elijah (John 1:23; Matt. 11:14); a second time by Elijah himself as one of the two witnesses in the future (Mark 9:11–12; Rev. 11:3–12).

Scriptures about the Messiah's appearance will have been fulfilled twice (Isa. 9:6–7; 61:1–2): once at Jesus' first coming; twice at Jesus' Second Coming.

Scriptures about Israel's return to their homeland have been fulfilled twice: once by Cyrus' decree to permit Jews in the Babylonian Captivity to go home starting from 537 B.C.; and again by the Aliyah (migration) before and after the Israel's independence in 1948. (See 1 Kings 8:34; Isaiah 43:6, 51:11; Jeremiah 25:12, 29:10, 30:3, 31:23; Amos 9:14.)

Therefore it should come as no surprise to us who understand the "law of double reference" that Daniel 9 may be fulfilled twice: once by the first coming;

a second time by His future coming. Just as the prediction of the First Coming was mathematically accurate, so too a prediction of the Messiah's return should be similarly accurate. Remember precise prophecy from God isn't meant to impress us, but to prepare us.

We shall revisit Daniel's prophecy again in the second to last chapter on 2020 and Beyond. Your patience will be rewarded!

72

72 IS A VERY USEFUL NUMBER IN FINANCE. People are interested in knowing how long it will take to double their investment. Bankers and brokers use the "rule of 72." The simplest way to estimate how long it will take to double your investment at a given interest rate is to divide 72 by the interest rate. The quotient represents the number of years it will take for your money to double.

For instance, if your investment gives you 5 percent interest, then it would take 72 divided by 5 or 14.4 years to double your money.

How many years would it take for your property to double in value? It depends on your rate of return. Some investors estimate that property value in Australia doubles every 7 years. That would be possible if the rate of return was an average of 10 percent, as 72 divided by 10 is 7.2 years.

The rule of 72 works whether you want to find out the number of years or the interest rate required to double your money. You can find out the interest rate needed to double your money by dividing 72 by the number of years in your investment time horizon. Say you were going to retire in 15 years and you planned to double your savings by then. What rate of return would allow you to reach your goal? Divide 72 by 15 years and you get 4.8 percent.

If you saved a percentage of your income (a practice the Bible recommends) and invested it consistently, it would actually not take a lot of financial skill or time to double your wealth. Remember the rule of 72!

Coincidentally, there were 72 rabbis who translated the Hebrew Scriptures into the Greek Septuagint. I wonder if it was an insightful Jew who made up the rule of 72!

74

74 IS THE NUMBER OF ANCESTORS OF JESUS from Adam to Joseph, according to Luke's genealogy. Luke's Gospel is written to a mainly Gentile audience and is interested in showing that Jesus is related to Adam and qualifies to be the Savior of the world.

Matthew's Gospel is different because it is mainly targeted to a Jewish audience and interested in proving that Jesus is related to the Jewish patriarchs and kings and qualifies to be the Jewish Messiah. Therefore Matthew starts from Abraham, continues through David's royal lineage, skipping 6 evil kings: Ahaziah, Joash, Amaziah, Joahaz, Jehoiakim, and Zedekiah, the last king of Judah before the Babylonian Captivity.* By Matthew's reckoning there were 42 generations from Abraham to Jesus (see chapter 14).

Contrary to the millions of years and hundreds of thousands of generations assumed by evolution believers, God counts only 74 people from the creation of Adam to the coming of Christ. Given this timeline, one can see how accurate information about God could be directly passed down to us through 74 people, some of whom were the godliest people who ever walked the face of the earth.

---

* Zedekiah, being an uncle of Jehoiachin and not the father, should not be counted any way.

80

80 IS A PRODUCT OF 8 (LIFE) AND 10 (LAW) and is a number associated with life under law. A Torah scroll is made of 80 skins of kosher animal. Human cells which have the ability to reproduce themselves can only do so 80 to 90 times in a lifespan. Why not more is a mystery of aging. According to the CIA's World Factbook (2010 estimates), the average human lifespan in the top 145 out of 223 countries and territories ranges between 70 and 80 years old.

The top 10 countries with the longest living citizens are Macau (average of 84 years old), Andorra (82.5), Japan (82), Singapore (82), Hong Kong (81.9), Australia (81.6), Canada (81.2), France (81), Sweden (80.9), and Switzerland (80.9). Even Iraqis, at number 145, live on average till 70. The bottom country is Angola (38.2).[1]

Many Christians have heard the teaching that God has given us 70–80 years to live. It comes from Psalm 90:10 (emphasis added).

> The days of our lives are seventy years; and if by reason of strength they are eighty years, yet their boast is only labor and sorrow; for it is *soon cut off*, and we fly away.

This is poor Bible interpretation. Most Bible students should know this rule: A text out of context is a pretext (for anything you wish it to say). We must keep Scriptures in their context. There are 5 contexts to consider: the immediate verses before and after, the same book, the same author (if he wrote other books we can compare with), other books in the same Testament, and the entire Bible. Here is the immediate context of Psalm 90:

> For we have been consumed by Your *anger*, and by Your *wrath* we are terrified. You have set *our iniquities* before You, our secret *sins* in the light of Your countenance. For all our days have passed away in Your *wrath*; we finish our years like a sigh. The days of our lives are seventy ears; and if by reason of strength they are eighty years, yet their boast is only labor and sorrow; for it is *soon cut off*, and we fly away.
>
> —PSALM 90:7–10, EMPHASIS ADDED

The context tells us God is not defining the ideal age humans should live, but the shortness of sinners' lives which are cut short by their sins.

Let's look at the author's context. Who wrote Psalm 90? It was not King David. In my Bible, there is a note under Psalm 90 which reads, "A Prayer of Moses." This is one of 2 Psalms written by Moses, and chronologically the oldest Psalm. What was Moses writing about?

The author's context is found in Numbers 14. Because of the unbelief of the 10 spies, all Jewish refugees above the age of 20 were sentenced to die in the wilderness without seeing the Promised Land. Most were dying at 70 to 80 years of age.

To apply this to all believers is a misapplication of Scripture. Moses was *lamenting* the fact that believers were dying so young, not living out their full age. What was the potential? Look at the godly men of the same generation. Moses at 80 was just starting out in ministry; he died at 120 (Deut. 34:7). Aaron his elder brother died at 123. Joshua died at 110 (Josh. 24:29). Caleb at 85 was just starting his conquest of the Promised Land. If he had lived another 25 years after the conquest, he would have also died around 110.

70–80 years of age applied only to the rebellious Israelites during the wilderness wandering. This verse in Psalm 90:10 was never intended to be the maximum life span of a Christian or the definition of a human generation. The ideal life span for man is defined in another book written by Moses:

And the LORD said, "My Spirit shall not strive with man forever, for he is indeed flesh; yet his days shall be *one hundred and twenty years.*
—GENESIS 6:3, EMPHASIS ADDED

This was, of course, the age Moses attained with perfect body and perfect eyesight. He climbed a mountain before he passed away! It is also the age of the oldest man in modern times, a certain *Shigechiyo Izumi* from Japan, who died in 1986 at the age of 120.

A broader context in which to interpret Psalm 90 is to look at other Scriptures concerning the same topic of aging. We find a relevant passage in Psalm 91, often called the great Psalm of protection. This was the second Psalm penned by Moses.

Because he has set his love upon Me, therefore I will deliver him; I will set him on high, because he has known My name. He shall call upon Me, and I will answer him; I will be with him in trouble;

I will deliver him and honor him. With *long life* I will *satisfy* him,
And show him My salvation.

—PSALM 91:14–16, EMPHASIS ADDED

God has given us a promise of longevity. You can live until you are "satisfied." If you reach 70 and are not satisfied, keep on living and serving God. If you reach 80 and are still not satisfied, keep on going. People don't stop and think about how these Scriptures apply to them. Instead they listen to secular news and live by worldly expectations. How long you want to live is really your choice. The Book of Proverbs tells us there are things we can do to "shorten" our days or "lengthen" our days.

To correctly interpret Psalm 90:10 its meaning must harmonize with the rest of Scriptures such as Psalm 91 and Philippians 1.

But if I live on in the flesh, this will mean fruit from my labor; yet *what I shall choose* I cannot tell. For I am hard-pressed between the two, having a desire to depart and be with Christ, which is far better. Nevertheless to remain in the flesh is more needful for you. And being confident of this, I know that *I shall remain* and continue with you all for your progress and joy of faith.

—PHILIPPIANS 1:22–25, EMPHASIS ADDED

Some people get the idea that "when it's time it's time" or "when you're number's up, you have to go." But the Bible tells us that Paul had a choice. Paul could choose to go, or he could choose to stay. At the time of writing the Book of Philippians while he was sitting in jail, Paul chose to stay as it was "more needful" for the believers. Paul's ministry was certainly a blessing and because he stayed, we today can enjoy the additional books he wrote: Titus and 1st and 2nd Timothy.

My Irish great-grandmother died at the age of 104. My Italian great-grandfather died at 96. My Thai great-grandmother died at 99. Don't let the devil rob you of your full potential. You can live to at least 80 and beyond. Believe God's Word, "With *long life I will satisfy him*, and show him my salvation."

92

92 IS THE NUMBER of naturally occurring elements on the earth. In other words, there are only 92 kinds of atoms on Earth. Why then do we have millions of different substances?

The answer is most atoms are unstable, so they must bond with other atoms in different combinations to become more stable. I think there is a lesson there for all of us. The Bible says:

> Two are better than one, Because they have a good reward for their labor. For if they fall, one will lift up his companion. But woe to him who is alone when he falls, For he has no one to help him up. Again, if two lie down together, they will keep warm; But how can one be warm alone? Though one may be overpowered by another, two can withstand him. And a threefold cord is not quickly broken.
> —ECCLESIASTES 4:9–12, EMPHASIS ADDED

Three, as we have already discovered, is a very important number. God is a Trinity. Many combinations of 3 become very strong or very important. When 1 oxygen atom (O) combines with 2 hydrogen atoms (H), it becomes water (H_2O). When 1 carbon atom (C) combines with 2 oxygen atoms (O), it becomes carbon dioxide (CO_2), the molecules plants breath and we exhale.

There are millions of combinations 92 elements can make. It's amazing how much variety God produces from just a few atoms!

120

120 IS A MULTIPLE OF 12 (GOVERNMENT) AND 10 (LAW), representing a great assembly.

The Talmud says that there were 120 scribes, sages, and prophets in the Great Assembly which completed the canon of the Old Testament. The Jewish name for this group of men was the "Great Knesset," from which the modern Israeli parliament gets its name and number. (However, unlike the original Knesset, the modern one is made up of mainly secular politicians.)

Who were the members of the Great Synagogue? Among the 120 were Ezra (the president of the group), Nehemiah, Zerubbabel, Joshua the high priest (not Joshua the successor of Moses), Mordecai (Esther's older cousin and adoptive father), Daniel, Shadrach, Meshach, Abednego, Haggai, Zechariah, and Malachi (the last 3 prophets of the Old Testament). These men decided to include the books of Ezekiel, Daniel, Esther, the 12 Minor Prophets, Haggai, Zechariah, and Malachi in the Bible.

It is amazing to realize that all these great men were contemporaries! These were the days after the 70-year exile in Babylon and leading up to the first coming of the Messiah. God knew He had a lot to do to prepare the nation of Israel for His Son. So God called many great men to accomplish great works before Jesus could come.

After 70 years of Babylonian captivity, exactly as God promised, King Cyrus of Persia issued a decree allowing Jews to go home. The Jewish captives returned in 3 major waves.

1. The first wave and biggest wave of 42,360 Jews was under Zerubbabel (Ezra 2:64). (See also Ezra 1–6.) The return was necessary as it brought back the ancestors of Jesus (Mary and Joseph's family). Zerubbabel was a common ancestor of both Joseph (Matt. 1:12–13) and Mary (Luke 3:27).* He started the

---

* Mary was related to King David through his son Nathan. Joseph was related to King David through his son Solomon. However, both these lines reunited in the person of Zerubbabel as both Joseph and Mary are related to Zerubbabel. Since his father Shealtiel/Salathiel came from Solomon, that means his mother had to come from Nathan.

rebuilding of God's Temple (which Jesus had to walk into to present Himself as Messiah).

2. The second wave of 1,754 Jewish men, not counting their wives and children, was under Ezra (Ezra 8:1–14). (See also Ezra 7–10.) While Zerubbabel was rebuilding the Temple, Ezra was rebuilding the spiritual vitality of the people. The Jews had to be prepared to understand the Bible and recognize their Messiah. Without this Biblical teaching and spiritual revival, the early apostles and disciples would not have so readily followed the Messiah.

3. The third wave was under Nehemiah (Neh. 1–13). Though the people had put away their foreign wives and experienced a short-lived revival, the city of Jerusalem was vulnerable and unprotected. Nehemiah, cup-bearer to King Artaxerxes of Persia, became God's wall builder. Nehemiah's efforts to rebuild the wall were fiercely opposed by Sanaballat the Horonite, Tobiah the Ammonite, and Geshem the Arab, indicating to us the groups of people who will also oppose Christ's Second Coming. Yet the rebuilding was complete, with a shovel in one hand and a sword in the other, in 52 days.

The preparation for Jesus' first coming could not be completed by priests, statesmen, and tradesmen alone. God had to call 3 more prophets to finish the work: Zechariah, Haggai, and Malachi.

Temple rebuilding had begun amid great excitement in 537 B.C. But early enthusiasm waned, and years later the Temple remained unfinished. God sent Haggai to tell them, "Finish what you started! Put My house first!" Haggai emphasized the natural side of giving and building a house for God.

> Now therefore, this says the Lord of hosts: "Consider your ways! You have sown much, and bring in little.... And he who earns wages, earns wages to put into a bag with holes." Thus says the Lord of hosts: "Consider your ways!...You looked for much, but indeed it came to little, and when you brought it home, I blew it away. Why?" says the Lord of hosts. "Because of My house that is in ruins, while every one of you runs to his own house.
>
> —Haggai 1:5–9

Notice that the poverty they were experiencing was not God's doing. It was not God's way. Twice Haggai said, "Consider your ways!" What had they done wrong financially? They had put the building of their own houses above that of God's house. God was not against them living in nice houses; in fact, God had promised them good houses and lands. But it was a matter of priority. The people had put themselves and their families before God's plan. By prioritizing their job over God's ministry, they worked hard but had little to show for it. It was as if they were putting all their money in a bag with holes in it. God wanted them to put Him first and allow Him to bless them materially.

God then commissioned Zechariah to join Haggai in motivating the people to prioritize God's house. As a great encourager, Zechariah told them the Temple will be no ordinary building, but will house the Messiah Himself. Zechariah emphasized the spiritual side of preparing God's house. All hands on deck, for the King is coming!

> Rejoice greatly, O daughter of Zion; shout, O daughter of Jerusalem: behold, thy King cometh unto thee: he is just, and having salvation; lowly, and riding upon an ass, and upon a colt the foal of an ass. [Jesus' royal yet humble entry into Jerusalem.]
>
> —ZECHARIAH 9:9, KJV

> And one shall say unto him, What are these wounds in thine hands? Then he shall answer, Those with which I was wounded in the house of my friends. [Jesus' crucifixion described 500 years ahead of time.]
>
> —ZECHARIAH 13:6, KJV

Finally, God called Malachi to finish the job. The exiles who had returned soon lapsed into their old ways: the priests dishonored God's sacrifices, offering the blind, lame, and sick lambs (which misrepresented Jesus); the men divorced their wives and married unbelievers; the people refused to bring their tithes and to serve God. They scoffed at the suggestion of serving God (3:14). Malachi assured them that the God of judgment was coming (2:17). Malachi reminded them that the Messiah must present Himself in the completed Temple (3:1). Malachi told them that before Messiah comes, one will come in the spirit of Elijah to pave the way! (3:1, 4:5) After this last warning, 400 years of silence fell on Israel.

No more prophetic voice was heard until a man named John, dressed in camel's hair and a leather belt, was shouting in the desert, "Repent, for the kingdom of Heaven is at hand!" (Matt. 3:2); and "Behold! the Lamb of God who takes away the sin of the world!" (John 1:29).

120 reminds us that God likes to call a team of very different people to fulfill His plan. Ezra was a priest whose main concern was the Temple and spiritual revival. Nehemiah was a government official whose main concern was the wall and natural order. In motivating people to complete the Temple, Haggai emphasized the importance of financial priority and stewardship—the natural side. Zechariah emphasized the importance of believing and preparing for the Messiah—the spiritual side.

When I think of Zerubbabel, Ezra, Nehemiah, Haggai, Zechariah, and Malachi all living at the same time and all called to prepare people for Jesus' first coming, I get excited to think of how many great men and women are alive right now and called to prepare people for the Second Coming of Christ. No matter how different your gift or call is from others, the 120 prove that you too can be used of God. It's amazing to be alive *together* at this hour!

120 is a number associated with fullness, especially the obedient saint's full blessing. God gave man the potential to live to a ripe old age of 120 years (Gen. 6:3; see chapters 80 and 2020 and Beyond); Moses died at 120, having faithfully completed his ministry (Deut. 34:7); Hiram sent David 120 talents of gold (1 Kings 9:14); the Queen of Sheba gave Solomon 120 talents of gold; Solomon sacrificed 120,000 sheep at the dedication of the Temple (2 Chron. 9:9); 120,000 children were spared by Jonah's preaching and Nineveh's repentance (Jon. 4:11); the Temple was 120 cubits tall (2 Chron. 3:4); 120 priests worshiped God when the glory fell on Solomon's Temple (2 Chron. 5:11–14); 120 disciples were praying in the upper room when the Holy Spirit fell on the first Church (Acts 1:14–15, 2:1–4).

All 120, including Mary the mother of Jesus, spoke in tongues on the Day of Pentecost. When I was a child, I was sent to a Catholic school and forced to attend Catholic mass. I did not understand much back then, but today I am confident that I now believe in Mary more than most Catholics do. I've followed Mary into the upper room and been filled with the Holy Spirit like she was. And I can speak in tongues like she did, too! Let's all follow the 120 into the fullness of the Holy Spirit's power.

144

144 IS THE 12TH NUMBER IN THE FIBONACCI SERIES (1, 1, 2, 3, 5, 8, 13, 21, 34, 55, 89, 144) and is a product of 12 x 12. There are 1,440 minutes in a day.

Biblically speaking, 144 seems to represent spiritual protection. There will be 144,000 Jews (12,000 from 12 tribes) who will be protected from the Anti-Christ and called by God to evangelize during the Tribulation.

There is a major Christian cult called Jehovah's Witnesses, whose founder, Charles Taze Russell, built a lot of doctrines around this number 144,000.

Back in the 1840s, "Pastor" Russell claimed that only he and his followers belong to the chosen group of 144,000 or the "Anointed Class." This meant that only 144,000 Jehovah's Witnesses could go to Heaven. A problem arose by the 1930s when membership to the Jehovah's Witnesses' Kingdom Halls outgrew 144,000.

Russell's successor, Joseph Franklin Rutherford, revised the doctrine by announcing a spiritual segregation. From 1935 on, there would be 2 classes of Christians from among the Jehovah's Witnesses: 144,000 belonging to the "Little Flock," an elite group who will go to Heaven; the rest belonging to the "Great Crowd," an earthly class of Christians who will enjoy "Paradise Earth."

This spiritual apartheid is why on their pamphlets and magazines, which they leave door-to-door, their covers often show colorful pictures of children hugging pandas and other cute earthly creatures. Most Jehovah's Witnesses have no hope of ever going to Heaven. Ask them, "Are you born again?" and they will tell you, "No!" Ask them, "Are you allowed to take communion?" and they will tell you, "No!"

During a Kingdom Hall service, the majority of Jehovah's Witnesses cannot partake of communion, which Jesus gave to every believer (see John 6:53). That privilege is reserved exclusively for a member of the 144,000. Even though their worldwide membership has grown to about 15 million, there are only about 8,000 who will go to Heaven and can have communion.

One must ask, "What ever happened to Jesus' words: There shall be *one* fold, and *one* shepherd?" (John 10:16, emphasis added). Did Jesus go through all the trouble of reconciling both Jews and Gentiles to Himself (Eph. 2:14–16), so that "there is neither Greek nor Jew, Barbarian [nor] Scythian" (Col. 3:11), only to reinstate a spiritual apartheid among the Jehovah Witnesses?

Before anyone persuades you who are the 144,000, why not see for yourself what the Bible actually says about the 144,000?

> And he [an angel from the east] cried with a loud voice to the four angels to whom it was granted to harm the earth and the sea, saying, "Do not harm the earth, the sea, or the trees till we have sealed the servants of our God on their foreheads." And I heard the number of those who were sealed. One hundred and forty-four thousand *of all the tribes of* the children of *Israel* were sealed:
>   of the *tribe of Judah* twelve thousand were sealed;
>   of the *tribe of Reuben* twelve thousand were sealed;
>   of the *tribe of Gad* twelve thousand were sealed;
>   of the *tribe of Asher* twelve thousand were sealed;
>   of the *tribe of Naphtali* twelve thousand were sealed;
>   of the *tribe of Manasseh* twelve thousand were sealed;
>   of the *tribe of Simeon* twelve thousand were sealed;
>   of the *tribe of Levi* twelve thousand were sealed;
>   of the *tribe of Issachar* twelve thousand were sealed;
>   of the *tribe of Zebulun* twelve thousand were sealed;
>   of the *tribe of Joseph* twelve thousand were sealed;
>   of the *tribe of Benjamin* twelve thousand were sealed.
> —REVELATION 7:2–8, EMPHASIS ADDED

The Holy Spirit anticipates every false doctrine before they occur. Lest any Jehovah's Witness should be deceived to think they are part of the 144,000, God recorded not only that they are all Jews, God also specified the tribes of their descent. (Dan is excluded, see chapter 13).

Ask any Jehovah's Witness which Hebrew tribe they come from and they will tell you, "I don't know," or, "It's spiritual." Could God be more unambiguous than to count the numbers and names of the tribes: exactly 12,000 from each 12 tribes of Israel?

Look furthermore to see what the Book of Revelation says about the 144,000:

> Then I looked, and behold, a Lamb standing on Mount Zion, and *with Him* one hundred and forty-four thousand, having *His Father's name* written *on their foreheads*. And I heard a voice from Heaven,

like the voice of many waters, and like the voice of loud thunder. And I heard the sound of harpists playing their harps. They *sang* as it were a *new song* before the throne, before the four living creatures, and the elders; and *no one could learn* that *song* except the hundred and forty-four thousand who were redeemed from the earth. These are the ones who were *not defiled with women*, for they are *virgins*. These are the ones who follow the Lamb wherever He goes. These were redeemed from among men, being firstfruits to God and to the Lamb. And in their mouth was found *no deceit*, for they are *without fault* before the throne of God.

—Revelation 14:1–5, emphasis added It is obvious that there are certain qualifications to being part of the 144,000. The first qualification is to be a Jew. Other criteria include: be without fault, speak without deceit, be a male, be a virgin, know a new song that no one else can learn, be with Christ on Mount Zion.

Ask any Jehovah's Witness who claims to be part of the Anointed Class, "Can you sing the new song of the 144,000?" and they will tell you, "I can't." Ask any of them, "Are you a virgin?" and most of them being elderly will tell you, "I'm not." So how can they qualify as part of the 144,000?

So many have been led astray because they followed Charles Russell and Joseph Rutherford instead of studying the Bible for themselves. They trust in other people's interpretation of the Bible, when the Bible offers a sure safeguard—let the Bible interpret itself. Everything that seems mysterious or difficult to understand at first is either explained in the immediate context or in a parallel passage somewhere else in Scripture. "Scripture interprets Scripture" is always a safe rule of Bible interpretation.

Like many cult leaders, Charles Russell and Joseph Rutherford suffered from a lack of knowledge of end times (or eschatology). They attended denominational Churches that did not teach such essential doctrines, and when they had unanswered questions, they fell away. A simple understanding of end-time prophecy could have prevented such a cult from arising in the first place. That is why I constantly try to demystify end times in my Church and in seminars I conduct.

Remember the Holy Spirit anticipates every false doctrine before it occurs. The Book of Revelation is the only book that gives a divine outline of itself for readers to easily follow. The Lord told John to write about 3 things:

Write the things which you *have seen*, and the things which *are*, and the things which *will take place* after this.

—REVELATION 1:19

The Book of Revelation is divinely divided into 3 parts:

+ a section on the *past* (chapter 1);

+ a section in the *present* (chapters 2–3 about the 7 Churches); and

+ a section about the *future* (chapters 4–22, starting with the Rapture of the Church, chronicling the events of the Tribulation, and ending with the Millennium and the recreation of a new Heaven and new earth).

Any Bible student with such a simple outline can read the Book of Revelation for herself and place the 144,000 Jewish evangelists in a *future* time frame. Chapters 7 and 14 come *after* the Rapture and *after* the start of the Tribulation. We are living in the Church age (chapters 2 and 3), not the 7-year Tribulation. Therefore the 144,000 have *nothing* to do with the present religious organization called Jehovah's Witnesses.

So much of end-time prophecy is misunderstood because it deals primarily with the Jews, using Jewish parlance and Jewish symbols. For instance, when Jesus refers to the "abomination of desolation" as the key event and midpoint of the Tribulation, it says nothing to the Gentile mind. But it means a great deal to the Jewish ears. The first "abomination of desolation" occurred in 167 B.C. when a Gentile ruler named Antiochus Epiphanes IV sacrificed a pig in the Temple of Solomon. No Jew can forget that because they still celebrate the cleansing of the Temple every year in a feast called Hanukkah.

The 144,000 clearly have to do with God's future dealing with the literal nation of Israel, something that didn't exist during Russell or Rutherford's time. Prior to 1948, these religious leaders could spiritualize Bible prophecy and misinform people that God had no more to do with Israel. However, God's covenant with Israel (and us) cannot be broken.

Thus says the LORD, Who gives the sun for a light by day, The ordinances of the moon and the stars for a light by night, Who disturbs the sea, And its waves roar (The LORD of hosts is His name): "*If those ordinances* [of the sun, moon, and stars] *depart* From before Me, says the LORD, *Then* the seed of Israel shall also *cease From being a nation* before Me forever." Thus says the LORD: "*If* Heaven above can be measured, And the foundations of the earth searched out beneath, I will also *cast off all the seed of Israel* For all that they have done," says the LORD.

—JEREMIAH 31:35–37, EMPHASIS ADDED

God says as long as there is sun, moon, and stars, so Israel's existence is guaranteed forever. Basically, Israel is indestructible!

Even though the Romans were used to judge Israel for her rejection of the Messiah at His first coming, and she was scattered worldwide in A.D. 70, she returned home as a nation on May 14, 1948. A myriad of end-time prophecies were fulfilled when Israel was rebirthed as a nation.

Now there is no denying God is not finished with Israel. He is about to complete His 70th week with Israel and to fulfill every detail of Daniel's 70-week prophecy. Part of His future dealing with Israel is to call out a young, bold, fresh army of 144,000 evangelists who will win people to Christ during the 7 years of turmoil on Earth. May they succeed in their mission!

150

PSALMS—DAVID'S DIARY, Israel's songbook, and until recently the Church's songbook—contains 150 chapters. It is unique for many reasons: it is the longest book of the Bible, it contains the longest chapter in the Bible (Psalm 119), the shortest chapter in the Bible (Psalm 117 with only 2 verses), and the middle verse of the Bible (Psalm 103:1–2). Psalms are significant.

> Bless the LORD, O my soul; And all that is within me, bless His holy name! Bless the LORD, O my soul, And forget not all His benefits.
> —PSALM 103:1–2

The Lord is at the heart of the Bible's message in the heart of all the verses. Whereas religions center on man, Christianity centers on the Lord Jesus Christ.

Charles Spurgeon said: "The delightful study of the Psalms has yielded me boundless profit and ever-growing pleasure!"[1]

Jesus said in Luke 24:44 (emphasis added), "These are the words which I spoke to you while I was still with you, that all things must be fulfilled which were written in the Law of Moses and the Prophets and the *Psalms concerning Me*." What is the main message of Psalms? Jesus!

While David holds the distinguished title of "sweet psalmist of Israel" in 2 Samuel 23:1, he is not the only composer of the Psalms. Roughly half (73) can be attributed to David and the other half to various authors such as Asaph (50, 73–83), Heman (88), Jeduthun (89), and the sons of Korah (42, 44–49, 84–85, 87). The earliest Psalms were written by Moses (90 and 91). One Psalm is attributed to David's son Solomon (127). Verse 20 of Psalm 72 suggests David wrote this Psalm, though Solomon is credited for adding the last verse. There are 2 Babylonian exile Psalms attributed to Jeremiah (137, possibly 74). There 3 post-Babylonian exile Psalms attributed to Ezra, Haggai, and/or Zechariah (107, 126, and 147). Many are called "orphan Psalms" whose authorship is anonymous (such as 1, 10, 33, 66, 72, and 102).

Psalms are in *numerical* order, but not *chronological*. For us who have been convinced that every detail in the Bible is there by design, the question is why.

There are 4 theories. The beauty of the Bible is that all 4 theories may be correct, as there are many layers to its codes.

THE RABBINICAL THEORY

Jewish Rabbis divide the Book of Psalms into 5 divisions each corresponding to the 5 Books of Moses).

+ Psalms 1–4 = the Genesis Book

+ Psalms 42–72 = the Exodus Book

+ Psalms 73–89 = the Leviticus Book

+ Psalms 90–106 = the Numbers Book

+ Psalms 107–150 = the Deuteronomy Book

According to this arrangement, a parallel exists between Moses and David. This is interesting and invites us to more study than we can afford here. Certainly, no one stands out more in Jewish history than Moses and David, until Jesus came. Jesus is by far the most famous Jew!

THE PERSONAL THEORY

It is customary among Jews to recite every day the Psalm which corresponds to one's age. For example, when you turn 13 (or enter your 14th year), you begin to say Psalm 14 out loud every day. This gives personal meaning and application to the Psalms. If you live to 150, you will not run out of Psalms to sing.

THE SCIENTIFIC THEORY

Don Christie in his book *Actual Proof of My Existence Signed: God of the Bible* explains how major science constants (numbers that are 10 "to the power" of another number) correspond to the number of the Psalm with the key scientific word in it. For instance

+ Psalm 24 contains "The earth is the Lord's."

+ Earth weighs 6 x 1024 kilograms.

+ Psalm 27 contains "The Lord is my light."

+ A photon or light particle has a minimum electron volt of

- 2.7.

- Psalm 33 contains "an instrument of ten strings."

- Super String Theory posits that the universe is made up of 10 dimensions, 6 curled up like strings at 10–33 centimeters (called Planck length).[2]

The theory of multidimensions is not so far fetched because the inspiration of the Word of God *assumes* God lives in and has the advantage of at least one extra dimension. We cannot see beyond our present, but God sees the past, present, and future. How can He if He were constrained by our single time dimension?

We cannot see into people's hearts, but God can hear all hearts and listen to all prayers at once. How is this possible?

The Bible's assumption is not merely that we have a very busy God, who runs around at breakneck speed to put His ear next to every person's mouth, but that we are dealing with a super-dimensional God who calmly sees the big picture, just like we who live in a 3-dimensional world could calmly lift a 2-dimensional piece of paper with our hands to view everything at once, whereas the hypothetical 2-dimensional beings on that piece of paper would hardly notice we were there at all. At best, the most intelligent 2-dimensional beings would describe our thumbs holding the edges of the paper as something like 2 dots at opposite ends of their universe. The advantage of adding just 1 extra dimension is great. Science has found at least 6 other dimensions. In my opinion, God may live in *infinite* dimensions! What He knows boggles the human mind. Yet He has revealed some of His plan to us in the Bible!

The definition of a *revelation* is information that did not originate from within our space-time dimension (such as where the Messiah will be born or Israel will become a nation in the end times), hence the information cannot be discovered, it must be "revealed." This is the nature of Biblical prophecies.

Psalm 44 contains "times of old." The smallest measurement of time is 10–44 seconds (called Planck time). This is the time it would take a photon traveling at the speed of light to cross a distance equal to Planck length. No smaller division of time has any meaning. We can say that the universe came into existence when it already had an age of 10–44 seconds, corresponding to Psalm 44.

Psalm 19 contains the words "heat" and "circuit." The charge of an electron, a subatomic particle that makes its circuit around an atom, is 1.602 x 10-19 coulombs. One electron volt equals 1.602 x 10-19 joules.

THE PROPHETIC THEORY

J. R. Church was first among Christians to discover a code in Psalms. He published his findings in his book *Hidden Prophecies in the Psalms*.[3] Psalms is the 19th Book, so Psalm 42 is prophetic of 1942. See if you think any of these messages are coincidences. Note the codes would not work if Psalms had been arranged in any other order, such as chronologically or by author.

+ The code is: 1900 + Psalm chapter = year in prophecy.

By reading the Psalm corresponding to the year, we should discover a prophetic message for that year.

In other words, when we see it on TV, it's old news. When you read it in the Bible, it's new news!

PSALM	YEAR	VERSES (KJV)	WORLD EVENT
42	1942	"Why art thou cast down...?"	World War II breaks out. Many humans suffer.
43	1943	"O, deliver me from the deceitful and unjust man...Why go I mourning because of the oppression of the enemy?"	Adolf Hitler kills 6 million Jews in the Holocaust.
45	1945	"My heart is overflowing with a good theme...Your arrows are sharp...the peoples fall under You...Instead of your fathers shall be your sons, whom you shall make princes in all the earth."	World War II ends. Many Jewish fathers died, but their sons return home.
46	1946	"He maketh wars to cease unto the end of the earth...	First full year of peace.

PSALM	YEAR	VERSES (KJV)	WORLD EVENT
48	1948	"Beautiful for situation, the joy of the whole earth, is mount Zion…the kings were assembled, the passed by together. They saw it, and so they marveled; they were troubled…Let mount Zion rejoice, let the daughters of Judah be glad…Walk about Zion…"	14 May 1948 the State of Israel reborn. 5 Arab neighbors (Egypt, Syria, Lebanon, Jordan and Iraq) simultaneously attack Israel from all sides and are defeated!
67	1967	"God shall bless us; and all the ends of the earth shall fear him."	Six Days War. Israel regains Jerusalem in only 6 days.
78	1978	"Marvelous things He did in the sight of their fathers, in the land of Egypt, in the field of Zoan [Ha–Awar]."	In 1977, Egyptian President Anwar Sadat meets with Israeli Prime Minister Menachem Begin at a conference organized by President Jimmy Carter. In 1979, Anwar Sadat becomes first Arab leader to sign peace treaty with Israel. President Carter wins Nobel Peace Prize.
80	1980	"You have brought a vine out of Egypt [usually bad place]…The boar out of the woods uproots IT [the vine out of Egypt] and the wild beast of the field devours IT…IT is burned with fire, IT is cut down.	Vine out of Egypt=Anwar Sadat Boar=Khalid Islambouli Cut down=assassination A warning! 1981 During a parade Anwar Sadat is assassinated.
89	1989	"Thou hast broken down all his hedges; thou hast brought his strong holds to ruin."	Berlin Wall separating East and West Germany falls on 9 Nov 1989.

Psalm	Year	Verses (KJV)	World Event
91	1991	Psalm of Protection "Thou shalt not be afraid for the terror by night; nor for the arrow that flieth by day...A thousand shall fall at thy side, and ten thousand at thy right hand; but it shall not come night thee."	First Gulf War. Saddam Hussein fires 39 SCUD missiles on civilian targets in Israel. Not one dies. Israel does not have to fear any terror. Pslam 91 is good to use for protection!
104	2004	"Let the sinners be consumed out of the earth, and let the wicked be no more..."-last verse	Earthquake near Aceh and tsunami on 26 Dec 2004 kills 300,000, at the end of the year.
107	2007	"Fools because of their transgression, and because of their iniquities, are afflicted...they reel to and fro, and stagger like a drunken man, and are at their wit's end...He poureth contempt upon princes"	Global Financial Crisis begins in 2007 due to greed and corruption of investment banks. Speculators reel at the shock in financial system. Even the wealthiest are hit hard. Real estate prices crash.
108	2008	"Give us help from trouble: for vain is the help of man."	The Western world looks to governments to solve their woes. Barack Obama elected in Nov 2008 on grand promises.
109	2009	"...the mouth of the deceitful are opened...lying tongue...Set thou a wicked man over him: and let Satan stand at his right hand."	Obama inaugurated 20 January 2009. Many soon disillusioned as government spending and national debt soars. Billions of $ of stimuls unaccounted for. Bankers bailed out, unemployment rises. Christian values marginalized.

153

153 DESERVES ATTENTION because it's the number of fish 7 disciples caught after the resurrected Christ told them where to cast their net (John 21:11). Why the Gospel writer did not round off the number to 150, why he specified 153 to be exact, is a mystery to most Bible commentators. 1, 3, and 5 are all significant numbers by themselves, but does the combination mean something more?

One clue can be found in gematria. The numeric value of the term "sons of God" (*ben ha Elohim*) is exactly 153. Perhaps this was Jesus' way of telling the 7 disciples who had gone back to fishing (their former profession before He called them into ministry) that they were still called to catch men—not fish! If this was Jesus' hint that they were still called to turn sinners into "sons of God," then it is solid evidence that Jesus expected his Jewish disciples to understand Hebrew gematria. Not surprising since the rabbis of their day preoccupied themselves endlessly with dissecting every word and computing the value of every letter in the Torah! If Peter was acquainted with gematria, then 153 should have confirmed to him that he was indeed a "fisher of men," called to turn lost souls into sons of God. (See chapter 276 for more.)

206

206 IS THE NUMBER OF BONES IN AN ADULT BODY, half of which are in our hands (27 x 2) and feet (26 x 2). This would have ensured maximum pain for Jesus as both His Hands and Feet were nailed to the Cross.

Yet Jesus fulfilled a startling prophecy written 1,000 years before His crucifixion, "He [God] guards all his bones [the Messiah's bones]; not one of them is broken" (Ps. 34:20). God protected Jesus' bones even though it was customary for the Romans to break criminals' legs to hasten the dying process of those hanging on a cross.

> Then the soldiers came and broke the legs of the first and of the other who was crucified with Him. But when they came to Jesus and saw that He was already dead, they did not break His legs.
>
> —JOHN 19:32–33

The reason His bones were protected was it was unnecessary for His bones to be punished. His blood was necessary and sufficient to wash away sins, not His bones.

> And according to the law almost all things are purified with blood, and without shedding of blood there is no remission [of sins].
>
> —HEBREWS 9:22

276

WHEN PAUL WAS SHIPWRECKED ON THE ISLAND OF MALTA,
Luke told us the precise number of passengers who were saved: 276 (Acts
27:37). Why didn't Luke round up the number to "280" or "about 300"? Luke
was not so careful when it came to recording how many people had gathered on
the day of Pentecost; he wrote "about 120" (Acts 1:15). It turns out the Holy
Spirit's hand is directly behind these sometimes strangely precise and other
times rounded figures. There are 4 three-digit numbers in the New Testament:

+ 120 (disciples in the Upper Room, post-Resurrection)

+ 153 (fish caught in Peter's net, post-Resurrection)

+ 276 (lives saved on a ship carrying Paul)

+ 666 (number of the Beast or the Anti-Christ)

Only 3 of these three-digit numbers are commonly discussed among
Christians, but 276 is rarely talked about. Numericist John Tng noticed that
all 4 numbers do not appear to be random, but interrelated. He observed the
following commonalities: Firstly, all of them are divisible by 3:

+ $120 \div 3 = 40$

+ $153 \div 3 = 51$

+ $276 \div 3 = 92$

+ $666 \div 3 = 222$

Secondly, all four are triangular numbers or numbers that can fill an
equilateral triangle perfectly. For instance the first four triangular numbers are
shown on right.

1   3   6   10

+ 120 = 15th triangular number

+ 153 = 17th triangular number

+ 276 = 23rd triangular number

+ 666 = 36th triangular number

Thirdly, the sum of these 4 numbers coincides with other significant gematria in the Bible. For instance, it equals the sum of the first 3 words in Genesis 1:1 "in the beginning" (913) and the last 3 words in Genesis 1:1 "and the earth" (302):

+ 120 + 153 + 276 + 666 = 1,215

+ 913 + 302 = 1,215

John Tng postulates that 1,215 may be a gemetria that is related to the first, middle and last names of the Anti-Christ. I only caution the reader to not follow gemetria but the plain text of the Bible in identifying the Anti-Christ. Micah 5:6 calls him "the Assyrian"; Isaiah 14:04 says he will be the "king of Babylon." A non-Middle Eastern head of state, such as an American president, cannot qualify as the Anti-Christ unless he is simultaneously the ruler of Iran or Iraq also. He can only be Anti-Christ who rules over the Middle East. Everyone else, no matter how powerful or seemingly evil, is pure conjecture.

Did Luke and John conspire to fabricate the above mathematical correlations for reasons known only to themselves? Or was it simply a coincidence that the numbers exhibit unique properties? Or is God communicating to us as He always has, through intelligent design?[1]

365

THE NUMBER OF DAYS IN A YEAR IS 365.25. That's why we have to add one day to February every 4 years or every leap year.

Coincidentally, Enoch lived for 365 years before God translated Him to Heaven. Genesis 5:24 (emphasis added): "And Enoch walked with God: and he was not; for God *took him*." Everyone else in that chapter "died" except Enoch who was "taken." He has been living in Heaven with his natural body for more than 5,000 years!

There has been a lot of misuse of the phrase "God took him." Often when somebody dies prematurely of sickness or in an accident, the grieving family is told, "God took him." But this is totally unscriptural!

There are 3 instances of people who were "taken" by God—Enoch, Elijah, and Jesus. Did it mean God made them sick or allowed them to be killed in an accident? Enoch was not "for God *took* him." The writer of Hebrews tell us, "By faith Enoch was *taken* from this life, so that he did not experience death: 'He could not be found, because God had *taken* him away.' For before he was *taken*, he was commended as one who pleased God" (11:5, NIV, emphasis added). In 2 Kings, "Elijah said to Elisha, 'Ask! What may I do for you, before I am *taken* away from you?'" (2:9, emphasis added). The angels said to the disciples, "Men of Galilee, why do you stand gazing up into Heaven? This same Jesus, who was *taken* up from you into Heaven, will so come in like manner as you saw Him go into Heaven" (Acts 1:11, emphasis added). Paul said that Jesus was "*taken* up in glory" (1 Tim. 3:16, NIV, emphasis added).

In none of these instances did the phrase "God took" mean God killed the person or made them sick. No! When God takes someone, it means that they did not experience sickness or death. That may not agree with the world's view of God, but that is the Biblical picture of our God. Our God is the one who safeguards and gives life!

Christians are waiting to be "taken" by God at the Rapture. Paul wrote about it. "Let me tell you a secret. Not all of us will die, but all of us will be changed" (1 Cor. 15:51, ISV). "For the secret power of lawlessness is already at work; but the one who now holds it back [the Church] will continue to do so till he is *taken* out of the way" (2 Thess. 2:7, NIV, emphasis added).

That means there will be a generation of believers who, like Enoch and Elijah, will be spared from ever experiencing death.

In a court of law, the testimony of 2 or 3 credible witnesses would be sufficient to establish a claim. We have just seen 7 Scriptures which prove when God "takes" someone, He spares them from sickness and death. Some people have been using the phrase "God took him" for so long that it's become a habit or religious tradition. Never let habit or tradition replace or take the place of Scripture!

Because Enoch never died, some Bible teachers believe he may be one of the two witnesses due to come preach in Israel as per Revelation 11:7. Other Bible scholars say Enoch will not be one of the two witnesses to come back to complete his life and die, because Enoch was a Gentile and the two witnesses appear to be Jews. Enoch's translation would then serve as a type of a mainly Gentile Church waiting to be raptured without seeing death.

In any case, Enoch left one of the most incredible testimonies of any saint. God used him to give the oldest prophecy recorded in the Bible.

> Now Enoch, the seventh from Adam, prophesied about these men also, saying, 'Behold, the Lord comes with ten thousands of His saints, to execute judgment on all, to convict all who are ungodly among them of all their ungodly deeds which they have committed in an ungodly way, and of all the harsh things which ungodly sinners have spoken against Him.'
>
> —Jude 1:14–15

The oldest recorded prophecy by a prophet is actually about the Second Coming of Christ. Enoch starting walking with God at the age of 65 and continued a deep relationship with God for 300 years. God found this man so irresistible He couldn't wait for him to die; God snatched Enoch up for Himself.

Enoch had this relationship with God without a Bible, the new birth, or the power of the Holy Spirit. How much easier should it be for New Testament believers to commune with God and walk with Him?

400

400 IS A MULTIPLE OF 40. Like 40, it can refer to a time of testing or waiting.

God said to Abraham: "Know certainly that your descendants will be strangers in a land that is not theirs [Egypt], and will serve them [the Egyptians], and they will afflict them four hundred years" (Gen. 15:13). Israel was in Egypt for approximately 400 years (Acts 7:6). Exodus 12:40 and Galatians 3:17 both tell us Israel was in Egypt for 430 years. Since God is usually exact, what accounts for the extra 30 years?

The Bible tells us that Moses was impulsive and tried to deliver Israel in his own strength, by killing an Egyptian guard! This was not God's way of demonstrating His saving power. No doubt the 40 years Moses spent tending sheep in the backside of the desert mellowed Moses out, but delayed God's plan. If God had allocated 10 years for Moses' ministry training, then his taking 40 years would mean 30 of those years were extra preparation time. That would explain why Israel came out 30 years late—all because of one man's impulsiveness. Our decisions do count in other people's lives!

After the conquest of Canaan, Israel went through turbulent times spiritually and politically under 13 judges. How long was this period? From Judges 3:8 to 1 Samuel 4:18, we can count the number of known years of servitude (111 years), plus the length of reigns of each judge (299 years), plus the span of Eli's judgeship (40 years), which equals 450 years. Or we can read Luke's sum in Acts 13:20, "All this took about 450 years." The prophet Samuel was a connecting figure who served the last judge, Eli, and anointed the first 2 kings of Israel, Saul and David.

From King David to the last the king of Judah named Zedekiah was 473 years.[1]

From Rehoboam, the first king of the divided kingdom of Judah, to Zedekiah, its last king, was 393 years. In this period of time, there was rampant ungodliness throughout society. Ezekiel was told to lie on his side for 390 days to represent the 390 years of sins of the nation (Ezek. 4:4–5). If the southern kingdom of Judah lasted 393 years, why did God require only 390? Second Chronicles 11 explains that after the kingdom split into north and south, the Levites left the northern kingdom of Israel to migrate to Judah where the Temple worship was. Then "those from all the tribes of Israel, such as set their heart to seek the LORD God of Israel, [also] came to Jerusalem to sacrifice to the LORD God of their fathers" (2 Chron. 11:16).

> And they [the migrant worshipers] strengthen the kingdom of Judah, and strengthen Rehoboam son of Solomon, for *three years*, because they walked in the way of David and Solomon for *three years*.
>
> —2 CHRONICLES 11:17, YOUNG'S, EMPHASIS ADDED

For 3 years after the death of Solomon, most Jews, including those from the north, continued to observe the Lord's feasts in Jerusalem and walked in the righteous ways of God. God subtracted these 3 years from the 393 year period of the divided kingdom, hence 390.

In 1 Kings 6:1, the Holy Spirit counted 480 years from the Exodus to the 4th year of Solomon. On the surface this seems to contradict Acts 13:20 which says the period of judges alone accounted for about 450 years. Adding 40 years of Israel's wandering in the desert, 25 years of Joshua's reign (according to Josephus), 40 years of Eli, Samuel, Saul, and David's leadership respectively, we should count at least 675 years between Exodus and Solomon.

Finnis Dake explained this 480 must be understood as counting the years of peace and prosperity since Exodus.[2] Therefore, starting with 675 years, we can minus 40 years of rebellion in the desert, 111 years of servitude in the time of the judges, 3 years of civil strife under Gideon's son Abimelech (the 6th judge), and 40 years of the people's choice King Saul; then we arrive at 481 years of actual peace and godliness. Since it's common practice to round years off, we can see that the Holy Spirit's accounting of 480 years is accurate.

The moral of the story is that when our years are wasted in rebellion and out of the will of God, God doesn't even count them! That's what it means to be "justified" by God's grace. Once we return to walking in His will, He accepts us "just as if" we had never sinned. He doesn't even bring up our past mistakes anymore. He doesn't count those lost years. Know that if you have ever walked out of God's will, He can erase that time out of your history. Now make sure to "redeem the time" you have left and serve Him to your best.

From Solomon's 4th year when Temple construction began to the year Nebuchadnezzar destroyed the Temple was 430 years.[3]

God told Daniel that there would be 483 years from the command to restore and rebuild Jerusalem until the Messiah's arrival. (See Daniel 9:25–26.) Since we know the Persian king Artaxerxes issued the command to rebuild Jerusalem on the 14ᵗʰ of March 445 B.C., we can know that the Messiah had to arrive around A.D. 32. No matter how you calculate it, using lunar or solar years, the Messiah is either long overdue or He has, in fact, already come. According to God's Word, He has come and died for the sins of the world.

After Malachi wrote the last book of the Old Testament, there was a period of prophetic silence for 400 years. That is, no prophet heard from God. No one wrote a message for God. This is called the intertestamental period (between the Old and New Testaments) or the "400 Years of Silence."

I'm sure it was a trying time for those Jews who had just returned from the Babylonian Captivity and were being oppressed by more Gentiles. During the next 400 years, Israel would be shuffled under 6 different rules: Persian;[4] Greek;[5] Egyptian;[6] Syrian;[7] Maccabean;[8] and Roman[9] (see chapter 6 Empires). During those times of mainly foreign rule, no prophet spoke. By the time Gabriel the archangel announced to Mary the arrival of Messiah, thousands of Jews like Peter, James, and John were thirsty to hear God's Word again. It's the thirst that makes the water so sweet.

Today we do not need to live in spiritual silence because God lives in all born-again Christians. *God in us* separates Christianity from every religion in the world! Our God is not distant. He is as close to us as any individual can be. We can hear God any time by picking up our Bible to read or by praying in the Spirit. Jesus told us, "My sheep hear My voice, and I know them, and they follow Me" (John 10:27). The only question is: Are we His sheep? Have we decided to make Him our Shepherd?

We can do so by saying,

> *Dear Lord Jesus,*
> *I call You my Lord and my Shepherd. I am Your sheep and You said I can hear Your voice. I believe You are leading me and guiding me in all the affairs of life. Thank You for sending Your Holy Spirit to help me! I believe He will teach me all things and remind me of everything You have told me (John 10:27).*

> He will guide you into all the truth…and he will tell you what is yet to come.
> —JOHN 14:26, NIV

400 years is a cycle of testing, trials and prophetic silence that is broken by Jesus Christ.

Significant Cycles	Years
From God's Promise to Abraham to God's fulfilment through Moses (Exodus)	430
From Othniel (Caleb's younger brother) the First Judge to Eli the Last Judge	450
From King David to Zedekiah the Last King of Judah (Davidic Dynasty)	473
From Exodus to Solomon's 4th year (Years of Peace & Prosperity only)	480
From Construction of Solomon's Temple to Destruction by Nebuchadnezzar	430
From Artaxerxes' Decree to Rebuild Jerusalem to Execution of Messiah	483
From Close of Old Testament (Malachi) to Opening of New Testament (Matthew)	400
From when the Turks took Jerusalem (1517) to when the Turks lost Jerusalem (1917)	400
From the First Adam to the "Second Adam"	4000

SYMMETRY IS A DIVINE CODE

We can see symmetry in Biblical chronology. Such parallels in timelines are by God's design, since the timeframes are outside the control of various patriarchs, prophets, judges, kings, and writers. They not only tell us that prophetically significant events occurred in cycles, but they may help us predict future events as well.

For instance, could Daniel's 70-week prophecy or 490 year cycle have dual application? Could the prophecy apply to both the First and Second Coming? We know there were 69 weeks or 483 years from Artaxerxes' decree to rebuild Jerusalem till the first coming of Messiah. Could there also be another 483 years from a more modern decree to rebuild Jerusalem till the Second Coming?

After the destruction of Jerusalem by the Romans in A.D. 70, Jerusalem laid in ruins for over a thousand years. Then Turkish Sultan Suleiman the Magnificent issued a decree to rebuild Jerusalem in A.D. 1537. He ordered the rebuilding of the current walls of the Old City of Jerusalem. This was a milestone year for Israel. Taking 1537 as the trigger date and adding 483 years brings us to a target date of 2020. Adding 490 years brings us to 2027.

Let me be clear: I am not predicting the end of the world in either 2020 or

2027. I am no date setter, only a student of Biblical patterns. God works in cycles, and the 400 year cycle is a major cycle of testing and waiting. If prophetic cycles show symmetry, then all I am asking is, "Could another significant event occur 483 years after the modern decree to rebuild Jerusalem?" We shall wait and see.

No matter how soon Jesus may return, I will not pack my bags and hide in a bomb shelter. I will continue to live in expectation that Jesus can come any time and call me to account at any moment. This is how we should live. If we are found faithfully serving our Church and pursuing God's interests up to the day He arrives, He will not punish us. He will reward us according to our faithfulness. No Christian should expect to be rewarded for living in a bomb shelter and hiding from the world. Whether Jesus comes tomorrow or in 40 years, every generation will be judged for believing His Word, walking in love, evangelizing the lost, and serving in Church.

Whereas 40 signifies short-term testing, 400 signifies intermediate-term testing, and 4,000 years is the grandest period of waiting from the first Adam to the second Adam.

613

613 IS THE TOTAL NUMBER OF COMMANDMENTS or *mitzvot* God gave the Jews in the Torah. When a Jewish boy turns 13, he enters adulthood and becomes a *bar-mitzvah*, which is Aramaic for "son of the commandments."

Who counted so many commandments in the Torah? Jewish tradition credits the ancient sage Maimonides. These commandments can be divided into two categories: 365 negative commands ("thou shalt not" types) and 248 positive commands ('thou shalt" types). 365 corresponds to the number of days in our year and serves as a reminder that humans break God's commandments every single day of the year.

Contrary to popular misunderstanding, it is not keeping the 10 Commandments that gets you into Heaven. It is perfectly keeping all 613 commandments every single day of your life.

Nobody in the Old Testament achieved this. Solomon acknowledged our universal failure when he said in 1 Kings 8:46, "For there is no one who does not sin" and in Ecclesiastes 7:20 (NIV), "There is no one on earth who is righteous, no one who does what is right and never sins." That is why atonement or covering of sins was necessary for every Jew.

Nor could anybody in the New Testament keep all 613 commandments, except for Jesus. Paul acknowledged our common fatal flaw in Romans 3:23, "For all have sinned and fall short of the glory of God." That is why redemption and forgiveness of sins is necessary now for every person in the world.

Neither does being able to keep some of the 613 commandments some of the time help our cause much, for James 2:10 (NIV, emphasis added) says, "For whoever keeps the whole law but fails in *one* point is guilty of breaking *all* of it." Does this seem harsh? Does it make sense?

It makes perfect sense legally. How many laws does someone need to break before becoming a criminal? Only one! A man who steals is not excused by a good judge because he did not murder. A woman who drinks and drives is not pardoned because she did not cheat on her taxes this year. Breaking one law is enough to make one a criminal; likewise committing one sin is enough to make one a sinner. One does not have to break every law in the book to be found a lawbreaker or a sinner!

The Supreme Court of Heaven has decided that "sin" is breaking any one of these 613 divine laws. No Jewish person today can keep all of God's laws, especially since many of them have to do with rituals in the Temple, which has been destroyed since A.D. 70. For instance, the Bible commands the Jewish high priest to sacrifice a goat in the holy of holies on the Day of Atonement (Lev. 16). The Bible further commands that no Jew must do any work on the Day of Atonement; "It shall be a sabbath of *complete rest* to you, and you shall humble your souls" (Lev. 23:32, NAS, emphasis added). All Jews live in disobedience to these laws today, so how do the modern rabbis justify it?

They claim that if the Jews do good on the Day of Atonement, they will absolve themselves of their sins. Yet this human theory violates the very principle of atonement, "For it is the blood that makes atonement for the soul" (Lev. 17:11). It also violates God's command for us to cease from our own strivings and efforts and to enter into complete rest by trusting in the blood of an innocent one to atone our sins.

Even though the earthly Temple was destroyed, there is a heavenly temple on which the earthly one was based. And Jesus the Messiah has placed His sinless blood on the heavenly mercy seat as an atonement for the sins of the world. Hebrews 9:22 (KJV) says, "Without the shedding of blood there is no forgiveness." We no longer have to strive to keep the 613 commandments. With the Temple erect, the Jews could not do it. Without the Temple today, how much less can we achieve it? But Christ being the perfect sacrifice has made an atonement for our souls, and by believing in Him we have forgiveness of all our sins.

I once heard rabbi say it is not necessary to keep the 613 *mitzvah* to be a "good" person. If this was so, how would we know which particular commandments we could ignore or violate without consequence? How many would we need to keep to qualify as a "good" person? The answer is: All of them! When we realize how high the standard is, we will realize how far we have fallen. That's why we all need a Savior. What is the function of God's 613 laws? "Wherefore the law was our schoolmaster to bring us unto Christ" (Gal. 3:24, KJV).

666

He [the Anti-Christ] causes all, both small and great, rich and poor, free and slave, to receive a mark on their right hand or on their foreheads, and that no one may buy or sell except one who has the mark or the name of the beast, or the number of his Name. Here is wisdom. Let him who has understanding calculate the number of the beast, for it is the number of a man: His number is 666.

REVELATION 13:16–18, EMPHASIS ADDED

666 IS ONE OF THE MOST INTRIGUING NUMBERS IN THE BIBLE. Both believers and doubters are familiar with the number and detect its evil connotation. What does it really mean?

666 is a triplicate of 6, the number of man. 666 means "**man man man**." It represents *man* without God or enthroning himself as god. John 6:66 is the lowest point in Jesus' ministry: "From that time many of His disciples went back and walked with Him no more."

666 is the number of the beast of Revelation 13, commonly known as the Anti-Christ. This title is sometimes misleading because the ultimate deceiver has 33 titles in the Old Testament and 13 titles in the New Testament. To some people's surprise, he is never once called the Anti-Christ in Revelation. In Revelation 13, there are actually 2 beasts commonly conflated as a single person called Anti-Christ. The first seems to be a military or financial leader. The second is often labeled by theologians as his false prophet; but I think it's better to understand him as his media man, image manager, or public face. Considering the amount of lies told by the financial powers through the secular media, it is believable that the 2 beasts are *already here* in a figure. But we are also expecting 2 real individuals.

Rejecting the Bible, most people are naive about the Anti-Christ and will embrace him unawares. The first prediction about Anti-Christ appears early in Scripture in Genesis 3:15. The same promise which predicted the birth of Christ, called the "Seed of the Woman," also predicted the coming of Anti-Christ, called the "Seed of the Serpent," meaning Son of Satan. Just as Jesus came literally, so too the Anti-Christ will come literally. The Bible unfolds with more clues about him. He is also known as: "The Prince that Shall Come," "The Little Horn," "The Lawless One," "The Man of Sin," "The Son of Perdition," and "The Beast."

The term *Anti-Christ* is only used in the epistles of John and sometimes appears in the plural. First John 2:18 (emphasis added) says, "Little children, it is the last hour; and as you have heard that the Antichrist is coming, even now *many* antichrists have come, by which we know that it is the last hour." Second John 1:7 (emphasis added) says, "For *many* deceivers have gone out into the world who do not confess Jesus Christ as coming in the flesh. This is a deceiver and an antichrist." These verses tell us the term "antichrists," as far as the Church is concerned, refers more to a spirit that comes against the Church than a singular person.

When speaking to the Jews, as the books of Daniel, Ezekiel, and most of Revelation do, the term "Anti-Christ" is never used. Why would the Jews look for an Anti-Christ when they have not yet embraced the *Christ*? No, Jews are more familiar with the long line of evil dictators who have oppressed and murdered them, starting from Pharaoh going down through Antiochus all the way to Adolf Hitler and modern terrorists. In the end times, Jews are to on the look out for the ultimate racist who should be better known as the Anti-Semite. His number and the number of his name will be 666.

FEARFUL SPECULATIONS

Some people unnecessarily fear that barcodes or scannable chips may have the number 666 on them. They fear getting a barcode printed on their foreheads or a microchip embedded in their hands (or even in their pets.).

Others like Seventh Day Adventists fear that the mark of the beast is worshiping on Sunday instead of Saturday. Nothing in the text identifies the mark of the beast with *days* of worship but an *object* of worship. This worship day teaching continues in spite of the fact that the New Testament advises us to avoid legalism: "One person esteems *one day* above another; another esteems *every day* alike. Let each be fully convinced in his own mind. He who observes the day, observes it to the Lord; and he who does not observe the day, to the Lord he does not observe it" (Rom. 14:5–6, emphasis added). "So let no one judge you in food or in drink, or regarding a festival or a new moon or *sabbaths*, which are a shadow of things to come, but the substance is of Christ" (Col. 2:16–17, emphasis added).

Still others fear that 666 will be related to a global or national identity card. But Revelation 13:17 teaches that this is the number of *his* name, not *our* name. This is not a mark that can be issued without our consent or that we get haphazardly. It is a mark associated with "worship" and received only after worshiping the *beast* or his *image*. Five verses of Scripture make this clear:

> If anyone *worships* the beast and his image, and receives his mark on his forehead or on his hand, he himself shall also drink of the wine of the wrath of God...and they shall have no rest day or night, who *worship* the beast and his image, and whoever receives the mark of his name.
>
> —REVELATION 14:9, 11, EMPHASIS ADDED

> A foul and loathsome sore came upon the men who had the mark of the beast and those who *worshiped* his image.
>
> —REVELATION 16:2, EMPHASIS ADDED

> He [the false prophet of the beast] deceived those who received the mark of the beast and those who *worshiped* his image.
>
> —REVELATION 19:20, EMPHASIS ADDED

> Then I saw the souls of those who had been beheaded for their witness to Jesus and for the word of God, who had not *worshiped* the beast or his image, and had not received his mark on their foreheads or on their hands. And they lived and reigned with Christ for a thousand years.
>
> —REVELATION 20:4, EMPHASIS ADDED

What separates the saved from the damned is not *when* we worship, but *whom* we worship. We believers worship Jesus Christ and have nothing to fear. This mark may not even be a physical mark considering the context of Revelation 13:14–18. The Bible was not originally written with chapter and verse (they were added later), so chapter 14 flows right on from the last verse of chapter 13. The first verse of chapter 14 contrasts the mark of the beast on unbelievers' foreheads with the "144,000 having His Father's name written on their foreheads." These are 144,000 Jews who will put their faith in the Messiah during the Tribulation. No Bible teacher I have heard believes that God will insert a chip into these 144,000 believers' foreheads. No Bible teacher I know teaches that God will put a scannable barcode on the believers' heads. Clearly a spiritual "ownership" is implied by having someone's name written on us. I doubt that a tattoo, barcode, chip, or something natural *on* our head is really going to determine our salvation. I believe it's what *in* that head that matters more to God.

Christians should never live in fear of such kooky doctrines. A person who fears is a person who doesn't really know how big our God is.

We should confess as the Apostle John did, "Greater is He who is in me than he who is in the world!" (1 John 4:4).

HAVE YOU SEEN THIS NUMBER 666?

If the number 666 is not a physical mark, what could it be about? We are sure of one thing: it is related to finance. Revelation 13:16–17 makes it clear: "He [the Anti-Christ] causes all, both small and great, rich and poor, free and slave, to receive a mark on their right hand or on their foreheads, and that no one may *buy* or *sell* except one who has the mark or the name of the beast, or the number of his name" (emphasis added).

The end-time mark has something to do with buying and selling, or in a word, *trading*. Could it be mere coincidence that when the global financial meltdown started in 2007, the S&P 500 index bottomed on the 6th of March 2009 at the infamous 666 points?

Millions of people around the world saw that number. It may not have registered spiritually or intellectually, but it was significant to Bible readers. God's prophecies are often fulfilled not by some obscure event, but by something so obvious it's staring all of us in the face.

The connection between the number 666 and the most watched stock market index in the world should not be ignored without due diligence.

CONSPIRACY THEORIES

I am not into conspiracy theories as most conspiracies cannot be verified except by insider or secretive information. Yet I cannot ignore all conspiracies completely. Why? Because the Bible is full of them! Adam and Eve fell not because of a head-on confrontation with an evil force, but because they were not aware of the conspiracy being fomented by the serpent.

The greatest conspiracy of all time was the plot to murder our Savior, the Lord Jesus Christ. Today we can read in plain language who the conspirators and co-conspirators were—Judas, the self-interested rabbis, and the powerful Romans, yet if we were alive on the day Jesus was crucified, those facts would have been hidden from our view. Any one of us could have easily been swept in with the crowds' roar, "Crucify Him! Crucify Him!" The crowd was not acting on their own volition; they were being moved by an idea planted by the ruling elite. It was the ultimate "inception," an idea that grew like a virus.

Only a few disciples could have suspected this was a set up, but by the time they caught on, Judas was dead and Christ had been murdered. One of the key events in the Bible was a satanic conspiracy to murder the Son of God. Powerful people were pulling powerful strings!

Could 666 be pointing to a financial conspiracy? Who controls or influences almost all our lives on this planet? One possibility is that the banks do. With one decision they can change the interest rates and everybody's lives are instantly affected. They are not elected, they are often unknown to the masses, and they don't seek the limelight. Governments come and go, politicians rise and fall, but bankers not only remain, but grow in power. Governments owe them money. Consumers owe them money. Their influence grows as both governments and people fall into more debt. Their control crosses borders and seems to know no boundaries. When they lose people's money, national governments bail them out with more money.

I am not one who has ever been convinced by conspiracy theories, but of all the conspiracy theories I've come across, the most plausible one is that the financial elite (by which I don't mean merely rich people or large corporations, but the central banks and investment banks) are the true rulers of the world. If 666 is a financial symbol, and it is, then the financial elite may be the players to watch in the last days. Their decisions affect everybody's lives, except those who choose to live free in Christ.

Christians are called to live in God's financial system by kingdom principles that include tithing and giving, but only 20 percent of Christians today offer their full tithe to God. Given a need to buy a house or a car, how many Christians today would immediately go to the bank, apply for a loan, and borrow money from strangers at interest, rather than tithe in faith, sow in expectation, and trust God to provide a harvest? To borrow and lend are not necessarily wrong, as God said believers will lend to many nations. But to pay interest without paying tithes is putting the world first instead of putting God first.

If Satan's system is the financial system, then I'm afraid too many Christians have already bought into his way of living. Too many Christians think it's impossible to tithe and survive. Too few believers believe tithing works and God's Word is powerful enough to help them acquire tangible things like homes and cars. Didn't Jesus say in Matthew 6:33, "But seek first the kingdom of God and His righteousness, and all these *things* shall be added to you"? If

God is powerless in most people's minds, then who has the power? Is there a possibility the bankers do?

What should God-fearing people be more concerned about: this financial system enslaving people in debt or being branded like a cow with the number 666? I believe Jesus told us who the enemy is: "You cannot serve God and mammon" (Matt. 6:24). *Mammon* is not just a pretentious word for money; it is the Canaanite god of money. It is a spirit that competes with God for our heart, our time, and our resources. Mammon demands worship, homage, and obedience. Jesus taught that Mammon is the anti-God. Could the head of the world financial system then be the Anti-Christ? The tentacles of the financial system easily qualify as a form of global control or one world governance. While prophecy teachers are waiting for a one world government to form in Europe or through the United Nations, they forget that the IMF and World Bank are already here. They do not need to be voted in. They are in power now!

Knowing Bible prophecy, I know that the Anti-Christ has to have a major connection to the Middle East. America, Europe, and China, these are but side issues to Bible prophecy. Where do the tentacles of the world financial system lead? The Middle East! When Thailand's richest billionaire and former prime minister Thaksin Shinawatra was ousted from government, to which region of the world did he flee? He hid in the Middle East! Every U.S. President shakes hands with Middle Eastern leaders. The Middle East swaps its depleting oil reserve for an ever growing gold reserve. When the world's fiat currencies tumble, the Middle East could reveal its strategic end-time importance at last— it's not the oil, but the gold money it holds, that will make them the lenders and the world their borrowers (financial slavery). While historians, economists, and prophecy teachers speculate about where the world's center stage is, the Bible has never lost focus that the *Middle East* is where the spiritual, financial, and military warfare will be happening.

666 IS ASSOCIATED WITH 3 PERSONS IN SCRIPTURE

The first person is a wise king who drifted away from God through his lust for unbelieving women—King Solomon. The number 666 is associated with his great wealth: "The weight of gold that came to Solomon yearly was 666 talents of gold" (1 Kings 10:14; 2 Chron. 9:13).

The second person is a relatively unknown character, *Adonikam*, whose Hebrew name means "my Lord has risen." This was an exile who returned to Israel from the Babylonian Captivity.

God had predicted that after 70 years of captivity in Babylon, the Jews would be released to go home by a future king to be named "Cyrus" (Isa. 44:28, 45:1). In 537 B.C. a Persian king named Cyrus issued a decree, just as God had predicted, for the return of the Jews to their homeland. Some Jews were reluctant to leave their new Gentile home, but those who were willing returned to the Promised Land in three waves: first under Zerubbabel; second under Ezra; and third under Nehemiah.

Ezra chapter 2 lists those Jews who returned with Zerubbabel by their family head and number. In verse 13 appears Adonikam's traveling group: "the people of Adonikam, 666" (v. 13).

How many descendants did Adonikam have? 666. Counting him with the group, a total of 667 people returned (Neh. 7:18). So Adonikam is a man with whom the number 666 is associated, but unfortunately we do not know much about him. Certain Scriptures[1] and typology* indicate that the Anti-Christ may have Jewish blood. Perhaps the Anti-Christ will be a descendant of Adonikam.

The third person associated with the number 666 is the Anti-Christ himself. "Here is wisdom. Let him who has understanding calculate the number of the beast, for it is the number of a man: His number is 666" (Rev. 13:18).

WHAT DOES ANTI-CHRIST MEAN?

The identity of the Anti-Christ has been unnecessarily mysterious to the Church. Biblically speaking, there are already many antichrists around because anyone who is *against* being saved by the blood of Christ is *anti*-Christ. Whoever puts anyone or anything in the place of Christ is *anti*-Christ.

Is the spirit of anti-Christ prevalent? How many people today believe that their good works will allow them to reach enlightenment or go to Heaven? Countless multitudes! By trusting their merits above those of Christ, they are by definition *anti*-Christ. How many people believe Jesus was merely another wonderful prophet or teacher, instead of who He claims to be—the Creator God who deserves worship and trust? Such deniers go *against* Christ's Person and Sacrifice, and are therefore *anti*-Christ. John told the Church, "Little children, it is the last hour; and as you have heard that *the Antichrist* is coming, even now *many Antichrists* have come, by which we know that it is the last hour" (1 John 2:18).

All self-righteous people possess the spirit of anti-Christ. The Anti-Christ will simply be the supreme charismatic leader around which all other anti-Christ's can rally and follow. What kind of leader will the masses follow? The Anti-Christ, being against Christ, must be a hater of Jews (Jesus is a Jew) and a

---

* Judas could be a type of the Anti-Christ.

hater of Christians (to whom Christ is Savior). The followers of the Anti-Christ must also hold the same views: they hate Jews and Christians.

Is there any violent group of people who currently fit this description? Would the masses be willing to follow a leader who echoes these sentiments? I think one can readily see that the world is poised to adore and follow the cruelest and evilest man without hesitation or batting an eyelid.

Mass media and public opinion are currently against the Jews and Christianity. A solution to end "the Jewish problem in the Middle East" and "the Christian problem in the religious world" is forthcoming, although we know it will be a losing one. No sooner than this agenda is proclaimed Christ will come back to rule and reign! For now the world awaits a political leader who will represent this satanic hatred publicly.

Since much of the world will fall in love with this leader without realizing they are following the devil's pawn, how can believers recognize him? The Bible warns us, "Let him who has understanding calculate the number of the beast, for it is the number of a man: His number is 666" (Rev. 13:18).

The phrase "him who has understanding" simply refers to a Christian who reads his Bible and is filled with the Holy Spirit. John, who wrote the Gospel of John, the Epistles of John, and the Book of Revelation, recorded Jesus' teachings on understanding. "When He, the Spirit of truth, has come, He will *guide you* into all truth; for He will not speak on His own authority, but whatever He hears He will speak; and He will *tell you* things to come" (John 16:13, emphasis added). And again, "But the anointing [of the Holy Spirit] which you have received from Him abides in you, and you do not need that anyone teach you; but as the same anointing *teaches you* concerning all things" (1 John 2:27, emphasis added).

A Christian's spirit is in union with God's Spirit, so we should not be in the dark about spiritual matters. We should expect God to give us understanding through His Word and His Spirit. To those who have the Holy Spirit, what does the number 666 tells us about the future Anti-Christ?

I do not think it will be a physical tattoo or microchip or any physical mark, any more than God's name written on the 144,000 Jewish believers' foreheads will be a tattoo, microchip, or physical mark. 666 is more likely symbolic or code.

666 IS CODE FOR 3 THINGS

First, 666 is an apt code of the unholy trinity of Satan, the Anti-Christ, and his false prophet during the 7 years on earth called the Tribulation. These 3 personalities are found in Revelation 13.

Second, most Bible teachers interpret 666 as the gematria of the Anti-Christ's name. One problem with gematria is which language will his name be in? I once heard Ronald Wilson Reagan was the Anti-Christ because "Ronald" has 6 letters, "Wilson" has 6 letters, and "Reagan" has 6 letters. This is the linguistic equivalent of grasping at straws and has been proven wrong since President Reagan's death.

The only languages in which Biblical gematria matters are Hebrew or Greek. The only other gematria for which a Biblical case can be made are Aramaic (which has exactly the same number of alphanumeric symbols as Hebrew, 22) and possibly Latin (which is incomplete because not every Roman letter has a corresponding numeric value, only I, V, X, L, C, D, M). Some try to use English gematria to suggest that a U.S. president, the pope, or some other European leader may be the Anti-Christ. I disagree with such use. Stick with the Biblical languages!

The preterist view is that Nero the 6th emperor of Rome was the Anti-Christ. The Hebrew gematria for "Neron Caesar" is 666.

N	R	O	N	K	S	R	TOTAL
50	200	6	50	100	60	200	666

Nero was certainly an evil man who persecuted Christians and burnt the first followers alive (see chapter on 10 Days). While he certainly fits the bill as *an* antichrist, he is not *the* Anti-Christ.

The historicist view is that different popes were historically anti-Christ. While I don't endorse anyone being anti-Catholic (I am pro-Jesus and anyone including Catholics can also be pro-Jesus), the historicist view was prevalent among Protestant Reformers and is still the view of Seventh Day Adventists. They make their argument not only from the Roman Church's bloody history, but also from gematria. Let's take a look at a few.

Starting with Latin, the first 6 Roman numerals add up to 666.

I	V	X	L	C	D	TOTAL
1	5	10	50	100	500	666

A Latin title appearing on the pope's mitre until 1963 was *Vicarius Filii Dei* or the "Vicar of the Son of God." *Vicar* is the root of *vicarious*, meaning "substitute for." *Anti* in Greek is a prefix that not only means "against" but also "in place of." Therefore, the Vicar of Christ is interpreted to mean someone standing in place of Christ, the substitute of Christ, or "*anti*" Christ. The Latin gematria is curious.

V	I	C	AR	I	U	S	F	I	L	I	I	D	E	I	TOTAL
5	1	100	-	1	5	-	-	1	50	1	1	500	-	1	666

Moving on to Greek, historicists calculate the gematria of the Latin language.

L	A	T	E	I	N	O	S	TOTAL
30	1	300	5	10	50	70	200	666

How does the Latin language point us to the Roman Church? Latin is an extinct language no longer spoken by anyone in the old Roman Empire except the religious hierarchy living in the Vatican. Pope Vitalian (papacy 657–672) issued the decree that Latin must be used in all Catholic masses and official documents in A.D. 663, or 666 years after Christ's birth. Catholic Church goers could not understand the service or sermon until 1965, when the Latin requirement was finally dropped.

There are some other interesting Greek gematria. The Italian Church is *Italika Ekklesia* in Greek. The Latin kingdom is rendered *He Latine Basileia*. Both have a gematria of 666.

I	T	A	L	I	K	A	E	K	K	L	E	S	I	A	TOTAL
10	300	1	30	10	20	1	5	20	20	30	8	200	10	1	666

H	E	L	A	T	I	N	E	B	A	S	I	L	E	I	A	
-	8	30	1	300	10	50	8	2	1	200	10	30	5	10	1	666

Two other Greek words relating to the end times have a value of 666: *apostates* meaning "apostate" or falling away (from Bible-based Christianity) and *paradosis* meaning "tradition," which is what Jesus condemned as an evil substitute for the Bible. Mark 7:13 records, "Making the word of God of no effect through your tradition which you have handed down."

A	P	O	ST	A	T	E	S	TOTAL
1	80	70	5	1	300	8	200	666

P	A	R	A	D	O	S	I	S	TOTAL
80	1	100	1	4	70	200	10	200	666

Turning to Hebrew, historicists make their anti-Catholic case with two more gemtaria. *Romiti* means the "Roman man" and *Romiit* means the "Roman kingdom."

R	O	M	I	T	I	TOTAL
200	6	40	10	400	10	666

R	O	M	I	I	T	TOTAL
200	6	40	10	10	400	666

Many Catholics would find the antagonism some Christians have towards the popes to be shocking, but it is a subject worth studying. The atrocities the popes committed during the Crusades and the Inquisitions against Jews and Protestants are undeniable. Pilgrims and Puritans migrated to America to avoid religious persecution by the Catholic Church. It was Catholic persecution that sparked the exit of Jews from Europe in 1492.

Bible-believing Christians do not hate Catholics, but they dislike being wrongly associated with the Crusades and Inquisitions. Christianity has been blasphemed worldwide because of the cruelty and crimes of a religio-political power in Italy which has nothing to do with born-again Christians. No, Christians could not have started the Crusades or Inquisitions because Christians, Jews, and Muslims were the victims of these Roman Crusades and Inquisitions.

One can sympathize with the historicists who believe the popes fulfilled the role of many anti-Christs in history; but I do not believe the pope can be *the* Anti-Christ because of the plain text of the Bible, such as what we will read in Daniel chapters 8 and 11.

WILL THE NEXT ANTI-CHRIST STAND UP?

The futurist believes that though the spirit of anti-Christ has been operating in the world since the first century, and tribulation has always been a promise of the Christian experience in one form or fashion, *the* Anti-Christ and *the* 7-year period called Tribulation are due at the close of the Church age. Who is this Anti-Christ? Futurists also turn to gematria for some clues.

One interesting insight from gematria is that the Hebrew "w" (pronounced "vav") is the 6th letter of the Hebrew alevbeth (alphabet) and has the numeric value of 6; which means www (the World Wide Web) is numerically written 666 in Hebrew.

Although I don't think the Internet is the Anti-Christ, I do think that the Internet is a tool the Anti-Christ would like to use. Many young people and married men have become addicted to pornography through the Internet. The Internet has made evil much more easily accessible to people. Intellectually and socially the Internet is also a dangerous place because it has no moderator and anyone can say whatever they want to say or pretend to be whoever they want to be. Many Web surfers create their own make-believe identities. Others smear the identity of people they disagree with. The Internet has truly become the new Sodom and Gomorrah. In many ways www does represent 666.

Contrary to many sermons preached, the gematria of "Satan" is *not* 666. Undoubtedly Satan is an anti-Christ for he opposes Christ from the beginning. Satan will also demon possess a political leader whom Christians know as the Anti-Christ. The Jews will know him instead as the anti-Semitic "beast."

What is the Hebrew gematria for Satan? 359. If 360 refers to days in a year*, then Satan has ruled man every day minus 1 day. What is this one special day? Rabbis say Satan's power vanishes on the Day of Atonement or the day the high priest enters the holy of holies to offer a perfect lamb. Christians would agree that Satan was dethroned on the Day of Christ's Resurrection or Easter Sunday.

The Greek gematria for Titan is 666. The Titans in Greek mythology are a corruption of the Chaldean *Sheitan* and Hebrew *Satan*. The Titans were the race of giant offspring that came when fallen angels violated the daughters of men. Goliath was one of the last Titans.

T	E	I	T	A	N	TOTAL
300	5	10	300	1	50	666

The story of the hybrid race of Giants is one of the most curious in the Bible. It happened just before Noah's Flood and is one of the often overlooked causes

---

* All ancient calendars had 360 days in a year until the days of King Hezekiah (about 700 B.C.) when the Bible records the turning back of the shadow by 10 degrees. Since then most civilization adjusted their calendars by adding 4 to 5 days to the year.

of the end of Noah's world. Jesus predicted, "But as the days of Noah were, so also will the coming of the Son of Man be" (Matt. 24:37). If there is a parallel between Noah's time and our time, then we may see an increase in "paranormal" activities. Titans come closest a Biblical description of what modern people would call "aliens." They are humanoid—part normal, part paranormal. If the Greek gematria of Titan is prophetic of the Anti-Christ, then he may be involved in some UFO or alien encounter.

WILL ALIENS SAVE THE HUMAN RACE?

It needs to be explained in no uncertain terms that I do not believe any human has encountered an actual alien from another planet. In terms of physics, the distance between stars is simply insurmountable. The nearest star to us, *Proxima Centauri*, is over 4 light-years away. (That is the distance light travels at 300,000 kilometers per second for 4 straight years.) The nearest spiral galaxy, *Andromeda*, is *2 million* light-years away. A remote galaxy has been detected *13 billion* light-years away. The distances that must be bridged for any alien to visit Earth are unfathomable.

But what if aliens have the technology to travel really fast? In sci-fi movies, aliens can travel at warp or faster-than-light speed. While that's true in Hollywood, Einstein's theory of relativity virtually makes a closed book case against space travel, as any vehicle approaching the speed of light would also approach infinite mass. Alien believers must resort to space-time bending and hyper-dimensions, which are still products of fiction, not the real world.

I do believe that people believe they have seen aliens. In the Bible, aliens are demons. "Close encounter" stories about UFO sightings and alien abductions confirm they are evil spirits rather than outer space visitors. Dr. Gary Bates has done extensive research into this phenomenon and found at least 3 common threads in alien stories:

1. The UFOs are never sighted as entering Earth's atmosphere, but are always observed as though already here.

2. Aliens are often reported to appear suddenly or walk through walls, which begs the question: how do physical entities walk through solid walls?

3. One group on Earth is entirely immune from alien abduction: born-again Christians. Alien abductions have been reported by people of all religions, no religion, and nominal Christianity. But not a single alien has abducted a born-again Christian.

What about born-again Christians make aliens so averse to them? The Bible teaches that Satan and his demons are afraid of Jesus and born-again believers who know how to use His name.[2]

THEORIES ABOUT THE U.S. PRESIDENT

Let's come back to Earth to find other candidates for the Anti-Christ. Many Bible prophecy teachers were excited to find the Hebrew gematria of the Arab name "Hussein" is 666.

H	U	S	S	E	IN	TOTAL
5	6	300	300	5	50	666

Of course, with the execution of Iraqi dictator Saddam Hussein on December 30, 2006, that candidate can safely be eliminated. But prophecy teachers are turning to another world leader whose middle name Hussein means "handsome": Barack Hussein Obama. There are numericists who think they have made an airtight case that Obama is the Anti-Christ, and their gematria are impressive. But we cannot follow gematria over the plain text of the Bible.

The challenge I have in accepting a U.S. president as the Anti-Christ is simple, and it will keep you safe when interpreting prophecy: the Bible is primarily not a book about America, Australia, or Western Europe; it is primarily a book about the Middle East. If a U.S. leader were the Anti-Christ, it would be *despite* the fact that he is American, not *because* he is American. A U.S. leader could theoretically qualify as the Anti-Christ if he has some relationship to the politics and religions of Middle East. And this is where Obama may qualify as a unique world leader.

While I am not convinced about this hypothesis, I will present pieces of evidence for you to consider. Barack Hussein Obama was born on August 4, 1961, which is the 216th day of the year (6 x 6 x 6 = 216). He is the first president to be born into a non-Christian family. His father was a Kenyan and his stepfather was an Indonesian. Obama was schooled in Indonesia until the age of ten. In 1971, he was sent to live with his maternal grandparents in Honolulu, Hawaii, a city at 21.6 latitude north (6 x 6 x 6 = 216). In 1985 he moved to Chicago, Illinois, where he attended a radical Christian Church known for its black supremacist view, but now rarely makes mention of his Church, his pastor, and his Christian faith. His apostasy from Christianity is noteworthy in light of the gematria of *apostates*—666. In November 2004, Obama was elected senator of Illinois State. The address for Obama in Chicago, Illinois, has the zip code 60606 (remove the 0's to read 666). On the 5th of November 2007, one day after the U.S. presidential election, the day Obama made his winning speech, the winning "Pick 3" lottery in his home state was 6-6-6. And of course, his middle name, Hussein, is an Arab word meaning "handsome" with a Hebrew gematria of 666.

As I stated before, a U.S. president doesn't impress me as the Anti-Christ, but if Obama continues his career after his presidency is over as an international dignitary or the head of a global agency involved in Middle Eastern affairs, then I will revisit these coincidences and pay closer attention to this American leader.

WHERE WILL THE ANTI-CHRIST COME FROM?

To review, 666 is code for 3 things: first, an unholy trinity; second, the gematria of the Anti-Christ; third, 666 is a code that corresponds to Scriptural evidence about the nationality of the Anti-Christ.

There have been 6 major world empires that have oppressed Israel: Egyptian, Assyrian, Babylonian, Medo-Persian, Greek, and Roman. The number 666 can be identified with one of these major Gentile empires. According to E. W. Bullinger, the duration of the Assyrian Empire was 666 years.[3]

Despite many prophets and teachers' predictions that the Anti-Christ will be an American or European, he cannot be either. Neither the German Hitler nor Italian Mussolini nor American Henry Kissinger could have been the Anti-Christ. The Anti-Christ is plainly called numerous times in Scripture the "Assyrian." (See Isaiah 10:24, 14:25, 30:31; Micah 5:5–6.) This means the Anti-Christ cannot come from any country *outside* the old Assyrian Empire. The Anti-Christ must come from *within* the territory of the old Assyrian Empire— which today encompasses modern Iraq, Iran, and Syria. All three are current enemies of Israel and are unstable enough to start something nasty. The Bible is amazingly predictive!

If any Biblical character were a type of the Anti-Christ (the Anti-Semite to the Jews), the Pharaoh of Exodus surely qualified as one. Casual Bible readers have missed the nationality of this Pharaoh.

When one reads the story of Joseph, a Jewish son who saved Egypt from 7 years of famine, one has to ask a simple question: how could the Pharaoh of Exodus forget the story of this Jewish savior and end up enslaving Joseph's people by the time Moses was born? There seems to be a disconnect between the end of Genesis (Pharaoh's gratitude for the Jews) and the beginning of Exodus (the new Pharaoh's hatred and enslavement of the Jews).

A Bible student has to wonder, *How could a royal descendant of the Pharaoh of Genesis have possibly missed his education about Joseph?* The answer is found in 2 Scriptures. Exodus 1:8 tells us, "Now there arose *a new king* over Egypt, who did not know Joseph." This Pharaoh in Exodus was not from the same dynasty of the Pharaoh in Genesis. In fact, this Pharaoh was not Egyptian at all! He was a foreign conqueror identified by Isaiah. From which country did the evil Pharaoh come? Isaiah 52:4 tells us: "My people went down at first Into Egypt to dwell there; Then *the Assyrian* oppressed them without cause." The Assyrian invader assumed the title of Pharaoh when he rose to power. However, he would not have shared the history or knowledge of the previous Pharaohs. In many ways and places, God has told us who the Anti-Christ will be.

This ancient power struggle between Egypt and Assyria is magnified in the prophetic writings. Two significant end-time chapters that get almost no mention by prophecy teachers are Daniel 8 and 11. Like many prophetic Scriptures, they have dual fulfillment—one in past history (near future to the writer) and one in the future (far future to the writer; now near future to us).

Daniel chapter 8 correctly predicted the rise of the "he-goat" or Alexander the Great before he came to power. (Goat is a symbol of Greece, just as goat cheese is still identified with Greek food today.) Daniel 8 also predicted the future reemergence of the Greek Empire in the latter times. Most prophecy teachers are looking west to the Roman Empire. However, in the Bible Greece is more significant than Rome. Greek is the *language* of the New Testament. Greek is synonymous with *Gentile* to the Jews. In other words, Greece is the one to watch out for in the end times, for the Anti-Christ will come from a country within the former Greek Empire: modern Greece, Turkey, Syria, or Egypt. Interestingly, three of them share radical elements that call for the death of Israel.

Will the Anti-Christ be a Greek, Turk, Syrian, or Egyptian leader? Daniel chapter 11 narrows the candidate down to one of two options: the king of the North (Syria) or the king of the South (Egypt). Daniel predicted these two powers would fight. Daniel's prophecy has already been fulfilled once by the ancient wars between the Egyptian dynasty of Ptolemy's and the Seleucid dynasty of Antiochus's. But Daniel's prophecy must be fulfilled once more in the end times. These two countries will be engaged in some future dispute and the winner of the final dispute will become the greatest anti-Semite the Jews have ever known. Christians call him *the* Anti-Christ.

You may be asking, "Who was the winner of the past conflict?" The winner was the king of the North—Antiochus Epiphanes IV. He was the infamous man who committed the "abomination of desolation" on December 25, 167 B.C, by erecting a statue of Zeus inside God's Temple and sacrificing a pig on the altar of Yahweh. Hanukkah today celebrates the cleansing of the Temple from this abomination in 164 B.C.

Who will be the winner of the future conflict between Egypt and Syria? The king of the North—that is, another Syrian. This winner shall be "a vile person" who "shall come in peaceably, and seize the kingdom by intrigue," and "shall do according to his own will: he shall exalt and magnify himself above every god, shall speak blasphemies against the God of gods…he shall regard neither the God of his fathers [a Jew] nor the desire of women [possibly a homosexual], nor regard any god [an atheist]; for he shall exalt himself above them all [*the* Anti-Christ]" (Dan. 11:21, 36–38). Would a man fitting the above nationality and description have the motive and means to attack Jews and Christians? You had better believe it!

WHAT IS THE MARK OF THE BEAST?

God has given us many clues, but the simplest clue I believe is the fact that the mark of the beast is a financial (and thus spiritual) mark. Finance always speaks of ownership. When you pay money for something, you own that thing. When your boss pays you, he owns your time. When you're in debt, the lender owns you or your asset. Finance is such a powerful force that Jesus said, "You cannot serve God and mammon" (Matt. 6:24). Jesus did not say, "You cannot serve God and the pope," or, "You cannot serve God and worship on Sunday." Jesus juxtaposed God with money. Money is the anti-God. It's the thing to watch out for in the end times. The mark of the beast is reiterating the same point. I believe Jesus is not warning us of some esoteric debate about worship days.

The world is not enforcing Sunday as the rest day. The world could care less, as it is working 7 days a week! The Anti-Christ could care less when you go to Church, as long as the rest of the 6 days of your life are controlled by money; as long as you make decisions to obey or disobey God based on money; as long as you say no to tithing, no to Church building, no to missions, because there just isn't enough money, Lord!

Here are the facts we know without a doubt:

1. The mark of the beast is a mark of spiritual ownership (just as the mark on the 144,000 means God owns them).
2. The mark of the beast is a financial mark.
3. The mark of the beast is a spiritual deception that will be rampant, an almost universal danger in the end times.

4. The mark of the beast is a barrier to salvation.

Given these facts, why would anyone believe that a microchip implant is the mark of the beast? Why would a microchip hinder someone from being saved?

Jesus said, "You cannot serve God and mammon" (Matt 6:24). What are we to make of Jesus' statement? You *cannot* serve God and love money at the same time. Again Jesus said, "For where your treasure is, there your heart will be also" (v. 21). This is a way of saying money is connected to the heart. If you want to know what somebody loves, look where they put their money.

In all my years of travel and ministry, I know of no deception more widespread than the false belief that Christians don't have to tithe because tithing is in the Old Testament. Therefore, some Christians act no differently from the world by hoarding all their money for themselves. These people serve God with their lips, but serve money with their lives. Given a choice to believe the mark of the beast is a microchip implant or the god of money, which controls the way Christians give, which would you choose?

I know many Christians will not believe this. But I wouldn't play around lightly with money. I know pastors who do not tithe, yet ask their flock to tithe. Isn't it deception? I know Churches which do not tithe on their tithe. Isn't this the attitude of a taker, not a giver? Isn't Christ a giver and Anti-Christ a taker? Who are we to follow?

I ask you to carefully consider the harmony of Scriptures. The Bible predicts that there will be widespread deception and many people will be marked by this *financial* mark. Do you think God is warning us about not using credit cards, barcodes, or utilizing microchip technology? Is there a possibility that there may be a bigger problem and darker deception that Christians *don't have* to tithe? Isn't that Mammon speaking? Doesn't that attitude oppose the God's number one priority for us, which is doing the work of the Gospel?

Why don't Christians tithe? While people may offer many excuses, the principal reason people withhold their tithe is because the spirit of anti-Christ has misled Christians to believe that if they gave God so much as 10 percent of their income, they would no longer be able to *buy and sell*. The spirit of anti-Christ has branded their hands and foreheads with the irrational fear that they cannot survive if they gave to God and trusted Him with their material well-being. In other words, they won't be able to *buy and sell*.

Is this an end times issue? The last warning in the Old Testament was about robbing God of tithes. Some Christians claim this warning in Malachi 3 doesn't apply to us anymore. But carefully examine the context for yourself. Isn't the same chapter about tithes also about the future coming of Elijah the prophet and the future judgment? Can we dismiss Elijah and judgment just because it's in Malachi 3? Christians may view Malachi as "old," but put yourself in the Jews' perspective, they see it as the "end." Malachi is to the Jews what Revelation is to Christians—a final warning about how God will judge the human heart. According to God, loving money and refusing to tithe will become a major end times issue.

What about the excuses? What are the religious-sounding reasons to not tithe? "Tithing is not in the New Testament. Tithing is part of the old covenant law, so those who follow the law will be judged by the law." Knowing the New Testament, I would feel embarrassed to make such a claim! Aren't these Scriptures on tithing in the New Testament: Matthew 23:23, Luke 11:42, and Hebrews 7:8–9?

> But word to you Pharisees! For you *tithe* mint and rue and all manner of herbs, and pass by justice and the love of God. These you *ought to have done*, without leaving the others undone.
> —LUKE 11:42, EMPHASIS ADDED

Did Jesus teach us to love God and do justice? If so, we must accept the rest of the verse: He also told us to tithe! Our Lord said you *ought to* tithe.

> Even Levi, who receives tithes, paid tithes through Abraham, so to speak.
> —HEBREWS 7:9

This is a New Testament confirmation that tithing to God was practiced by every patriarch including Abraham through to Levi, hundreds of years before Moses was born or the Mosaic Law was instituted. Abraham gave tithes to Melchizedek, not because it was required by law, but because tithing is an eternal principle practiced by all godly people.

> Here [on Earth] mortal men receive tithes, but *there* [in Heaven] *he* receives them, of whom it is witnessed that he lives [that is *Jesus*].
> —HEBREWS 7:8, EMPHASIS ADDED

Does God care about tithes? The New Testament says the Lord Jesus personally receives tithes in Heaven when we give to His servants on earth. Just as every president or prime minister receives taxes through delegated authority (the tax office), God receives tithes through delegated authority (the

Bible-believing Church). What teaching could be clearer in the New Testament? Tithing matters because money represents people's heart, love, and desires.

The Old Testament prophets warn us about loving money. The Gospels warn us about loving money. The Epistles warn us about the loving money. The Book of Revelation is not a bizarre out-of-place message. If you will listen, it is the same message written by the same Author. Why are we searching high and low for an obscure invention that is not mentioned in the rest of the Bible, when something that is consistently talked about in the Bible can right now steal people's hearts away from God? It is very possible that the mark of the beast is an apocalyptic warning that those who love money may receive the Anti-Christ's spiritual branding on their hands and foreheads.

The Anti-Christ's system is a global financial system that enslaves people to debt and endless toil to pay off interest on debt. God's system is supernatural—tithe, sow, contribute selflessly and sacrificially, then your reward on earth and in Heaven will be great! Jesus said, "There is no one who has left house or brothers or sisters or father or mother or wife or children or lands, for My sake and the Gospel's, who shall not receive a hundredfold *now in this time*—houses and brothers and sisters and mothers and children and lands, with persecutions—*and* in the age to come, eternal life" (Mark 10:29–30, emphasis added).

Another excuse people use is this: tithing was bringing money, grains, and animal sacrifices into the Temple; since the Temple has been destroyed, we can no longer tithe. This is legalism. It is missing the *heart* of God by following the *letter* of the law. The heart of tithing in the Temple was to acknowledge God's ownership in every area of life and to support the ministry of God's work. Now that "One greater than the Temple" (Matt. 12:6; 23:17) is here, isn't it even better to tithe to *Jesus* directly (without having to go to Jerusalem) and to support the work of His *true* temple—the local Church and its work?

WHO IS THE ANTI-CHRIST?

The Anti-Christ cannot be anybody Christians don't like. He must meet certain qualifications delineated long ago in the Holy Scriptures. He must be from the Middle East, specifically the region of former Assyria or Syria proper. Something that seems to complicate the matter is he is called the Assyrian (Isa. 10:5, 12, Mic. 5:5–6), the Greek (Zech. 9:9–16), and the King of Babylon (Isa. 14:4; implied by Zech. 5:11 and Rev. 17–18). How can he be from all three places? Firstly, those ancient empires occupied overlapping territories. Secondly, Jesus was also predicted to be from 3 places: Bethlehem, Egypt, and Nazareth (Mic. 5:2, Matt. 2:1–6, Hos. 11:1, Matt. 2:13–15, Judg.

13:5, Matt. 2:23).[4] He fulfilled all 3 prophecies by being born in Bethlehem, hidden in Egypt for a season, then moving to Nazareth. Thirdly, in today's global village, one can be "from" many places. To take President Obama's case for an example, he could be from Kenya, Indonesia, Hawaii, Illinois, or Washington D.C., but one place he is *not* currently from is the Middle East. That could change. He could be "from" there if his future job relocates him there. Unless and until that happens, Christians should not be calling him the Anti-Christ.

The Anti-Christ will probably be the top henchman for a global financial system, whose center appears to be in New York or London, and may be shifting to China or India, but ultimately the Bible indicates the buck stops in the Middle East. The Middle East controls the world's energy resources and collects gold for currency reserves. It is the secret epicenter of the Anti-Christ's interests.

His one world government is not waiting to be built or elected. It is outside of election, above law, and beyond national boundaries. Only its full power and power players are waiting to be revealed. It controls the people of the nations and is seeking to control believers' lives. The only way to break free from it is to live a supernatural life in Christ and not believe that we cannot buy, sell, and live our lives unless we obey its demands and disobey God's commands.

OVERCOMING THE SPIRIT OF ANTI-CHRIST

Too many are serving Mammon instead of God. Too many are robbing God of tithes because they are in crippling debt to the world. Too many are serving the banks and financial institutions by skipping Church to work and pay off excessive debts and compounding interest. If you cannot afford to pay your loans or credit card bills, it's better that you give up your credit cards and luxury items and be able to honor God in practical ways. Your life will be less stressed, more blessed, and you will have more time and money left with which to serve God. We either serve God or Mammon. We either serve Christ or Anti-Christ.

God loves Christians in marketplace ministry. God blesses and prospers some of His saints with great wealth. Deuteronomy 8:18 says, "And you shall remember the LORD your God, for it is He who give you power to get wealth, that He may establish His covenant." It is not wrong for Christians to pursue business. But it is wrong to forget prosperity's purpose: to establish God's covenant, to save lives, and to spread God's Word. It is not wrong to be rich, but it is wrong to put riches first and tithing to God last. Guard your hearts by giving at least 10 percent of your income towards your local Church.

Some people do not know how to calculate their income. Let me help you. If you spend it, it's your income. If you're a student with no job but you pull $10 out of the ATM, $10 is your income and 10 percent or $1 belongs to God. If you have a business, you must minus your expenses from your gross income. Because that is more calculating, some Christian businessmen don't tithe but instead "owe God." Let me give you a tip. If your business buys you a $50,000 car, that's your income and you should have enough money to tithe at least $5,000 to God. It's better if you made exact calculations, but that is a rough guide that helps you put God first instead of ignoring Him while you spend money on yourself. God meets everyone at their level. Don't make excuses to not tithe. To not tithe is to make an idol out of your income. Idolatry, more than a national ID or scannable barcodes, is a risk I'm not willing to take.

I told the Lord, "People won't believe that the mark of the beast is a financial mark." (I speak to the Lord like I speak to a real person—He is *more* real than we are.) I told Him, "People will question, 'Are you saying salvation is linked to giving?' or they may object, 'God doesn't care that much about money!'" He told me, "You have Scriptures to show them." Here are the 3 New Testament cases He gave me.

First, wasn't Cornelius saved because of his giving heart? Acts 10 verses 4 and 31 record what the angel said to Cornelius before he heard the Gospel from Peter and was saved.

> Your prayers and your *alms* have come up for a memorial before God....Cornelius, your prayer has been heard, and your *alms* are remembered in the sight of God.
> — ACTS 10:4, 31, EMPHASIS ADDED

Listen to other translations!

> Your prayers and *charities*, he replied, have gone up and have been recorded before God....Cornelius, your prayer has been heard, and your *charities* have been put on record before God.
> —ACTS 10:4, 31, WEYMOUTH, EMPHASIS ADDED

> Your prayers and *offerings* have come up to God, and he has kept them in mind....Cornelius, your prayer has come to the ears of God, and your *offerings* are kept in his memory
> —ACTS 10:4, 31, BBE, EMPHASIS ADDED

Second, didn't Jesus connect Zacchaeus' salvation to his giving? Luke 19:8–9 records (emphasis added),

> Then Zacchaeus stood and said to the Lord, "Look, Lord, I *give half* of my goods to the poor; and if I have taken anything from anyone by false accusation, I restore fourfold." And Jesus said to him, "Today *salvation* has come to this house."

Zacchaeus did not pray the conventional sinner's prayer, which I believe in. Zacchaeus simply showed his genuine faith by his giving. In English we even say someone is genuine when they "put their money where their mouth is."

Third, did God care about how people treated offerings? In at least two instances, Jesus was watching how two women gave. In Luke 21:1–4, Jesus commended the woman who put in two mites (copper coins), "And He looked up and *saw* the rich putting their gifts into the treasury, and He *saw* also a certain poor widow putting in two mites. So He said, 'Truly I say to you that this poor widow has put in more than all; for all these out of their abundance have put in offerings for God, but she out of her poverty put in all the livelihood that she had'" (emphasis added). In Matthew 26:6–13, Jesus commended the woman who poured an alabaster box of costly oil on His head. Then He linked her offering to the Gospel, "Assuredly, I say to you, wherever this *gospel* is preached in the whole world, what this woman has done will also be told as a memorial to her" (v. 13, emphasis added). In all my years of travels, going to Churches, and listening to perhaps thousands of sermons, I have never heard someone connect this woman's giving to her salvation—have you?

Evidently giving placed a divine mark on Cornelius, Zacchaeus, and these two women. Giving shows the heart of someone who is ready to get saved or is saved. Is it not entirely possible and congruent with the rest of Scripture that *not* tithing places a spiritual mark on those who are stingy, selfish, or scared to trust God in the most private area of life? In life there are 2 groups of people: "givers" and "takers." In a real sense, salvation is based on Christ's giving. "For God so loved the world that He *gave* His only begotten Son" (John 3:16, emphasis added). When we become Christian, we become givers like Christ. In your opinion, who owns the "takers": Christ or the Anti-Christ?

SIGNS OF THE TIMES

The global financial crisis (GFC) since 2007 is only a symptom of Mammon's grip over people and governments at the highest levels. Remember Revelation 13:16–17 predicts, "He causes all, both *small* and *great, rich* and *poor*, free and slave [we would say self-employed and employed], to receive a mark on their right hand or on their foreheads, and that no one may buy or sell except one who has the mark" (emphasis added). What enslaves everybody on earth, the rich and the poor alike, the individual and the corporations alike, is lifelong debt and compounding interest. It is impractical, uneconomical, and unrealistic to inject everyone on the planet with a microchip. But it is not impractical at all to enslave everyone to interest payments which make them serve Mammon all their life.

The stage is set, but not for every human to have microchip implants or global ID. The stage is set, but not for the pope to control the world by making everyone worship on Sunday. These are theological fairy tales that make some people feel good about the group they are in and look down on others. The Bible is not about denominational debates or religious theory. It is about real life. The stage is set for the Anti-Christ to compete against God for the hearts, minds, and time of people by shackling them to the master of materialism and debt.

ANCIENT CODES STILL RELEVANT TO OUR TIMES

The divine codes about the ends times are more relevant than ever. The Middle East continues to be the center of political, economic, and religious turmoil. The Anti-Christ will be in the middle of all this.

God intended these time-bending predictions about the Anti-Christ and his financial system to be a major proof that His Word is divinely inspired. To those of us who have no prejudice for or against the Bible, we have before our eyes ample evidence of its trustworthiness. Don't let the spirit of anti-Christ deceive you!

969

HERE'S A RIDDLE POSED BY BIBLE COMMENTATOR CHUCK MISSLER, "WHO IS THE OLDEST MAN IN THE BIBLE, YET HE DIED BEFORE HIS FATHER?"[1] I would respectfully add to this riddle, "Who is the oldest man in the world who lived longer than his son but died before his father?"

His name was Methuselah, meaning "his death shall bring." Bring what? The worldwide Flood! Methuselah died at 969 years old, on the year Noah (his grandson) entered the ark and the Flood waters broke up from under the earth and the rain fell.

There are 2 big issues worth discussing about Methuselah. Firstly:

WHO KNEW ABOUT THE WORLDWIDE FLOOD?

Was it only Noah? Though little is known about Methuselah, enough evidence is given to tell us that the Flood was not a surprise to anyone who believed God. Enoch, Methuselah's father, must have known about the Flood, for he named his son "his death shall bring." Enoch never lived to see the Flood because he walked with God and was translated from this earth without ever dying.

Methuselah then named his son Lamech, meaning "sorrow," knowing the impending danger upon a sinful world. Lamech then named his son Noah, meaning "comfort" or "rest," indicating he already knew his son's destiny as the one to build the place of rest for survivors.

What the story of Methuselah brings out is a beautiful picture of how caring God has always been in revealing a rescue plan for mankind and how well-informed the first humans were. Because of evolutionary indoctrination, even Christians have a hard time believing that the earliest humans were intelligent just like us and in some ways better than us—for one, they lived healthier, longer lives. Evolutionists assume that the farther back we look, the more primitive and ape-like our ancestors were. Don't believe it!

People indoctrinated with an evolutionary mindset regularly confront historical evidence contradicting their theory, such as the ancients' ability to build pyramids in Egypt and the Mayan jungle (technology we no longer possess). They will stand in front of a pyramid in awe.

When told we can't even rebuild anything like it today, they are so shocked that the only explanation they can come up with is aliens must have built them. I suggest the other possibility is that evolutionary thinking is simply wrong. (Gasp!) The ancients were always intelligent because humans were made in the image and likeness of God and evolution is not true.

Whenever evolutionary thinking contradicts historical evidence, we have 2 options: take off our evolutionary glasses to see clearly; or add another pair of myopic lens on top of our evolutionary one to create a really blurred vision of a fanciful theory (like aliens came, built the pyramids, and left—nice work, Spock! Or was it a Klingon?).

When we refuse to admit evolution contradicts plain evidence, we end up seeing an absurd picture of reality in our minds. Now I don't expect non-Bible-believing readers to be convinced by this one chapter (I, as a hard-core evolutionist, took many years of persistent questioning and in-depth studying before coming to my conclusion), but I do expect Christians to read the Bible from a Biblical perspective instead of an evolutionary perspective.

Why is it important we question the evolutionary philosophy of the power elite? Because it affects the way people think about everything. A common question believers ask is, "How did people get saved before they knew about Jesus?" The question assumes that we know more than the ancients. The question is an assumption that the farther back we go, the less informative people were. But in fact, the opposite case is true. Adam should have been the most well-informed man in the world. First-century Jewish historian Flavius Josephus recorded that Adam was in possession of the knowledge of both the world wide Flood and the end of the age by fire.

> They [Seth's sons] also were the inventors of that peculiar sort of wisdom which is concerned with the heavenly bodies, and their order. And that their inventions might not be lost before they were sufficiently known, upon Adam's prediction that the world was to be destroyed at one time by the force of *fire*, and at another time by the violence and quantity of *water*, they made two pillars, the one of brick, the other of stone: they inscribed their discoveries on them both, that in case the pillar of brick should be destroyed by the flood, the pillar of stone might remain, and exhibit those discoveries to mankind; and

also inform them that there was another pillar of brick erected by them. Now this remains in the land of Siriad to this day.

—Josephus, The Antiquities of the Jews, 2.3, emphasis added

This has been in the history books for 2,000 years, yet I don't know one history teacher in our school system who is aware of it or knows what to do with this information. Adam was informed about the Flood! Adam was also informed about our modern race to a nuclear holocaust. Because of antediluvian longevity, Adam would have lived to see the birth of Lamech (Noah's father), which meant Adam and Noah would have been separated by only a generation. (Noah lived long enough to see Abraham.)[2]

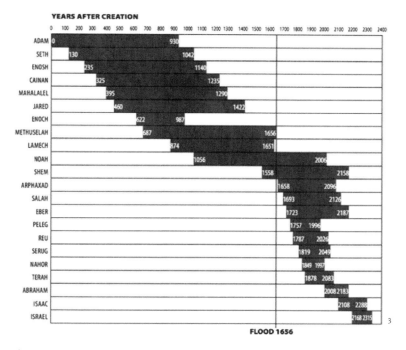

Information could have been transmitted accurately and personally from Adam to Enoch, Methuselah, and Lamech. Enoch was so well-informed about the Flood, he named his son Methuselah, or "his death shall bring." A New Testament writer records that Enoch was already knew about the Second Coming of Christ!

> Now Enoch, the seventh from Adam, prophesied about these men also, saying, "Behold, the Lord comes with ten thousands of His

saints, to execute judgment on all, to convict all who are ungodly among them of all their ungodly deeds which they have committed in an ungodly way, and of all the harsh things which ungodly sinners have spoken against Him [a clear reference to the Second Coming and Judgment Day].

—JUDE 1:14–15

Secular historians and some Christians now assume evolution is the answer and everything else has to fit this paradigm. This is neither open-minded nor scientific. Because of evolutionary indoctrination, we constantly make mistakes in understanding history and ignoring historical evidence. Understanding reality correctly helps us answer many spiritual questions, such as, "How did people get saved before they knew Jesus?" The answer is, "They had always known about Jesus. The New Testament didn't invent Jesus; it revealed His name to us." But the first humans who took God seriously also took the Messiah seriously. Adam knew a Blood sacrifice was an identifying marker of the coming Savior. Enoch knew the Savior would come with His saints to execute judgment on defiant and unrepentant sinners. Methuselah knew the world could not be saved except by faith in the Lord's wooden ark, a picture of the Lord's wooden cross. Everybody who has ever and will ever be saved can only be saved by faith in the one Savior of mankind.

The second issue some will ask about:

DO YOU REALLY BELIEVE PEOPLE COULD LIVE THAT LONG?

"Why did some people live long?" is not as interesting a question as "why do we die at all?" Originally God made us eternal and we were never meant to die. Biologically we have the potential to live forever. All our cells have the potential to rejuvenate endlessly. This is what the "stem cell" debate is about—how can scientists harness the body's innate ability to rejuvenate cells and hence organs and tissues? Physically man is capable of living on and on, scientists just don't know why there seems to be a "kill switch." For all our science, death is still a fundamental mystery.

It remains a mystery unless one is open-minded to the Biblical account of how things began, then history makes sense and our future becomes clear. God made both the earth and man perfect. Man was created to live and never to die. Environmentally, the universe was made to sustain life. Then a murderer named

Lucifer intruded on the happy scene. Adam and Eve obeyed this killer, sinned against the Creator, and since then death has lorded over mankind.

Instinctively we know death is a robber and an intruder. Why should we feel that way if evolution were true? Evolution presupposes millions of years of death and suffering, so shouldn't we feel death is natural by now? Why haven't we evolved to the point of enjoying evolution? Most of us feel death is morbid and in a real way "unnatural." Even the death of a fictional movie character can bring tears to our eyes. Again, why should this be so if evolution were true?

The Bible introduces death not as something natural or intended by God but as a "punishment" for sin and an "enemy" to be put down by the resurrection of the dead. Sin causes death. Sin is the reason we face the doom none of us look forward to. When compared to the life God intended for us to live, even a thousand years is a tragically short life. Our question every day should be, "Why do we live so short?"

Once we accept the Biblical perspective, we can look back into history with the correct premises. Research meteorologist Dr. Raul Lopez wrote:

> Analysis of the lifespans of Patriarchs and rulers in the Old Testament shows that the lifespan values over time clearly define a sigmoid curve. There is a regularity and order in the data that does not support the idea that Old Testament longevity values are mythological or manipulations of the Hebrew writers ... Acceleration of aging could conceivably be attributed to two major effects taking place— progressive changes in the genetic control of aging and progressive changes in environmental conditions that would accelerate cell deterioration.[4]

There are 3 identifiable stages of age decline. Before the Flood, the ages of the patriarchs were fairly stable at 895–969 years, except Lamech who lived up to his name (sorrow) and died at 777. A steep declined occurred after the Flood. Tracing Noah's descendants to Abraham, we see: Shem (lived to 600), Arphaxad (438), Shelah (433), Eber (464), Peleg (239), Serug (230), Nahor (148), Terah (205), and Abraham (175). Then another decline occurred after Exodus: Aaron (123), Moses (120), Joshua (110), and David (70).

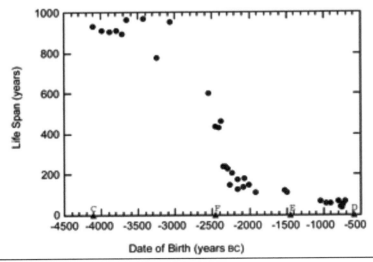

Life spans of Old Testament individuals on vertical Y axis. Year of their birth on horizontal X axis. Triangle abscissa point to 4 major events: Creation (C), Flood (F), Exodus (E), and Babylonian Deportation (D).

5

Dr. Lopez, who analyzes data for atmospheric science for over two decades, noticed the basic similarities within these 3 groups:

1. Not too many patriarchs died young
2. Most died at similar ages
3. Not too many lasted much longer than most
4. There is an upper limit to longevity in each period.

This kind of data suggests the Bible is not trying to record myths, but facts. It is worth mentioning that the Sumerian Kings List also recorded similar longevity in similar times as the Bible. My question is not, "Why did they live so long?" but, "Why do we now live so short?"

When it comes to theories about the aging process, there are two main sides: nature and nurture. On the nurture side, scientists attribute cellular aging to a number of factors: poor diet, free radical damage, immune system decline, increased stress, and disease. On the nature side, scientists claim aging and death may be preprogrammed into our genes or result from the accumulation of genetic mutations. Both sides could be right. Let's combine what we know to the Biblical account of history.

The Fall was a global disaster that made death possible. Yet given ideal conditions both environmentally and physically, it was reasonable that our early ancestors lived for hundreds of years. In the first 10 generations before the Flood, our environment was adversely affected by the Fall, yet still at its closest state to perfection. The Bible hints at the possibility that there was a protective canopy over the earth before the Flood. This could have blocked out much of the cosmic rays that harm life today. The condition of the soil and quality of food would have been near optimal. The first humans would have eaten perfect nutrition, drank pure mineral-rich water, and breathed perfect air. Mankind had not had time to dump toxic chemicals into the water, air, and soil. Our first ancestors would not have yet accumulated all the genetic mutations that we have today.

Notice after the second planetary disaster, Noah's Flood, the patriarchs' life spans decreased dramatically until it reached present levels. The Flood itself explains a lot. It would have caused a near-extinction "bottleneck" or huge loss of genetic information from the human population and a "founder effect" or concentration of similar genes, including similar genetic mutations, from the limited genome of 4 couples. The earth's conditions were never the same after the Flood. The canopy of Genesis disappeared from our atmosphere. The soil and food quality declined, implied by God's injunction for Noah to start eating meat for nutrients (Gen. 9:3).[6] We are no longer living in the Garden of Eden.

From the Bible's perspective, our bodies and environment have been much damaged by sin, and it's not over. The Bible predicts more diseases and disasters leading up to the very end. Why? God knew it would happen, but God is not to blame for giving us free choice. We are simply reaping what we sow. Many seeds of sin have been sown on the earth. The "end times" doesn't mean the end of the world, but a harvest time of every seed man has sown. We can still change our destiny by sowing humility, repentance, faith, and forgiveness. Will we do it?

People seem to live up to their names. Methuselah (his death shall bring) lived till the year of the Flood, God prolonging his life till 969 years; Lamech (sorrow) died the youngest of the 10 pre-Flood patriarchs (tragically before his father) at the age of 777; and Noah (rest) survived the Flood and found rest on the other side, living till the age of 950.

Until the millennial age of the Messiah, Methuselah will hold the record as the oldest man to live on Earth.

1948

MAY 14, 1948, is the birthday of the modern state of Israel.

Abraham, the father of Jews and Christians, was born in 2052 B.C.[1] If we express this in years after Adam's creation, Abraham was born on 1948 A.M. (*Anno Mundo*).[2] Coincidence? As the rabbis say, "Coincidence is not a kosher word!"

Multiplying Abraham's birth year by a factor of 3, we get another interesting number: 1948 x 3 = 5,844. The Torah contains 5,845 letters. Why 1 short, I don't know, but is this coincidence, too?

If Abraham's birth foretold the rebirth of the modern state of Israel, what might Isaac's birth tell us? Isaac was Abraham's son of promise (Gen. 18:10; Rom. 9:9; Gal. 4:23), therefore his birth could point to the coming of God's Son of Promise, Jesus Christ. No one should be dogmatic about it, but it is an interesting divine code to watch. Isaac was born 100 years after his father, which is 2048 A.M.

2048 happens to be one "Genesis generation"[3] away from the rebirth of Israel. Jesus said, "Assuredly, I say to you, this generation will by no means pass away till all these things take place" (Matt. 24:34; Mark 13:30; Luke 21:32). See chapter 2020 and Beyond.

1967

1967 IS THE YEAR Israel recaptured Jerusalem from Gentile control. This is the second most important prophetic date in modern Israeli history, prophesied about by the prophets including Daniel.

> Therefore the male goat [symbol of Greek Empire] grew very great; but when he became strong, the large horn [Alexander the Great] was broken [he died at the age of 33], and in place of it four notable ones [his 4 generals] came up toward the four winds of Heaven [Greek Empire broke up into today's Greece, Turkey, Syria, and Egypt]. And out of one of them [a descendant of 1 of the 4 generals] came a little horn [a double reference to a historical Gentile king who trampled Jerusalem, and also a future Anti-Christ who will repeat the process] which grew exceedingly great toward the south [Egypt], toward the east [Syria/Iran], and toward the Glorious Land [Israel]. And it grew up to the host of Heaven; and it cast down some of the host and some of the stars to the ground, and *trampled* them. He even exalted himself as high as the Prince of the host [historically both Ptolemy I and Antiochus I gave themselves the title *Soter*, which means Savior]; and by him the daily sacrifices [not the *yearly* atonement, but the *daily* burnt offerings or sacrifices of praise] were taken away, and the place of His sanctuary was cast down. Because of transgression, an army was given over to the horn to oppose the daily sacrifices; and he cast truth down to the ground. He did all this and prospered. Then I heard a holy one speaking; and another holy one said to that certain one who was speaking, *"How long* will the vision be, concerning the daily sacrifices and the transgression of desolation, the giving of both the sanctuary and the host to be *trampled underfoot?"* And he said to me, "For 2,300 days [NIV, NLT, NAS, and ESV all say "2,300 evenings and mornings"]; then the sanctuary shall be cleansed.
>
> —DANIEL 8:8–14, EMPHASIS ADDED

Jesus related this "trampling" idiom to Jerusalem falling under Gentile control.

> And Jerusalem will be *trampled by* Gentiles until the times of the Gentiles are fulfilled.
>
> —LUKE 21:24, EMPHASIS ADDED

We are given a precise number in an interesting idiom: "2,300 evenings and mornings." The literal level of interpretation means 2,300 literal evenings and mornings, or 1,150 days or a little over 3 years. This was literally fulfilled when 1,150 days[1] passed from Antiochus IV Epiphanes' abomination of desolation (a Gentile king defiled the Jewish Temple with an idol and pig sacrifice) till the cleansing of the Temple by the Maccabees, a victory celebrated each year at the feast of *Hanukkah*.

Why didn't Daniel just say "1,150 days"? One reason is that the daily sacrifices were offered twice a day, so 2,300 is the number of sacrifices that ceased from the abomination of desolation. But could God be giving us more divine codes?

On a prophetic level of interpretation, 2,300 becomes an important number if a day is also code for a year.[2] Literalists oppose this "day-year" principle. They see a day is only a 24 hour period, and that is true in most cases. However, when it comes to prophetic passages, the Law of Double Reference applies. Both the literal day and the symbolic year interpretations can be correct. The beauty of the Bible is both sides who love God's Word can be right! Take a look at the evidence below and decide for yourself whether 2,300 years was prophetic of Israel's future.

Daniel predicted that starting from a Gentile king trampling on Jerusalem till a future restoration would be 2,300 years. When was the trigger date for us to start counting? There are 2 viable options.

In 332 B.C., Alexander the Great invaded Jerusalem. 332 B.C. + 2300 years = A.D. 1967. (Less 1 year for no year "0.") 1967 is the year Israel re-captured Jerusalem after a decisive victory in the Six Day War.

In 319 B.C., one of Alexander's 4 generals, Ptolemy I Soter (Ptolemy the Savior), invaded Jerusalem.[3] Converting 2300 Biblical years of 360 days each to our modern year of 365.25 days, we get 2267 years. 319 B.C. + 2267 years = A.D. 1948. 1948 is the year Israel fulfilled prophecy by reemerging as a sovereign nation state.

Coincidence? (For more calculations and updates beyond the scope of this book, visit the bonus section of our website: www.discover.org.au/2020).

2011

PROPHETIC SIGNIFICANCE OF 11

11 SPEAKS OF DISORDER, disintegration and things falling apart for the ungodly, according to prophetic teacher Henry Pillai. The 11th hour is the last hour of a clock. World War I ended at the 11th hour (French time) of the 11th day of the 11th month of 1918. Prophetically we have been living in the 11th hour of human history since. On 20 April 2010, British Petroleum (BP)'s Deepwater Horizon oilrig exploded in the Gulf of Mexico, killing 11 people. I think we will all remember where we were when President Obama announced Osama bin Laden was shot dead. I was sitting in the car of a Bible school director in Brisbane. It was Monday morning Australia time, but it was the 11th hour of Sunday, May 1, 2011 in Washington D.C. time! I do not recall any other president delivering a televised statement at the 11th hour before midnight!

2011 was characterized by political upheaval in the world and chaos in Nature. The Middle East descended into chaos in 2011, at first rioting over higher food prices, but then protesting against corrupt governments after the region was encouraged by the ousting of Egyptian President Hosni Mubarak on February 11.

The greatest earthquake that ever struck Japan occurred on the 11th of March 2011, tilting the earth's axis by 10cm, triggering a tsunami that reached 10km (6 miles) inland, killing over 28,000 people and igniting a nuclear reactor crisis. 2011 saw a bizarre range of natural disasters: From December 2010 to January 2011, Queensland, Australia experienced flooding that killed 35 people and cost at least $1 billion of damage; in January a week of monsoon floods killed 23 people in Sri Lanka and left 1 million homeless; in the same month flash flooding killed 500 in Brazil; on 22 February a 6.3 magnitude earthquake struck Christchurch, New Zealand, killing 181 people; on 24 March a 6.8 magnitude earthquake struck the Shan State of Burma, leaving 120 dead. These are the signs of what Jesus called "birth pangs" or the earth going into contraction before the Second Coming of Christ.

Here are some significant modern events falling on the 11th:

DATE	EVENT
11th December 1917	JERUSALEM: General Allenby was commanded to invade Jerusalem and set the city free from the Turks.
11th September 2001	USA: The spirit of terror was released on this planet when terrorists commandeered 4 airplanes into the Twin Towers, the Pentagon, and a field in Pennsylvania.
11th February 2010	IRAN: anti-government demonstrations on the 31st anniversary of the Islamic Revolution of 1979 which had replaced a Westernized monarchy with the Shi'a theocracy of Ayatollah Khomeini.
11th February 2011	EGYPT: President Hosni Mubarak left office after 30 years of corrupt rule. While in power, he reportedly amassed a personal wealth of $70 billion, which would make him the world's richest man.
11th March 2011	JAPAN: 9.0 earthquake and tsunami killed over 28,000 and caused nuclear radiation contamination.

September 11 marked a milestone in terror. It was the worst terrorist attack on American soil. The symbols of this tragedy were the Twin Towers, which look like number "11". Other patterns of 11 are associated with this terrorist attack.

Date of the terrorist attack was 9/11	$9 + 1 + 1 = 11$
September 11 is the 254th day of the year	$2 + 5 + 4 = 11$
Number of floors in the Twin Towers	110 or 11 x 10
The first plane to hit the Twin Tower	Flight 11
Number of passengers on Flight 11 was 92	$9 + 2 = 11$
Number of passengers on Flight 77 was 65	$6 + 5 = 11$
Number of passengers on Flight 93 was 38	$3 + 8 = 11$

Number of letters in the official name of the President during the attack: George W. Bush	11 letters
Number of letters in the code name Secret Service assigned to the President: Trailblazer	11 letters
Number of letters in the official name of the most devastated target: New York City	11 letters

2012

THANKS TO THE MOVIE **2012** everyone seems to know something significant is predicted to happen very soon, maybe even the end of the world as we know it. However, what the moviegoers are told is not the most interesting part about this number 2012.

Why is it that the Mayans, who were meticulous timekeepers, predicted that the world would end on precisely the 21st of December 2012? Let me say first of all that as a Christian, I do not believe the Mayan calendar as much as the Hebrew calendar, but before we get to that, let's explore what the Mayans thought.

The Mayans believed that God (or gods) created 4 different ages, and we are currently living in the 4th age. The 1st age had no human beings in it. The 2nd and 3rd ages included human beings, but they were destroyed both times. In the 4th and final age, human beings have been given a remaining 5,126 years to live and please God (or gods).

If the Mayan belief that our present age should last about 5,000 years is correct, we should want to find out when the Mayan countdown started. According to the Mayan "long count" calendar, the present world had its beginning in 3114 B.C. Counting forward 5,126 years, we arrive at 2012. The date touted, December 21st, simply coincides with winter solstice or the darkest day of 2012.

Of course, none of this was taught in the movie *2012*. Why? Because on the one hand, Hollywood wants us to believe the Mayans were extremely skilled mathematicians (they were!), but on the other hand, they don't want us to know the same Mayans believe humans have been on earth for about 5,100 years. These intelligent people were obviously *not* evolutionists and did *not* believe humans have been evolving for 5 million years.

But it's hard to shake off bias. People interpret data to fit their own frame of reference. One evolutionist conjectured whether these Mayan ages actually refer to stages of human evolution, but the timeline is incongruent with their own theory. 5,000 years is not enough time for any macro-evolutionary change much less speciation. Humans were 5,000 years ago exactly as humans are today!

If you start out believing in millions of years and evolution as facts, and then you confront the incredibly precise calculations of the Mayans telling you they believe the world will end in 2012 because this current world was created in 3114 B.C., you would have a dilemma on your hand. Were these people really intelligent or were they dumb-dumbs?

On the one hand, evidence points to their genius in science. The Mayans had advanced forms of astronomy, mathematics, art, and architecture. They built great pyramids in the middle of a thick tropical jungle. They engineered a pressurized water system before the arrival of Europeans.[1] Their astronomers calculated the length of a solar year to a precision. Our present Gregorian calendar counts 365.2425 days in a year; the Mayan calendar counted 365.2420 days; and modern astronomy counts 365.2422 days. The Mayans were off by only 0.0002 day, making them more accurate than the Gregorians! Their astronomers also figured out that 5 Venus years roughly equals 8 Earth years (5 x 584 days = 8 x 365 days). I don't know what they did with that fact, but that's pretty interesting!

On the other hand, some may argue, "Why should we believe these barbarians? Didn't they practice human sacrifice?" We do not believe their morals because they were godless people, but we can take their math seriously because they were great mathematicians.

At the end of the day, an evolutionist selectively chooses to believe the mystical 2012 and dismiss the "nonsensical" date 3114 B.C. because of bias. But that is not intellectually honest.

Leave the bias aside and ask yourself what makes 5,000 years ago a special starting date. Did you know that in 2010, major ancient civilizations like Greece, China, and Japan all celebrated "5,000 years of history"? According to Dr. John Heffner quoting PBS, "No single artifact, inscription, pottery, or anything has been found in any place to predate Egyptian civilizations more than 5,000 years ago."[2] If humans have been around for 5 million years, have you ever asked yourself why we have no written record, no stanza of poetry, no line of music, no piece of legislation, dating further than 5,000 years? It appears as if the major civilizations sprung up overnight 5,000 years ago, complete with written language, legal codes, magnificent architecture, and advanced sciences. How could this happen?

The Bible records a significant event about 5,000 years ago which wiped out a previously thriving human population: the global Flood. Only 8 people—Noah and his family—survived on a mega large ark. This is corroborated by other global flood stories from all around the world. Might this be the event which started the Mayan countdown around 5,000 years ago? The coincidence is uncanny.

Furthermore, we know another calendar that dates the age of humanity at about 5,000 to 6,000 years: the Hebrew calendar. Now if there ever were a people who were meticulous counters, it was the Jews. Jewish rabbis actually counted the number of letters in a Torah (Old Testament) manuscript to verify whether or not it's been faithfully copied. One missing letter meant the entire copy had to be buried and the copyist job restarted. Unfortunately, a lot of numerology and mysticism have arisen from the well-known fact that the Jews are exact counters.

What year is it on the Hebrew calendar? Add 3,760 years to our Gregorian year and you will roughly get the Jewish year.[3] For instance, the Gregorian 2010 is the Hebrew 5770. In other words, the Jews believe that it has been roughly 5770 years since the creation of Adam. The Jewish estimate of creation at 3761 B.C. is startlingly similar to the Mayan estimate of 3114 B.C.

It is hard to imagine 2 cultures that would be more different than the Jews and the Mayans, yet they had a consensus on the date of the creation of the world. They were not alone. Here are some other creation dates[4] from history:

- 5555 B.C.—the 1st century Jewish historian Josephus' date
- 5507 B.C.—a Persian date
- 5493 B.C.—the Ethiopian Church's date
- 5490 B.C.—the Syrian Church's date
- 5481 B.C.—a second estimate by Josephus
- 4004 B.C.—the date of both Dr. John Lightfoot, a 17th century Anglican minister, and Irish Archbishop James Ussher (1581–1656)
- 3993 B.C.—estimate by German astronomer Johannes Kepler (1571–1630)
- 3761 B.C.—Jewish calendar
- 3114 B.C.—Mayan calendar

So is 2012 the year of the end of the world? It depends on your calculation. Jews and Christians have traditionally held the view that God gave man 6,000 years to steward the earth before a day of reckoning. How soon that day is coming depends on your starting point, so an accurate creation date is quite significant to end-time prophecy buffs.

We will revisit the Hebrew calendar again in the last 2 chapters.

LAST THOUGHTS ON 2012

Before we leave the year 2012, two more comments. First, the Mayans are not the only ones pointing to 2012. Some scientists are also concerned that the sun follows an 11-year cycle and its solar storm peak is due in 2012. This is a time when the solar poles can reverse (see chapter 11). Of relevance to our lives, a powerful magnetic storm can harm astronauts in space, disrupt communication on Earth, and even melt our power grids.

Second, to what were the Mayans referring when they said we are living in the 4th and final age, and what were the other 3 ages before ours? Of course these Mayan ages do not fit within the evolutionists' millions of years. Rather they fit surprisingly well with the Scripture's account. The 1st Mayan age where no humans existed fit well with the age in which angels lived with God and one-third of the angels rebelled with Lucifer. God's expulsion of the fallen angels out of Heaven closed the 1st age. The 2nd and 3rd ages included humans, but both were ended unhappily. These coincide well with the Fall of Adam which ended the age of innocence and Noah's Flood which ended the age of gross immorality on the earth. The 4th and final age corresponds to our time period, in which God promises not to destroy the earth again by flood (therefore there will be no repeat of the previous age), and extends the gift of salvation to us for a limited time (the *final* opportunity for redemption).

2013-2014

WHILE THE MAYANS MAY HAVE BEEN LOOKING FOR A MAJOR EVENT IN 2012, God does not follow the Mayan calendar. But, as we will see, the Mayans may not have been too far off.

UNDERSTANDING GOD'S CALENDARS

God's calendar is the Hebrew calendar, not the Mayan calendar or Gregorian calendar. When God created the world in Genesis 1, he called the first month Tishri, not January. So much confusion about the end times and Biblical prophecy originates from the fact that we tend to read Scriptures with Gentile eyes and hear sermons with Gentile ears, rather than with the original Hebrew understanding. The Bible tells us, in fact, that the Jews had 2 calendars: one civil starting with Tishri 1 as the New Year (called Rosh Hashanah in Hebrew); the other religious starting with Nisan 1.

Why might this be? Everything in the Old Testament is fully revealed or fulfilled in the New Testament. In the Old Testament, Tishri the 1st signified either the creation of the world on day 1 or the birth of Adam on day 6. Naturally this was a good starting point for humanity's calendar. But then God chose a people group to receive His Word and His Messiah—the Hebrews. These people's lives, struggles, and victories would become a drama of God's plan of salvation for the rest of humanity. After the Hebrews fell into slavery in Egypt, they were brought out, not by their own strength or through their own efforts, but by God's grace activated by their faith. These slaves of Egypt were saved from the angel of death by the Blood of the Passover lamb. When this salvation occurred on Nisan the 14th, God told Moses: Start a new calendar! "This month is to be for you the first month, the first month of your year" (Exod. 12:2, NIV).

What is the spiritual significance of this new start in the Old Testament? Nisan the 14th—the day the Jews were saved by the Blood of a lamb and enjoyed a fresh start—happens to be the very day Jesus Christ shed His Blood on the cross and the whole world was given the opportunity to have a new beginning. And yes, the entire world started a new calendar to commemorate Jesus as the Savior of the world! The parallels between the events at Passover and the Cross are uncanny. Whose mind but God's could have predicted and orchestrated such global events to harmonize with Scripture?

The 2 Jewish calendars have prophetic application, global application, and also personal application. Every Christian knows that he or she has 2 birthdays: the first is the one none of us chose, our natural birthday; the other is the one we get to choose, the day we are born again through faith in Christ. Every Christian, in effect, runs on 2 calendars—a natural one that started on one's entry into the world (with no choice) and a spiritual one that started on one's entry into the kingdom of God (by our choice).

God's calendars were a shadow of the personal experience of the new birth, a new beginning we instantly get when our sins are washed away! But there's more to God's calendars.

APPOINTED TIMES ON GOD'S CALENDARS

Once we make the switch from sin to salvation, from natural life to spiritual life, from civil calendar to sacred calendar, so-to-speak, there are divine landmarks God has set in our spiritual calendar. They are the 7 feasts of God or 7 annual appointments with God. Please read the chapter on 7 Feasts to understand how they were designed not only to be commemorative, but also predictive.

For instance, if any ancient believer had studied the first 4 Biblical feasts carefully, he would have been able to tell the exact month and day on which:

1. Jesus would be crucified,
2. Jesus would be buried,
3. Jesus would rise from the dead, and
4. the Holy Spirit would descend on the Church and fill the believers with power!

The only unknown would have been which year would these events occur on God's calendar? The month and day were predetermined by God's calendar and predicted by the prophets when God set out His "appointed times." This begs the question: if the first 4 feasts were fulfilled to the exact month and day, is there any reason the last 3 feasts shouldn't also be fulfilled to the exact month and day? They should!

2 questions remain: what events will fulfill the last 3 feasts? and in which year? The answer to the first question is easy. Whereas the first 4 feasts pointed to events during the first coming of Messiah, the last 3 feasts now point to events relating to His Second Coming. Specifically, trumpets point to the Rapture of

the Church, Yom Kippur points to the Second Coming and national salvation of Israel, and Sukkot points to the millennial reign of Christ.

The answer to the second question requires us to dig deeper into the calendars and feasts of God.

THE SUN AND MOON

All Jewish feasts (and all description of time for that matter) ultimately have their basis in the movement of sun and moon. The first of every Jewish month always falls on a new moon, called Rosh Chodesh (head of the month), and is a minor holiday. While Gentiles are not as fastidious about counting moon cycles, Gentiles have *months* because of the *moon's* orbit around the earth.

Because of the simple relationship between time, the sun, and the moon, it has come to the attention of end-time teachers that we may need to pay more attention to the sun and moon to discern the "signs of the times." This is not astrology, but simple astronomy. It was God who said in Genesis 1:14 (emphasis added), "Let them [sun, moon, and stars] be for *signs* and for *seasons* [Hebrew *moed*, the same word as "feasts" or God's appointed times], and for days and years." Other Scriptures confirm we should take this direction.

> The sun shall be turned into darkness, and the moon into blood, before the great and terrible day of the LORD come.
> —JOEL 2:31

> The sun shall be turned into darkness, and the moon into blood, before the great and notable day of the Lord come.
> —ACTS 2:20, KJV

> Immediately after the tribulation of those days the sun will be darkened, and the moon will not give its light.
> —MATTHEW 24:29

> Then I saw the lamb open the sixth seal. There was a powerful earthquake. The sun turned as black as sackcloth made of hair, and the full moon turned as red as blood.
> —REVELATION 6:12, ISV

All 4 passages relate to the end times. All 4 passages tell us what to look at in the end times: Look up! Didn't Jesus tell us in Luke 21:28 (emphasis added),

"Now when these things begin to happen, *look up* and lift up your heads, because your redemption draws near"? What's up above our head? The sun, moon, and stars! Who made them? Not the devil. Our God did, and He made them to point to His Son Jesus. If you want to see a sign, look at what God made in the sky!

For years Bible teachers have puzzled over what the sun turning into darkness and moon into blood could mean. When in doubt, I believe the simplest, most literal answer is the best one. There is no need to spiritualize the literal or obscure the obvious. What if the Bible was simply referring to solar and lunar eclipses?

A total solar eclipse blocks out the light of the sun. A total lunar eclipse is called a "blood moon." Jewish rabbis have long associated solar eclipses with judgment on the Gentiles and lunar eclipses with judgment on the Jews. Dark signs for dark times! By searching the NASA website for past, present, and future eclipses, we find some eclipses that coincide with God's appointed feasts. First, we should understand a special astronomical pattern called a *tetrad*, that is, 4 consecutive blood moons or total lunar eclipses. If an eclipse falls on a Jewish holiday, it would be significant. But if 4 consecutive lunar eclipses all fell on 4 Jewish holidays, that would be remarkable!

Pastor Mark Biltz found the following tetrads occurring not only on God's feast days, but also near significant events relating to God's dealing with the Jews. 1967 and 1948 are without doubt 2 of the most significant years for Israel in modern history. Were there any fearful sights and great signs from Heaven?

Tetrad on 4 Feasts near the time the Israel regained Jerusalem in the Six Day War of 1967

24 April 1967	18 Oct 1967	13 April 1968	6 Oct 1968
Passover	Sukkot	Passover	Sukkot

Tetrad on 4 Feasts immediately after the rebirth of the State of Israel in 1948

13 April 1949	7 Oct 1949	2 April 1950	25 Sep 1950
Passover	Sukkot	Passover	Sukkot

Were these mere coincidences? How often do tetrads occur? Twice in the 1900s, none in the 1800s, none in the 1700s, none in the 1600s, six times in the 1500s, but none fell on Passover or Sukkot. If we go back one more century, we find another amazing tetrad.

Tetrad on 4 Feasts around the time of the Spanish Inquisition and Jewish Diaspora in 1492

2 APRIL 1493	25 SEP 1493	22 MAR 1494	15 SEP 1494
Passover	Sukkot	Passover	Sukkot

If we go forward in time, we find that tetrads will occur 6 times in this century, but only 1 string of blood moons will coincide with God's Feasts. A tetrad on God's Feasts will never occur again in our lifetime, except on these dates:

15 APR 2014	8 OCT 2014	4 APR 2015	28 SEP 2015
Passover	Sukkot	Passover	Sukkot

If lunar eclipses on the Jewish feasts qualify as the "moon turning into blood", solar eclipses should qualify as the "sun turning into darkness." Let's overlay some solar eclipses on our timeline. There will be a total solar eclipse on 20 March 2015. What's significant about that? It happens to be 1 Nisan 5775 on the Hebrew calendar, or the Religious New Year! There will be a partial solar eclipse on 14 September 2015. What's interesting about that date? It happens to be 1 Tishri 5776, the Civil New Year, or the Date of Creation!

15 APR 2014	8 OCT 2014	20 MAR 2015	4 APR 2015	14 SEP 2015	28 SEP 2015
Passover	Sukkot	Religious New Year	Passover	Civil New Year	Sukkot
Lunar Eclipse	Lunar Eclipse	Solar Eclipse	Lunar Eclipse	Solar Eclipse	Lunar Eclipse

Truly the sun and moon are for signs! God is giving us a clue He is coming soon! When the prophet Joel said, "The sun shall be turned into darkness, and the moon into blood, before the great and terrible day of the LORD come," we can read it this way in modern language, "Before the great and terrible day of the LORD come, there will be a total solar eclipse and a total lunar eclipse." The concentration of eclipses on God's Feast Days on God's calendar around 2014-2015 is a sure sign something big is about to happen!

This does *not* mean the Second Coming will be in 2014 or 2015, but if past patterns are prophetic, then we should expect a major event involving Israel around the time of 2014–2015. If I had to make an educated guess, I would say that the major event will involve an announcement regarding Jewish rights to the Temple Mount and the rebuilding of the Third Temple on that site. Nothing could be a better symbol of peace than Jews and Muslims sharing the use of the Temple Mount, with the Al Aqsa mosque and Jewish Temple coexisting side-by-side. However, this will be the *false* "peace and safety" before "sudden destruction comes" (1 Thess. 5:3).

Yet another divine code is the fact that 2014 will be a *shmita* or sabbatical year. According to the Bible, the Jews must rest the land every 7th year. Then after 7 cycles of 7 years (49 years), the Jews are to celebrate a *Jubilee* year. The Jubilee is a year of releasing all debts and complete rest. It points to the ultimate jubilee we find in Christ, who releases us from our debt of sin and gives us rest from the condemnation of the law. The Jubilee is a fitting type of Christ and His millennial reign, when the curse of the world will be lifted.

When will the next Jubilee be? Jewish rabbis have lost count of when the Jubilee should be, but we know that a Jubilee can only follow a *shmita* year, so 2015 may qualify as a Jubilee! We also know that a Jubilee can only be proclaimed on Yom Kippur or the Day of Atonement, and Yom Kippur 2015 may be a very special date indeed. (See chapter on 70 Sevens.)

What this conjunction of signs means is things will not always remain as they are now, and God's Word is about to be proven true once again. The Tribulation is soon, the Anti-Christ is waiting in the wings to be revealed, and the Second Coming of Christ is closer than many think. It certainly won't hurt to "watch" and "pray." It won't hurt to expect our Lord's coming soon. It's time to live holy and seek first the kingdom of God. Jesus told us in Luke 21:28 (emphasis added), "Now when these things begin to happen, *look up* and lift up your heads, because your redemption draws near."

2020

AND BEYOND

ONE OF THE BIGGEST PHOBIAS in the body of Christ is "date-setting." If you skipped the entire book to find out whether I will set a date for the Second Coming, please save your theological bullets (to shoot date-setters) and read the previous chapters first.

Undoubtedly I will not be able to convince all to keep an open mind. No matter how much I explain, some will be bent on criticizing any hint of "date-setting" without understanding I offer no dogma or date. I present the codes; you decide. I do not claim to know when the Second Coming will be.

I believe Matthew 24:36 (NIV), "About that day or hour no one knows, not even the angels in Heaven, nor the Son, but only the Father.'" At the same time I also believe other Scriptures like:

> But you, brethren, are *not* in darkness, so that this Day should *overtake* you as a thief. You are all sons of light and sons of the day…Therefore let us *not sleep*, as others do, but let us *watch* and be sober."
>
> —1 THESSALONIANS 5:4–6, EMPHASIS ADDED

The Holy Spirit told Christians that whereas the Second Coming will seem to come suddenly, unexpectedly, or without warning to *unbelievers*, it should not overtake us the *sons of light* by surprise!

We do not know the exact hour, but we are not to fall asleep like the 5 virgins just before the Bridegroom comes! We are to watch. What for? For the

---

* This doesn't mean the Son doesn't presently know the date of His own Second Coming, for He would not be God if He were ignorant of that fact. He only laid aside His omniscience and other privileges as God while He walked on the earth. Philippians 2:7 explains this and it's helpful for students to read this passage in many translations. The New American Standard reads, "But [He] emptied Himself, taking the form of a bond-servant, and being made in the likeness of men." The New Living Translation, "Instead, he gave up his divine privileges; he took the humble position of a slave and was born as a human being." Weymouth Bible says, "Nay, He stripped Himself of His glory."

Bridegroom's arrival, for Christ's Return! In other words, we should be aware of the approximate season of His coming.

But I am concerned, as Jesus was, that many have fallen asleep just before the wedding. Not only are so many disinterested in keeping their lamps burning in anticipation of the Bridegroom, they want to put out the lamps of the 5 virgins preparing for and talking about His arrival!

> You must understand that in the last days scoffers will come, scoffing and following their own evil desires. They will say, "Where is this 'coming' He promised? Ever since our fathers died, everything goes on as it has since the beginning of creation."
>
> —2 PETER 3:3–4, NIV

If anyone is a scoffer, they will find themselves not contradicting the Bible, but fulfilling what it says! For the Bible has the audacity to predict it will not only be around for eternity, but it will be so captivating that public interest in its codes will be raised to fever pitch near the end, pricking the ire of scoffers and confirming the blessed assurance of believers.

WHEN IS THE END?

For the reader who is genuinely interested in when the "end of the world" might be, I have some good news and bad news. The good news is the Bible promises there will be no end of the world, not in the sense of human extinction or a planetary explosion. No! God assures us that He made this Earth to be inhabited forever, and we humans are eternal spirits that will live on forever. In His love, He has destined the earth and us to be a part of His plan, if we so choose. That's the good news.

The bad news? Depending on how you look at, things are not going to continue as they are forever—and that's bad news for some and more good news for others. Undoubtedly there are portents indicating that the earth is in contraction or as Jesus forewarned 2,000 years ago "in labor pangs" waiting to both expel sinners off the face of the planet and deliver up the "sons of God" unto resurrection. No, the world will not be destroyed and humanity will not go extinct, but this present age of rebellion and grace is coming to an end. The pertinent question is *how soon?*

As far as speculation and imagination, there is no shortage when it comes to date-setting. 1998 was going to be the end because 666 + 666 + 666 = 1998. When that failed, 2,000 was going to be the end because 2,000 ÷ 3 = 666.666.

Scripture does not give us the liberty to add, subtract, divide, or multiply 666 any way we so choose. As far as sound Biblical interpretation of end-time chronology, there seems to be little rigorous or systematic application of the conventional rules of interpretation. Simply put, we must stick to the Bible.

I would encourage you to study particularly chapters 2012 and 2013–2014 and understand them thoroughly before reading on. Having done that, you can be prepared to understand that what I am about to say is not intended to minimize the importance of those approaching dates.

A major event will occur to Israel in the vicinity of 2012–2014. I hope it will be the rebuilding of the Temple in Jerusalem. It could be the Ezekiel 38 invasion from the north, a war which Israel is predicted to win since 3,500 years ago, when the book of Ezekiel was written. It could even be the Second Coming of Christ, but it does not have to be. Why? Because there are divine codes pointing towards 2015, 2020, and beyond.

My intention is not to cause any controversy about how soon or how long prophetic events will transpire, but to report the divine codes and let you decide the timeline. The codes exist and they are real. But to which event they refer cannot be stated dogmatically.

Codes that relate to 2020 and beyond could be pointing to post-Second Coming events, such as events in the Millennium (1,000 year reign of Christ), or they could be pointing to Tribulation events or the Second Coming itself. It's hard to tell until we get closer to the time.

Interestingly, while the mystics are looking to 2012, economists like Harry Dent and trends analysts like George Freidman are pointing to 2020–2022 as a focal point for major change. Christ overthrowing the present world system and setting up global peace from the city of Jerusalem would constitute the ultimate "major change." Dent even predicts we will emerge out of the present "winter" season into "spring." A fitting metaphor of the Rapture and the Resurrection! Do the divine codes point to 2020 as that kind of "spring"?

Some would be elated if I said the codes tell us the end is closer than that; say "goodbye" to your earthly toils! Others would be upset there's not more time. Some would be relieved if I said the end is not for a while; there may be more years to work, reach lost souls, and live fruitful lives. Others would be disappointed by the identical sentence! I wish I could comfort all your emotions. Only Christ can.

He evidently wants us to live in this balance between a sense of *urgency* on the one hand and a sense of *long-term* investment on the other hand. We are to both eagerly expect His coming at any moment and faithfully build as if we were passing the baton to many generations to come. Apparently no divine code resolves this tension in the Christian life. My job is to report the evidence of divine codes. It's up to the reader to decide what you believe and how you will live. I present the possibilities.

BEFORE THE END

Prophetically speaking, it is possible to look further out into the future than 2014. Before I tell you other significant years, I want to tell you two reasons why I don't think the "end of the age," the Rapture of the Church, or the Second Coming of Christ has to occur as soon as 2014. It is often stated by Christian teachers that no event has to precede the Rapture of the Church. It is "imminent" or it can happen any unexpected time. While this is true of the Rapture of the Church, the end of the age has many conditions that must first be fulfilled.

One major prophecy left unfulfilled is the reconstruction of the Third Temple in Jerusalem. If the Anti-Christ is to walk into it and defile it (an event called the "abomination of desolation" by both Daniel and Jesus), this assumes the Temple has to exist to begin with. It does not at the moment. The Al Aqsa mosque occupies the southern side of the Temple Mount and the Dome of the Rock (Jerusalem's prominent golden dome) occupies the center of the mount. There is no Jewish temple there.

Some may argue the Temple could be constructed after the Rapture or within the first half of the Tribulation. That gives 3 ½ years for such a project to get completed before the Anti-Christ walks in and commits the "abomination of desolation" at the midpoint of Tribulation. That's a very short time for a major building project. Of course, miracles have happened before in the land of Israel. Never say anything is impossible in the Middle East!

Historically it took 7 years for Solomon to construct the First Temple, 8 years for the Athenians to construct the Parthenon, and 46 years for Ezra to reconstruct the Second Temple. "Then the Jews said, 'It has taken forty-six years to build this Temple, and will You raise it up in three days?'" (John 2:20). Keep in mind the ancients had the benefit of round-the-clock slave labor. How long will it take to build the Third Temple? However long, it has to be built before the anti-Semite Anti-Christ is revealed to the Jews and before the Second Coming of Christ.

A second major prophecy is unlikely to be fulfilled within a matter of 3 or 4 years. The Bible clearly predicts that Babylon will once again become a major center of commerce. Its reconstruction and sudden destruction are both predicted.*

The reconstruction is occurring right now. But it does not seem complete. By the time it is destroyed in Revelation 18, the financial world will be rocked by its destruction in a similar way as the world reels when there is a crash on Wall Street. I don't see Iraq so prominent yet as to warrant market shock at its collapse.

Iraq has to be stabilized first, then the world will trade with it, and most likely tourism there will flourish. The thought of tourism to Iraq at the moment does not seem all too appealing to most vacationers. Commercially Iraq has great potential, but again, not too many investors would feel certain about putting their money in Iraq just yet.

This gives me pause and leads me to the possibility we may have a few more years to go before a major Biblical event like the "end of the age." Rebuilding Iraq should not happen as quickly as the next 3 years, but then I would venture to say it shouldn't take 30 years either. We are not sure when Babylon will rise, but we are not far. We are in the season of the end.

The only way I see that the world can circumvent the rebuilding of Iraq and move straight into the Tribulation is if Babylon does not refer to modern Iraq, but to Saudi Arabia. This is the possibility put forward by Walid Shoebat, a former PLO terrorist turned Christian evangelist. Ancient Babylon was much bigger than modern Iraq. Isaiah 21:1 (NLT) locates Babylon by a sea: "This message came to me concerning Babylon—the desert by the sea." Iraq has no sea, but Saudi Arabia is flanked by both the Red Sea on the west and the Persian Gulf on the east. Bob Cornuke has also raised the profile of Saudi Arabia by investigating the possibility that Mount Sinai is not in the so-called Sinai Peninsular, but is the restricted mountain with a blackened peak, Jabal al Lawz, in Saudi Arabia. That would put Saudi Arabia in the center of one of the most important events in Biblical history. If the Babylonian system refers to Saudi Arabia, an oil rich nation where many religious fanatics are funded, then the financial world is already poised to bend, bow, and break at the will of Babylon. This scenario would put us much closer to the end of the timeline!

---

* Either the literal city by that name within Iraq or a symbolic city in Saudi Arabia, all of which used to be called the Babylonian Empire. See Zechariah 5:5–11, Revelation 17–18, Isaiah 13:19, and Jeremiah 50:40.

LET'S REVIEW HOW JEWISH RABBIS
INTERPRET THE BIBLE

As explained in the chapter Decoding Numbers, Jewish rabbis are taught to search for 4 levels of meaning:

1. *Pashat* (simple, literal meaning).

2. *Remez* (hinted, implied meaning).

3. *Drash* (searched out, homiletical, metaphorical meaning). This includes teaching on types and shadows. I will show you a *drash* interpretation of the Parable of the Good Samaritan soon.

4. *Sod* (secret or mystical meaning). This includes counting a day as 1,000 years and analyzing other numbers. This is the one we're about to discover in the divine codes about future dates.

POSSIBILITIES WORTH WATCHING
FOR AND PRAYING ABOUT

What are some significant upcoming prophetic dates according to the divine codes? Let me give you 7 options to consider. This will be our longest chapter together, so please take it in stride. Feel free to pause and let the numbers soak in. We will start with the longest-term projection and work our ways towards nearer-term projections.

1. A Code from the Jewish Calendar

God works on the Jewish calendar. The Jews, who are known as good accountants, count the start of their calendar from the creation of Adam or 3761 B.C. That means the Gregorian year 2010 is the Jewish year 5770. (Or add 3760 years to the present year to find roughly the Jewish equivalent.).

According to Jewish tradition, such as recorded in the *Seder Olam Rabbah* quoted by Rashi and the Babylonian Talmud, God has allocated to human history six 1,000 year periods corresponding to the 6 days of Creation, to be followed by a millennial sabbath of 1,000 years corresponding to the 7th day rest. The early Church fathers held this view also. In a non-canonical, 2nd century Epistle of Barnabas,* we read that Christians understood the idea of a 6,000-year-plan:

---

* Barnabas is an early Church father writing cited by Clement and Origen, not to be confused with the later *Gospel of Barnabas*, a long-winded and heretical book (222 chapters in Italian) that contradicts the New Testament, denies the Trinity, claims Jesus escaped crucifixion, and mentions Mohammed by name.

Give heed, children, what this meaneth; He ended in six days. He meaneth this, that in six thousand years the Lord shall bring all things to an end; for the day with Him signifyeth a thousand years; and this He himself beareth me witness, saying, Behold, the day of the Lord shall be as a thousand years. Therefore, children, in six days, that is in six thousand years, everything shall come to an end. And He rested on the seventh day. This He meaneth; when His Son shall come, and shall abolish the time of the Lawless One, and shall judge the ungodly, and shall change the sun and the moon and the stars, then shall he truly rest on the seventh day.

—BARNABAS 15:4–5, J. B. LIGHTFOOT TRANSLATION

If we adopt the view that God gave man a lease to the planet of 6,000 years, after which the earth returns to her Owner for a sabbatical rest of 1,000 years, then we should look for the end of the present age at the Hebrew year 6,000.

If the Jewish count were right (A.D. 2010 is actually 5770 years since Adam), then we may have to wait another 230 years before a significant change to take place in 2240. Theoretically this is the maximum time allowed by any divine code I have ever come across for things to continue the way they are before the Second Coming.

But it is highly doubtful we will be around till 2240 due to the accelerating events fulfilling Bible prophecies, especially those concerning Israel. So might there be a mistake in the Jewish calendar?

That is my personal conclusion. We know the Jews did in fact make an error in reading Daniel 9. By missing the timing of the Messiah's first coming, they erroneously applied Daniel's 490 years to the Temples instead 483 years till the Messiah (see chapter on 70 Sevens).

If they tried to make Daniel's 490 years fit the interval from the destruction of the First Temple in 586 B.C. to the destruction of the Second Temple in A.D. 70, they would have introduced a 166-year error (656 - 490 = 166).[1] Even the noted Orthodox Rabbi Shimon Schwab (1908–1995) agreed that there are at least 165 missing years from the current Hebrew calendar. That would mean 2010 should be at least 5936 on the Hebrew calendar. This would put the *maximum* projection for humanity's 6,000th anniversary to the year 2074.

2. A Code from the Torah

I came across a divine code in the Torah, or the first 5 books of the Bible, in Perry Stone's book *Breaking the Jewish Code*. In it, Perry Stone uncovered a *sod* level of interpretation of the Torah:

> The Hebrew Bible was divided into chapters and verses in 1448 by Rabbi Nathan. Although the chapters and verses were placed by men in the Scripture, a strange and amazing pattern emerges when counting the verses in Deuteronomy and comparing the verses to the actual Jewish year. This is the concept that each verse in the Torah corresponds with a date on the Jewish calendar.[2]

For instance, starting from Genesis 1:1 and counting 5,708 verses, we come to Deuteronomy 30:3 which promised, "That the LORD your God will *bring you back* from captivity, and have compassion on you, and *gather you again* from all the nations where the LORD your God has scattered you" (emphasis added).

What year did Jews escaping the Holocaust come back into their motherland? The Hebrew year 5708 or the Western year 1948. Verse 5708 in the Torah matched the Hebrew year 5708!

An obvious question is, "How many verses are there in the Torah?" Tradition says 5845. If each verse corresponds to a Hebrew year, then the last year in this code is 5845. Which year is that on our calendar?

5845 - 3760 = 2085. Does this mean the Second Coming will be in 2085? Not necessarily, as 2085 could refer to an event within the millennial reign of Christ. Why not? All we know is God has marked out 2085 as a prophetic date to watch out for (if you're around)! If Jesus were to come back in 2085, then we must subtract 7 years to arrive at the beginning of the Tribulation. 2085 - 7 = 2078.

This is the mystical level of interpretation. It doesn't alter any doctrine in the Bible and it doesn't contradict any truth we all hold dear. It affirms that God knows the future, He knows every detail of our lives and "Jesus is coming soon!"

3. A Code from "This Generation"

A Scripture often misused in calculating the end of the age is:

> Now learn this parable from the *fig tree*: When its branch has already become tender and puts forth leaves, you know that summer is near. So you also, when you see all these things, know that it is

near—at the doors! Assuredly, I say to you, *this generation* will by no means pass away till all these things take place.

—MATTHEW 24:32–34, EMPHASIS ADDED

The trigger for knowing when the end time is near is the "fig tree." What is the fig tree? Most Bible commentators have assumed this refers to Israel's national rebirth in 1948.

The next question is, "How long is a generation?" Since Jesus said the generation that sees the fig tree puts forth leaves will not die till all these things take place, we should know the definition of a generation. Many commentators have assumed a generation lasts 40 years. 1948 + 40 = 1988. Thus one author wrote a booklet, "88 Reasons Why the Rapture Will Be in 1988."

Such predictions are based on man's theory about what a fig tree is and how long a generation lasts. The fig tree is a symbol of Israel, but it could refer to Israel's independence in 1948, or Israel's recapturing of Jerusalem in 1967, or Israel's rebuilding the Temple.

We should not rely on man's theories and medical reports to define what a generation is. What is the Bible's definition of a generation? Having read chapter 80, you know it is not 40 or 70 or 80. Yet there are speculators now setting new dates for Jesus' return based on these assumptions (e.g., 1948 + 70 = 2018). Genesis 6:3 tells us that God defines a generation as 120. Is that realistic? That's precisely how long Moses lived. Among the verified oldest living people, we know a French woman named Jeanne Calment died in 1997 at the age of 122. A Japanese man named Shigechiyo Izumi died in 1986 at the age of 120. My own Irish great-grandmother lived to 104.

We can also calculate a generation from Genesis 15.

Then He said to Abram: "Know certainly that your descendants will be strangers in a land that is not theirs, and will serve them, and they will afflict them *four hundred years*....But in the *fourth generation* they shall *return here*, for the iniquity of the Amorites is not yet complete.

—GENESIS 15:13, 16, EMPHASIS ADDED

People get carried away when it comes to end-time Scriptures. For some reason they forget the ordinary standards of interpreting literature and they make up their own interpretations. But the same rules apply to interpreting end-time Scriptures as to interpreting salvation Scriptures or giving Scriptures. We cannot make up our own definitions. We must be honest enough to allow the Bible define its own terms and idioms. Let "Scripture interpret Scripture."

Even a cursory glance at Genesis 15 will inform us: if 4 generations = 400 years, then 1 generation = 100 years (at least!).

But if we want to be more precise, we know that 400 years was only a rounded figure, because the Israelites actually spent 430 years in Egypt as slaves (Exod. 12:40–41, Gal. 3:17). Upon leaving Egypt, they hadn't "returned here" or fulfilled the prediction of Genesis 15:16 yet. They wandered for another 40 years. After Moses died and Joshua assumed leadership, they took another 5 years in their conquest to resettle in the Promised Land. So from the time they became "strangers" in the land of Egypt to the time they "returned here" was:

- 430 as slaves + 40 wandering + 5 conquering = 475 years

- 475 years ÷ 4 generations = 119 years per generation.

Shall we round up to 120? This number is confirmed by Genesis 6:3. So let's apply these numbers to the fig tree and see how long this generation can last till "all these things take place." I shall include the 100 year = 1 generation as a possible (still Biblical) factor.

- 1967 + 120 = 2087

- 1948 + 120 = 2068

- 1967 + 100 = 2067

- 1948 + 100 = 2048

I do not subscribe to these dates because there may be a flaw with the assumption made by prophecy teachers. If we look at the Matthew 24:32–34 in the context of other Scriptures, we find a parallel passage in Luke which elucidates the Matthew passage.

Then He spoke to them a parable: "Look at the *fig tree*, and *all the trees*. When they are already budding, you see and know for yourselves that summer is now near. So you also, when you see these things happening, know that the kingdom of God is near. Assuredly, I say to you, *this generation* will by no means pass away till all things take place.

—LUKE 21:29–32, EMPHASIS ADDED

Any attempt to identify the fig tree as Israel or Jerusalem seems nullified by this verse, "Look at the fig tree and *all the trees.*" If the fig tree were Israel, then all the trees would mean all the nations of the world. That wouldn't to narrow it down at all!

Let us not mitigate the importance of Israel in prophecy. Far from it, her rebirth fulfills many prophetic Scriptures and is a necessary condition for many other end-time passages to make sense. But her rebirth is not necessarily "the fig tree and all the trees" blooming. Therefore calculations based on the "fig tree" theory have been unreliable so far.

The idiom is about spring. It's that simple. The signs of prophetic spring were given in the preceding verses of Matthew and Luke: the sun darkening, the moon turning to blood, stars falling (meteor showers or asteroid impact), distress of nations, rise in natural disasters, and false religions claiming Christ while denying His deity. If we look at the immediate verse preceding this passage in Matthew 24, it might give us a clue as to what exactly "spring" may be.

> And He will send His angels with a great sound of a trumpet, and they will gather together His elect from the four winds, from one end of Heaven to the other.
>
> —MATTHEW 24:31

Here is what I believe "spring" may be: the Rapture. Spring is a most apropos metaphor for the Rapture. We will literally "spring" up and away! Could Jesus be indicating this: the generation which sees the Rapture, this generation will not pass away till all is fulfilled?

We don't normally hear this interpretation because popular Christian novels have led the body of Christ to assume that the Tribulation must soon follow the Rapture, but no Scripture mandates this. There could be many years, even many decades, between the Rapture and the start of the Tribulation. I believe when Christians are gone, the world will immediately sink into a worse state. But life will go on. And if it goes on for more than 7 years, then many who trusted in Christian novels instead of the Bible will lose heart and become deceived, thinking Christ is not coming back at all. On the contrary, Christ will return within a generation of the fig tree and all the trees giving up their representative fruits or the saints. The assurance here may be that no more than 120 years (one Biblical generation) will pass from the Rapture till all these things take place.

4. A Code from the Book of Psalms

Having read chapter 150, you have had a glimpse of the fascinating codes and prophetic implications of the Book of Psalms. J. R. Church is credited for discovering that each chapter in the 19th Book may be alluding to end-time events starting from the year 1900. Psalm 48 matches 1948 and so forth.

Combine J. R. Church's discovery with the special place that the Book of Psalms hold in Jewish tradition, and we discover some interesting clues.

All Jews know Psalms 113–118 constitute the "Hallel." *Hallel* in Hebrew means "praise," from which we get *hallelujah* or "praise the Lord!" These 6 Psalms are recited during the 3 great feasts of Passover, Weeks (Pentecost), and Tabernacles, and during the 8 days of Hanukkah (a feast that both looks backward to the defiling and cleansing of the Second Temple and looks forward to the defiling by the Anti-Christ and cleansing by Jesus Christ). If the Hallel has a prophetic meaning, it is pointing to the years 2013–2018 as significant. Once again, there is a conjunction of signs that begin on 2013.

The Hallel is never recited at Rosh Hashanah (civil new year on Tishri 1st) or on Yom Kippur (Day of Atonement). These 2 festivals are 10 days apart and prophetic of Israel's national salvation. Rosh Hashanah is the first of 10 high holidays called the "Days of Awe" (*yamim noraim*) or the "Ten Days of Repentance" (*asseret yemei teshuva*), culminating in *Yom Kippur*, the Day of Atonement. All these feast names point to a time when Israel will fulfill prophecy by repenting:

> I will return again to My place [meaning He had come once and is now in Heaven] till they acknowledge their offence [Israel offended God in a major way prior to A.D. 70 when their holy temple and city were destroyed. 40 years earlier they crucified their most famous prophet, Yeshua ha Mashiyach]. Then they will seek My face; In their affliction [during Tribulation] they will earnestly seek Me.
> —HOSEA 5:15

> Then they will look on Me whom they pierced [Jesus' hands and feet were pierced]. Yes, they will mourn for Him as one mourns for his only son [God's Son], and grieve for Him as one grieves for a firstborn.
> —ZECHARIAH 12:10

One third of national Israel will one day recognize that Messiah had come for her and she missed Him. They will most likely repent at Rosh Hashanah and get saved on Yom Kippur. Since these feasts are so fitting for the timeframe of Israel's salvation, it begs the question why the Hallel is *not* prayed during this timeframe. I do not know. It may simply mean Israel will be in Tribulation and it will not be the time for her to rejoice.

What are some other significant Psalms and their corresponding years? Immediately after the last Hallel is Psalm 119, the longest Psalm, possibly prophetic of a very "long" year in 2019.

Psalm 136 is called the "Great Hallel" which may signal a great year of praise in 2036.

There is another group of 6 Psalms known as the Hallel or "Hymnal Verses" (*pesukei dezimra*). They are recited daily during Jewish morning services. Rabbi Jose initiated their use in the 2nd century and Maimonides supported it in the 12th century. This Hallel is to me the "true" Hallel, in the sense that every Psalm in this group actually begins and ends with the words *hallelujah!* The 6 Psalms are Psalms 145–150.

If one assumes the last Psalm matches the last year in prophecy, then by adding 150 to 1900 we arrive at the year 2050. Could this be the latest possible date for a significant event? As far as the Psalms code go, there are no further dates.

Let me be absolutely clear: I do not believe that the Second Coming will occur in 2050. Of course it could. But 2050 may also be a significant year inside the post-Second Coming era.

The conjunction of codes point to earlier dates for major world-changing events. Can we predict what these events will be based on the Psalms code? It would have been nearly impossible to predict the fall of the Berlin wall in 1986, even though Psalm 86 contained the prophetic words, "Thou hast broken down all his hedges." This appears more than coincidental since the word "hedges" occurs only one other time in 2,461 verses of the Book of Psalms. The application became obvious only after the event.

Therefore, I cannot make any firm predictions based on the Psalms code, but I am willing to satisfy the curiosity of readers who ask, "What *might* happen in the next few years according to the Psalms code?" If you understand that I am not making any dogmatic predictions, I offer these Psalms, their corresponding years, key words, and possible future events for your interest.

PSALM	YEAR NO.	VERSES	PROPHETIC EVENT
112	2012	"Blessed is the man who fears the Lord…Wealth and riches will be in his house…His horn will be exalted with honor. The wicked will see it and be grieved…The desire of the wicked shall perish."	Based on this it appears 2012 may not be the financial disaster some economists are predicting. Or else it means believers will have a great opportunity to prosper while the wicked's wealth perishes.
113	2013	Key words: "sun," "high," "heavens," "high," "raises," "lifts up".	Something happening in the sky—solar activity, asteroid passing, or so-called UFO sightings. Rapture of the Church would qualify.
114	2014	"Tremble, O earth…"	A major earthquake or geopolitical shaking
120	2020	"Lying lips," "deceitful tongue," "hates peace," "war"	Opposite to keys words in Psalm 46 about post-WWII peace in 1946. Psalm 120 hints at the Anti-Christ being revealed or a war that prepares him to be revealed (possibly Ezekiel 38-39).
122	2022	"I was glad when they said to me, Let us go into the HOUSE of the Lords…Jerusalem is BUILT…Pray for the peace of Jerusalem…Because of the HOUSE of the Lord our God I will see your good."	This psalm has many positive words about Israel. This may be the year the House of God—the Third Temple—is built. It may also indicate a false peace brokered by the Anti-Christ.

If these things come to pass, do not call me a true prophet. If they come to pass in part or do not come to pass at all, do not call me a false prophet. I already explained the codes are there but they are not obvious till after the fact. My faith is based on God's Word and so should yours.

5. A Code from "2 days"

Numerous Scriptures indicate that after 2 days or 2 years, the Messiah will come (from the Jews' perspective) or return (from the Christians' perspective).

A "day" can be interpreted literally and figuratively when it comes to Bible prophecy. This "day-year" principle was introduced by God in the Torah.

> According to the number of the days in which you spied out the land, forty days, *a year for each day*, you shall bear your iniquity forty years, and you shall know my displeasure.
> —Numbers 14:34, esv, emphasis added

God endorses the "day-year" principle in other Scriptures.

> As for you, lie down on your left side and lay the iniquity of the house of Israel on it; you shall bear their iniquity for the number of days that you lie on it. For I have assigned you a number of *days corresponding to the years* of their iniquity, three hundred and ninety days; thus you shall bear the iniquity of the house of Israel. When you have completed these, you shall lie down a second time, but on your right side and bear the iniquity of the house of Judah; I have assigned it to you for forty days, *a day for each year*.
> —Ezekiel 4:4–6, nas, emphasis added

> But, beloved, do not forget this one thing, that with the Lord one day is as a thousand years, and a thousand years as one day.
> —2 Peter 3:8

Prophecy teachers are familiar with the idiom the "Day of the Lord," which appears repeatedly throughout Scripture. On a literal level, it is the 24-hour day in which Christ will judge the world, but it is also on a prophetic level a much longer period of time starting from the Tribulation and lasting until the Great White Throne Judgment at the end of the Millennium. Hence the "Day of the Lord" is both a 24 hour period and a 1,000 year long event.*

---

* The Law of Double Reference is *not* an "either or," but a "both and" proposition. Be careful not to twist this principle to mean the 6 days of creation in Genesis do not really mean 6 literal 24-hour days. They were literally 6 periods of 24-hours *and* they allude prophetically to 6 periods of 1,000 years comprising human history.

Let me show you 5 examples of "2 days" Scriptures and how to apply them prophetically.

1. Hosea 6:2 predicted, "After two days He will revive us." This can be applied literally and figuratively, as most prophecies can be without clash or contradiction. Literally, Jesus will come 2 days after national Israel repents and prays for the Messiah to deliver them from the anti-Semite Anti-Christ. Prophetically, Jesus could come 2,000 years after He "returned to His place" in Heaven according to Hosea 5:15.

2. God intended for interval between the Exodus and entry into the Promised Land to be 2 years. Through disobedience the Jews delayed God's plan by 38 years. However, the type is not destroyed. (Just as Moses disobeyed God by striking the rock twice instead of speaking to it; yet the type remains valid that Christ the Rock would be struck only once, and after that we may obtain fresh waters by speaking God's Word.) If the interval between Exodus and the Promised Land is a type of the interval between Christ's ascension and Christ's return, then we should enter the Millennium 2,000 years after Christ's ascension.

3. In John 4:40, the Samaritans (symbolic of Gentiles or the Church age) "urged Him to stay with them; and He stayed there two days." Samaritans represent the non-Jews or Gentiles. Jesus, the Jewish Messiah, has stayed with a predominantly Gentile Church for 2 days or 2,000 years.

4. Jesus said in Luke 13:32, "Go, tell that fox, Behold, I cast out demons and perform cures today and tomorrow, and the third say I shall be perfected." This applied literally to Jesus' perfect work on the cross at the First Coming, but it may also apply prophetically to Jesus' perfect work in defeating the Anti-Christ at the Second Coming. When will He accomplish His perfect work? He said after 2 days.

5. One of the most famous passages of Scripture has a prophetic implication that has often been overlooked by teachers. It is the parable of the Good Samaritan. Let us read the passage in full then shed light on its meaning and possible codes.

Then Jesus answered and said: "A certain man went down from Jerusalem to Jericho, and fell among thieves, who stripped him of his clothing, wounded him, and departed, leaving him half dead. Now by chance a certain priest came down that road. And when he saw him, he passed by on the other side. Likewise a Levite, when he arrived at the place, came and looked, and passed by on the other side. But a certain Samaritan, as he journeyed, came where he was. And when he saw him, he had compassion. So he went to him and bandaged his wounds, pouring on oil and wine; and he set him on his own animal, brought him to an inn, and took care of him.

—LUKE 10:30–34

On a literal level, this is a story about 5 groups of men—a wounded victim, a bunch of thieves, a priest, a Levite, and a Samaritan. The only one who helped the wounded man was the least expected to do so—the Samaritan. The moral? Go love the person you love least, then you can claim you love God and love your neighbor as yourself. If we come short of such love, we need a Savior to wash our sin.

On an allegorical level, this story of full of symbols that make great fodder for the evangelist and Bible teacher! It summarizes the entire Gospel and God's plan for man. Let's translate what each element in the story points to.

PARABLE	MEANING
A certain MAN	Adam
Went DOWN	Fell into sin.
From JERUSALEM	From a high point. Jerusalem is on a hill, so leaving Jerusalem is always going "down". The road from Jerusalem to Jericho, known as the "Bloody Way," is a descent. Leaving a relationship with God is a descent for mankind.
To Jericho	Religion. Jericho was a priestly city with at least 12,000 priests living there. The descent from God leads us into human formality, rules and religion. Remember it was the tree of the "knowledge of good and evil" that killed Adam. Religion traps us in right and wrong. Christianity offers us life or death.

PARABLE	MEANING
Fell among THIEVES	Satan and his demons. Jesus called Satan a thief in John 10:10. "The thief does not come except to steal, and to kill, and to destroy." Jesus also categorized religious teachers who deceive men into thinking that they can climb their way into Heaven with their knowledge of right and wrong as thieves and robbers in John 10:1. Our problem is not ignorance of right and wrong; our problem is committing sin despite knowing it's wrong. Sin is the enemy that robs and kills us.
STRIPPED him	Satan stripped Adam of his innocence and right-standing with God.
WOUNDED him	Satan wounded Adam with sin consciousness, guilt, fear and shame.
Leaving him HALF-DEAD	Adam immediately died spiritually, but he didn't die physically till 930 years later. Adam, like us, was a walking dead. Without Christ, we are dead on the inside while walking out the remainder of our short lives on the outside.
A certain PRIEST... passed by	Religion offered no help
A certain LEVITE... passed by	Religious people offered no help. They give rules of do's and don'ts, but not life to a dying man.
A certain SAMARITAN	JESUS! This was the unexpected turning point of the story. The solution did not come from religion or religious people, but from the one they least expected. The hero of this story is someone first-century Jews hated and rejected—the Good Samaritan, representing Jesus Christ!
He JOURNEYED	Christ from Heaven came a long way!
Came WHERE HE WAS	God came to our level. He was born as a baby in a little town. God walked with us!
Had COMPASSION	This was the chief characteristic of Jesus and the impetus fro the Redemption Plan.
BANDAGED his wounds	Jesus came to heal. The Gospels prove He is the Good Samaritan who healed!
Pouring on OIL and WINE	Wine a symbol of the Blood that cleanses us from sin; Oil a symbol of the Holy Spirit that empowers us to live again for God.

PARABLE	MEANING
Set him on his own ANIMAL	The Holy Spirit and anointed ministers of God are often depicted in Scripture as an ox, donkey or beast of burden.
Brought him to an INN	The Church. Every new believer is brought into the Family of God where they can be nurtured and grow spiritually.

If Jesus' parable had ended there, we would already have a very clear picture of the Gospel and the plan of God for our lives! But here is the finish to the story. It is deeply meaningful and I believe prophetic.

> On the next day, when he departed, he took out two denarii, gave them to the innkeeper, and said to him, "Take care of him; and whatever more you spend, when I come again, I will repay you."
> —LUKE 10:35

PARABLE	MEANING
When he DEPARTED	Jesus left! He literally ascended into Heaven ("raptured" if you will) after giving His Church the Great Commission and His Holy Spirit.
He took out TWO denarii	Literally 2 days' worth of wages, or 2000 years of grace! Remember that numbered items in dreams and parables are divine codes for years. For instance, Joseph interpreted the 7 fat cows as 7 years of prosperity and the 7 lean cows as 7 years of famine. Joseph did not go to modern Bible schools, but he correctly interpreted Pharaoh's numbers as years.
Gave them to the INNKEEPER	the Holy Spirit. If the Inn is the local church you attend, then the Innkeeper represents the Pastor of your local church.
Take CARE of him	Teach My people My Word for the next 2 days or 2000 years.
When I COME AGAIN	the Second Advent of Christ.
WHATEVER more you spend	"There is no limit to what I will pay for them," Jesus is saying. You cannot bankrupt Jesus!

PARABLE	MEANING
I will REPAY	Jesus will come and give eternal rewards to every Christian who searches for lost sheep and brings them into the safety of the Inn. Whatever price we need to pay, whatever effort we need to spend, God will repay us, for He is no man's debtor!

The parable of the Good Samaritan is the 5th example of how God predicted 2 days before Jesus returns. The question becomes, 2 days starting from when? What is the trigger?

Luke 10 interestingly gives us one of the clearest answers. Prophecy teachers have assumed it will be 2 days or 2,000 years after the birth of Christ. This was the rationale behind the hysteria surrounding the year 2000. If the turn of the millennium marked 2,000 years after Jesus' birth, shouldn't Jesus return on the year 2000?

Since I study and teach Biblical prophecy, I didn't take any notice of the new millennium celebrations and just spent time with my family. Too many Christians are taken in by the media and even "Christian hype" before thoroughly investigating their own Bibles.

So when is the start of the prophetic countdown of 2,000 years? Luke 10:35 tells us, "When he *departed*, he took out two denarii" (emphasis added). The trigger was not Jesus' birth, but Jesus' resurrection and ascension into Heaven. Christians have tended to make more ado about Christmas than Resurrection Day (Easter, as it's misnomered). But Jesus' resurrection is far more important than Jesus' birth. He could have come and backed out of His plan to save mankind. He could have said, "It's not worth it." He could have said, "My will and not the Father's will be done." But He submitted to the gruesome death of the cross and suffered the torments of hell for 3 days, after which He resurrected and 40 days later ascended into Heaven.

Adding 2,000 years to the year of His ascension takes us to the prophetic date of 2032. If His Second Coming marks the 2,000[th] anniversary of His victory over death, hell, and Satan, then we would have to subtract 7 years for the start of the Tribulation.

+ A.D. 32 + 2,000 years = A.D. 2032

+ A.D. 2032 - 7 years = A.D. 2025 (latest start of Tribulation according to this code)

That would put the Rapture of the Church any time *before* 2025. It seems that no matter which code we turn to, all are pointing to this vicinity as the "last days" and our generation as the last generation.

6. First Code from Daniel

There is an often overlooked Scripture predicting the timing of the resurrection.

> At that time Michael [the guardian angel of Israel] shall stand up, The great prince who stands watch over the sons of your people; And there shall be a time of trouble, Such as never was since there was a nation, Even to that time. And at that time your people shall be delivered, Every one who is found written in the book. And many of those who sleep in the dust of the earth shall awake [resurrect from the dead], Some to everlasting life, Some to shame and everlasting contempt.
>
> —DANIEL 12:1–2

When shall these things happen? God gave Daniel a precise time!

> From the time that the daily sacrifice is abolished and the abomination that causes desolation is set up, there will be 1,290 days. Blessed is the one who waits for and reaches the end of the 1,335 days.
>
> —DANIEL 12:11–12

The Bible gives a countdown: "from" a particular trigger event "to" a particular target, there shall be 1,290 days. David Rogers suggested that we apply the day-year principle to this Scripture, and count 1,290 years from the trigger to the target.[3] Let's read the trigger again:

> And from the time that the continual burnt offering shall be taken away, and the abomination that maketh desolate set up, there shall be 1,290 days.
>
> —DANIEL 12:11, ERV

The trigger is when the "continual burnt offering" was taken away. We prophecy teachers tend to leap forward from Daniel's era to a future event like Antiochus Epiphanes IV's sacrificing a pig on the altar of God in 166 B.C., or

Roman General Titus' destroying the Temple in A.D. 70. Certainly both of these events would have interrupted the daily or continual offering.

But we must remember by Daniel's time, the Temple had been desolate and the burnt offerings had ceased. When Daniel prayed in chapter 9, verse 17, he described the condition of the Temple, "Cause Your face to shine on Your sanctuary, which is desolate." Although there is prophetic application to future defiling of the Temple, Daniel was probably referring to offerings stopping in his time, during the Babylonian Captivity. The question becomes: When did the daily offerings stop? Daniel answers it!

> In the *third year* of the reign of Jehoiakim king of Judah, Nebuchadnezzar king of Babylon came to Jerusalem and besieged it. And the Lord delivered Jehoiakim king of Judah into his hand, along with some of the articles from the temple of God. These he carried off to the temple of his god in Babylonia and put in the treasure house of his god.
>
> —DANIEL 1:1–2, NIV, EMPHASIS ADDED

Nebuchadnezzar's first invasion occurred in the 3rd year of Jehoiakim's reign. It was at this time that he and/or his men entered into the Temple and removed some of the holy vessels. In Judaism, not even a common Jew could enter the holy place without defiling it. Only sanctified priests could enter the holy place, and only the high priest could enter the holy of holies and only once a year! Any unauthorized entry would defile the Temple and halt the offerings until the place could be cleansed.

Therefore, the presence of a Gentile army robbing the Temple vessels necessarily meant the daily sacrifice or continual offering had to stop. In context, the trigger point for this clock's countdown came in the 3rd year of Jehoiakim. Encyclopedia Britannica says Jehoiakim ascended the throne in 609 B.C.,[4] therefore the continual offering was interrupted or taken away in 607 B.C.

We have a trigger point, now we want to find the target. What is the abomination that causes desolation? This idiom may seem strange to untrained ears, but it is used 5 times in Daniel 9:27, 11:31, 12:11, Matthew 24:15, and Mark 13:14. Because Jesus warned the Jews to flee "when you see the 'abomination of desolation,' spoken of by Daniel the prophet, standing in the holy place," we have always assumed that it had to be a person or an idol standing on the Temple Mount. But there is something standing smack in the middle of the holy place today that qualifies as an abomination that makes worship desolate to the Jews.

It is Jerusalem's architectural landmark—the golden Dome of the Rock. Why is this beautiful building an affront to the Jews? Because since its construction, Jews have not had the freedom to enter the site and worship God as they used to. At various times Muslims, who control the Temple Mount, have forbidden Jews and Christians from walking on the Temple Mount or entering the Dome of the Rock where the holy of holies most likely used to stand. If this is the target, then we want to know: When did construction of the Dome of the Rock begin? In A.D. 684.[5]

From the time the continual offering was interrupted in 607 B.C. to the abomination of desolation standing in the holy place in A.D. 684, how much time transpired? 607 + 684 - 1 (no year 0) = 1,290 years!

Daniel's prophecy is quite accurate so far. He continues to report the words he heard, "Blessed is the one who waits for and reaches the end of the 1,335 days." The question is: Is the next period of 1,335 years a new prophecy with a new starting date, or the old 1,290 years prophecy starting at the same starting point but ending 45 years later (1335 - 1290 = 45)? Put another way, are the 1,335 years concurrent or contiguous with the 1,290 years?

If they were concurrent, then the resurrection should have occurred 45 years after the Dome of the Rock was set up in A.D. 684. Since Jesus did not return and the resurrection of the dead did not occur in A.D. 729, we can safely assume that the next 1,335 years began after the 1,290 years. Here's the math:

+ 607 B.C. (daily sacrifice halted) + 1,290 years = A.D. 684.

+ A.D. 684 (abomination of desolation) + 1,335 years = A.D. 2019.

If Daniel's 1,335-year prophecy is as reliable as his previous 1,290-year prophecy, then a major event such as the resurrection of the dead is due in the year 2019.

While this is a very interesting theory, I am not convinced that the Dome of the Rock is the ultimate abomination of desolation, because Jesus said, "When you see the 'abomination of desolation,' spoken of by Daniel the prophet, standing in the holy place...then let those who are in Judea flee to the mountains" (Matt. 24:15–16). If we accept Jesus at His Word, then the Jews should have been fleeing Jerusalem for as long as they've seen the Dome of the Rock stand—which it has for the last 1,300+ years.

While there is a structure that makes Jewish worship desolate, Scriptures indicate there will also come a man who will defy the Jews and defile the Temple personally. "Don't let anyone deceive you in any way, for that day will not come until...the man of lawlessness is revealed....He will oppose and will exalt himself over everything that is called God or is worshiped, so that he sets himself up in God's Temple" (2 Thess. 2:3–4, NIV, see also Daniel 11:36 and Revelation 11:2).

7. Second Code from Daniel

> Know therefore and understand, that *from* the going forth of the command to restore and rebuild Jerusalem [not the temple] *until* Messiah the Prince [not the temple], there shall be *seven weeks* and *sixty-two weeks* [69 sevens = 483 years]; the street shall be built again, and the wall, even in troublesome times.
>
> —DANIEL 9:25, EMPHASIS ADDED

Daniel could not have been clearer! From the time a decree is issued to rebuild Jerusalem to the time Messiah appears as King (Hebrew *nagid* means prince, ruler, leader), there will transpire an interval of 483 lunar years (or 477 solar years). That leaves 1 more week of 7 years for God's dealing with Israel, completing the entire 70 weeks of Daniel 9:24–27 or 490 years.

Had the rabbis studied Daniel 9 carefully, they would have applied 483 years to the time span from Artaxerxes' decree to rebuild Jerusalem (Daniel's trigger was the city, *not* the Temple) in 445 B.C. to the triumphal entry of the Messiah riding on a lowly donkey in A.D. 32 (Daniel's target was the Savior, *not* the Temple). The rabbis missed the Savior of the world while fixated on the Temple. Jesus tried to open their eyes when He said (speaking of Himself), "Yet I say to you that in this place there is One greater than the Temple" (Matt. 12:6). Instead they applied 490 years (the whole 70 weeks prophecy) to the interval between the construction and destruction of the Second Temple, completely ignoring the Messiah's appearance in between! Ancient Jews misapplied the prophecy to the Temple, and now modern Jews studying to become rabbis are *forbidden* to calculate the 70 weeks prophecy to verify the coming of the Messiah.

How could they be forbidden to read their own Scriptures? Jewish rabbi Maimonides (Rambam) justified it this way:

> Daniel has elucidated to us the knowledge of the end times. However, since they are secret, the wise [rabbis] have barred the calculation of the days of Messiah's coming so that the untutored populace will not be led astray when they see that the end times have already come but there is no sign of the Messiah.[6]

If Scripture-loving Jews are willing to revisit this ancient prophecy again, though they missed the First Coming, they will not have to miss the Second Coming! How can they apply Daniel's prophecy again in modern context?

THE LAW OF DOUBLE REFERENCE

There is a law of double reference which we can apply to Daniel's famous "70 weeks" prophecy. The law of double reference or dual application is a hermeneutical principle that says prophetic Scriptures can be applied to the near future and the remote future. That is why the famous Scripture quoted during every Christmas season can apply to both the First Coming and the Second Coming:

> For unto us a Child is born [referring to the Incarnation of God in the flesh, hence First Coming], Unto us a Son is given [referring to the return of God the Son, hence the Second Coming]; And the government will be upon His shoulder [clearly a Second Coming timeframe when He shall rule over all humanity]. And His name will be called Wonderful, Counselor, Mighty God, Everlasting Father, Prince of Peace.
>
> —ISAIAH 9:6

In one Scripture we have the prediction of both the First and Second Coming. And we also have the humanity and deity of Christ revealed in one breath! The Child representing His humanity could be "born," but the Son representing His divinity can only be "given." His identity will be revealed in His name: He is none other than Mighty God. The divinity of Christ was long established before His incarnation.

Turning back to Daniel 9, we apply the law of double reference. The first trigger point for a prophetic countdown came in 445 B.C. when Artaxerxes issued the decree to rebuild Jerusalem. Was there a more remote decree (from Daniel's perspective) or a more recent decree (from the modern Jews' perspective) which could serve as another trigger to a prophetic countdown of the Messiah's arrival?

There is! After the Romans destroyed Jerusalem and its Temple in A.D. 70, Jerusalem laid waste for centuries. Then, a more recent decree to rebuild Jerusalem and its walls was issued. Based on this newer decree, there is a possibility that the Jews can estimate the time of the Second Coming.

But first, let's re-read Daniel's prophesy:

> Know therefore and understand, that *from* the going forth of the command to restore and build Jerusalem *until* Messiah the Prince, there shall be *seven weeks* and *sixty-two weeks*; the street shall be built again, and the wall, even in troublesome times.
>
> —DANIEL 9:25, EMPHASIS ADDED

Converting 69 weeks or 483 lunar years to 476 solar years or 173,880 days, we came up with this equation in the chapter on 70 Sevens:

- March 14, 445 B.C. + 173,880 days = April 6, A.D. 32 (or 10 Nisan)

Thus we arrive at Jesus' triumphal entry into Jerusalem on 10 Nisan, 4 days before His crucifixion for the sins of the world.

Since then Jerusalem was destroyed by Roman General Titus in A.D. 70. But we see that Jerusalem and its city walls are not in ruins today. The question is, "When was the modern command issued to restore and rebuild Jerusalem and by whom?"

The answer is by Ottoman Sultan Suleiman (Solomon) the Magnificent in A.D. 1537. Applying the same equation, we calculate:

- A.D. 1537 + 476 years (173,880 days) = 2013

Could this be the year of something prophetically significant, like the Ezekiel 38–39 war, or the Rapture or the start of Tribulation? I don't know. But we won't go to hell for expecting Biblical prophecy to be fulfilled very soon! There might even be a prize in Heaven for those who came closest to guessing the right date!

All I know is the magis were blessed to see the Child Jesus at the predicted time. And Jesus was upset with the Jews when they didn't believe Daniel 9:27. In Luke 19:43–44, He predicted their city and Temple would be destroyed "because you *did not know* the *time* of your visitation" (emphasis added).

What happens to the city of Jerusalem is correlatively significant to the timing of the Messiah's coming. The first decree to restore and rebuild Jerusalem was by Artaxerxes in 445 B.C. The second, more recent decree to restore and rebuild Jerusalem was by Suleiman in A.D.1537.

There is a third important date relating to Jerusalem that we should be aware of: that is the recapturing of Jerusalem on June 7, 1967. Next to Israel's independence on May 14, 1948, this is the most important date in the modern Israel's history. Could this date also be applied to Daniel's prophecy?

Sir Isaac Newton, a great creation scientist, was a lover of Scripture and of Israel. When he read Daniel 9:27, he noticed that God intentionally segmented the 69 weeks into "7 weeks and 62 weeks."

This is an odd way of saying 69 weeks, as God could have easily said the Messiah would come "69 weeks" after the decree to rebuild Jerusalem. Why didn't He?

According to Newton, the 69 weeks referred to Jesus' first coming, but the 7 weeks were isolated to refer to the Second Coming. Converting 7 weeks to 49 lunar years or 17,640 days, we can calculate:

• June 7, 1967 + 17,640 days = September 23, 2015[7]

What's exciting about this date is it happens to be *Yom Kippur* or the National Day of Repentance for Israel!

Furthermore, Yom Kippur is the only day that a Jubilee year can start! Rabbis have lost count of when the Biblical Jubilee year should fall. They only know the *shmita year* or the 7th year in a 7-year cycle falls on September 23, 2015 (1 Tishri 5776). Could a Jubilee year be proclaimed exactly 49 years after Jerusalem was restored back to her people? Time will soon tell.

And this Yom Kippur is 5 days before a total lunar eclipse coinciding with Sukkot or the Feast of Tabernacles on September 28, 2015. To understand the significance of lunar and solar eclipses on God's Feasts, please reread the chapter 2013-2014.

There is a matrix of divine codes that are tightly packed into this timeframe from 2014 to 2015. Both Passovers and Sukkots in these 2 years occur on lunar eclipses. Both the religious and civil new years occur on solar eclipses.

15 APR 2014	8 OCT 2014	20 MAR 2015	4 APR 2015	14 SEP 2015	23 SEP 2015	28 SEP 2015
14 Nisan 5775	15 Tishri 5775	1 Nisan 5775	14 Nisan 5775	1 Tishri 5776	10 Tishri 5776	15 Tishri 5776
Passover	Feast of Tents	Religious New Year	Passover	Civil New Year or *Rosh Hashana*	Yom Kippur Atonement	Feast of Tents

15 APR 2014	8 OCT 2014	20 MAR 2015	4 APR 2015	14 SEP 2015	23 SEP 2015	28 SEP 2015
Lunar Eclipse	Lunar Eclipse	Solar Eclipse	Lunar Eclipse	Partial Solar Eclipse		Lunar Eclipse

Why should we who are interested in divine codes pay close attention to the 23rd of September 2015? What makes Yom Kippur 5776 so special? This date alone:

- fulfills a double reference in Daniel 9,

- marks 49 years since the capture of Jerusalem,

- falls on a *shmita* year which is the only year that could be declared a Jubilee year (a symbol of freedom, forgiveness, and the millennial age),

- is preceded by 2 Hebrew new year celebrations that coincide with solar eclipses, and

- is sandwiched between 4 consecutive blood moons coinciding with the Jewish Feasts of Passover and Sukkot—a coincidence that *will never happen again in our life time (in the 21st century)*.

The conjunction of 5 divine codes is absolutely uncanny. Did not the Lord say that the "Day of the Lord" will be surrounded by darkness?

> Is not the day of the LORD darkness, and not light? Is it not very dark, with no brightness in it?
>
> —AMOS 5:20

> "And it shall come to pass in *that day*," says the Lord GOD, "That I will make the sun go down at noon, And I will *darken* the earth in broad daylight."
>
> —AMOS 8:9, EMPHASIS ADDED

> *That day* is a day of wrath, A day of trouble and distress.... A day of *darkness* and gloominess, A day of clouds and thick *darkness*.
>
> —ZEPHANIAH 1:15, EMPHASIS ADDED

> The *sun* shall be turned into *darkness*, And the *moon* into *blood*,
> Before the coming of the great and awesome *day* of the LORD. And
> it shall come to pass That whoever calls on the name of the LORD
> Shall be saved.
>
> —JOEL 2:31–32, EMPHASIS ADDED

No matter how we slice and dice it, the divine codes are telling us something of great significance is approaching in the vicinity of 2012–2015.

For those who may wish to apply Daniel's prophecy more liberally, there is one more date we could extract from this one Bible passage. (Truly we will never plumb the depths of a single verse of God's Word! Every inspired word is profound.) What if God knew that our calendar would change from 360 day years to 365.25 day years? What if we could apply our solar calendar to the Hebrew prophecy, what year would we arrive at?

+ A.D. 1537 + 483 years = 2020

I call this a liberal interpretation as it is a *Gentile* interpretation, but the Word of God works on many levels. If this Gentile figure 2020 correlates to the Gentile Church's Rapture, then the Jewish Tribulation could start shortly after 2020, and the Second Coming could occur in the vicinity of 2027.

+ A.D. 1537 + 490 years (70 weeks of Daniel) = 2027

CAUTION: Please be careful *not* to assume that the Rapture necessarily signals the start of the Tribulation! No passage of Scripture indicates that. It is a common but unfounded assumption of prophecy writers.

The Rapture can occur, and many days or years pass before the Tribulation begins. The trigger for the Tribulation is *not* the Rapture of the Church, *nor* the signing of any treaty by Anti-Christ. The trigger is defined by the prophet Daniel. There is no need to add your opinion or some commentator's interpretation when the literal meaning of the passage is clear.

> Then he [Anti-Christ] shall *confirm* a covenant with many for one
> week [7 years]; But in the middle of the week [3 ½ years into it]
> He shall bring an end to sacrifice and offering. And on the wing
> of abominations shall be one who makes desolate, Even until the
> consummation, which is determined, Is poured out on the desolate.
>
> —DANIEL 9:27, EMPHASIS ADDED

The Tribulation is the most well-defined period of time in the Bible. It is a 7-year period that starts with a powerful man *confirming* a treaty with Israel. The English Revised Version translates the word *confirm* as "make firm." Young's Literal Translation renders it as "strengthen." This speaks of *enforcing* any of the numerous unenforced international treaties and UN resolutions concerning Israel. No one has been charismatic or influential enough to bring peace to the Middle East. The Anti-Christ will pretend to for 7 years, and then break his promise only half way through, at the 3 ½ year mark or midpoint of the Tribulation. The abomination both Daniel and Jesus refer to should be reminiscent of what Antiochus Epiphanes IV did to the Jewish Temple when he erected a statue of Zeus in the Temple and offered a sacrifice of pig on its altar. Something as offensive and idolatrous as that will occur again. Then 3 ½ years later Christ will come to destroy the Anti-Christ, save the repentant Jewish people, and kick off the Millennium.

Applying the divine code in Daniel 9:25 to the modern "ear that hears" takes us to a revolutionary date of 2020.

NUMBER OUR DAYS

So teach us to number our days, That we may gain a heart of wisdom.
—Psalm 90:12

THE TWO HARDEST CONCEPTS for man to handle are "infinity" and "eternity." It's hard for the finite human mind to even think of either one, so we rarely do. Yet every pursuit in life becomes futile if it ends abruptly in an unprepared death.

The average life expectancy globally is now 66 years. In Japan it is stretched to 82 years. The Psalmist prayed, "So teach us to number our days, That we may gain a heart of wisdom." It is wisdom to ask ourselves, "How many days do I have left to live on earth and how shall I spend them?"

- 82 years = 29,951 days—the longest average life is but a few days!

- 66 years = 24,107 days—the global average is 5,844 days shorter.

How many days do you have left on earth? No one but God knows, but suppose you had an idea. We can put it in perspective by calculating your remaining days. If you were to live another:

- 50 years—then you have 18,263 days left

- 40 years—14,610 days left

- 30 years—10,958 days left

- 20 years—7,305 days left

- 10 years—3,653 days left

- 5 years—1,827 days left

True story: a 55-year old man who hosted a radio show on Saturdays figured he could live till 75. He calculated that he had about 1,000 Saturdays left on radio, so he went and bought himself 1,000 marbles and put them all into a jar. Every Saturday he would faithfully take 1 marble out of the jar. Every week there was one marble less. One Saturday, he took out the last marble. He got on radio and announced that week that he had emptied his jar, and if he was back on radio next week, God had given him extra time. He would consider every week from that point on a bonus from God.

Actually, every day is a gift from God. "Teach us to number our days," the Psalmist said, and then we can live more purposefully, more intentionally.

How many Saturdays do you have left to live? If you were to live another:

- 50 years—then you have 2,600 Saturdays left

- 40 years—2,080 Saturdays left

- 30 years—1,560 Saturdays left

- 20 years—1,040 Saturdays left

- 10 years—520 Saturdays left

- 5 years—260 Saturdays left

Clearly our days on earth are but a scratch on the infinite line of eternity. But we hold on to the scratch as if it were everything we've got. God says there's an eternity in Heaven to be gained and a hell to be shunned. The way to stretch our time is to repent of our sins and believe in His Son.

Charles Finney said it best when he described the "moral insanity" of a man who refuses to consider his own future. "See this madness manifested in his relative estimate of time and of eternity. His whole life declares that, in his view, it is by far more important to secure the good of time than the good of eternity....O give me the joys of time: why should I trouble myself yet about the trivial matters of eternity?"[1]

Numbers don't lie. Having nearly finished this book, dear friend, I ask you to pause and calculate the risk of ignoring eternity and the rewards of preparing for it. Take a moment.

Our days are numbered. Our time is short. May be shorter than you think! Even if you lived one thousand years, from God's perspective, it is as a day. Soon it is all over.

Time is short. Time doesn't pause. Time is a slow-marching army, a relentless traveler, an unstoppable force. When a day is gone, you can never get it back.

There is no use trying to beat time or fight against the clock. It's a losing battle. The purpose of life is not to stop the clock or reverse your age. The purpose of life is in summarized by Rick Warren in 3 simple words: "Prepare for eternity!"[2]

Although we must all travel on the train of time, our destiny is eternity. To hang on to time as if it's all we got is like a man refusing to get off a train because he's been on it so long; he doesn't know whether he would like to see the destination or not! To say, "I don't care about death and where I'm going after I die," is like getting on a train and saying, "I don't care where it takes me. The destination matters not." We call such people homeless. Time is only a vehicle, not the goal. No matter how much success we achieve in time, no matter how much money we accumulate in life, we will never feel as if we have "arrived." Only when we enter eternity do we arrive!

Why is the true meaning of life found in eternity, and not in this time in which most people are preoccupied? For the simple reason that only in eternity, a life can be fully evaluated, and all rewards and judgments will be meted out. It's fair to say that during life some good deeds go unnoticed and some evil deeds escape justice. But not so in eternity. In eternity, every thought and every decision is being counted. Did we love the way we should? Did we give as much as we could? Did we doubt the lies and believe the truth? If and when we fail, God gives us time to repent and believe in His Son. "The Lord's patience gives people time to be saved" (2 Peter 3:15, NLT).

ADDING ETERNITY TO YOUR LIFE

You cannot have a relationship with numbers, but you can have a relationship with the God who invented numbers. The God who wrote the Bible is unique in that His divine codes are hidden in the Bible, in our anatomy, and throughout the universe.

There is literally no other book, no other religion, and no other God, that can claim responsibility for the 7-day week, for the multiples of 6 relating to man (the day he was created, the continents he lives on, the atomic number of his main element carbon, the temperature of his planet's core), or for the 10 Commandments upon which entire civilizations have been built. Both external reality and our internal conscience have been stamped with these numbers. God is making it easy for us to identify Him.

> For since the creation of the world His invisible attributes are *clearly seen*, being understood by the things that are made, even His eternal power and Godhead, so that they are *without excuse*.
> —ROMANS 1:20, EMPHASIS ADDED

For instance, the Biblical 10 Commandments are not only written into many countries' legal codes, they are also written within our human hearts. Try this out (I have). Ask any person who hasn't studied religion if she knows the main pillars, precepts, or tenets of any religion, and she usually cannot guess them. Now ask the same person if she thinks murdering is wrong, she will tell you, "Yes!" Who told her murder is wrong? Animals don't know that. God has placed a seed of His law in our human heart (Rom. 2:14–15). Now ask her if she thinks adultery is wrong, she will adamantly tell you, "Yes!" How does she know this? Who told her adultery is wrong? Now ask her if she thinks lying is wrong, she knows the answer is, "Yes!" These are just 3 out of God's top 10 Commandments. I have tried this out with people of every major religion, and the answer always comes back the same, even when their own religion did not teach about God's 10 Commandments. We know them because we are more than animals, we are moral spirits made in the image and likeness of our Creator.

It is not difficult to figure out which God made us to be morally pure like He is. Even without reading the Bible, our conscience attests to the truth of God's Holy Laws. What does all this mean to *you* personally?

1. One: the God of the Bible is unique.
2. Two: the God of the Bible is intelligent.
3. Three: the God of the Bible is counting.

Yes, according to Jesus, God is counting the very hair on your head! "But the very hairs of your head are all numbered. Do not fear therefore; you are of more value than many sparrows" (Luke 12:7).

I love our daughter beyond words, but I have never counted the strands of hair on her head. God loves us so much He counts. No one can say, "God doesn't know me." No one can say, "God doesn't care about me." I doubt that you know the number of hairs on your own head. God knows more about you than you know about yourself!

If God is counting the most minor things, then shouldn't we expect God to be counting the major things like our private thoughts, words, and actions? Every thought, word, and action is being recorded in the Book of Deeds (Rev. 20:12, NAS). While our memories tend to be short on things we've done wrong and long on things we've done right, God's memory is perfect.

Our initial reaction is to rationalize our wrongdoings, "I probably have done some foolish things, but overall I've tried to do more good than harm." That is both bad morals and bad math. You know that a million times negative one still comes out to a negative number (1,000,000 x -1 = -1,000,000). Legally, all it takes is one crime to make someone a criminal. You don't have to break every law in the book to be a lawbreaker; you need only break one.

> For whoever shall keep the whole law, and yet stumble in one point, he is guilty of all.
>
> —JAMES 2:10

All it takes is one sin to make us a sinner. This makes sense morally, legally, and mathematically. God has given us 10 fingers to remind us of the 10 Commandments written on our hearts, which point to the 10 Commandments written only in the Bible, which point to the only Savior Jesus Christ.

Once we realize we have sinned and our sins are being numbered, then we will look for a Savior. Becoming aware that "all have sinned and fall short of the glory of God" (Rom. 3:23) should not lead us to complacency, but to take urgent action!

We will all face a Perfect Counter when we die. Yes, no good deed will go unnoticed. But no evil deed will go unpunished. "For the wages of sin [singular] is death" (Rom. 6:23).This is why Jesus chose to die to pay the price of our sins. He didn't have to, but He, as the only sinless Savior, chose to pay the penalty of our sins. It is perfect math, boundless grace, and infinite mercy.

As long as we think our account is in the positive, we will risk eternal ruin by ignoring both our sins and the Savior's gift. Knowing Christ' sacrifice, we should not delay, but receive God's gift of salvation now. "The gift of God is eternal life in Christ Jesus our Lord" (Rom. 6:23).

God is making it easy. He has written His message everywhere, in both words and numbers that are easy to discern. Every 7-day week reminds us the God of the Bible created the world. Our 10 fingers remind us we will be evaluated on the basis of 10 Commandments. Every New Year celebration reminds us how many years ago the Son of God came to save the world. No matter what religion or nation we are from, we all count how many years it has been since Christ's birth. Even for the atheist, it is a new year only in relation to God's arrival. Did you know when Jesus came to Earth, He split time in two? He can also divide our lives into two—*Before Christ* (B.C.) and *After Deliverance* (A.D.)!

If you are ready to begin a relationship with a moral and loving God who counts Christ's sacrifice as sufficient payment for your mistakes, then pray this prayer out loud to repent and receive eternal life:

Dear Heavenly Father,

I'm sorry for my sins, too many for me to count. Thank You for offering to make me pure and give me a new life. Today I believe that Jesus Christ is the Son of God. He came and died on the cross to take away my sins. I believe He rose again on the third day and is alive and able to help me now. I invite Jesus to be my only Savior, my only Lord, now and forever. Amen.

Welcome to the family of God! Christ has reconciled you and given you an eternal relationship with God. Now is a great time for you to read the Bible for yourself, pick a good Bible-believing Church to attend, and ask them to baptize you! I would love to hear your testimony: care@discover.org.au.

APPENDIX 1

THIS IS A SUMMARY of some calculations found in this book. While it is not a prediction of the Second Advent, it is a table of significant years in which major predicted events are likely to occur.

PARABLE	MEANING
1537 A.D. + 476 years	2013
Passover and Sukkot on Lunar Eclipses	2014
7 June 1967 + 17,640 days	23 Sep 2015 *Yom Kippur*
Passover and Sukkot on Lunar Eclipses	2015
1967 + 50 (*Jubilee Year*)	2017
Psalm (1900) + 113 to 118	2013-2018
281 B.C. + 2300 years*	2018
684 A.D. + 1335 years*	2019
1537 A.D. + 483 years	2020
US crisis of 50: 1970 + 50	2020
US Presidential election	2020
1537 A.D. + 490 years	2027
32 A.D. + 2000 years	2032
US 50th President elected**	2032
Psalm (1900) + 136	2036
US 50th president finishes first term	2036
Next year with 7 eclipses	2038
1948 + 100 years	2048
Isaac's birth in Creation years	2048
Psalm (1900) + 146 to 150	2046 to 2050

CONCLUSION

No matter which code we look at or which equation we punch in, the numbers are telling us we are in the vicinity of a great transitional age. Time is less like a clock than a stopwatch. Time is not winding up nor moving in circles, it is clearly counting down towards a target. We are moving inexorably towards a goal, a destiny, an "appointed time." God is about to do something great; His Word will be vindicated once and for all, and no person reading this has an excuse to delay his decision to believe.

*(For more calculations and updates beyond the scope of this book, visit our website: www.discover.org.au/2020).

** Assuming six more one-term presidencies from 2012 on (see chapter 50).

APPENDIX 2

1. How many twins were in the Bible?
2. Do men and women have different numbers of ribs?
3. How many individual cases of healing did Jesus perform?
4. How many bones are in the human body?
5. How many types of prayers are taught in the Bible?
6. Who had 666 descendants?
7. How many generations were there from Abraham to Jesus?
8. How high was Mount Calvary?
9. How many apostles were there in the New Testament?
10. How many chromosomes are in a human cell?
11. How many kinds of chemical elements are there on Earth?
12. What was the minimum age for a Jewish man to go to war?
13. How many annual feast days were appointed for Israel?

TEST YOUR KNOWLEDGE

1. Why is "13" considered bad omen?
2. Who are the 144,000 in the Book of Revelation?
3. Do you keep the 10 Commandments?
4. How did 70 percent of people in the New Testament receive healing?
5. What do you think the infamous 666 represents?
6. Which future date on God's calendar concerns you the most and why?
7. What does it mean to "number our days"?

NOTES

PREFACE

1. Avraham Steinberg, *Encyclopedia of Jewish Medical Ethics* (Nanuet, NY: Feldheim, 2003), 819. Other scientific sources vary by 2 days, estimating the average human gestation period at 273 days.

INTRODUCTION

1. "The Letters of the Torah," Torat Emet, http://www.aishdas.org/toratemet/en_ pamphlet9.html (accessed January 16. 2011).

DECODING NUMBERS

1. Peter Plichta, *God's Secret Formula: Deciphering the Riddle of the Universe and the Prime Number Code* (Shaftesbury, UK: Element Books Ltd, 1998), chap. 17.

2

1. Anne Marie Helmenstine, "What is the Most Abundant Element?" http://chem-istry.about.com/cs/howthingswork/f/blabundant.htm (accessed February 1, 2009).

2. *Babylonian Talmud Sukkah*, 52a; *Yerushalmi Talmud Sukkah*, 55b.

3. We know this 45 day theory is against Scripture because Revelation 11 tells us Elijah as one of the two witnesses will be killed before the 7th trumpet, before the 7 bowl judgments are poured out, before the judgments on Babylon. This most likely puts the end of Elijah's ministry at the midpoint of the Tribulation, around the time the abomination of desolation occurs. That would separate the ascension of Elijah from the appearance of Messiah by 3 ½ years, not 45 days.

2 DOUBLES

1. "What is the average rate of inflation in the United States?" http://heartsofthegods. blogspot.com/2007/07/what-is-average-inflation-rate-in.html (accessed February 9, 2009).

2. Human Population Milestones, http://en.wikipedia.org/wiki/User:Noe/World_ population_milestones (accessed December 29, 2010).

3. John Heffner, "World Population Debunks Macroevolution," http://www.youtube. com/watch?v=CuJ_-5JZ4xc (accessed October 19, 2010).

4. "Big Numbers," http://pages.prodigy.net/jhonig/bignum/indx.html (accessed February 13, 2009).

5. Heffner, "World Population Debunks Macroevolution." See also Don Batten, "Where Are All the People?" http://creation.com/where-are-all-the-people (accessed October 19, 2010).

6. Henry Morris, *The Biblical Basis for Modern Science* (Grand Rapids, MI: Baker, 1984), part 4, chap. 15.

7. Don Batten, "Where Are All the People?" http://www.answersingenesis.org/creation/v23/i3/people.asp (accessed February 13, 2009).

3

1. Kevin Conner, *Interpreting the Symbols and Types* (Portland, OR: City Christian, 1992).

3.1415

1. Mishnah, The Artscroll Series, 1983: *Seder Moed*, Vol. 1(b): *Eruvin*, Mesorah Publications, New York, page 22.

2. John P. Boatwright, "Proof Pi is Not Given as 3.0 in the Bible," http://home.teleport.com/~salad/4god/pi.htm (accessed February 4, 2009).

4

1. Chuck Missler, "The Camp of Israel," www.idolphin.org/camp (accessed March 16, 2009). Used by permission.

4 ANGELS

1. *Jewish Heritage Online Magazine*, "Angels in the Talmud," http://jhom.com/topics/angels/talmud_fourangels.htm#5a (accessed October 12, 2010).

2. A prayer of the Jews according to *Israel Today Magazine*, no. 75, April 2005, 12.

5

1. Thomas Samuelian, *Armenian Origins*, 8. Accessed March 28, 2009, at http://ararat-center.org/upload/files/ TomasSamuelyan_Origins_2004.pdf.

2. Richard Maybury, *The Daily Crux: An Interview with Richard Maybury*, http://radiopatriot.wordpress.com/2011/04/19/the-wisdom-of-richard-maybury/?like=1 (accessed April 18, 2011).

6

1. "Life Expectancy at Birth," www.cia.gov/library/publications/the-world-factbook/rankorder/2102rank.html (accessed October 7, 2010).

2. Total immediate deaths, excluding post-war deaths from the effects of the atomic bombs, are difficult to determine. Figures vary between 50 to 70 million, so the acceptable average figure is 60 million, a horror to imagine!

7

1. 1591, 1656, 1787, 1805, 1917, 1935, 1982 found at "A Catalogue of Eclipse Cycles," www.phys.uu.nl/~vgent/eclipse/eclipsecycles.htm (accessed October 25, 2010). The next year with 7 eclipses of any kind will be 2038.

2. W. E. Filmer, *God Counts: A Study in Bible Numbers* (Strathpine, QLD: Evangelistic Literature, 1984).

3. Dr. Ivan Panin, "God is a Mathematician," http://www.bereanpublishers.com/Apologetics/god_is_a_mathematician.htm (accessed April 17, 2009).

4. *Half-age-plus-seven-relationship-rule*, http://en.wikipedia.org/wiki/File:Half-age-plus-seven-relationship-rule.svg (accessed April 17, 2011).

7 FEASTS

1. Chuck Missler, *Personal Update*, September 1995, 14.

2. Roy Reinhold, "Paganism in Christmas," http://members.aol.com/prophecy04/Articles/Christianity/christmas.html (accessed September 29, 2004).

8

1. Martin Armstrong, "The 8.6 Year Cycle and the Forces of Mother Nature," http://armstrongeconomics.com/writings (accessed November 28, 2010).

2. *British Journal of Cancer* 19, no. 2 (June 1965): 217–226.

3. E. W. Bullinger, "Numbers in Scripture, Its Supernatural Design and Spiritual Significance," http://philologos.org/__eb-nis/eight.htm (accessed on February 11, 2009).

10 DAYS

1. This was Antiochus' birthday. The same day 3 years later marked the restoration of Temple worship in 164 B.C. The 25th of Kislev is now commemorated by Jews as Hanukkah or the winter Feast of Dedication. Jesus acknowledged this feast in John 10:22.

2. *Halley's Bible Handbook* (Grand Rapids, MI: Zondervan Publishing House, 1965).

3. The Nicene Creed quoted nowadays is not from the First Council of Nicea in A.D. 325, but from the First Council of Constantinople in A.D. 381. Both Councils agreed on the Creed; the substantive change by the later Council is an elaboration on the Holy Spirit.

10 COMMANDMENTS

1. The 10 Commandments are based on Exodus 20; Deuteronomy 5, 6:5; Mark 12:30 and Luke 10:27.

11

1. "Ireland and Northern European Countries to Benefit from Global Warming," http://www.finfacts.ie/irelandbusinessnews/publish/article_10008594.shtml (accessed August 6, 2010).

13

1. Home of future King Saul and capital of Israel under Saul.

2. Judges 19–20, total death 19:35, total survivors 19:47. Both King Saul and Saul of Tarsus descended from one of these 600 survivors. One Saul became an apostate king, the other Saul became the mighty apostle Paul. Thank God for the remnants who survived!

3. Samuel recounted this cycle of sin and savior in 1 Samuel 12:9–11.

4. Gideon was also called Jerubbaal. (See Judges 9:2, 1 Samuel 12:11.)

5. Dan, along with Reuben, Gad (Gilead), and Asher refused to fight with Deborah against the Canaanites.

6. Perhaps uncomfortable with having a serpent as a sign of its tribe, Dan later modified it to an eagle with a serpent in its mouth.

7. According to Perry Stone, *Breaking the Jewish Code* (Lake Mary, FL: Charisma House, 2009), 84.

8. *Maimonides' 13 Foundations of Faith*, translated by Marc Mermelstein, http://www.mesora.org/13principles.html and *The Thirteen Articles of Maimonides*, http://www.jewishvirtuallibrary.org/jsource/Judaism/The_Thirteen_Articles_of_Maimonides.html (accessed 21 April 2011).

18

1. *Shema* comes from the first Hebrew word of Deuteronomy 6:4, "Hear, O Israel, The Lord our God, the Lord is one!" The prayer continues with Deuteronomy 11:13–21 and Numbers 15:37–41.

2. See Matthew 5:5–13 for this model prayer.

19

1. R. H. Charles, trans., *The Book of Jubilees* (Oxford: Clarendon Press, 1913), 4:30–31, 23:9.

19TH BOOK

1. Charles Spurgeon quote found at http://www.biblebb.com/files/SPURGEON/TOD/chstodpr.htm (accessed January 25, 2011).

19 HEALINGS

1. For further study along this line, I recommend the resources of Doug Jones Ministries and Keith Moore Ministries.

2. Healing continued after Jesus gave us His same Holy Spirit—Acts 5:16, Mark 16:15–18.

20

1. Shaunti Feldhann and Lisa Rice, *For Parents Only* (Colorado Springs: Multnomah Books, 2007).

22

1. "Definition of Bones in the Head," http://www.medterms.com/script/main/art.asp?articlekey=8644 (accessed October 11, 2010). There would be 29 bones in the human head if we counted the 6 auditory ossiciles or tiny bones inside the middle ears.

23

1. David DeWitt, "Chimp Genome Sequences Very Different from Man," http://creationontheweb.com/images/pdfs/tj/j19_3/j19_3_4-5.pdf (accessed March 24, 2009).

2. Ibid.

3. Carl Weiland, "Steve Jones and the 'End of Human Evolution,'" http://creation.com/steve-jones-and-the-end-of-human-evolution (accessed February 11, 2009).

4. *The New Scientist* 194, no. 2608 (June 16, 2007): 48–51.

5. John Sanford, *How Evolution Hurts Science*, DVD by Creation Ministries International.

6. "Was Dawkins Stumped?" www.creationontheweb.com/content/view/5712 (accessed March 4, 2009).

24

1. Finnis Dake, *The Dake Annotated Reference Bible* (Lawrenceville, GA: Dake, 1989), NT, 142.

26

1. *Interlinear Translation of the Greek Scriptures* (New York: Watchtower Society, 1969), 23. *Aid to Bible Understanding* (New York: Watchtower Society, 1971), 885.

2. Stone, *Breaking the Jewish Code*, 49.

38

1. Raul Lopez, "Temporal Changes in the Aging of Biblical Patriarchs," http://creation.com/temporal-changes-in-the-aging-of-Biblical-patriarchs (accessed October 11, 2010). Enoch is included even though he did not die, but was translated at the age of 365 (Genesis 5:23–24).

40

1. Harry Dent Jr., *The Great Depression Ahead* (New York: Simon & Schuster, 2009), 4.

50

1. George Friedman, *The Next 100 Years* (Melbourne, AU: Schwartz Media, 2009), 121.

66

1. "Life Expectancy at Birth," www.cia.gov/library/publications/the-world-factbook/rankorder/2102rank.html (accessed October 7, 2010).

2. Dake, *The Dake Annotated Reference Bible*, OT, 730.

70

1. Dake, *The Dake Annotated Reference Bible*, Cyclopedic Index, 83.

2. Chuck Missler, "*The Appointed Times*," http://www.khouse.org/articles/1998/61/ (accessed February 4, 2009).

3. Sir Robert Anderson, *The Coming Prince* (London: Hodder & Stroughton, 1894).

80

1. "Life Expectancy at Birth," www.cia.gov/library/publications/the-worldfactbook/rankorder/2102rank.html (accessed October 7, 2010).

150

1. Spurgeon quote found at http://www.biblebb.com/files/SPURGEON/TOD/chstodpr.htm.

2. Don Christie, *Actual Proof of My Existence Signed: God of the* Bible (Longwood, FL: Xulon Press, 2003).

3. J. R. Church, *Hidden Prophecies in the Psalms* (Oklahoma City: Prophecy Publications, 1986).

276

1. John Tng, "Revelation 13:18 Decoded: The 666 Riddle Solved!" http://www.fivedoves.com/rapture/2009/Obama_Rev1318.html (accessed October 25 2010).

400

1. King David's 40 years + Solomon's 40 years + 19 Kings of Judah's 393 or 394 years = 473 years.

2. Dake, *The Dake Annotated Reference Bible.*

3. Add Solomon's remaining 36 years to the 393-year reigns of 19 Kings of Judah equals 429 years. Since the years of kings' reigns are rounded figures, we can round the total up to 430 years.

4. Predicted by Daniel's interpretation of the writing on the wall in 5:28 and the vision of the bear in 7:5.

5. Predicted by Gabriel's interpretation of the he-goat in Daniel 8:21 and again by the angel Gabriel in 10:20.

6. Reign of the Ptolemies, or the King of the South, predicted by Daniel 11.

7. Reign of the Seleucids, or the King of the North, predicted by Daniel 11.

8. Reign of the Hasmonean Dynasty, starting with the revolt of the priest Mattathias Maccabeus and his sons Judas, Jonathan, and Simon.

9. Reign of the Herodian Dynasty: starting with Herod Antipater, then Herod the Great, Herod Agrippa I, and Herod Agrippa II.

666

1. Such as Daniel 11:38 and the conspicuous absence of Dan in Revelation 7.

2. Gary Bates, *Alien Intrusion: UFOs and the Evolution Connection*, Master Books, 2005.

3. Bullinger, "Numbers in Scripture."

4. Also Christ is called the "Branch" or *netser* in Isaiah 11:1, which may be a play on word with where He would live *Nazareth.*

969

1. Chuck Missler, "The Gospel in Genesis," http://www.joshuanet.org/articles/missler/gen5.htm (accessed October 3, 2010).

2. The *Book of Jasher 13:9*, an extra-Biblical source, says Noah died when Abraham was 58 years old.

3. Patriarchs from Adam to Israel © Answers in Genesis, www.answersingenesis.org/articles/2009/01/20/ancient-patriarchs-in-genesis.

4. Lopez, "Temporal Changes in the Aging of Biblical Patriarchs."

5. Diagram used by permission of Creation Ministries International www.creation.com.

6. This was in contrast to Genesis 1:29, which indicates the original diet was vegetarian.

1948

1. John Pratt, "Divine Calendars Testify of Abraham, Isaac and Jacob," http://www.johnpratt.com/items/docs/lds/meridian/2003/abraham.html. Corroborating source http://freepages.genealogy.rootsweb.ancestry.com/~mgholler/Caden/a75.htm (accessed October 13, 2010).

2. "Ages of the Patriarchs," http://www.arksearch.com/nabefore.htm (accessed October 13, 2010).

3. Genesis 15:13–16 defines 1 generation as 100 years. See chapter 2020 and Beyond for more analysis.

1967

1. See Fred P Miller's study on how to reconcile the dates of the abomination of desolation and cleansing of the Temple given by 1 Maccabees 4:52–53 with Daniel's 1,150 days. http://moellerhaus.com/2300.htm.

2. A principle God uses in Numbers 14:34, Ezekiel 4:4–6, and 2 Peter 3:8.

3. "Biblical Chronology," www.bible.ca/b-bible-chronology-genesis-5-world-events.htm (accessed May 13, 2011).

2011

1. Grace Assembly, Petaling Jaya. *Apostolic Prophetic Insight*, no. 1 (2011).

2012

1. Emily Laut, "How the Maya Did Their Plumbing," http://www.msnbc.msn.com/id/37023595/ns/technology_and_science-science (accessed August 9, 2010).

2. John Heffner, Interview by Dr. Carl Baugh on TV program *Creation in the 21st Century, Today's World Population Debunks Evolution*, http://wn.com/Today's_World_Population_Debunks_Evolution_Dr_Carl_Baugh (accessed August 9, 2010).

3. The Jewish year does not start on January 1st with ours, but on Nisan 1st or the Passover Feast for the religious calendar, and on Tishri 1st or *Rosh Hashanah* for the civil calendar.

4. "Estimates of the Age of the Earth," http://www.religioustolerance.org/ ev_date1.htm (accessed August 10, 2010).

2013–2014

1. Mark Biltz, *Stipulating Eclipse Comments*, http://www.elshaddaiministries.us/stipulation.html (accessed December 1, 2010).

2020 AND BEYOND

1. However, there may be other errors in the Hebrew calendar which would make the timing of the Second Coming even closer See Grant Jeffrey, *Armageddon: Appointment with Destiny* (Colorado Springs: WaterBrook, 1997).

2. Stone, *Breaking the Jewish Code*, 51.

3. David Rogers, "The Time of the Resurrection," http://bibletruth.cc/Daniel12.htm (accessed December 1, 2010).

4. Information on Jehoiakim found at http://www.britannica.com/EBchecked/topic/302380/Jehoiakim (accessed December 1, 2010).

5. Dome of the Rock information found at http://www.greatbuildings.com/buildings/Dome_of_the_Rock.html (accessed December 1, 2010).

6. *Iggeret Teiman* (al-Risala al-Yamaniyya, Maimonides' answer to the Yemeni Jews' questions in 1172), chap. 3, 24.

7. Jim Bramlett, *Prophetic Perspectives 2008-2015*, http://www.prophecyforum.com/bramlett/prophetic_perspectives.html (accessed February 9, 2009).

NUMBER OUR DAYS

1. Charles Finney sermon, "Moral Insanity" http://truthinheart.com/EarlyOberlinCD/CD/Finney/OE/560910_moral_insanity.htm (accessed January 27, 2011).

2. Rick Warren, http://www.goodreads.com/author/quotes/711.Rick_Warren (accessed January 28, 2011).

ABOUT THE AUTHOR

STEVE CIOCCOLANTI, B.A., M.ED., is the founder and director of Discover Ministries (www.discover.org.au). He has traveled to more than 35 countries ministering in churches, leadership seminars, Bible schools, and on TV and radio. With a Masters of Education, Steve has the unique gift of researching complex concepts and presenting them in simple, practical ways. Steve does it again in this book: *The Divine Code: From 1 to 2020*, which brings understanding and revelation to a wide range of topics hidden behind Bible codes and numbers.

A sought-after seminar speaker, Steve appears on a weekly TV program in Indonesia and pastors a church in Melbourne, Australia, where he currently resides with his family.

RESOURCES BY STEVE CIOCCOLANTI

OTHER BOOKS BY STEVE CIOCCOLANTI
From Buddha to Jesus: An Insider's View of Buddhism & Christianity (English, Chinese, Indonesian, Thai).
Zoe Life Reality

CD TEACHINGS BY STEVE CIOCCOLANTI
Discovering Your Destiny (3 CDs)
The Life of David (18 CDs)
9 Types of Prayer (4 CDs)

DVD PRESENTATIONS BY STEVE CIOCCOLANTI
A Christian Tour of Greece
A Christian Tour of Turkey
A Christian Tour of Thailand
End Times Package (6 DVDs)
Redeeming the Time (2 DVDs)
The Book of Revelation (10 DVDs)
4000 Years of History: From Creation to Christ (12 DVDs)

DVDS THAT COMPLEMENT
THE DIVINE CODE: FROM 1 TO 2020

Numbers DVD Series
1 Word from God Can Change Your Life
I Am Number 2
6 Suicides
9 Prayers of the New Testament
19 Healings of Christ

Order These Powerful, Life-Changing Resources from Discover Ministries at

www.Discover.org.au

CONTACT THE AUTHOR

To book Steve Cioccolanti for a speaking event
or
To obtain more teaching videos and audios, contact

DISCOVER
MINISTRIES

2020@DISCOVER.ORG.AU

WWW.DISCOVER.ORG.AU

The meaning of numbers is an ongoing study that may never be exhausted. If you wish to contribute helpful ideas, we welcome you to contact us! Fresh insights may be posted online.